RESIST!
The Art of Resista

Snapshot of an Exhibition
at a Certain Place
at a Certain Time

Introduction

> »The great force of history comes from the fact that we carry it within us, are unconsciously controlled by it in many ways, and history is literally present in all that we do.«
>
> James Baldwin, *The Price of the Ticket – Collected Nonfiction 1948–1985*

Why this book?

RESIST! The Art of Resistance was an exhibition at the Rautenstrauch-Joest-Museum (RJM) in Cologne that explored over five hundred years of anti-colonial resistance in the Global South. It examined rebellion and the desire for freedom, subversive resistance and colonial trauma, as well as self-empowerment and the will to survive.

RESIST! was originally conceived as a collaborative and participatory project. The exhibition opened to visitors on 1 April 2021, closed just one week later, before eventually remaining open from June 2021 until 9 January 2022 with major constraints. Changes to scheduling due to Covid-19, travel restrictions, futile visa applications, vaccination regulations, illness, quarantine and hygiene measures, the cancellation of planned events, limited visitor numbers, and increased bureaucracy all made the project extremely complex.

As a result of the coronavirus pandemic, the exhibition opening was delayed five times and most of the invited curators and artists could not be present in Cologne. Not knowing if and when we would be able to welcome visitors, we decided to launch *RESIST!* digitally on 29 January 2021. For this event, artist-in-residence Bahar Gökten choreographed *(RESI)STANCE ONE SHOT*, a dance performance by nine young urban dancers through the five chapters of the deserted exhibition. We interviewed four curators of the *It's Yours!* spaces, Peju Layiwola, Esther Utjiua Muinjangue, Elizaveta Khan, and Tímea Junghaus; together with artist-in-residence Kiri Dalena, we showed footage of the Cologne Black Lives Matter movement by photographer-in-residence Francis Oghuma and two video performances by Selma Selman and Ayrson Heráclito. A live DJ set by artist-in-residence Rokia Bamba brought the launch event to a close.

At the same time, *RESIST!* was enriched by countless international online discussions and an increased media presence of prominent intellectuals from the Global South, which immensely increased the public pressure on museums with colonial collections to restitute looted cultural artefacts and make significant changes.

All of this had a profound impact on the exhibition project.

Although the structure of the book follows the organisation of the exhibition into five thematic chapters, it is not an exhibition catalogue but a snapshot. It is an attempt to chronicle the whole period of the *RESIST!* project and to place it in the context of the ongoing worldwide discussions at the time about the continuities of racism and colonialism which had assumed unprecedented proportions globally. This book also aims to describe the extent to which the *RESIST!* project itself gave rise to internal, local and international debates and controversies.

While the exhibition closed on 9 January 2022, it led to further events and projects at the museum that are important for the understanding of *RESIST!* and its contemporary social and political context, which is why we decided to continue this snapshot beyond the end of the exhibition period.

For this reason, we are also discussing *I MISS YOU: About Missing, Giving Back and Remembering*, an intervention in the permanent exhibition of the RJM that opened on 29 April 2022 and presents what are commonly referred to as the Benin Bronzes – artworks from the court of the Kingdom of Benin (Nigeria) – after they were shown in their entirety for the first time in *RESIST!* We must also mention the panel discussion "Why Restitution Matters", which was held on 9 July 2022 to coincide with the visit of a royal delegation from Fontem (Cameroon) to the RJM and focused on their demand for restitution of a sacred statue that had been exhibited in the exhibition introductory room of *RESIST!*

The time frame covered by this book ends in December 2022 with the signing of an agreement between the City of Cologne and the Federal Republic of Nigeria regarding the transfer of ownership of all 92 Benin court artworks. The exhibition project began in the summer of 2019 and continued to evolve against the backdrop of extraordinary local and global historical events. *RESIST!* was particularly influenced by the murder of George Floyd by a white police officer on 25 May 2020, which sparked one of the strongest public protest movements in history against systemic racism, discrimination, and police violence, strengthening the BLM movement as well as the Rhodes Must Fall movement, which led to the toppling of colonial monuments around the world in subsequent years.

At the same time, negotiations about the restitution of works of art from Africa that had been looted during the colonial period gained new momentum, especially with regard to the Benin court artworks.

In early 2021, the German translation of Michael Rothberg's book, *Multidirectional Memory: Remembering the Holocaust in the Age of Decolonization*, led to discussions about the complex terrain of multidirectional memory, how the Shoah is remembered compared to other crimes against humanity, and the ways in which these relate to each other or not.

The years leading up to 2022 were also marked by the heated anti-antisemitism debate in Germany involving many postcolonial intellectuals and artists from the Global South, beginning with the controversy surrounding Achille Mbembe during the music and arts festival, the Ruhrtriennale in spring 2020, and culminating in 2022 with documenta 15, to which Selma Selman and Kiri Dalena, whose works were shown in *RESIST!*, were also invited, as well as yasmine eid-sabbagh and the Nest Collective, who participated in other special exhibitions at the RJM.

In spring 2021, the remains of 215 children were discovered at the former Indian Residential School in Kamloops (British Columbia, Canada). Tania Willard and Lawrence Paul Yuxweluptun, Indigenous artists from British Columbia, represented in *RESIST!*, are both victims of Indian Residential Schools, where between the late 1800s and 1996, more than 150,000 First Nations children were separated from families, "re-educated" and forbidden from speaking their languages. Many of them were pourly nourished and experienced physical and sexual abuse. Canada's Truth and Reconciliation Commission estimates that more than 6,000 children died while at Residential Schools.

In Portugal, the last colonial power to grant independence to its colonies, increasing pressure from its citizens and immigrants of African heritage has prompted contemplation of its colonial history. In April 2021, on the day commemorating the Carnation Revolution, President Rebelo de Sousa urged Portuguese citizens to openly reflect on Portugal's colonial history for the first time.

The Reconciliation Agreement negotiated between Germany and Namibia in May 2021 to make reparations for the German genocide of the Herero and Nama people sparked fierce criticism, has been rejected by Herero and Nama representatives, and is yet to be implemented. In *RESIST!*, the Nama and Herero curators and activists Esther Muinjangue and Ida Hoffmann dedicated their autonomous *It's Yours!* space, *Not About Us without Us*, to the topic of the first genocide of the twentieth century. The agreement was intensively discussed in the *RESIST!* online debate "Herero & Nama Voices from Namibia" on 18 August 2021.

On 20 June 2021, the Belgian Prime Minister Alexander De Croo returned the only known remains – a tooth – of the Congolese Independence leader Patrice Lumumba, who was assassinated in 1961, to the Democratic Republic of Congo after the Belgian parliament established a commission in June 2020 to address Belgium's colonial past in the wake of the BLM movements. However, in December 2022, the appointed commission failed to reach a consensus on a parliamentary resolution for the Belgian state to formally apologise and pay reparations for the atrocities committed.

Around the same time, Dutch Prime Minister Mark Rutte apologised for the Netherlands' role in the transatlantic slavery, 150 years after its abolition. After a comprehensive study concluded in February 2021 that Dutch troops had used "systematic and widespread extreme violence" in Indonesia's War of Independence (1945–1949), including against civilians, Rutte's apology to Indonesia followed.

In short, former colonial empires – and their museums – are struggling with the ghosts of their colonial past.

Between spring 2019 and the end of 2022, the debate about the restitution of looted colonial artefacts not only intensified, but also took on concrete forms.

The books *The Brutish Museums: The Benin Bronzes, Colonial Violence and Cultural Restitution* (2020) by Dan Hicks, *Africa's Struggle for Its Art: History of a Postcolonial Defeat* (2021) by Bénédicte Savoy, and Götz Aly's book *Das Prachtboot* (2001) about how Germans raided South Sea Culture triggered a new wave of discussions about restitution. While Hicks' book is a detailed account of the massacre that accompanied a British raid on Benin City and the theft of thousands of royal artworks from the palace, Savoy's book aimed to describe the long history of the debate, illustrating numerous attempts at restitution and demonstrating that claims for the return of artefacts had been taking place for decades. Aly's book focuses on the history of collecting in the Pacific ocean, a part of Germany's violent colonial past that has received little attention until now; he presented it to the general public during *RESIST!* on 9 June 2021.

On 9 November 2021, France returned 26 sculptures from the royal treasures of the Kingdom of Dahomey that were looted by the French army in 1892 to the Republic of Benin.

In a large-scale public discussion *RESIST! – Conversations All in One* on 3 December 2021, Bénédicte Savoy compared the possible return of the "Benin Bronzes" to the fall of the Berlin Wall.

On a local level, here in Cologne, the city became the first local authority in Germany to make the N-word illegal in May 2020 on the initiative of the "N-Wort

Stoppen" movement (Stop the N-Word) and began the process of coming to terms with Cologne's colonial past in October 2021 with its project "The City of Cologne's (Post-)Colonial Legacy".

This book is thus not only a book about an exhibition on anti-colonial resistance, but also a publication about a contentious and contested project in the context of local, national, and global resistance movements and social critique, as well as internal and external resistance movements around a site of resistance, the museum. *RESIST!* cannot therefore be reduced merely to an exhibition or a temporary project. Rather, it is a project that reflects on the museum and its future, as well as how to find a solution to prevent the museum from ending as a result of self-preservation and ultimately destroying itself through its own principles.

On 9 January 2022, the last day of the exhibition, a small group of young *RESIST!* mediators referred to as live speakers led a demonstration in the exhibition: *Widerstand ist keine Sonderausstellung!* (Resistance is not a special exhibition!) From their point of view, there is no place for a special exhibition on anti-colonial resistance in a museum that is still rooted in the colonial past, as the institution itself is a place where the continuities of colonialism can still be felt in its structures and forms of communication, and microaggressions are commonplace, they argue.

This is precisely the paradox of this exhibition project. Consequently, *RESIST!* must be transformed into a permanent project that redefines and gradually transforms the museum in light of its colonial past.

RESIST! established a creative and collaborative space in the midst of a system focused on the past and proposed strategies to counter power imbalances in the narrative of colonial history. *RESIST!* was thus a project that had a reflective and self-critical approach. *RESIST!* challenged museum paradigms, exposed power dynamics, structural and institutional racism, and sought to subvert them through new curatorial and narrative methods. Continuing *RESIST!* means opening the museum to marginalised, subversive, and disruptive narratives and re-integrating its collection into a multivocal and multidirectional story.

All this raises the fundamental question: Is *RESIST!* actually over?

Nanette Snoep, Vera Marušić, Lydia Hauth, Ricardo Márquez García
Cologne, December 2022

ACKNOWLEDGEMENTS
The *RESIST!* exhibition, the accompanying programme, and lastly this book were made possible by the generous support of the German Federal Cultural Foundation, the programme 360° –Fund for New City Cultures, Peter and Irene Ludwig Foundation, the F. Victor Rolff Foundation, the Museum Association RJM e.V. and the Federal Agency for Civic Education. We thank them for their trust in this experimental project.

Table of Contents

- 002 — **Introduction: Why this Book?**
  Nanette Snoep, Vera Marušić, Lydia Hauth, Ricardo Márquez García

- 008 — **There was Once a Pair of White Sandals**
  Nanette Snoep

- 018 — **A Reflection by raumlaborberlin on their Design for *RESIST!***

- 023 — **Introductory Text to the Exhibition *RESIST! The Art of Resistance***

- (029) — **Chapter 1**
  ## Liberation Struggles, Uprisings, Protests

- 036 — **King Asabaton Fontem Njifua Restitution Claim for a Sacred Sculpture**

- 038 — **Why Restitution Matters**
  Asabaton Fontem Njifua, Diane Ngolefe Acha-Morfaw, Charles Ngulefac Morfaw, Beatrice Folefac Emenkeng, Josephine Ngimafac Talieh, Chief Charles Taku, Martin Nkefu, Emigdas Nkem

- 064 — *It's Yours!* space
  ## Esther Utjiua Muinjangue and Ida Hoffmann
  ### Not About Us Without Us

- 066 — **A luta continua**
  Esther Utjiua Muinjangue and Ida Hoffmann

- 070 — **Conversation: Not about Us without Us**
  A Conversation between Esther Utjiua Muinjangue and Nanette Snoep

- 075 — **Conversation: Herero & Nama Voices from Namibia**
  Esther Utjiua Muinjangue, Sam Geiseb, Kambanda Nokokure Veii, Mbakumua Hengari, Israel Kaunatjike, Joshua Kwesi Aikins

- (087) — **Chapter 2**
  ## Subversion and Refusal

- 094 — *It's Yours!* space
  ## Peju Layiwola
  ### Benin 1897

- 097 — **Claims for restitution of the Benin Court Artworks**
  Peju Layiwola

- 098 — **List of Benin Court Artworks Owned by the RJM**

- 100 — **Context of the Restitution Debates in Recent Years in Germany**

- 110 — **Conversation: Benin 1897**
  A Conversation between Peju Layiwola and Nanette Snoep

- 116 — **I MISS YOU. About Missing, Giving Back and Remembering**

- 117 — **I Have Come to Take You Home**
  Peju Layiwola

- 118 — **Back to Benin-City! Agreement of the Transfer of Ownership of 92 Benin Court Artworks on 15/12/2022**

- 120 — **Timeline of the Restitution of the Benin Court Artworks at the RJM, February 1897–20/12/2022**

122 **Conversation: Africa's Struggle for its Art**
A Conversation between Bénédicte Savoy and Nanette Snoep

123 **Conversation: *RESIST! All in One***
A Conversation between Felwine Sarr, Ciraj Rassool, Nana Oforiatta Ayim, Bénédicte Savoy, Andreas Görgen, Peju Layiwola, Elizaveta Khan, Rahab Njeri

(127) Chapter 3
Own Stories, Own Narratives

138 *It's Yours!* space
Tímea Junghaus
Roma Resist!

146 **RomaMoMa**
A European Manifesto for Roma Cultural Inclusion
ERIAC European Roma Institute

148 **Conversation: Roma Resist!**
A Conversation between Tímea Junghaus and Nanette Snoep

(155) Chapter 4
Trauma & Transformation

170 *It's Yours!* space
In-Haus e.V.
No Resistance Fits in a Box!

172 **A look back on In-Haus' participation in *RESIST!***
Elizaveta Khan, In-Haus e.V.

176 ***RESIST!*-Box**
In-Haus e.V.

(191) Chapter 5
Cultural Resilience or the Art of Survival?

202 Artists

206 Credits & Imprint

Nanette Snoep, Initiator and Curator-at-large of the exhibition *RESIST! The Art of Resistance*, Director of the Rautenstrauch-Joest Museum since 2019

There was Once a Pair of White Sandals

»I believe in memory not as a place of revival, but as point of departure – a catapult throwing you into present times, allowing you to imagine the future instead of accepting it.«

»Poor History had stopped breathing : betrayed in academic texts, lied about in classrooms, drowned in dates, they had imprisoned her in museums and buried her, with floral wreaths, beneath statuary bronze and monumentable marble.«[1]

Eduardo Galeano, *Memory of Fire*, 1985

This essay is my personal contribution to question the various efforts made by ethnological museums to "decolonise" themselves. Which, ultimately, raises the question of whether we can "decolonise" ourselves at all.

Since I began working in ethnological museums in 1995, there have been numerous brilliant texts about the act of "decolonising" museums, about "unlearning" or "decentering". However, true decolonisation requires the radical transformation – or rather dismantling – of power relations and white privilege. This is painful and provokes resistance. Despite all the international, national, and local debates and initiatives, museums have not fundamentally changed. Are ethnological museums genuinely committed to "decolonisation", or are they primarily concerned with maintaining the status quo and saving face?

I became acquainted with museums at an early age. As a director of art museums in the Netherlands, my father imparted a love of that unique scent of dust in museum repositories and a passion for "unloved" works, the "black sheep" of a collection, objects that are unusual and do not conform to conventional canons; although they are never exhibited, once they have been inventoried, they are intended to remain part of the collection forever. My father loved the little stories hidden behind the objects and passed this on to me.

I began my professional career in ethnological museums as an intern at the Museum of Mankind in Paris in 1995. For the exhibition "Treasures of the Marquesas Islands", I had to clear out the Oceania gallery to make room for an extravagant, exotic backdrop made out of papier-mâché with a reproduction of a cave landscape and lush greenery. An older staff member who was on the

[1] Eduardo Galeano, *Memory of Fire. Genesis. Part One of a Trilogy*, New York: Nation Books 1985, XV

verge of retirement led me through the storeroom for the Oceania collection. We walked through a maze of overflowing shelves reaching up to the ceiling. This petite older lady was wearing delicate white sandals and was happy to finally have someone to chat with about the heat (the offices and storerooms had no air conditioning), the problems with the underground trains, and her work stresses. Suddenly, she stopped in front of a large grey metal cabinet to show me something. When she opened it, I saw several rows of human skulls, at least twenty. I now know that they were *Toi moko*, mummified, ancestral heads of Māori from New Zealand. The little lady in her delicate white sandals proudly showed them to me and said, in a victorious, self-satisfied tone, that a delegation from their country of origin had recently come to honor their ancestors, but she had kept them hidden. I don't think I replied to her. But at that moment I was seized by a strong sense of dismay towards museums, an awareness of a deep injustice that I still feel today. This moment of inequity has profoundly influenced my museum career. For example, the first restitution – after twenty-six years of struggle – of ancestral remains to Hawaii, which had been in the repositories of the State Ethnographic Collections of Saxony until 2017, where I was director from 2015 to 2018, reminded me of this moment in time. The transfer of ownership of the 92 Benin court artworks back to Nigeria from the RJM in December 2022, following decades of demands for their return, was also a continuation of this. This may explain why working with collections characterised by invisibility and colonial violence has become one of the main concerns of my museum practice. Twenty-seven years have passed since my encounter with the little old lady in the white sandals. Since then, I have been trying to communicate new narratives and change hegemonic museum structures.

We live in a time between old and new power relations and major geopolitical changes – what Antonio Gramsci referred to as an "interregnum" or a transitional period. "The crisis consists precisely in the fact that the old is dying and the new cannot be born: in this interregnum, a great variety of morbid symptoms appear."[2] And so, ultimately, the museums that are deeply connected to the colonial past have also become diseased organisms. The project *RESIST!* was an attempt to heal this so-called sick organism.

2   Antonio Gramsci, *Selections from the Prison Notebooks*, New York: Quintin Hoare and Geoffrey Nowell Smith, 1971, p. 276

Whose stories are being told in ethnological museums?

These so-called ethnological collections were largely compiled at the peak of the European colonial empires, when the colonial powers felt entitled to bring millions of artefacts and photographs of people from the Global South to Europe and establish ethnological museums. Unfortunately, these collections are now lost in a dense fog of anonymity: millions of portrait photographs from ethnological collections are unidentified. The names of the creators and original owners of artefacts are rarely known, and the narratives and notes about the collected artefacts are virtually never from first-hand sources. Until now, ethnological museums were convinced that THEY alone could tell the stories about these people and the artefacts they created and used. Today, however, we must recognise that these museums, as a result of their one-sided, European, and still colonial perspective, have erased the various stories and meanings of these artefacts collected during the colonial era. Indeed, the way we conceive of and understand colonialism is embedded in the colonial structures and power relations that persist to this day. Colonialism consequently still controls our mentality through a hegemonic epistemic system. So, shouldn't the task of ethnological museums be to communicate the multidirectionality of memory from the colonial era?[3]

How can we address the power imbalances in the creation of narratives about the colonial past? How can we link specific looted artefacts to anti-colonial resistance in order to chronicle a multidirectional history of colonialism?

The aim of RESIST! was to rewrite, pluralise, and reinterpret narratives about the colonial past. It was a project that opposed the idea of the "single story". In order to do this, previously silenced stories were told and voices from the Global South which had been silenced were made audible.

But how can this be achieved in a white hegemonic system designed to exclude those affected by colonialism and racism? Although we currently live in a post-migrant society, the staff and directors in ethnological museums – like me – are rarely from or have family ties to the same countries of origin as the objects in their collections.

[3] Michael Rothberg, *Multidirectional Memory. Remembering the Holocaust in the Age of Decolonization*. Stanford: Stanford University Press, 2009

RESIST! was an exhibition about the resistance of men and women against the colonial regime, a system that – I am paraphrasing Aimé Césaire here – drained societies of their essence, undermined their institutions, confiscated their land, smashed their religions, and destroyed their material culture. RESIST! was a story about colonial violence and systematic oppression, about the structural racism that eats away our society like a cancer, pervading the museum too, and under which so many people still have to suffer. And if these stories are not told, if they do not become part of the museum narrative, then the ghosts of colonialism will never be exorcised.

The fundamental problem of ethnological museums is the negation of historicism, that is, of the historical dimension of societies and the colonial relationship. Who has interpretative sovereignty over colonial history? Who produces history? As the Haitian historian and anthropologist Michel-Rolph Trouillot points out in his book – one of the books that inspired me to start this project – history is the history of power, the history of the victors. It is "the fruit of power, but power itself is never so transparent that its analysis becomes superfluous. The ultimate mark of power may be its invisibility; the ultimate challenge, the exposition of its roots."[6]

In ethnological museums, voices from the Global South are suppressed and museum institutions retain power over the narrative. This is paradoxically demonstrated by myself, a white museum director of Dutch nationality, who initiated and led RESIST! and who is writing this essay from a position of power.

What does the "dialogue of cultures" that museums have venerated for so many decades look like in reality? What does this so-called equal cooperation with countries of origin look like? What do restitution and decolonisation, words uttered so readily by every museum director nowadays, actually mean? If perspectives from the Global South on objects and stories remain invisible, and only Western monocultural perspectives are reflected in our structures and our programming, then the so-called decolonisation of the museum as an institution will not succeed. Museums should focus on voices from the regions of origin – and by that, I mean perspectives that are not translated or

»Colonial domination involves the deliberate destruction of other cultures. The destruction of knowledge (besides the genocide of indigenous people) is what I call epistemicide, the destruction of the knowledge and cultures of these populations, of their memories and ancestral links and their manner of relating to others and to nature. Their legal and political forms – everything – is destroyed and subordinated to the colonial occupation«[4]

Boaventura de Sousa Santos, *Epistemologies of the South and the Future*, 2016

[4] Boaventura de Sousa Santos, „Epistemologies of the South and the Future", in: *From the European South: a transdisciplinary journal of postcolonial humanities*, 1, 2016, 18

[5] Michel-Rolph Trouillot, *Silencing the Past. Power and the Production of History*. Boston: Beacon Press 2015 (1995), 147

[6] Ibid., p. 5

»... the problem of historical representation is how to represent that ghost, something that is and yet is not..«[5]

Michel-Rolph Trouillot, *Silencing the Past. Power and the Production of History*, 1995

[7] Édouard Glissant, "The Quarrel with History", *Carribean Discourse: Selected Essays*, Charlottesville: University Press of Virginia, 1992, p. 64

mediated by museum curators. Édouard Glissant[7] rightly says that history should not be exclusively left to university historians. We need a museum that disseminates a multitude of histories, a "polyphonic museum" with different perspectives on the collections and colonial history, and even beyond colonial history, because history did not begin with colonialism, and this must be integrated into every level of museum work.

With *RESIST!* we wrote a new, multivocal, non-linear, and non-hierarchical narrative that was reflected in the labyrinthine staging and patchwork of narratives, an assortment of historical objects from the RJM collection, documents, film, music, contemporary artworks, and recorded conversations with a wide range of relevant figures. The exhibition gradually became a progressively louder cacophony of voices from freedom fighters, artists, thinkers, activists, musicians, and visitors from the past and present.

RESIST! is a strategy to view our own collection through the lens of colonial violence and resistance. Telling the story of anti-colonial resistance through the objects themselves is also a way of reinscribing them in the history of colonialism, which only needs to be rewritten and made multidirectional.

> »*RESIST!* is perhaps the first time a museum has sought to interrogate its ethnological history through the idea of resistance, through the idea that in an object you can see not just an essence of who people are, not an ethnicity, but a history of resistance. And this is a move by which an ethnological museum seeks to re-inscribe itself as a history museum, in a sense, as a museum about societies from Africa and other parts of the Global South in which they are rendered historical.«
>
> Ciraj Rassool in *RESIST!-Conversation Benin 1897–Köln 2021*, online discussion, 14/05/2021

At the beginning of the research for *RESIST!* it was virtually impossible to identify objects in the collection that could tell these stories about resistance, because most of the objects are hardly documented. *RESIST!* is therefore also a long-term research project that goes beyond classical provenance research, because the research does not begin at the time the object was looted, but seeks to focus on the period before this occurred, in other words, the period when a population was resisting their colonisers. Consequently, *RESIST!* is also an attempt to give these objects agency and to allow them to once again become part of a history that had been silenced.

Even the Benin court artworks, which were looted during the massacre by the British colonial army in February 1897, are evidence of resistance. The Kingdom of Benin did not want to submit to the British and their claims to power. Any interpretation of the Benin artworks from Nigeria, then, is only complete if the resistance of the Kingdom of Benin is also taken into consideration.

RESIST! methods

With *RESIST!* we wanted to initiate a process of transformation, aiming to arrive at a museum that could serve as a tool for communities to present themselves in the public sphere. The scenography of the exhibition established the framework and the basis for starting negotiations and conversations between the various people involved.

The unique aspect of the *RESIST!* approach was to establish relationships rather than to proclaim factual, in this case "ethnological explanations".

RESIST! was a living and organic space that allowed for the negotiation and restructuring of conflictual relationships in a collaborative process.

RESIST! was conceived as a heterogeneous platform that sought to realise a redistribution of knowledge and experience and make a multitude of voices, media, and formats audible. Activists, thinkers, and politically engaged artists were invited to speak for themselves. The museum's influence over the creation of the stories in the exhibition was to be kept to a minimum. The goal of RESIST! was not only to fragment the dominant discourse of colonial historiography and make space for multiple voices, but also to actively promote the necessary process of simultaneous reflection, recognition, and negotiation of history within different societies and communities. RESIST! was intended as a kind of "factory" for the production of new narratives, a gigantic platform for micro and macro narratives from all times and places.

Over 40 international, national, and local artists took part in RESIST!, including already renowned artists such as Kader Attia, Belkis Ayón, and Kara Walker, but also less established artists, such as the Nigerian rapper Monday Midnite and young urban dancers from Cologne led by choreographers Bahar Gökten and Daniela Rodriguez, as well as musicians and theatre actors from Lomé (Togo), to name just a few. As the role of women in the history of anticolonial resistance is largely underestimated, the exhibition has given priority to female voices, and the vast majority of works in the exhibition have therefore been produced by women artists.

A team of museum mediators, whom we called "live speakers", made up mainly of people affected by racism themselves, worked as hosts in the RESIST! exhibition and interacted with visitors. Each person thus brought their own biography and voice into the exhibition. Quotes from artists and thinkers, comments from visitors left at the Library of Resistance or the It's Yours! space by In-Haus e.V., resistance music selected by artist-in-residence DJ Rokia Bamba, and the RESIST! Conversations (digital

»The role of institutions such as archives and museums in the ›preservation‹ of the past is the effect of a vast enterprise of destruction conducted at the expense of and as a substitute for destroyed worlds. [...] If what they preserve is extracted from living worlds, and if living worlds are producing objects whose destination is the museum and archive, their study cannot be confined to what is in them but should include the role they play in this enterprise of world destruction – in the production of what Hannah Arendt calls worldlessness.«[8]

Ariella Aïsha Azoulay, *Potential History. Unlearning Imperialism*, 2019.

[8] Arielle Aisha Azoulay, *Potential Histroy. Unlearning Imperialism*, London: Verso, 2019, p. 19–20

»If you allow only the colonialists to record history, they record it to their own glorification. I wanted to take that position of power, of historical painting, and put it into my own hands – take possession of history. I'm just an Indian trying to emancipate myself, but I still will look at these things. I may be under colonial occupation, but I will think about these things.«

Lawrence Paul Yuxweluptun, artist exhibited in *RESIST!*

talks with the *It's Yours!* curators, debates on the restitution of the Benin court artworks and the Reconciliation Agreement between the Federal Republic of Germany and Namibia regarding the German genocide of the Herero and Nama) were added over the duration of the exhibition. Historical documents, including portraits of enslaved people who successfully resisted their enslavement on the ship Amistad in 1839, contributed individual and personal elements to the narratives of resistance. In this supposed chaos, in this cacophony of voices, objects from our collection told their own micro-stories.

»Look at the power structures within your institution and question yourself how they came to be. Are you willing to make sacrifices and to give up your privileged position for a more just and equal world? It's not up to Black people to educate you. Ignorance is a privilege too.

I don't know enough about the situation in Germany during Covid 19 but in the Netherlands none of the cultural institutions grabbed the opportunity to make themselves politically relevant. They were all complaining about money and the importance of art instead of opening up there spaces to give shelter to homeless people.

And another thing to keep in mind: Nothing about us without us.«

Patricia Kaersenhout, 2021, artist exhibited in *RESIST!*

9   Nur Sobers-Khan, „The Islam in Europe Exhibition and the World of Islam Festival", in: Osur Öztürk, Xenia Gazi, Sam Bowker: *Deconstructing the Myths of Islamic Art*. New York/London, 2022, p. 57

»Failure as curatorial practice can represent a fertile site for thinking, and a generative source for the creation of narratives, especially disruptive narratives. Failure permits a glimpse into the inner workings of the institutional complex and its relation to its collections and the communities it claims to serve. Failure can highlight the unspoken fault lines of an institution – its structural racism, its misogyny, its Islamophobia, its general mismanagement, the ways in which its origins in violent colonial history reinscribe colonial hierarchies and power dynamics on the present – and how these fault lines can suddenly illuminate the limitations of the cultural heritage sector and its origins in imperialist violence.«[9]

Nur Sobers-Khan, *The Islam in Europe Exhibition and the World of Islam Festival*, 2022

RESIST! thus gradually became a monumental and collective sculpture in which chance encounters between people, ideas and historical facts were intentional. *RESIST!* gave space to heterogeneous narrative forms within a structure composed of five chapters, which are reproduced here in the book: Chapter 1 – Liberation Struggles, Uprisings, Protests, Chapter 2 – Subversion and Refusal, Chapter 3 – Own Stories, Own Narratives, Chapter 4 – Trauma and Transformation, Chapter 5 – Cultural Resilience or the Art of Survival?

RESIST! became a "performative installation", a rhizomatic exhibition of stories in which objects and artworks functioned both as witnesses and as active players, forming a complex of snippets and remnants of resistance connected by the red beams that formed and supported the labyrinthine structure of the exhibition. Within this complex, four autonomous spaces, the so-called *It's Yours!* spaces, spaces for self-determination, were erected. The first *It's Yours!* space *Not About Us without Us* by Ida Hoffmann and Esther Utjiua Muinjangue addressed the German genocide of the Herero and Nama and referred to Germany's role in European colonial history. In the second *It's Yours!* space, *Benin 1897*, Peju Layiwola displayed the RJM's 92 Benin court artworks from Nigeria for the first time and explored the connection between museum collections and colonial violence, as well as the struggle for restitution. She first conceived this space back in 2020, at a time when no one would have believed that the restitution of the Benin court artworks would actually take place only two years later. The third *It's Yours!* space, *No Resistance Fits in a Box* by the Cologne grassroots organisation In-Haus e.V., was dedicated to the fight against racism in Cologne. And in the fourth *It's Yours!* space, *Roma Resist!*, the curator Tímea Junghaus highlighted the resistance of the Roma and the Sinti, the largest European minority, against the "colonial regime" within the borders of Europe. The *It's Yours!* autonomous spaces thereby not only "occupied space" in the physical sense, but also in the institutional context of "curatorial activism" in a public space. The principle of these four autonomous *It's Yours!* spaces was to facilitate both the physical and symbolic "occupation" of an institutional space and discourse. To distinguish them from the labyrinthine architecture of their surroundings, the four *It's Yours!* spaces were simple white cubes and were designed by the *It's Yours!* curators.

I first implemented this practice of "giving space" as director of the Grassi Museum of Ethnology in Leipzig in 2018. In the exhibition *Megalopolis: Voices from Kinshasa*,[10] I gave a collective of artists from Kinshasa "carte blanche" to curate an exhibition about their own city. "Carte blanche" in this context meant freedom of action based on mutual trust. For a museum institution that struggles to envisage such an experimental arrangement and whose bureaucratic structures are inflexible, granting a "carte blanche" or creating an *It's Yours!* space was and is a challenge. In order to overcome this, a trusting relationship between the "colonial museum" and the "colonised" curator is essential. After all, even in instances where a "carte blanche" is granted or *It's Yours!* spaces are created, the museum remains the rule-maker in its own institution, deciding who has agency there and who does not. Here we can clearly notice the limits of efforts to decolonise institutions.

10 Nanette Snoep, "Carte blanche for Kinshasa – A future instruction book for the museum?", *Megalopolis: Voices from Kinshasa*, Leipzig: Grassi Museum für Völkerkunde, 2019, pp. 36–46

> »It is well known in the Roma community that the ethnographic museum is a *benga*, Romanes for ›devil‹. It is hell for Roma culture.«[11]
>
> Tímea Junghaus *It's Yours!* curator, January 2021

11 *RESIST!* Conversations, January 2021. Tímea Junghaus, *It's Yours!* curator of *ROMA RESIST!* in conversation with Nanette Snoep

As can be seen from the exhibition plan shown on page 22, the four *It's Yours!* spaces formed the core structure of the exhibition, which were then surrounded by contemporary artworks dealing with the theme of resistance and objects from the museum collection, as well as historical documents bearing witness to acts of resistance. Modular spaces such as the *Library of Resistance*, the *Repair Atelier*, *Young Rebels*, and *No resistance without music* offered places for discussions, reading, writing, music sessions, and watching films.

The arrangement took the form of a labyrinth of narratives, historical events, voices, artistic works, and objects of resistance, presented not in chronological order, but as pieces of a gigantic puzzle.

RESIST! – not without resistance

The realisation of the exhibition was not without resistance, pain, and conflict. This colonial wound, these lingering traumatic memories in a colonial place, accompanied the exhibition and permeated the relationships between the museum director, the museum staff, artists, curators, museum mediators, the administration team, cooperation partners, communities, activists, the Museum Friends association, the regular mostly white audience and the new and more diverse and younger audience that had formed thanks to the *RESIST!* exhibition.

The live speakers' experiences of the exhibition were often painful, partly because of sometimes discriminatory behaviour of visitors, and partly because the museum could not create a safe space for them. The rigid administrative routines of the museum, such as questions about if and what kind of contracts could be made, humiliating visa procedures, and restrictions relating to the museum security were perceived by many participants from the Global South and from diasporic communities as the instrumentalisation of power and the manifestation of institutional racism. All of this made it difficult to build trusting relationships.

Thus, in our attempts to make *RESIST!* a place where diversity and multi-directional memory is lived out, the difficulties and limits of decolonising the ethnological museum soon became apparent. What does it mean when an institution rooted in the colonial past tries to include people affected by racism, but when this same institution was designed to exclude them?

One possible solution to these dilemmas was demonstrated by the role of In-Haus e.V., a grassroots organisation based in Cologne, whose director Elizaveta Khan was one of the four *It's Yours!* curators. This organisation acted as a point of contact for the other *It's Yours!* curators who could not be on site because of the pandemic. Among other things, In-Haus e.V. added protest signs by the *It's Yours!* curators Esther Utjiua Muinjangue and Ida Hoffmann to the exhibition that expressed their dissatisfaction with the negotiations relating to the so-called reparation agreement between Germany and Namibia that were going on at that time. It also supported *It's Yours!* curator Peju Layiwola in her fight for the restitution of the Benin court artworks on a local level, and planned exhibition visits for school groups to increase their awareness of the topic of restitution. In-Haus e.V. thus became an important mediator and ultimately ensured that the museum did not remain the sole rule-maker and facilitator.

Was *RESIST!* ultimately a form of collective therapy? How can we imagine the future of the ethnological museum, if it has one? Should it be seen as a place of mourning, a museum that lays bare wounds and allows society to heal? What might it mean for ethnological museums to play an active role in the healing process?

Should the ethnological museum be transformed into a "storytelling" museum, which means storytelling as a method for healing colonial wounds and developing resilience? But isn't this mission doomed to failure in a place so marked by colonial violence because of the history of its collections and its institution?

And now?

While we talk about a "colonial" conquest at the end of the nineteenth century, we are currently experiencing a so-called "decolonial" conquest, an ironic situation in which ethnological museums today are competing to "win" at decolonisation. In this interregnum period, decolonisation is on the lips of every ethnological museum director and staff member. Since realising that restitution is part of decolonisation and can help them to be viewed in a sympathetic light, they have changed their attitudes towards it. There are people who were staunchly opposed to returning artefacts just a short time ago who are now at the very forefront of decolonisation and restitution efforts. When we developed the concept for *RESIST!* in the summer of 2019, restitution was not yet an accepted museum practice for ethnological museums; now, as I write these last few sentences in December 2022, the ownership of the 92 Benin court artworks in the RJM was formally transferred to Nigeria on 15 December 2022 and the first three Benin court artworks have already been returned to Nigeria. My current fear is that, by consenting to restitution, ethnological museums already see themselves as absolved of their role in the continuation of the colonial system, and therefore do not believe they need to renounce their power and white privilege. How can we prevent decolonisation from becoming nothing more than an empty catchword?

We must remain vigilant that museums, in their "decolonial conquest", do not establish a new hegemony that is still based on the exclusion of the people that are most affected by racism and colonialism. To ensure this does not happen, critical voices need to be integrated into museum structures in order to drastically change them, so that people from the Global South and from the diaspora here in Europe can determine the future or not of ethnological museums themselves. This will be the challenge in the years to come.

RESIST!
Cologne, December 2022

»The easy adoption of decolonizing discourse by educational advocacy and scholarship, evidenced by the increasing number of calls to ›decolonize our schools‹, or use ›decolonizing methods‹, or, ›decolonize student thinking‹, turns decolonization into a metaphor.

The easy absorption, adoption, and transposing of decolonization is yet another form of settler appropriation.«[12]

Eve Tuck, K. Waye Yang, 2012

[12] Eve Tuck, K. Waye Yang, „Decolonization is not a metaphor" in *Decolonization: Indigeneity, Education & Society, Vol.1*, No. 1, 2012, pp. 1–40

[13] Audre Lorde, *Sister Outsider*, Penguin Random House, 2019 (1984), pp. 103–106

»The master's tools
will never dismantle the
master's house.«[13]
Audre Lorde, *Sister Outsider*, 1984

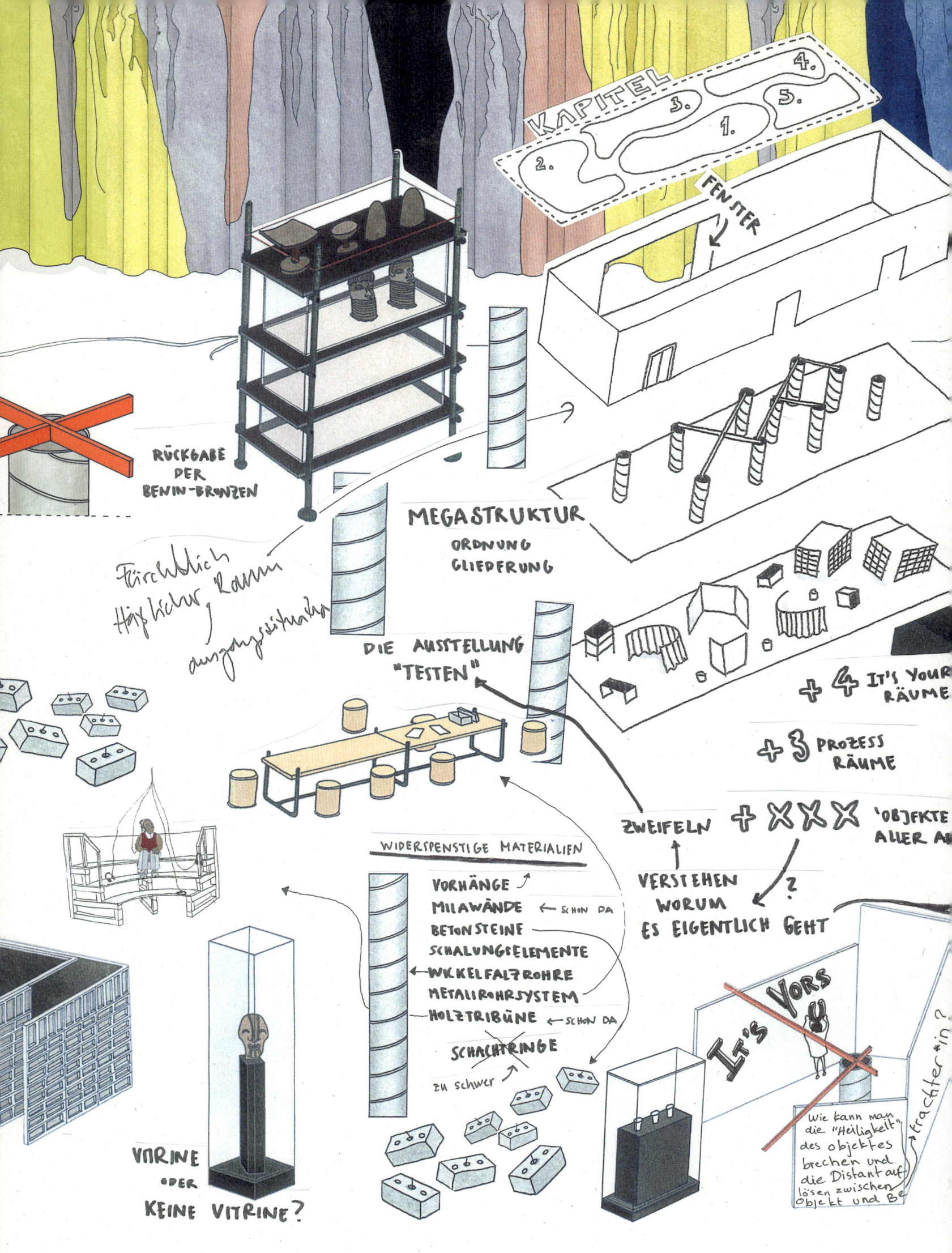

A reflection by **raumlaborberlin** on their design for *RESIST!*
more information: raumlabor.net/resist

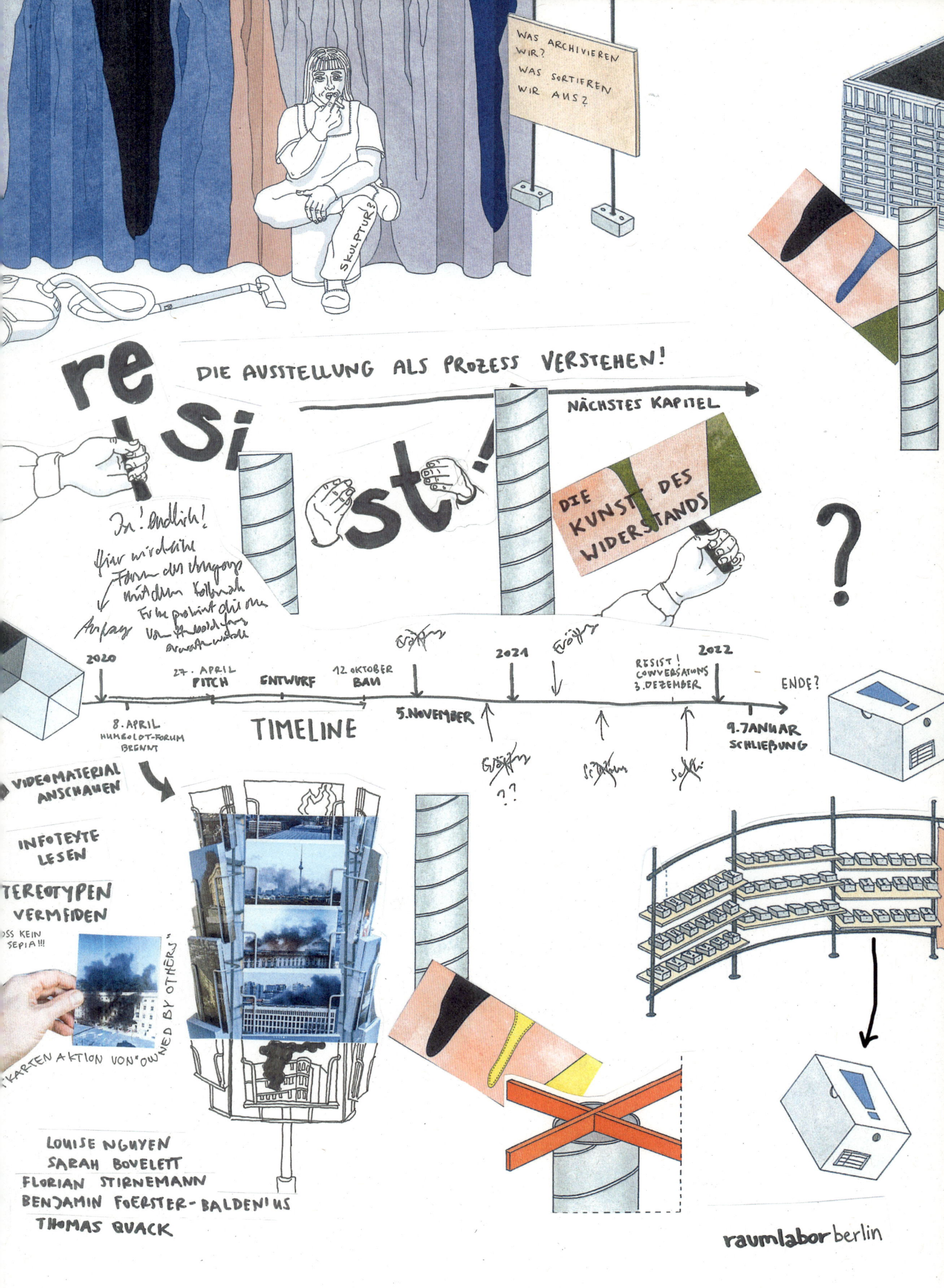

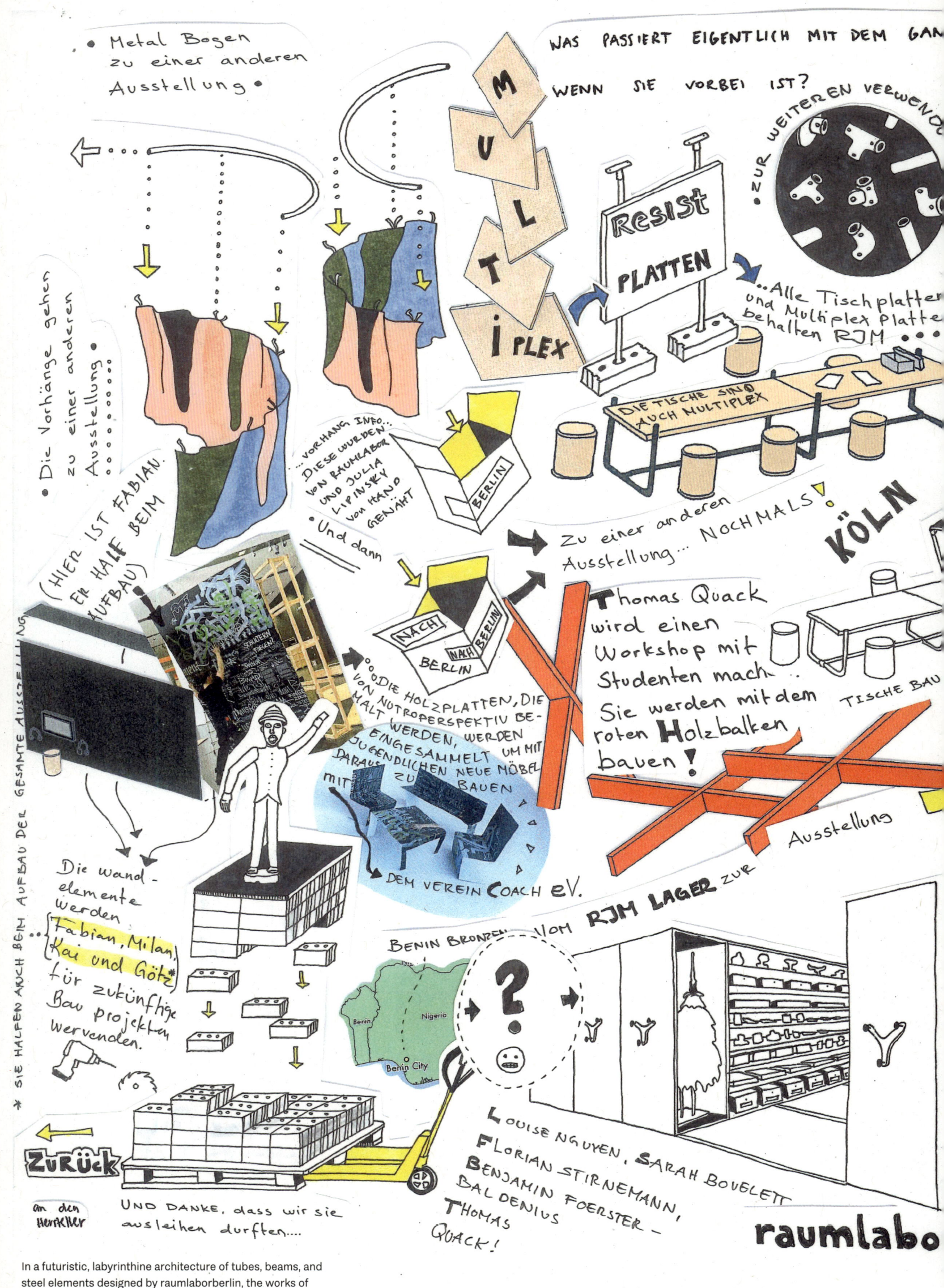

In a futuristic, labyrinthine architecture of tubes, beams, and steel elements designed by raumlaborberlin, the works of over forty contemporary artists from the Global South and the diaspora told stories of rebellion and war, violence and trauma, survival and resilience.

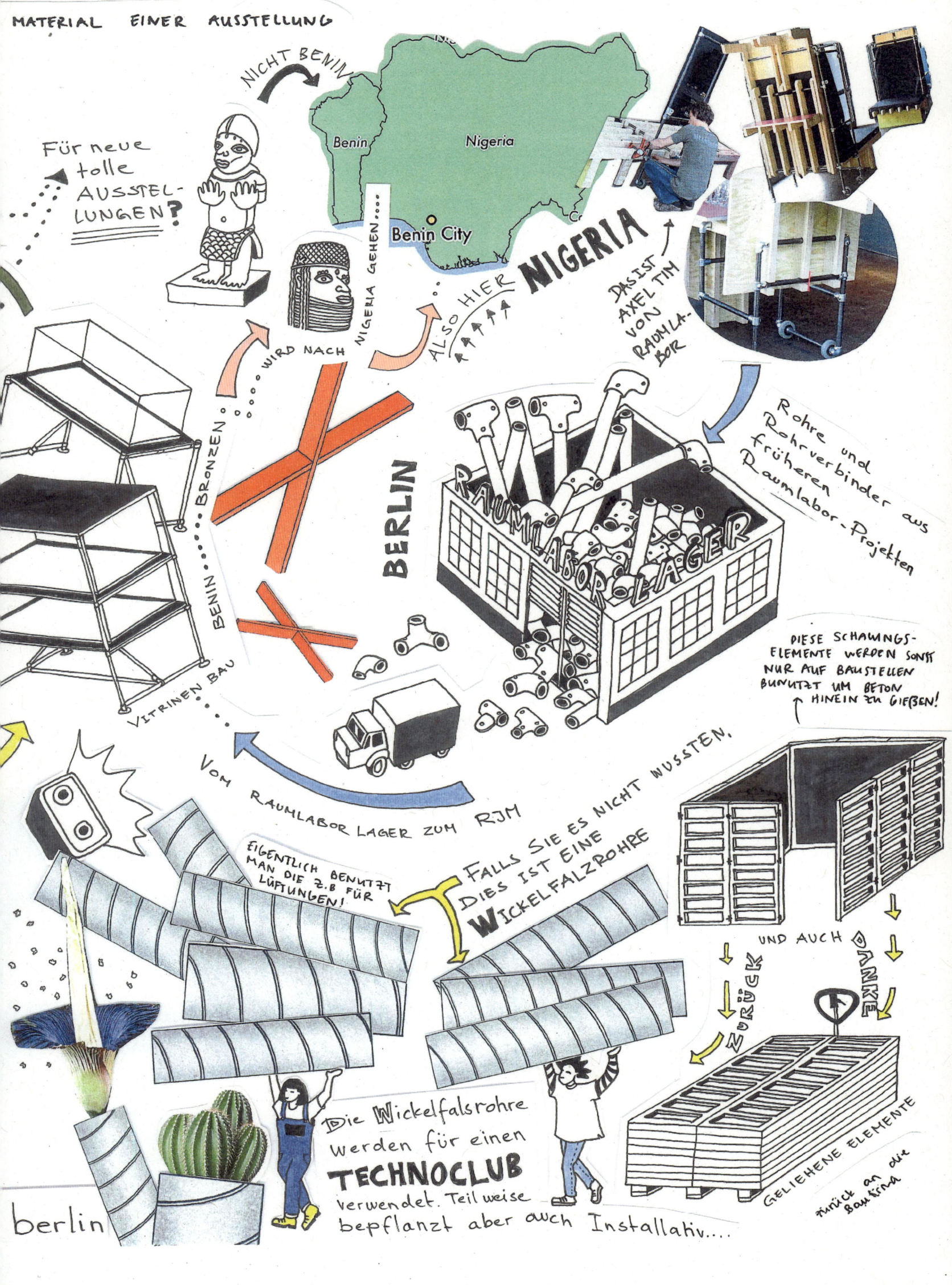

29/01/2021–09/01/2022

It's Yours! space
Peju Layiwola
Benin 1897

It's Yours!-space
In-Haus e.V.
No Resistance fits in a Box!

Chapter 3
One's own Stories, One's own Narratives

Chapter 4
Trauma and Transformation

It's Yours! space
Tímea Junghaus
Roma Resist!

Library of Resistance

Young Rebels

Repair Atelier

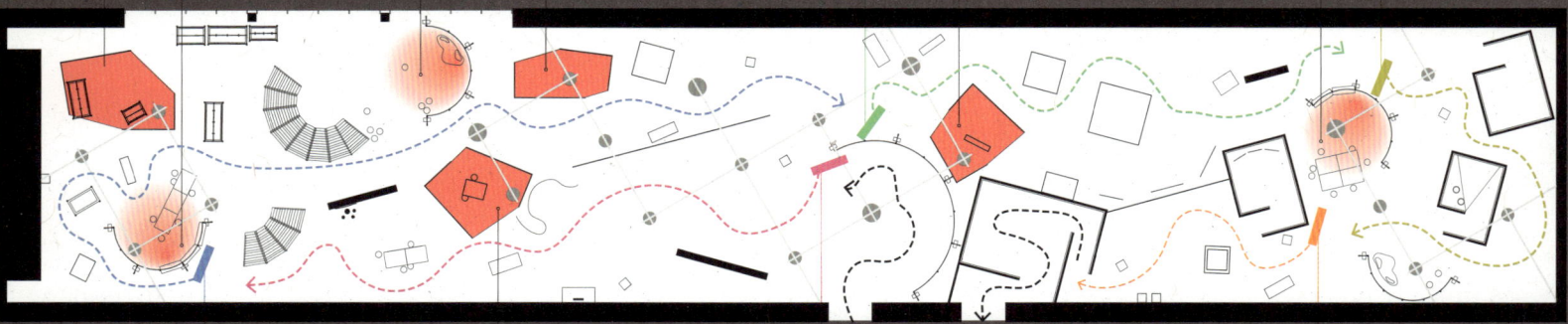

Entrance   Exit

Chapter 2
Subversion und Refusal

It's Yours! space
Esther Utjiua Muinjuangue & Ida Hoffmann
Not About Us without Us

Leave a Comment

Chapter 1
Liberation Struggles, Uprisings, Protest

Chapter 5
Cultural Resilience or the Art of Survival?

»When we revolt it's not for a particular culture. We revolt simply because, for many reasons, we can no longer breathe.«
Frantz Fanon   *The Wretched of the Earth*, 1961

022

Rautenstrauch-Joest Museum—Cultures of the World

RESIST! The Art of Resistance

The Art of Resistance is dedicated to the human struggle for freedom, self-determination and survival. RESIST! is about survival strategies and self-empowerment. The exhibition is a tribute to the people who have resisted in various ways and whose stories are still rarely told or heard today.

European colonialism is a 500-year-old system of violent conquest and appropriation of foreign territories in the Global South, plus the associated subjugation, exploitation and enslavement – up to and including the extermination of entire populations. Resistance against Western domination has been unceasing since the arrival of Christopher Columbus in America in 1492. That struggle has been individual and collective, secret and open, covert and open. The impact of colonial traumas and continuities, unequal power dynamics and institutional racism can still be felt today. The BlackLivesMatter movement, the worldwide destruction of colonial monuments, the demands for the restitution of cultural objects looted from the Global South: all these illustrate the liberation process.

In Silencing the Past (1995), the Haitian ethnologist Michel-Rolph Trouillot stresses the continuity of anti-colonial resistance: this continuity, he argues, suggests that an anti-racist present and future is possible. RESIST! follows this claim to create a space for repressed and marginalised voices. The exhibition exposes wounds and presents the unfinished process of healing – while openly asking whether one can meaningfully represent resistance in a museum whose very collections and institutional history are so directly intertwined with colonialism.

Different strategies of resistance are narrated using contemporary art, historical sources and objects from the museum's own collection without any claim to a comprehensive historical overview. In a kaleidoscope of images, voices, things and stories, the exhibition presents five chapters about revolt and protest, refusal and subversion, self-determination and the rewriting of history, trauma, transformation and resilience.

RESIST! is an interactive and constantly-changing exhibition in which over 40 artists and activists from the Global South and the diaspora tell their stories. Through the use of polyphony it attempts to dismantle the previous narrative that has been far too one-sided. Within this labyrinth, four autonomously curated rooms bring to light additional perspectives: Namibian activists Esther Utjiua Muinjangue and Ida Hoffmann tell a German-Namibian story – the story of the first genocide of the 20th century, directed against the Herero and Nama people in Namibia. Nigerian artist Peju Layiwola deals with cultural objects looted from the Kingdom of Benin (Nigeria), many of which form part of the RJM collection. To address colonial apparatuses in Europe, Hungarian curator Tímea Junghaus recounts the struggle of the Sinti and Roma for self-determination, and the Cologne-based post-migrant association In-Haus e.V. denounces racism in Germany.

Addressing colonialism and its unconscious legacy in the present is not easy and evokes different reactions and emotions, ranging from defensiveness, feelings of fragility, guilt and sadness to compassion, solidarity and understanding. In a nutshell, RESIST! is a platform for critical engagement with the colonial past and its continuities, which creates spaces for speaking, listening, networking, togetherness and solidarity.

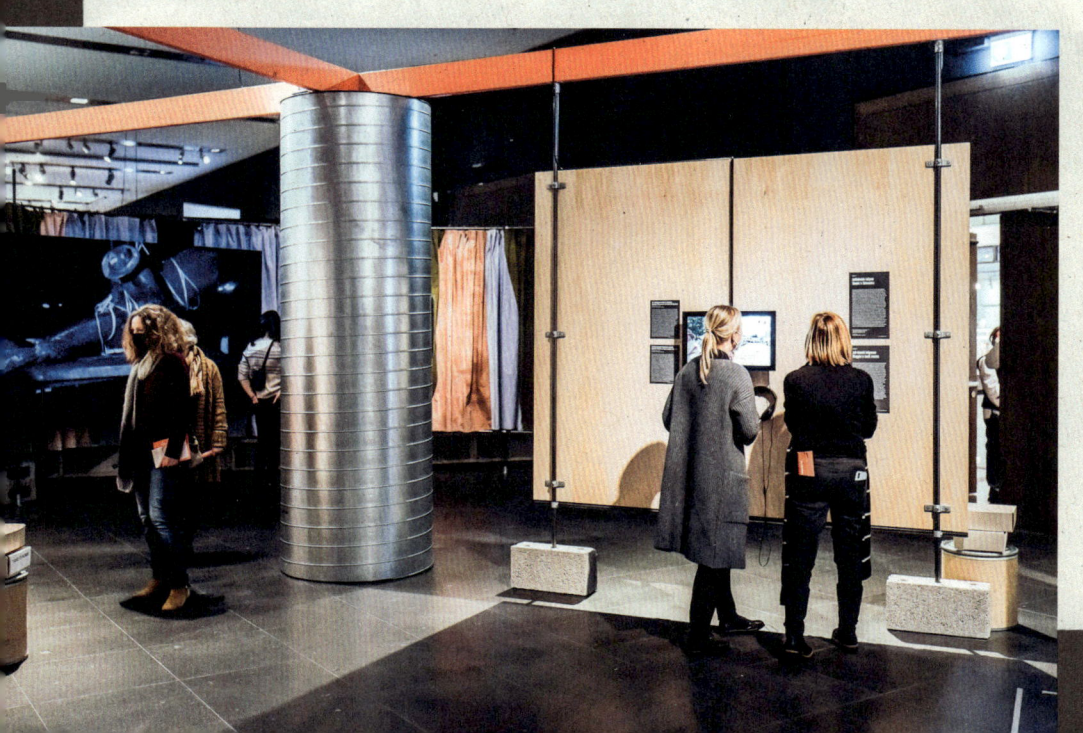

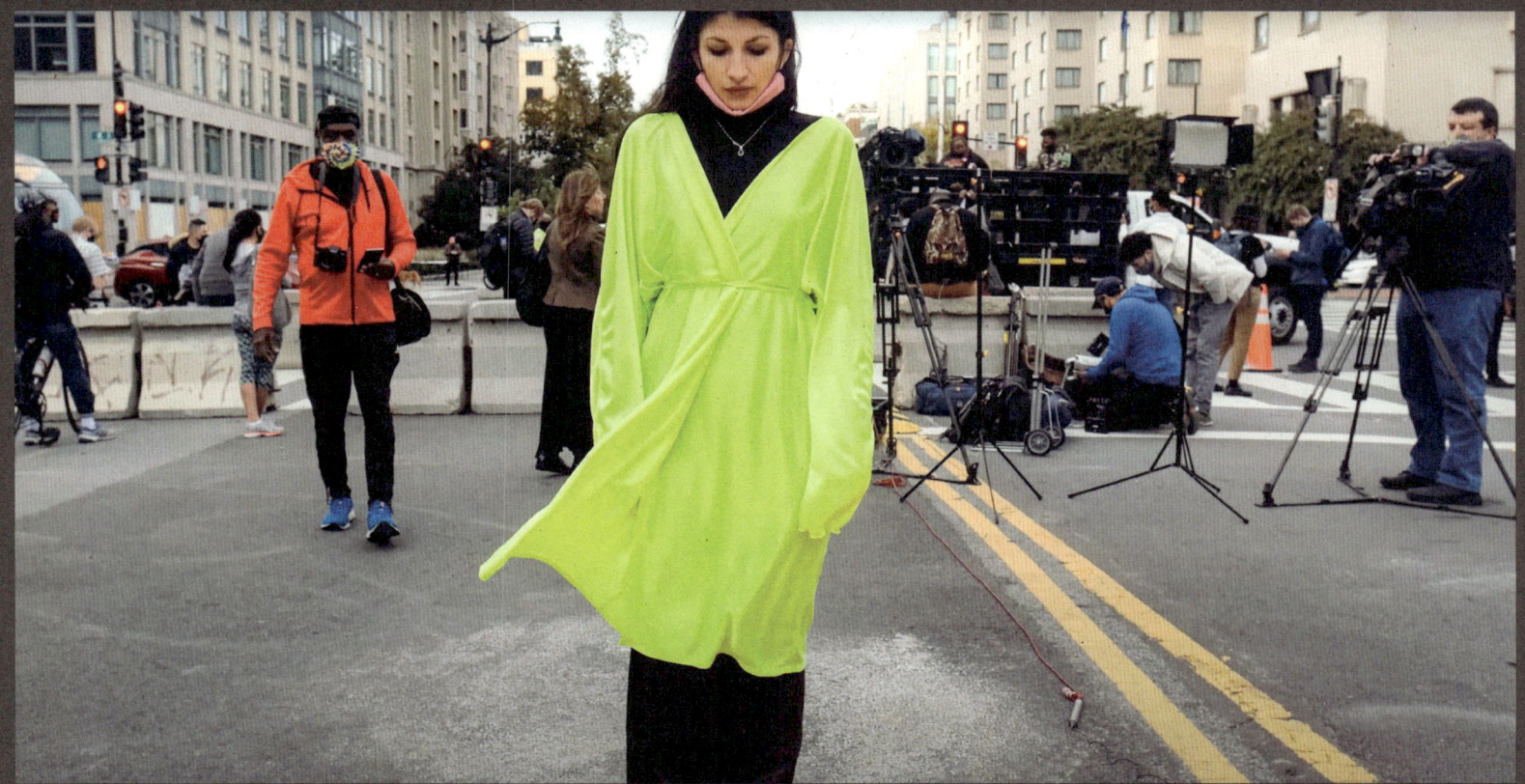

Selma Selman: *You Have No Idea*
3/11/2020, US Presidential Election Day, performance between BLM Plaza and the White House, Washington, DC, video, 5 min.

This video performance was part of the *It's Yours!* space Roma Resist! by Tímea Junghaus. Selman, shouting the same words over and over again, walks down BLM Boulevard in Washington, DC on Election Day 2020. Photojournalists from all over the world follow the artist while the crowd films her with their smartphones, expressing their fascination or disapproval.

»This performance is very personal: It is my frustration brought to life. You have no idea. You have no idea about my life as a whole. You do not know who I am; nor do you know my joy or my sorrow. You do not know whether there is pain in my life or not, or how I feel at that moment. You have no idea, no idea ...« *Selma Selman*

Washington, USA 03/11/2020

Removal of the Equestrian Statue of Mouzinho de Albuquerque Lourenço Marques (now Maputo)

Video, 08:11 min., RTP Arquivos (Rádio e Televisão de Portugal)

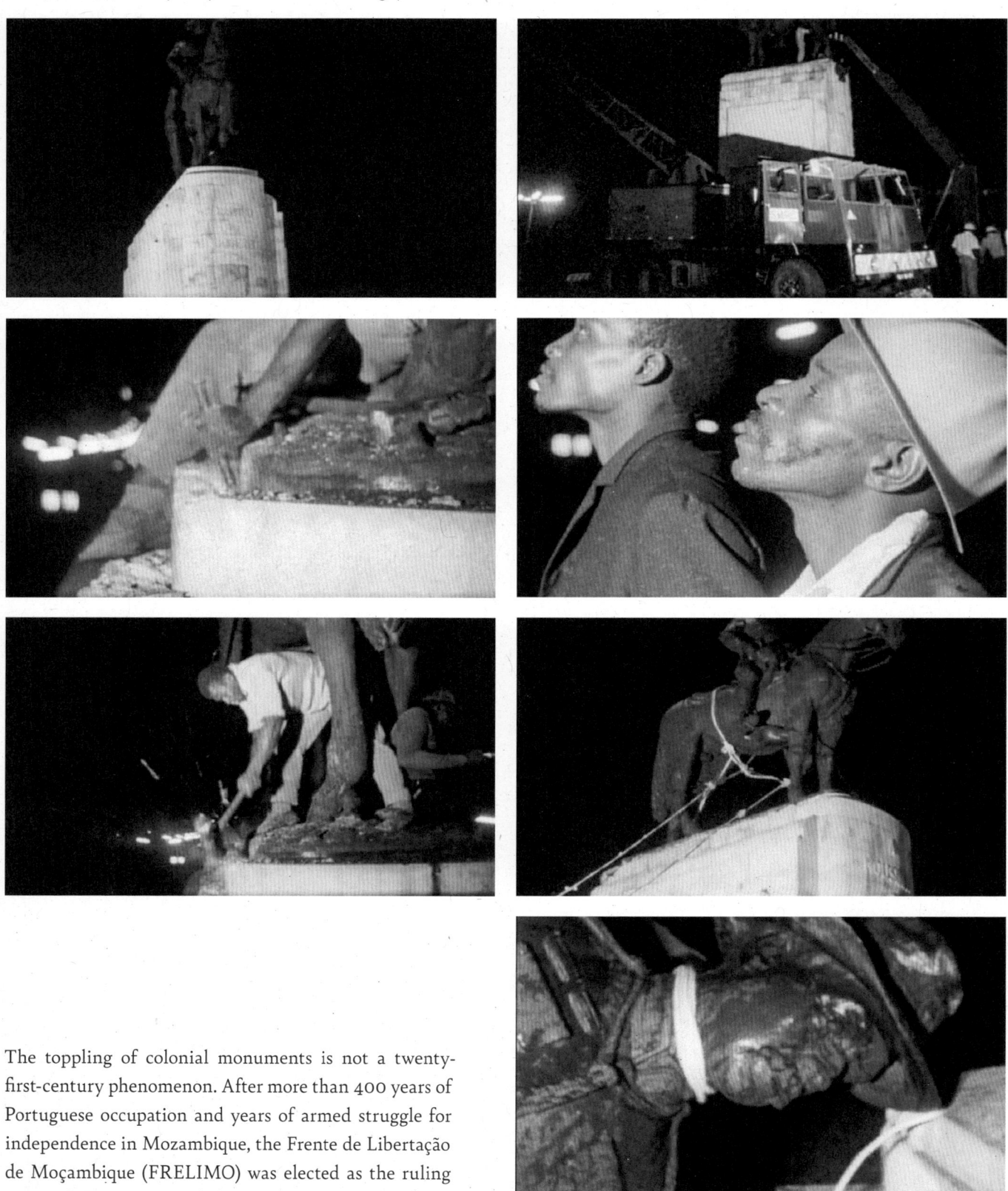

The toppling of colonial monuments is not a twenty-first-century phenomenon. After more than 400 years of Portuguese occupation and years of armed struggle for independence in Mozambique, the Frente de Libertação de Moçambique (FRELIMO) was elected as the ruling party of the independent Republic of Mozambique on May 21, 1975. Shortly after the proclamation of independence, FRELIMO destroyed and removed many colonial statues and monuments, such as this statue of Joaquim Augusto Mouzinho de Albuquerque (1855–1902), one of the most prominent figures in the colonial government of former Portuguese East Africa. For FRELIMO, he was the ultimate embodiment of the the arrogance of colonial rule. This footage shows firefighters and soldiers removing the equestrian statue of the unpopular colonial ruler from in front of the town hall in the middle of the night.

Maputo, Mozambique 21/06/1975

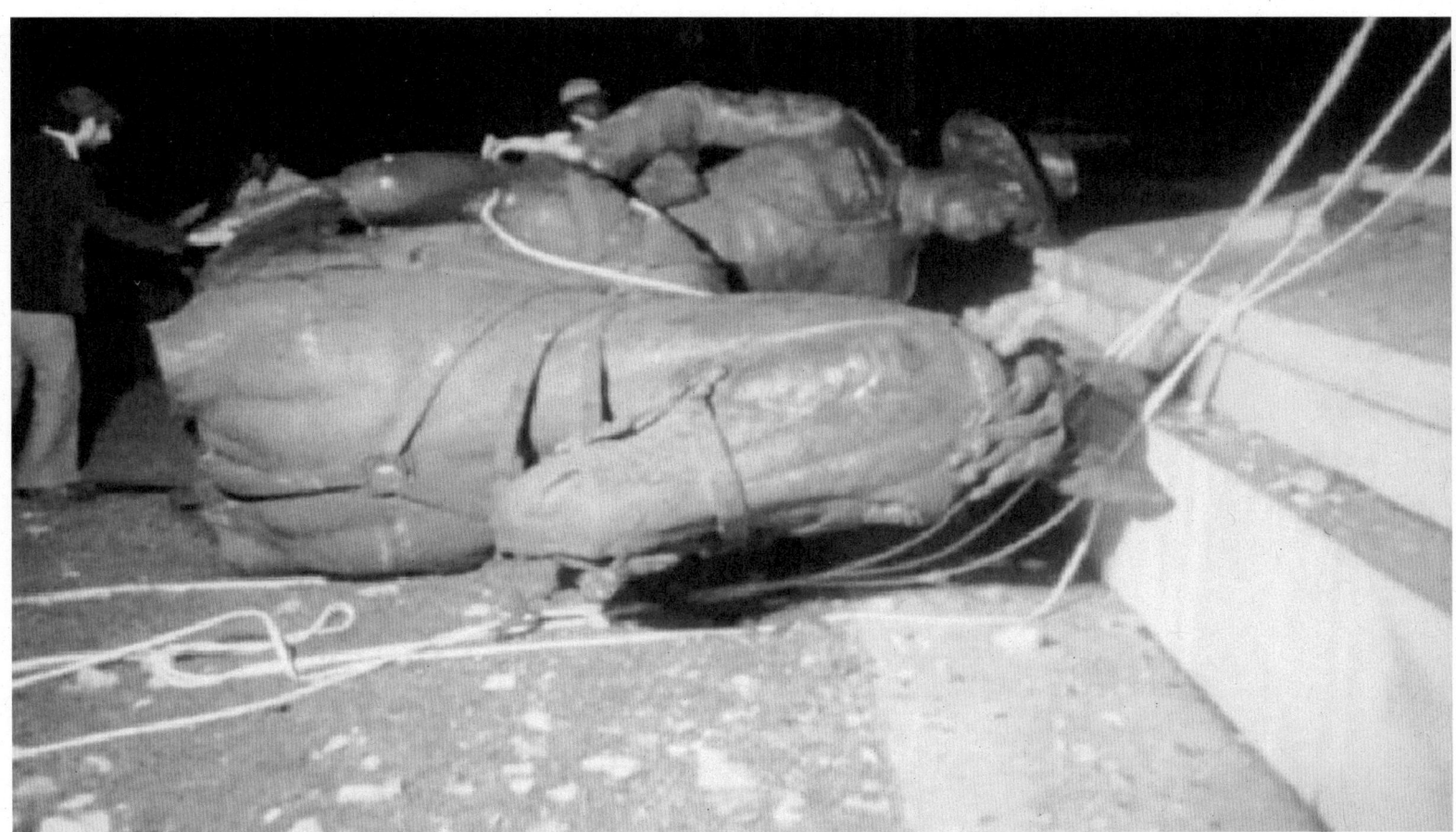

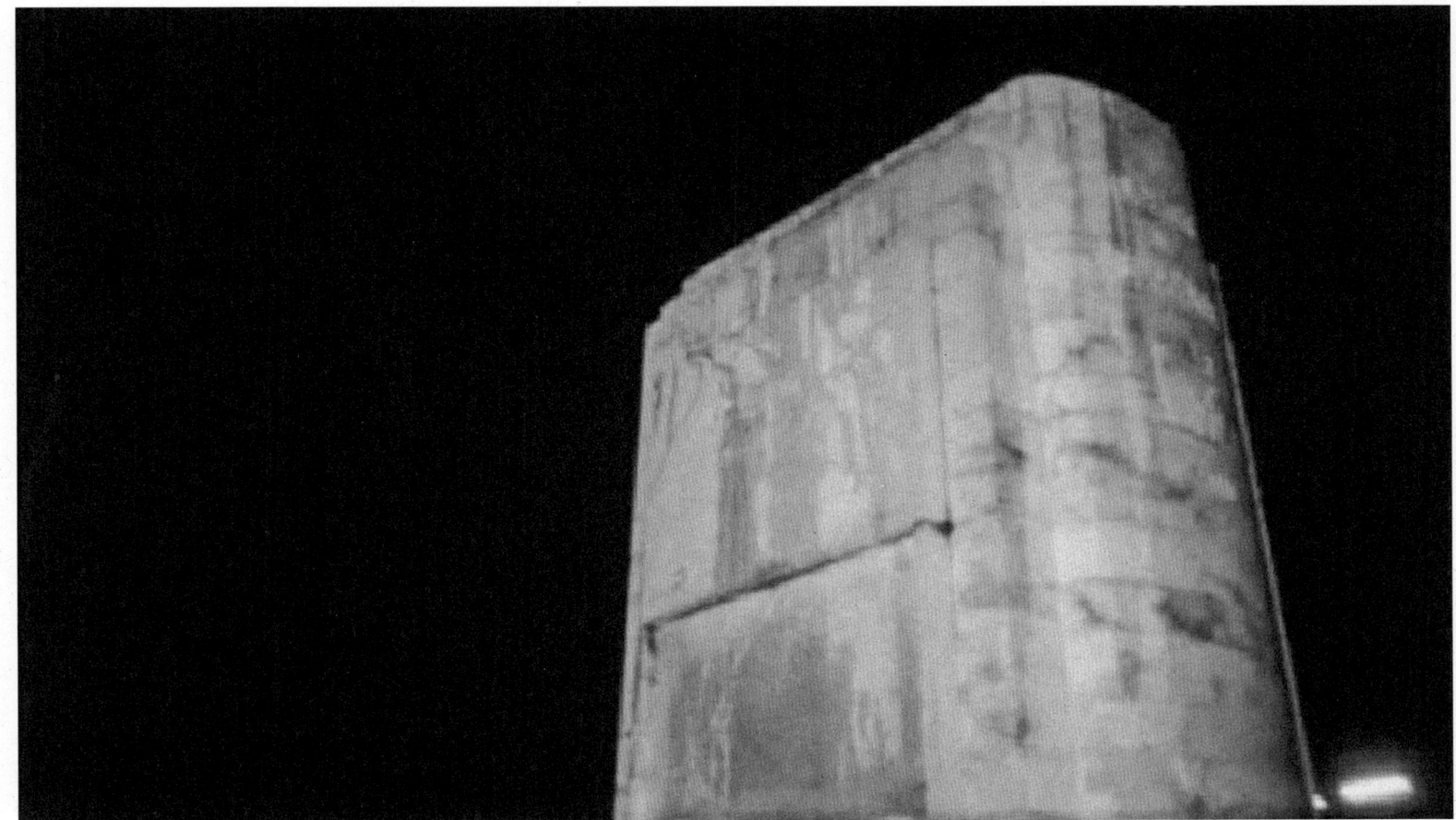

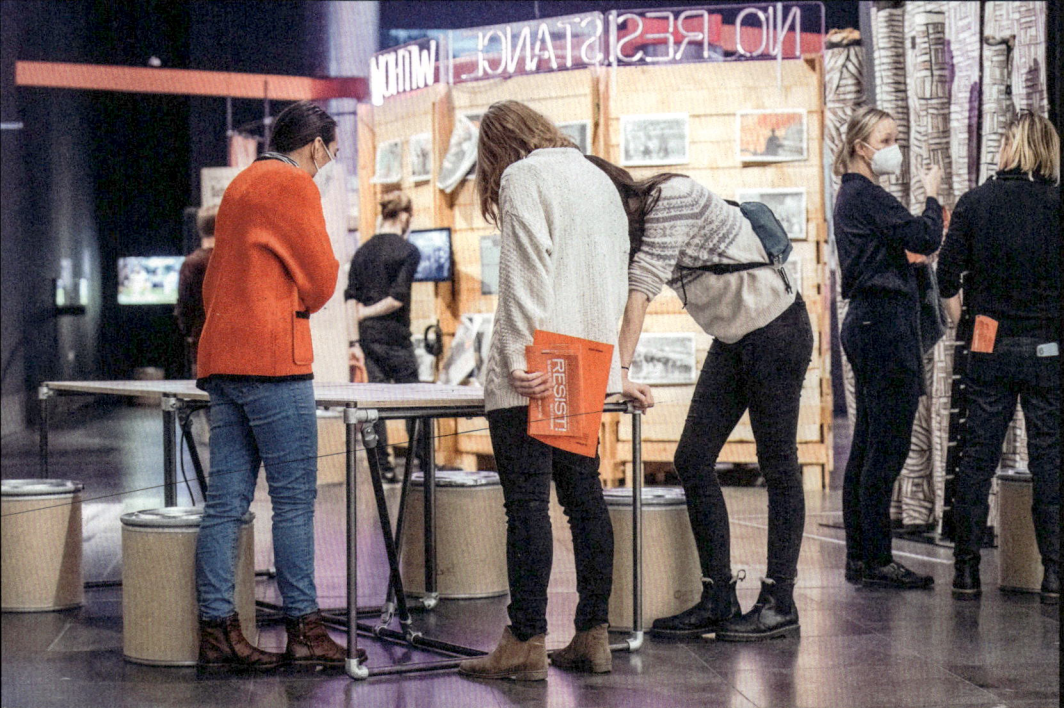

Liberation Struggles, Uprisings, Protests

"I look around and wherever there are colonizers and colonized face to face, I see force, brutality, cruelty, sadism, conflict [...]. No human contact, but relations of domination and submission which turn the colonizing man into a classroom monitor, an army sergeant, a prison guard, a slave driver", wrote Martinique-born Aimé Césaire in French in his 1955 book Discourse on Colonialism, which became the rally cry against colonial relations of domination, exploitation and their continuities.

Colonialism is part of our modern world – a history of conquest and violence, of trading human beings like commodities, of questing for resources, of a hegemonic knowledge system and of exploitation up to and including the extermination of entire population groups. Enslaved and colonised people were central agents of their own liberation. It was them who initiated radical breaks with the existing conditions. Even though each unfolding of anti-colonial protest must be considered in its contextual complexity, all resistance has one thing in common: oppression and violence was followed by resistance. The repertoire of resistance is broad, but struggles for independence and uprisings against colonial rule were a historical constant. In his book Black Skin, White Masks, the Martinique-born psychiatrist and writer Frantz Fanon explains how the colonised were driven to violence because there was no other way out. Minimised in historiography, these struggles and revolutions were often well organised. Frequently, they combined elaborate strategies with sophisticated tactics, and oftentimes, women played an important role in them.

In order to legitimise all colonial wars and exploitation and thus justify European colonialism even after the abolition of slavery, theories based on racism and "social Darwinist" were developed and disseminated from the 1860s onwards. The same period also saw the emergence of apartheid policies in South Africa and segregation in the United States, which have left deep wounds in society that still hurt today. After 1945, colonial empires began to dissolve, starting with India and ending with Angola and Mozambique, which became independent in 1975 after many years of bloody warfare. In 1989, Namibia gained its independence from South Africa. The process of decolonisation must be seen as a totality in which many different people (and peoples) in many places performed smaller and larger acts of resistance, enabling radical upheavals and establishing new forms of resistant thought and action, which have great influence on current struggles. Fanon described the relationship between

Cologne, Germany November 2020

colonisers and the colonised as a world divided in two, based on centuries of colonial violence. Have the relations between (ex-)colonisers and the (ex-)colonised changed since?
In a labyrinthine and provisional architecture, RESIST! tells of a noisy world full of broken images, cracks, disturbances and voids – but also of successful protests and uprisings that testify to the inexhaustible power of people to fight for freedom, independence and fairness.

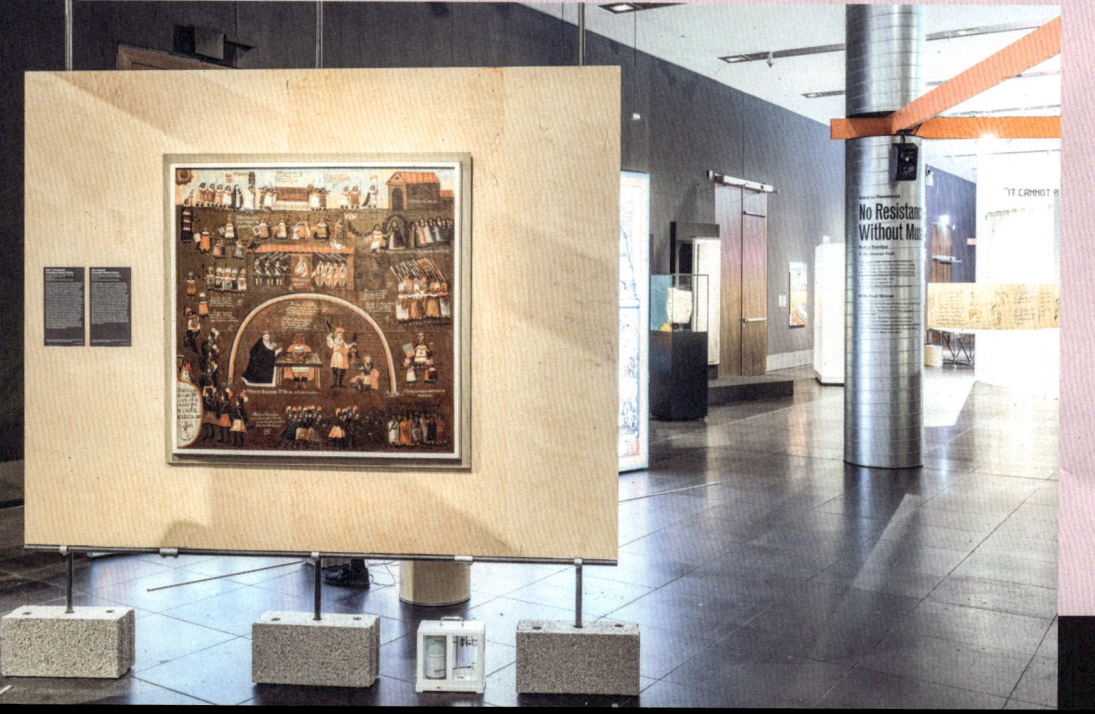

The Decapitation of Atahualpa in Cajamarca

Cajamarca, Peru **1533**

Artist not recorded
Original title *Degollación de Atahualpa en Cajamarca*, Peru, mid-eighteenth – early nineteenth century, oil on canvas

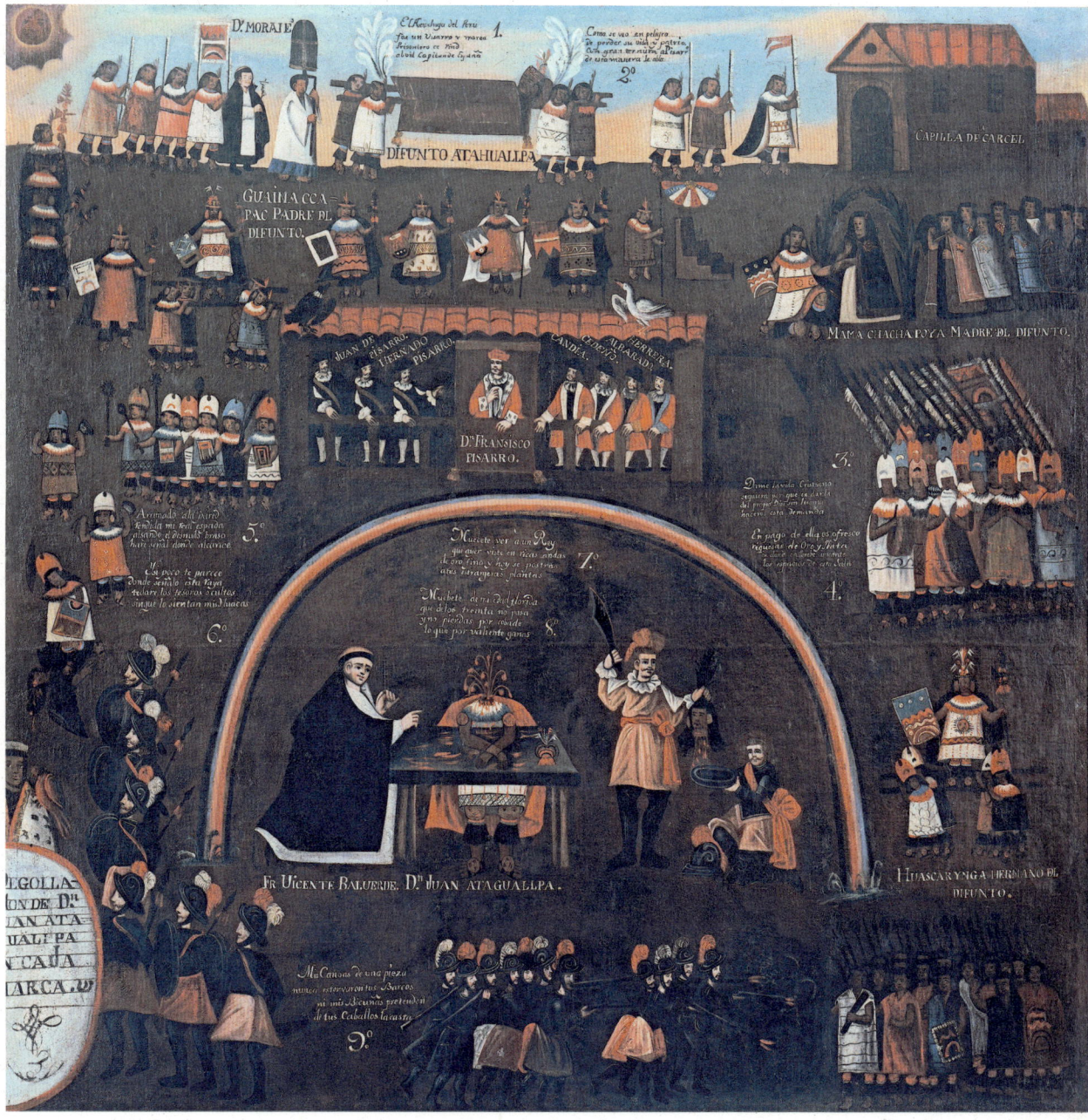

The Spanish colonial period in Latin America was marked by various resistance movements against colonial rule. They began with the first invasion of the Caribbean islands in 1492 and ended with the abolition of slavery in Cuba in 1886 and the conclusion of the last independence movements and wars in 1898. In modern-day Peru, the resistance and survival tactics of the Inca ruling dynasty began with the violent Spanish invasion of 1532: at their very first meeting in Cajamarca, the Spanish Captain General Francisco Pizarro took the Inca ruler Atahualpa hostage in order to use him for the further conquest of the Inca Empire. Atahualpa was executed by the Spanish in 1533. After more than forty years of resistance, the Inca Empire was officially considered "conquered" in 1572.

This painting depicts the execution of the Inca ruler Atahualpa by the Spanish in 1533. It was painted by an Indigenous artist whose style reflects the colonial reimagining of Inca imagery. Atahualpa, who was baptised by the monk Vicente Valverde (left) shortly before being beheaded by his executioners (right), sits under a rainbow. Above him stands Francisco Pizarro and his followers. At the edges of the picture, Inca soldiers resist the troops of the Spanish conquerors. Although eyewitness accounts state that the Inca ruler was strangled, his assassination is depicted as a beheading – a reinterpretation that can be traced back to Felipe Guamán Poma de Ayala's chronicle of Indigenous history from 1615. Later, in the course of the eighteenth century, the Inkarri myth emerged. It prophesied that the pre-Hispanic order of the Inca Empire could be restored by Atahualpa's body growing anew from his severed head. This myth, unknown to the Spanish, was also applied to Túpac Amaru II, who was actually beheaded in 1781 after his failed rebellion against the Spanish colonial rulers. While this image of Atahualpa may have been circulated after his death as a deterrent, it covertly represented a symbol of hope in the context of the Inkarri myth. Although the rebellion was unsuccessful, Túpac Amaru II was later glorified and went on to influence numerous Latin American resistance movements, including the Tupamaros guerrilla movement in Uruguay. In the context of the Inkarri myth this painting by an anonymous indigenous artist also represents a symbol of hope and survival.

Coraje Inka TV
The 239th Anniversary of Túpac Amaru II's Revolution

Documentation, 48:56 min., Coraje Inka TV

Tungasuca, Peru   2019

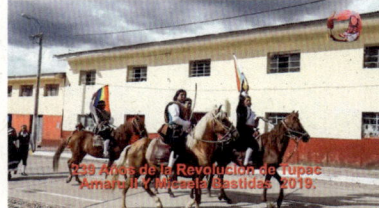
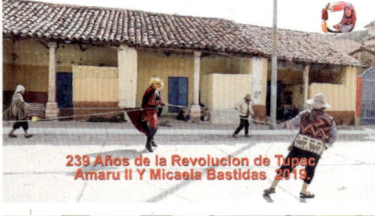
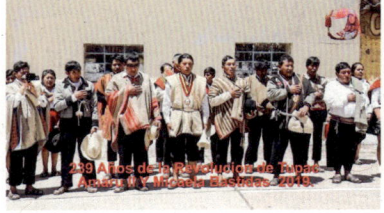
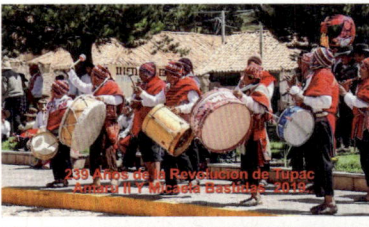
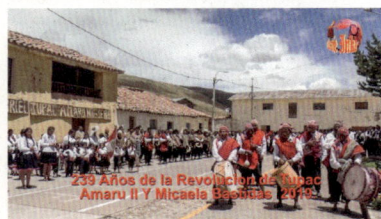
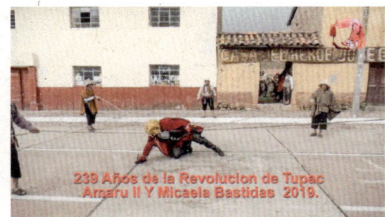
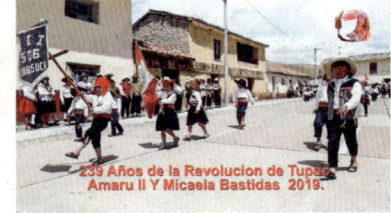
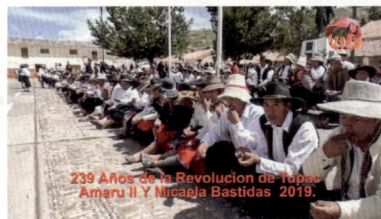
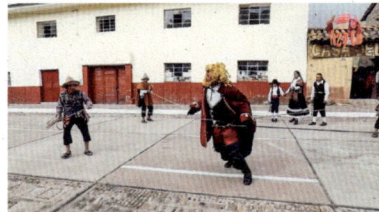
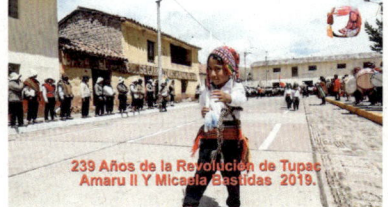
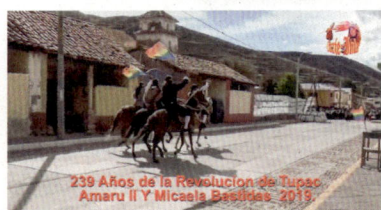
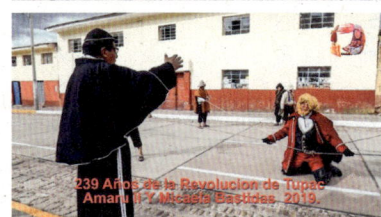

This documentary by the independent television channel Coraje Inka TV shows people celebrating the 239th anniversary of the rebellion led by Túpac Amaru II (1738–1781). José Gabriel Condorcanqui, the owner of a large estate and the descendant of Inca nobles, christened himself "Túpac Amaru II", explicitly positioning himself as the successor to the last Inca ruler, Túpac Amaru I. He initiated one of the largest Indigenous rebellions of the eighteenth century (1780–1783) against the Spanish in modern-day Peru, leading its initial phase together with his wife Micaela Bastidas Puyucahua. The rebellion was directed against the "Bourbon Reforms" of the Spanish colonial power, which were intended to put the native population at an even greater economic disadvantage. Condorcanqui and Bastidas were executed by the Spanish in 1781. The rebellion was continued by other leaders until its final failure in 1783. Today, images of Túpac Amaru II adorn T-shirts, posters, and the like. To commemorate the anniversary of these events, scenes from his struggle are re-enacted annually at major sites in Peru, as shown in this video from Tungasuca. With an army of around 80,000 fighters, Túpac Amaru II and his wife conquered southern Peru. Micaela Bastidas was active as a commander and also oversaw the recruitment and logistics of the resistance movement. The death of Túpac Amaru II and his wife marked the beginning of widespread guerrilla action by Indigenous people throughout South America. Their rebellion is considered the initial spark for the independence movements that led to the end of Spanish colonial rule four decades later.

The People Behind the Liberation Uprising on the Spanish Slave Ship Amistad

North Coast, Cuba — 01/07/1839
Freetown, Sierra Leone — November 1841

22 pencil drawings, 1839–42, William H. Townsend

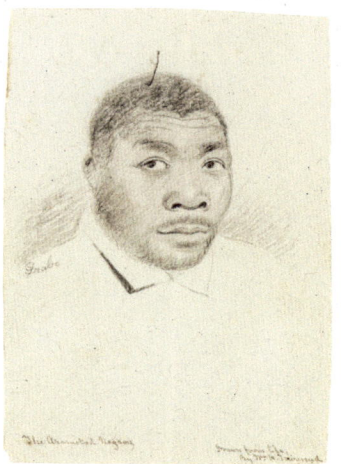

Grabeau

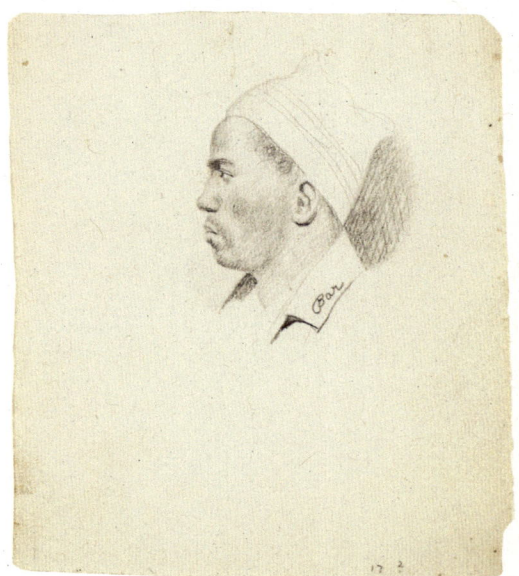

Bar

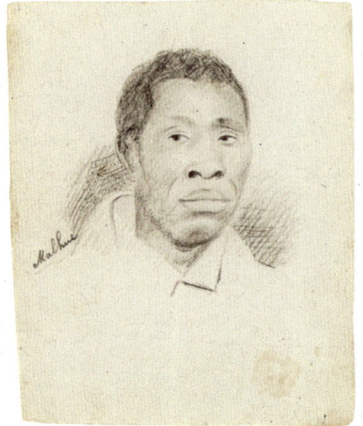

Malhue

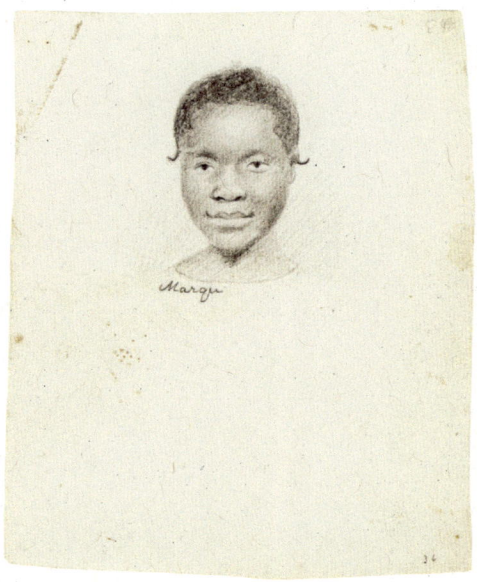

Marqu

The transatlantic slave trade (ca. 1500–1850) is one of the greatest crimes against humanity: over the course of 400 years, some 17 million people were taken from Africa to the Americas and enslaved. From the very beginning, there were rebellions among those enslaved. Many revolts were already beginning on the slave ships, but most were brutally suppressed. A pivotal moment in the history of slave rebellion is the Amistad Mutiny. One of the rare successful uprisings on a slave ship, it has been very well documented. These portraits depict twenty-one men and a 9-year-old girl. They came from Lomboko, Sierra Leone with twenty-nine other men, two young girls, and a boy aged between 8 and 12; enslaved in 1839, they were shipped to Cuba. While the Amistad was sailing to Havana, the 25-year-old Sengbe Pieh (or Joseph Cinqué or Joseph Cinquez), assisted by Grabeau (portrayed here), started a mutiny. Many of the insurrectionists belonged to a secret society called the Poro, which had taught them warfare and other skills. The girls (see here on the right a portrait of Marqu), who were unchained, supplied the men with weapons they had found on the ship. After taking over the ship and killing most of the crew, the forty-three surviving resistance fighters wanted to go back to Africa, but were captured off the coast of Long Island, New York. They were acquitted after a long trial, thanks to the support of American abolitionists. Sengbe Pieh, Grabeau, and the others were able to return to Sierra Leone as free people in November 1841.

Courtesy of Beinecke Rare Book and Manuscript Library, Yale University

The People Behind the Liberation Uprising on the Spanish Slave Ship Amistad

22 pencil drawings, 1839–42, William H. Townsend

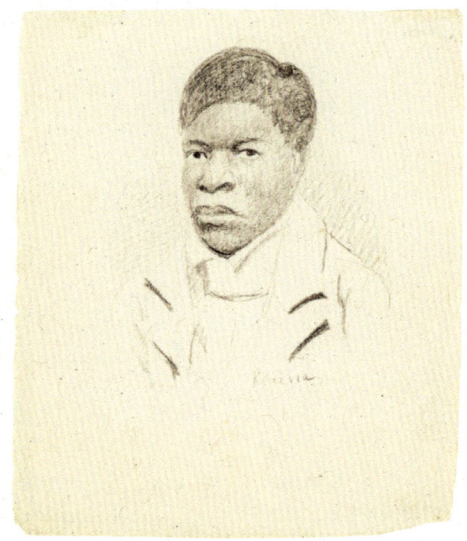

Kezzuza

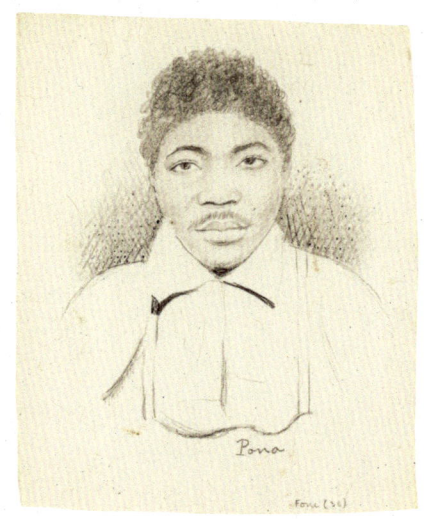

Pona

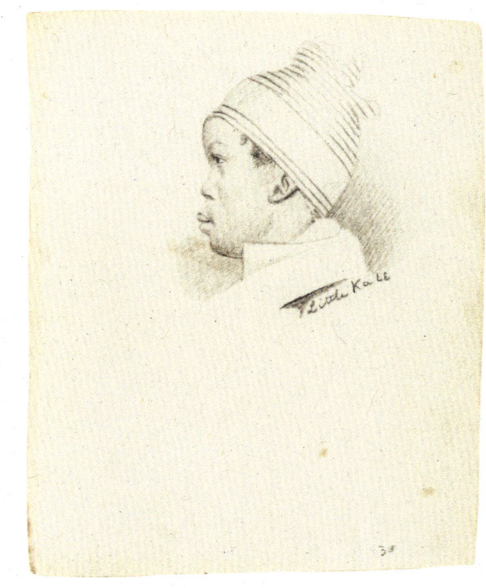

Little Kale

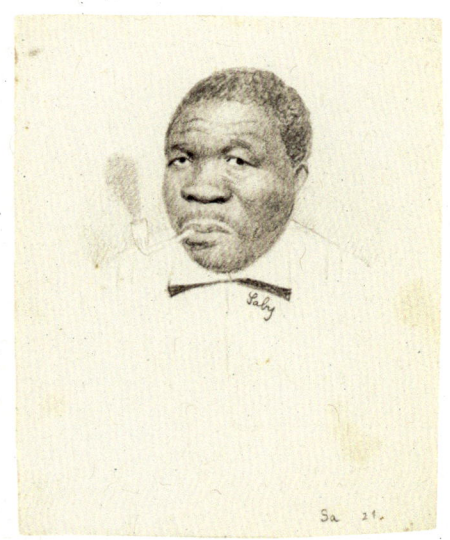

Saby

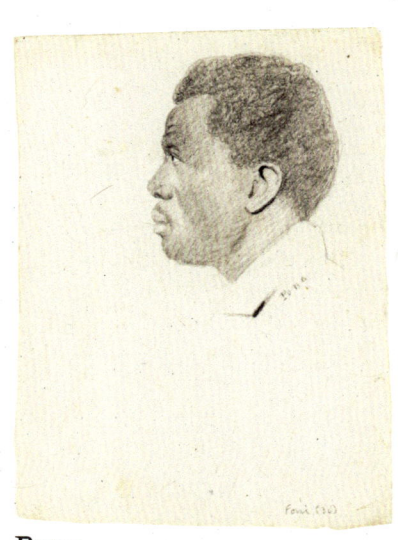

Pona

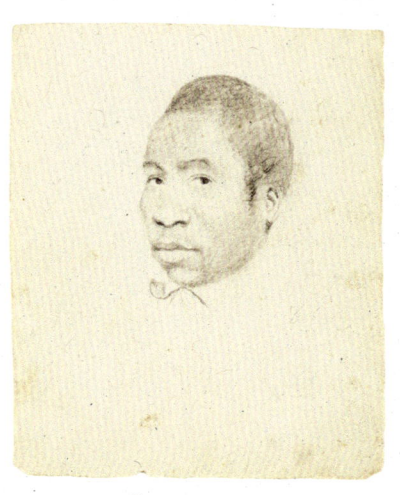

Name unknown

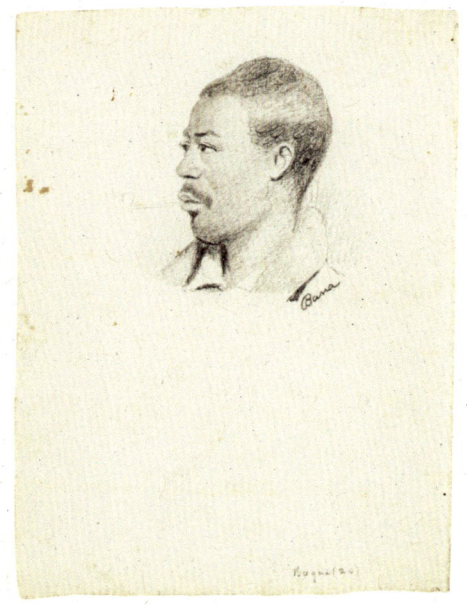

Bana

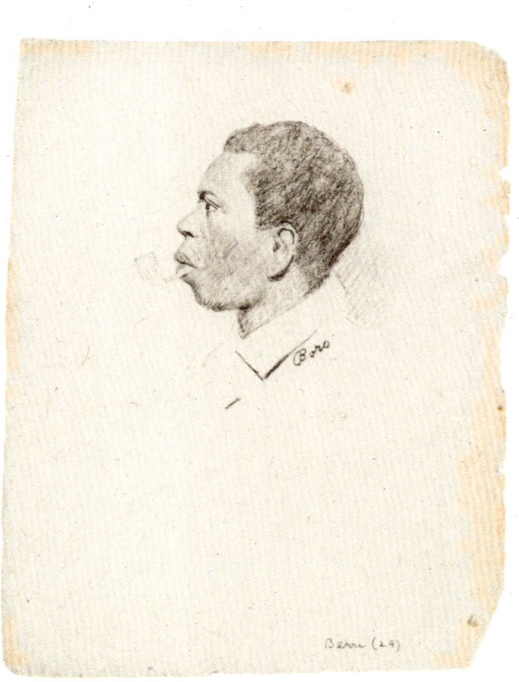

Boro

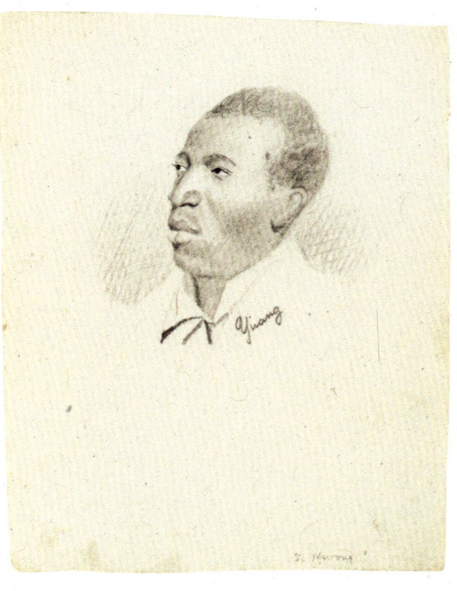

Yuang

North Coast, Cuba 01/07/1839
Freetown, Sierra Leone **November 1841**

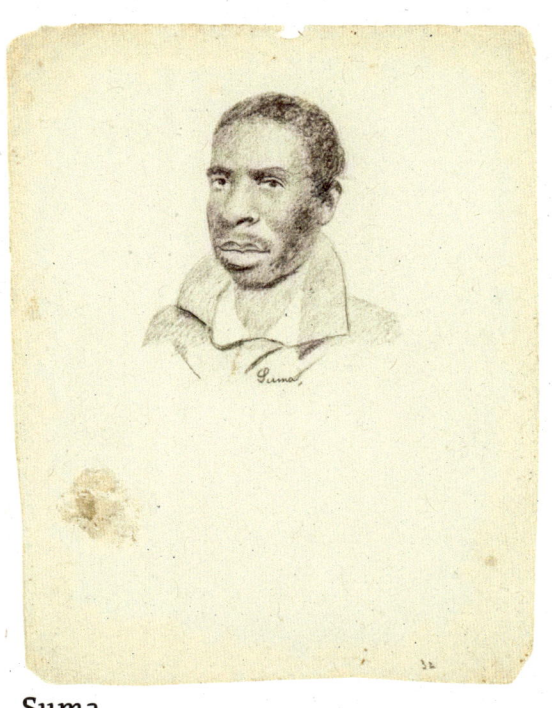
Suma

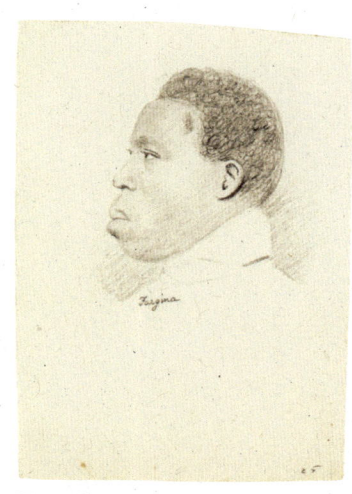
Fargina

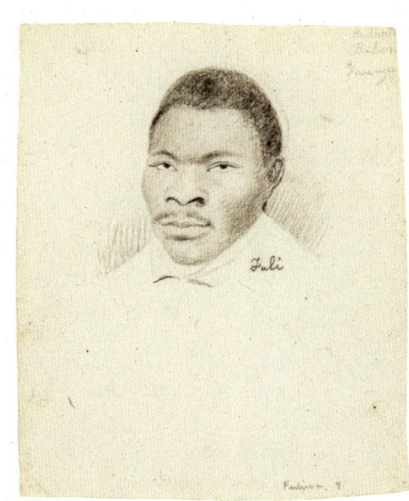
Fuli

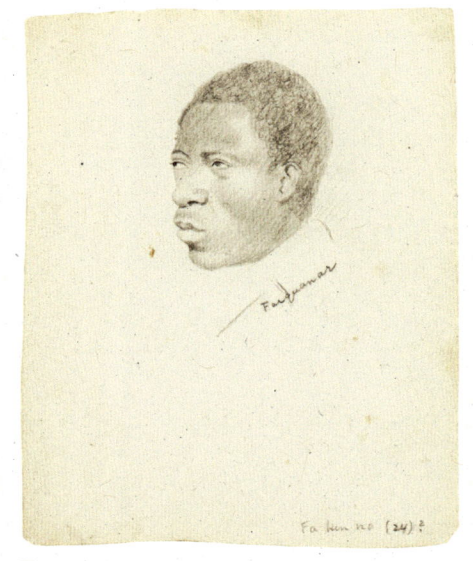
Faquarna

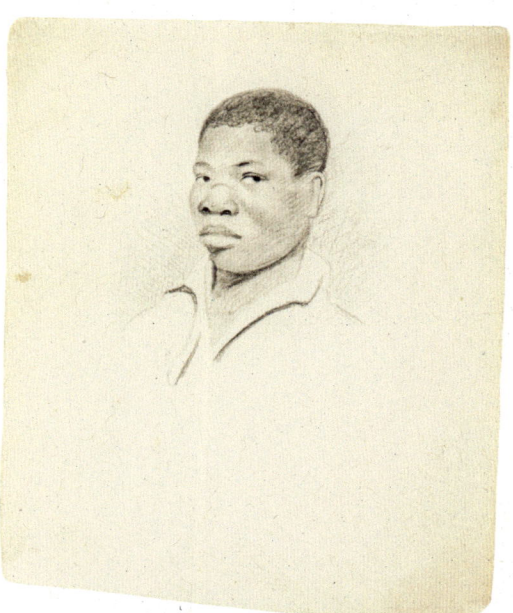
Name unknown

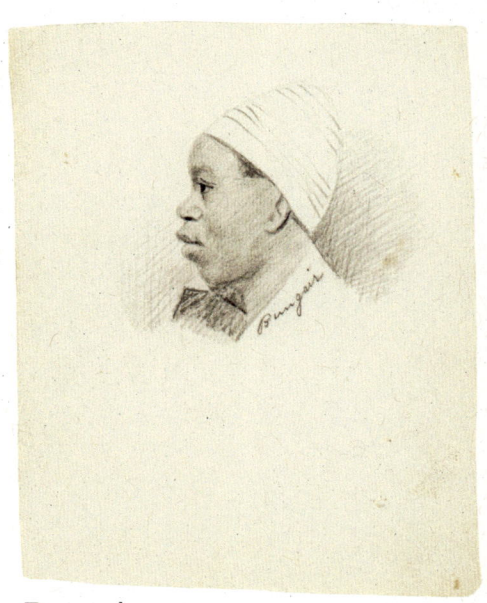
Bungair

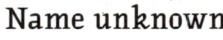
Sar

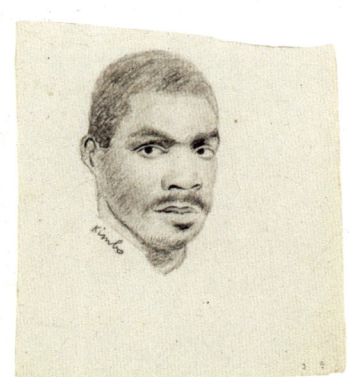
Kimbo

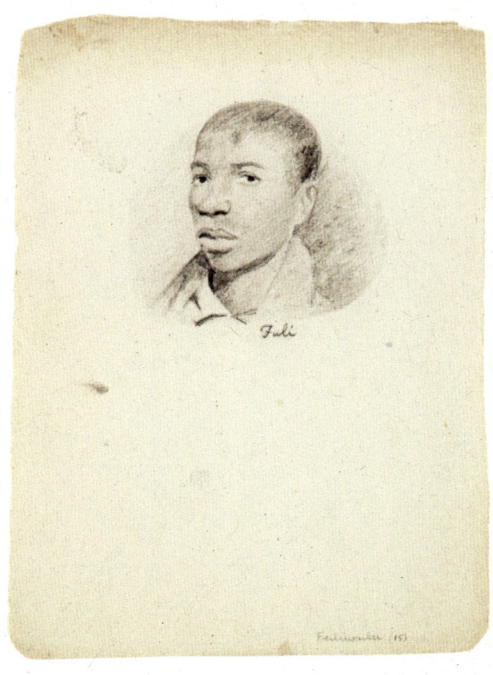
Fuli

King Asabaton Fontem Njifua
Restitution Claim for a Sacred Sculpture

Statement by Chief Charles Achaleke Taku, International Lawyer, Lead defence counsel at the International Criminal Court and great grandson of the Bangwa King Fontem Asunganyi, on his first visit to the Rautenstrauch-Joest Museum in Cologne, 21/07/2021

»My name is Chief Charles Taku, I am a traditional ruler from the Bangwa, from Fontem, from Cameroon. I came here in the name of His Majesty King Asabaton Fontem Njifua and the family and the people of the Bangwa and Fontem. I came here in order to attempt to connect with what we call the culture and conscience of the Bangwa people, in order to commence the vitally important process of bringing them back to where they belong, back to all of the memories of our parents and all of our history and our own existence. To reconnect with the links, the cultural and spiritual links of our people, of our ancestry, of our history. I believe there is a profound disconnection, a void and an emptiness. I believe that with His Royal Highness here at the Rautenstrauch-Joest Museum, and other leaders in different museum collections, a part of our humanity is not lost but hidden here.

> And we need to heal, we need to regain our cultural identity. We need to reconnect with our ancestry once again. We need to reconnect with the present, the past, and the next generations. We need that continuity, we need that harmony, that creative harmony, that spiritual harmony that has been disrupted. We need to be able to reconcile, to bring it together to form a whole. This is our contribution to Black civilisation, and therefore it belongs to us, so that Black civilisation can find its meaning and its contribution to humanity once again.

We need to bring back His Royal Highness here, as well as all the other leaders and cultural artefacts and symbols with spiritual values that are kept in museums and scattered all over the world. I came here to Germany to start a dialogue for their return, for their repatriation, but also to create new cultural links, talks, relations, which will replace colonial and cultural imperialism. Diversity is a blessing to the world, not a curse. Diversity was ordained by God for his own glory and that of we human beings. And this is the beginning of that dialogue, to find that true meaning of that humanity and diversity and to start this new connection.« *Chief Charles Taku*

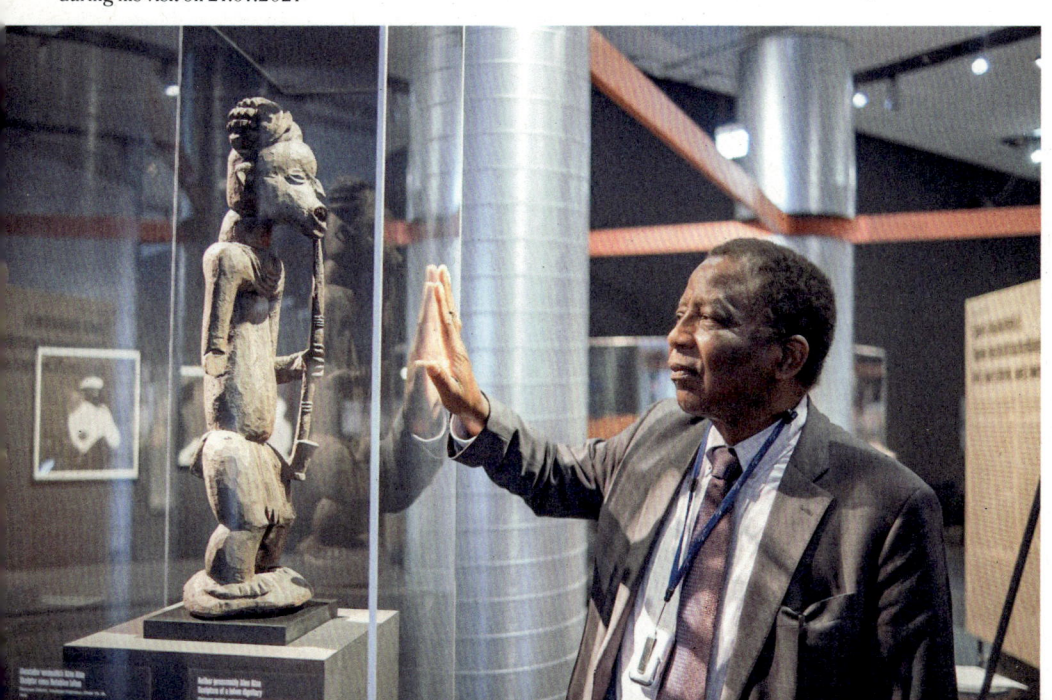

Chief Charles Taku in front of the sacred sculpture *Lefem* in *RESIST!* during his visit on 21.07.2021

This wooden commemorative statue of a dignitary comes from the Bangwa region situated in the south-west highlands of the Cameroon Grasslands. This statue was an important symbol of royal power and an emblem of the powerful *Lefem* society. Such statues were kept in secret places and were only shown to the public during initiation, enthronement, and transfer of power ceremonies. This statue was probably sculpted by Ateu Atsa (ca. 1840–1910).

In 1901, during the violent German colonial occupation of Cameroon (1884–1919), this sculpture was looted by the German colonial army after years of resistance by the Bangwa people.

Gustav Conrau (1865–1899), a German colonial agent, trader and collector, came to the Bangwa Highlands in 1898 to recruit workers for the German plantations on the coast. King Asunganyi (ca. 1880–1952), one of the nine kings of the Bangwa region, provided Conrau with labourers to work on the plantations. A year later, however, Conrau returned without the labourers, which sparked rumours about their deaths. When he asked for more workers, a conflict broke out and Conrau was arrested by King Asunganyi. Conrau then fled and probably shot himself during his escape attempt. Holding King Asunganyi responsible for Conrau's death, the Germans retaliated with violent raids on Bangwa villages that lasted four years due to the persistent resistance of the Bangwa people. As a result, the German Lieutenant Kurt Strümpell (1872–1947) was responsible for the "punitive war retribution payments", which is when he seized this sacred *Lefem* sculpture as well as other war booties. He donated this statue to the Braunschweig Municipal Museum in 1902. In 1955, the Düsseldorf collector Klaus Clausmeyer received it in exhange for other artefacts and subsequently gave it to the RJM in 1966.

Chapter 1

Fontem, Cameroon & Cologne, Germany — July/August 2021

Njifua, I hereby submit this request for the restitution of the artefacts which were looted from the Royal Palace of His Majesty Fontem Asunganyi during the German punitive expeditionary campaign. This campaign commenced on 8 February 1900 and lasted about nine years. The punitive expeditionary campaign inflicted an unjustified, unwarranted and disproportionate existential devastation on our spiritual and cultural values, our economy and on our civilization. The impact of this punitive campaign, endures until today.

The expeditionary campaign breached the laws and customs of war even by the then standards of colonial rule. It targeted our civilian population, our civilization, our cultural, spiritual and religious values and the very essence of our human existence. Our King, Fontem Asunganyi was abducted and detained far from our Kingdom and several punitive measures were imposed on our people. Looting and the imposition of severe fines; forced labour during which many of our people disappeared with no explanation and/or justification; this amounted to collective punishment.

A German military officer named Kurt Strumpell, stood out among other military commanders as one of the most effective enforcers of the punitive colonial expeditionary campaign. Apart from the brutality of the punitive campaign, he looted arts of spiritual value which were the symbols and attributes of power; and not just for pecuniary gain but also in order to subdue, weaken and humiliate His Majesty Fontem Asunganyi and all the people within the Kingdom.

More than a century and two decades after these artefacts were looted and taken to Europe and other distant lands far away from their natural environment, we have suffered tremendous violations, depravations, calamities, spiritual and existential voids. These have arisen from the perversion of our ancestral arts, which are the essence of our spiritualism, our civilisation, our culture and our way of life. We were and still are disconnected from our spirituality and our cultural values and are still tormented by the spirits of our ancestors and by the memory of our people who disappeared and were, and still are, unaccounted for.

We believe that the colonial independence which we were granted remains incomplete. This is due to the fact that a significant part of our way of life, and our humanity is kept far away from us. Bringing back our artefacts will reconcile us with our spirituality, our civilization, our cultural values and our humanity. This, Honourable Mayor, is the underlying justification for our request for the return of our artefacts to their rightful home, the Kingdom of Fontem.

Honourable Mayor, permit me to state that despite the harm and pain we suffered, we were in an unprecedented moment of joy and renewed hope, when we received an invitation from Dr. RJM NanetteSnoep, Director Rautestrauch-Joest-Museum, to Chief Charles Taku (who is a great grandson of King Fontem Asunganyi), to visit the Municipal Museum of Cologne.

When Chief Charles Taku received the invitation, he immediately notified me and I authorized him to accept. I gave him the commission to see and to offer prayers to our ancestors on our behalf and to seek for the return of our beloved artefacts. He was also given a mandate to begin a discussion on cooperation with the Municipal Museum of Cologne. His visit therefore, was a significant step in the development of new relations between our Kingdom and The Municipal Museum of Cologne where many of our ancestral artefacts are found.

Chief Charles Taku has informed us, and we are grateful, that the Municipal Museum is keen on enriching the historical record with our perspective of the colonial relations between the Germans and our kingdom. The outreach effort made by the Cologne Museum through this invitation, is a significant development which will contribute to the understanding of the significance of our ancestral arts, our history and German colonial rule in our kingdom. While the history of the past cannot be eviscerated, a new dawn in our relationship may be developed by the restitution of our looted artefacts.

Chief Charles Taku, conveyed to Dr. RJM NanetteSnoep, our willingness to visit the Municipal Museum of Cologne with a small delegation from my kingdom, if invited. This will advance the discussion on the significance of our arts and the establishment of friendly relationship with the museum. I look forward to taking the opportunity to meet your honour.

Sincerely,

HM THE FON OF FONTEM

His Majesty, Fon
Asabaton Fontem Njifua
First Class Paramount Fon of Fontem
Civil Administrator

The *Lefem* looted by the German colonial army in 1901. The King of Fontem submitted a restitution request to the Mayor of Cologne in 2021. RJM Collection No. 48796

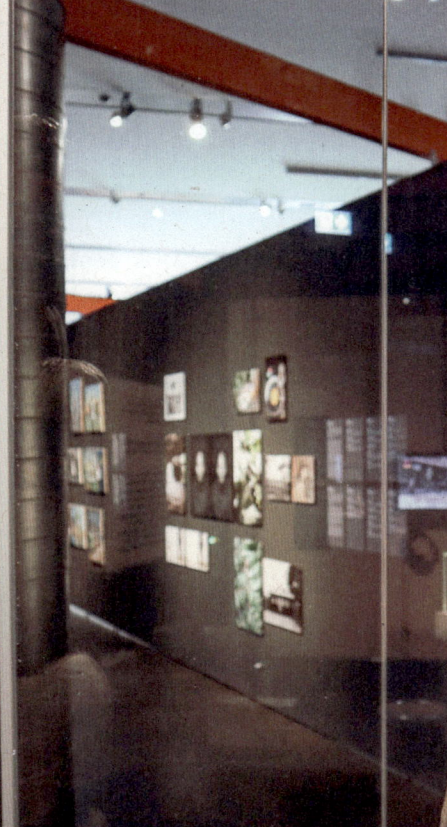

Panel Discussion
Why Restitution Matters

Speech by His Majesty King Asabaton Fontem Njifua on his visit to the RJM on 09/07/2022

Ladies and Gentlemen,

I wish to express my heartfelt thanks to Director Nanette Snoep for inviting me and my delegation to Cologne. This invitation comes as a welcome response to the request for the restitution of our ancestral artefacts. These artefacts were looted during the German expeditionary campaign that subjugated our people to collective punishment and misery.

One of our revered artefacts, which was looted from our Lefem, the most sacred ground where matters concerning the life of our kingdom are discussed, is found here in this museum in Cologne. Prior to being looted, the designated place for this artefact was at the entrance to the ground of the Lefem. The Lefem is a fearsome commander endowed with natural and spiritual powers. A spirit medium through which enemies of the Kingdom and evil spirits were prevented from gaining access to the sacred grounds of the Lefem to avoid desecration and harm to the King.

The looting of this artefact, which led to it being held in captivity far from its natural environment, deprived us of spiritual protection provided to us by our ancestors and by God.

> **The desecration of our Lefem and the theft of this artefact is one of the egregious collective punishments that has greatly impacted our cultural and spiritual norms, leading to societal dysfunction.**

Honourable Director, your letter of invitation dated 01/07/2021 highlighted the fact that this revered artefact was on display in the temporary exhibition *RESIST! The Art of Resistance* in the municipal museum. We are here to reiterate and emphasise the request for restitution that we have sent to the Mayor of Cologne. We consider the invitation you have extended to us as the beginning of the restitution process, putting an end to the agony of our ancestors and the generations to come.

Honourable Director, our presence here today is also an expression of our support for the new era of collaboration and friendship that you highlighted in your letter of invitation. This visit has received the endorsement of our people and our ancestors, who consider it an important step towards providing a solution to the individual and collective punishment we have endured for over a century.

After having set our eyes on this revered symbol of cultural and spiritual existence today, we can at last hope that it will be returned to its homeland, so that the emptiness, disruptions, nightmares, and enduring shame and humiliation we have been subjected to can come to an end.

I am accompanied by direct descendants of His Majesty Fontem Asunganyi and notable figures of our Kingdom who

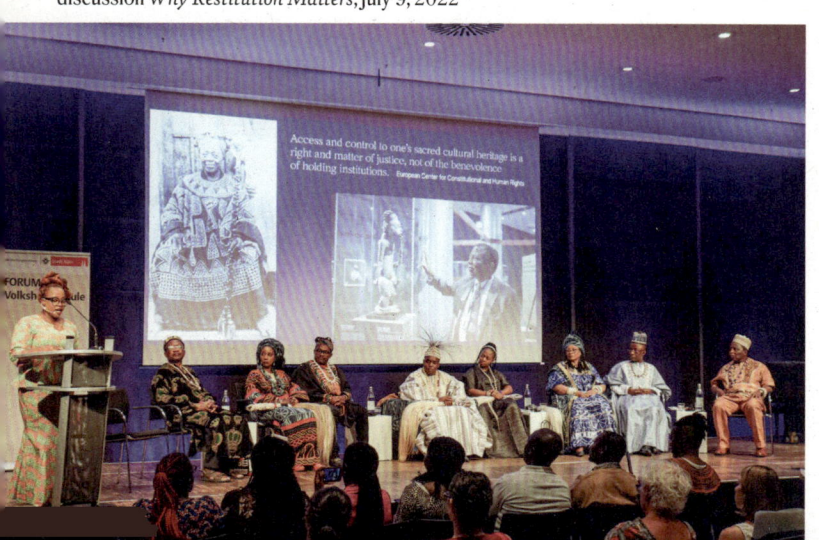

The royal delegation from Fontem / Bangwa during the public discussion *Why Restitution Matters*, July 9, 2022

The panel discussion took place as part of the visit of a royal delegation from Bangwa to the RJM and shed light on the reasons behind their request for the return of the *Lefem* sculpture that was exhibited in the entrance area of *RESIST!* and was put back in its display case in the museum's permanent exhibition after the exhibition was closed in January 2022. King Asabaton Fontem Njifua of Fontem/Bangwa travelled to Cologne in July 2022 with other important Bangwa representatives: Diane Ngolefe Acha-Morfaw, Charles Ngulefac Morfaw, Beatrice Folefac Emenkeng, Josephine Ngimafac Talieh, Chief Charles Taku, Martin Nkefu, and Emigdas Nkem. This visit by the King and his companions followed Chief Charles Taku's visit to the RJM a year earlier and served as an opportunity for the delegation to personally inspect and honor the sacred sculpture at the RJM as well as establish a direct dialogue with the museum and the civil society in Cologne – particularly the Cameroonian diaspora – about the request for restitution they submitted to the Mayor of Cologne, Henriette Reker, in August 2021. At the time of publication of this book, in December 2022, the request for the return of the *Lefem* from Fontem is still pending.

Chapter 1

Cologne, Germany   09/07/2022

have come to witness this historic moment and to support our request for restitution. They have also come to commence a new era of collaboration between us, the museum, and the municipal authorities of Cologne.

> The restitution of our artefact will mark a significant conclusory step in the decolonisation of Africa. Because the independence of Africa cannot be deemed complete when the very heartbeats of our civilisation, our spiritual and cultural fabric, are imprisoned, far removed from their natural environment. The return of our artefact to its natural environment will mark a new era of collaboration in which the ghosts of our violent colonial past will no longer haunt us or the successive generations to come.

We are hopeful that this visit will open the gateway for the restitution of our artefacts, which are held in about 14 other museums in Germany and across other countries in Europe, making them one of the largest number in European colonial possession. From this platform in Cologne, we wish to make an impassioned plea for all our artefacts to be returned to us without further delay.

I take this opportunity to extend my profound thanks to the people who have turned up to witness this historic event. In particular, the Bangwa diaspora and the Focolare Movement, who have accompanied us on this long journey of love and unity despite the multiple general challenges we have collectively endured.

Honourable Director, thank you so much for your hospitality.
King Asabaton Fontem Njifua

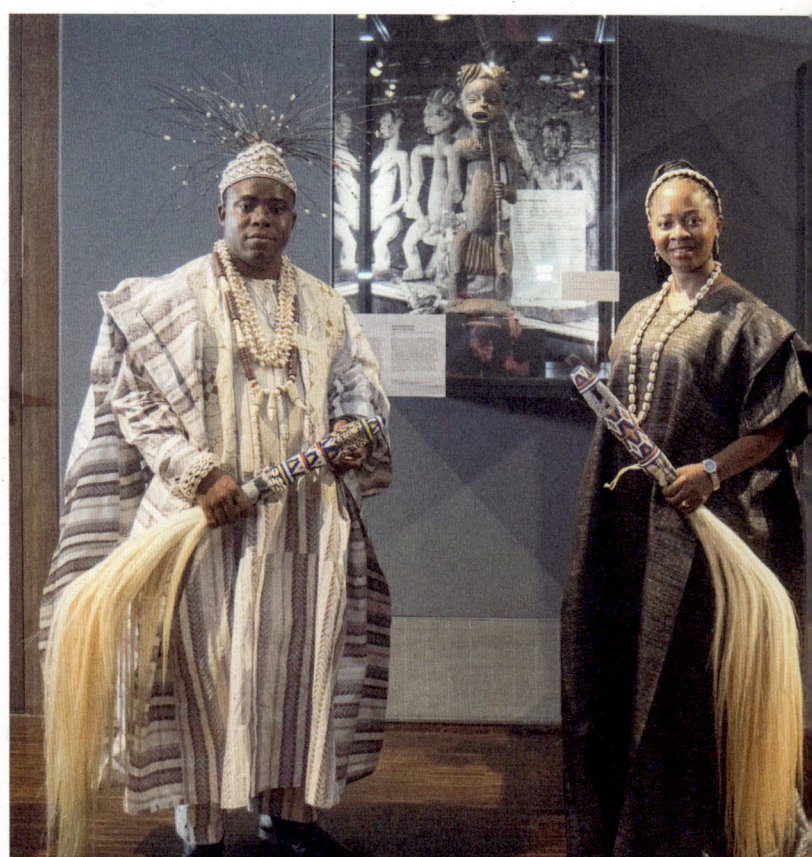

King Asabaton Fontem Njifua and Queen Folefac Emenkeng Beatrice in front of the *Lefem* in the permanent exhibition of the RJM during their visit on 09/07/2022

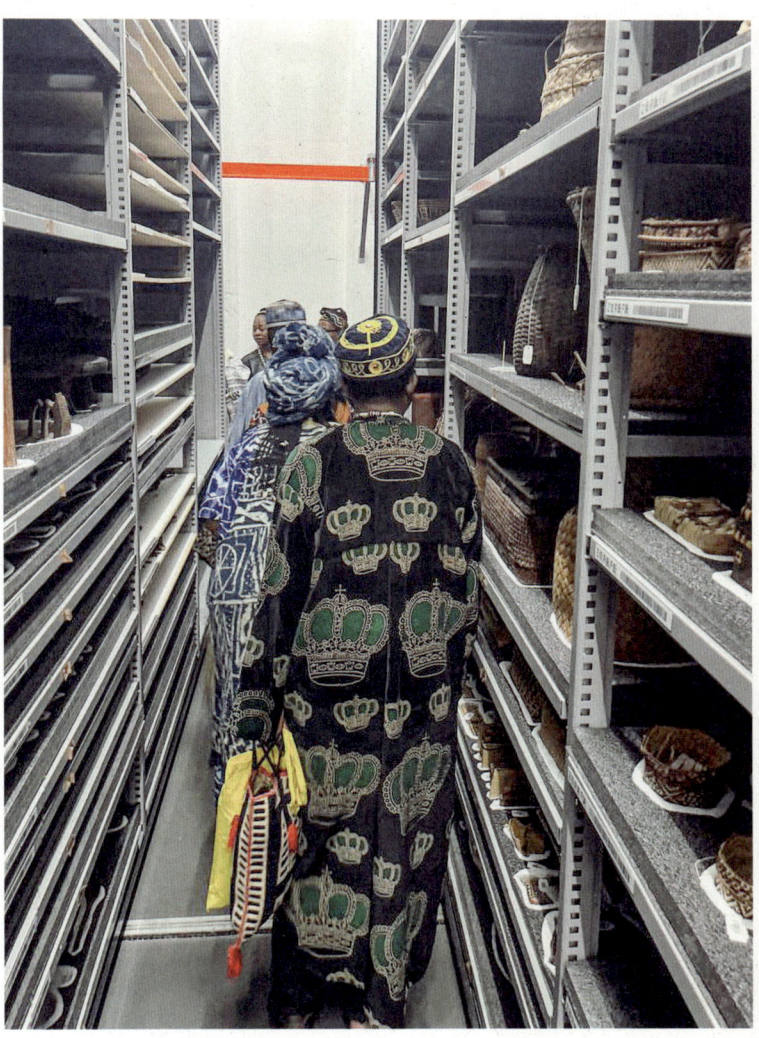

The delegation in the storages of the RJM

The Singh Twins
Jallianwala: Repression and Retribution, 2019

In India, a Crown colony of the British Empire from 1858 to 1947, there was continuous resistance to colonial rule and oppression. Mahatma Gandhi, was a key figure of the fight for independence. From 1914 onwards, he called for non-violent resistance, sending a clear message about independence from the British Empire and its exploitation through actions such as the Salt March in 1930, which he led with Sarojini Naidu, a female Indian poet and politician. Smaller and larger protests and uprisings went on across the subcontinent for decades, including the April 1919 demonstrations in the northern Indian city of Amritsar in Punjab, where up to 20,000 people gathered to march against the colonial government's tightening of police laws, the arrest of opposition figures, and the ban on Gandhi entering the province. Hundreds of people were killed when the British army opened fire on the demonstrators. The brutality of the colonial power aimed to suppress the emerging resistance movement but in fact had the opposite effect. The Jallianwala massacre intensified the protests and is considered a turning point in Indo-British history.

The detailed textile triptych *Jallianwala: Repression and Retribution* by the British artists The Singh Twins was created to mark the 100th anniversary of the Amritsar massacre. While the central panel of the triptych focuses on the event itself, the left and right panels explore its historical context as well as its aftermath and legacy. In the centre, we see the two key figures of the Indian independence movement, Mahatma Gandhi and Udham Singh – a legendary revolutionary of the Indian liberation movement who exacted revenge for the Amritsar massacre by assassinating the British politician responsible, Sir Michael O'Dwyer, two decades later.

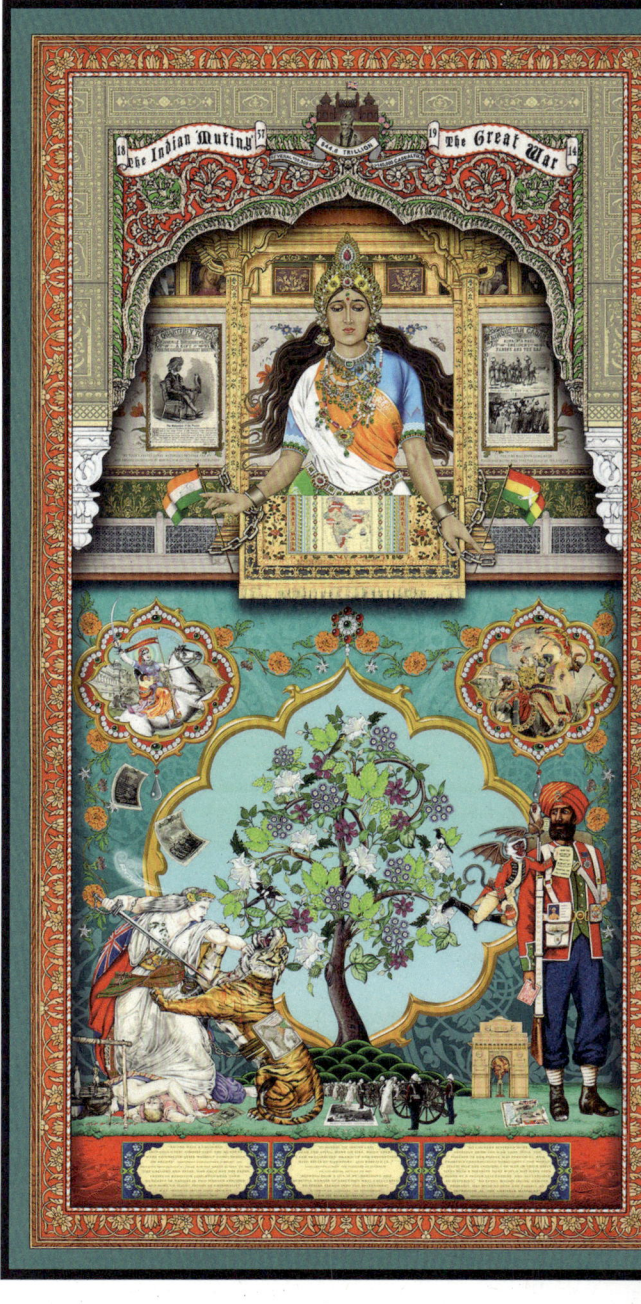

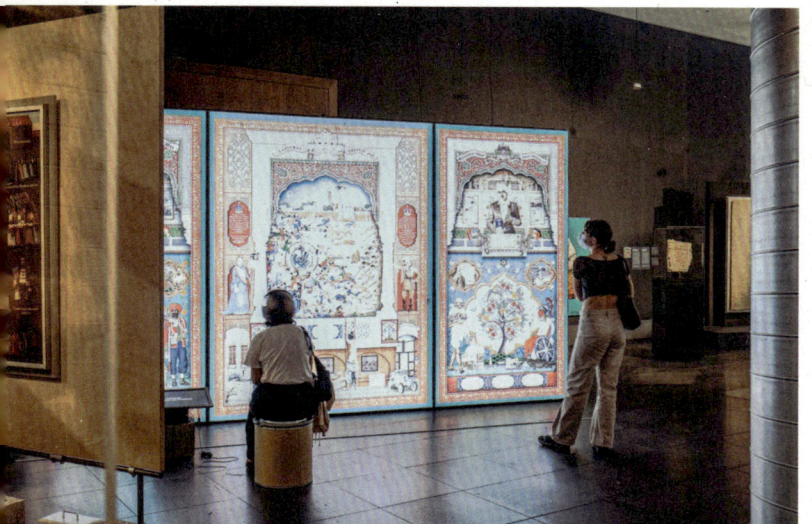

»We have always believed in the purpose of art as social and political commentary and documentation. In our own art, the importance we give to exploring colonial narratives pertaining to our own Indian identity and heritage stems from a conviction that not telling our own stories is like walking in the sand and leaving no footprints.« *The Singh Twins*

Amritsar, India **April 1919**
Liverpool, GB **April 2019**

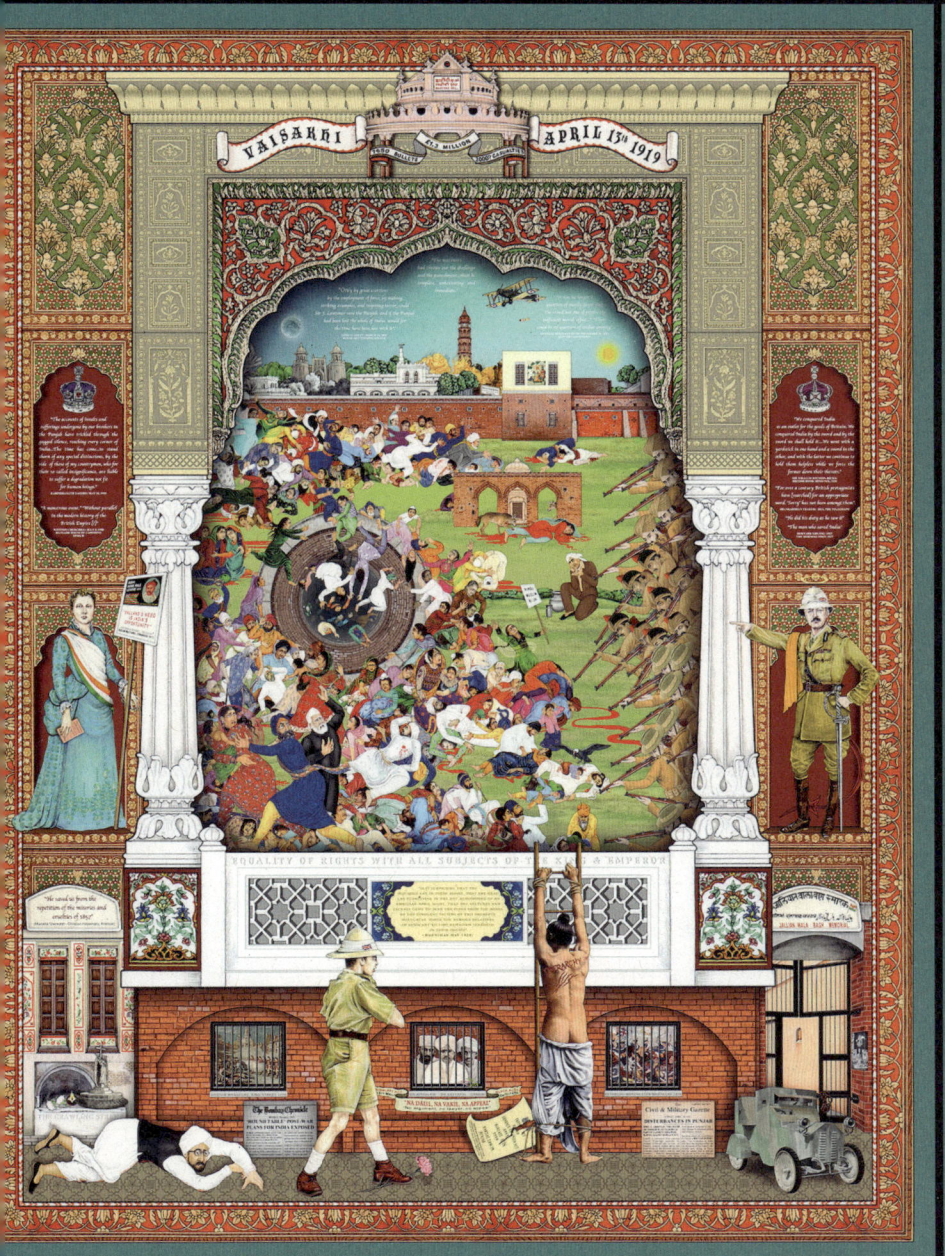
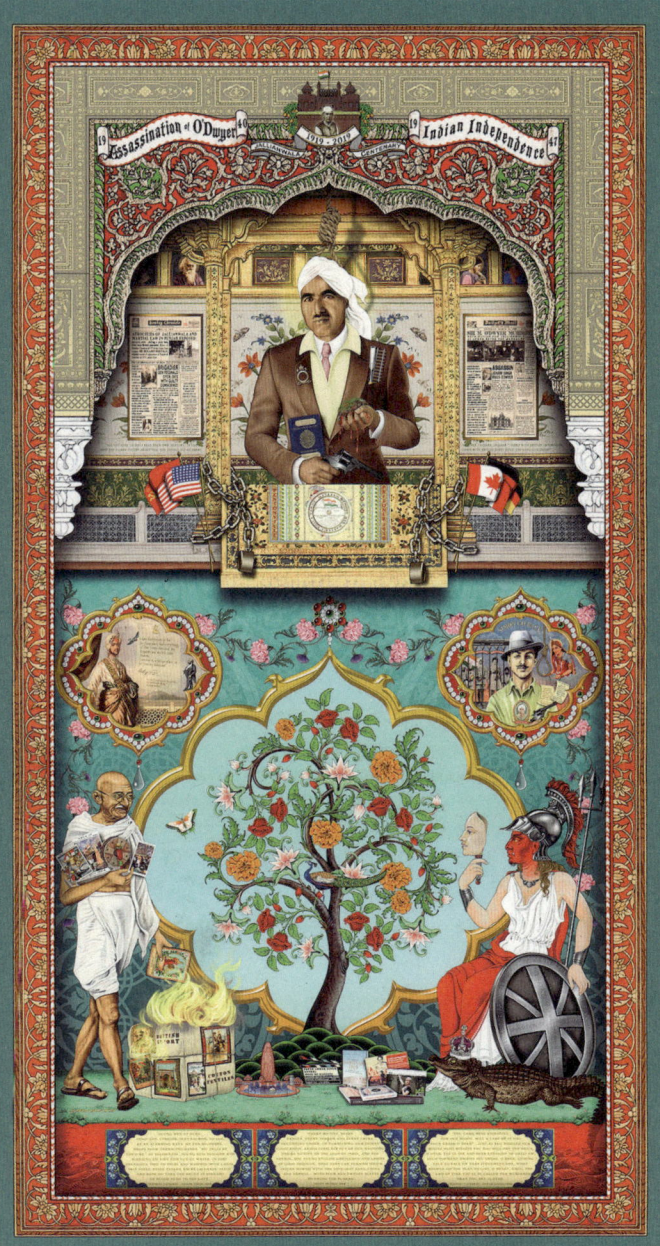

Courtesy of the Artists

Nura Qureshi
Are You Calling Me a Dog?, 2018

Villagization, 2016
Villagization was the British programme of forced resettlement to cut off Mau Mau supply lines. Residents of the Kiambu, Nyeri, Murang'a, and Embu Districts were forced to move into "protected villages" behind barbed-wire fences and watchtowers.

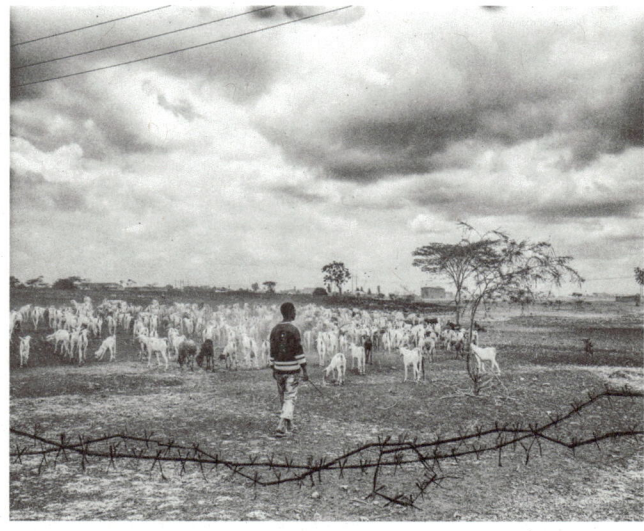

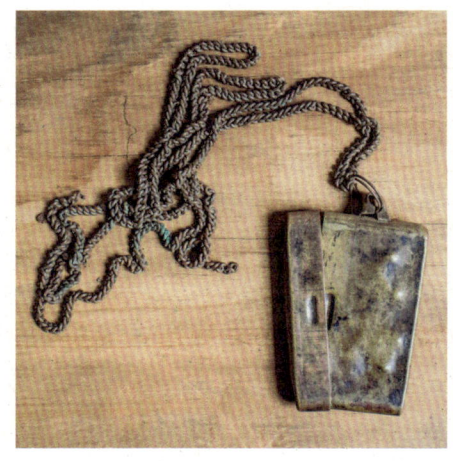

The Oath Administrator, 2018
Oath administrators were responsible for introducing new members to the movement and reading vows to be repeated by those swearing their allegiance to the resistance.

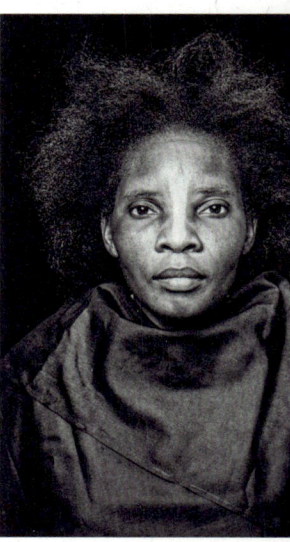

Between Banana Leaves, 2018
The Mau Mau used torches in banana trees to signal their presence.

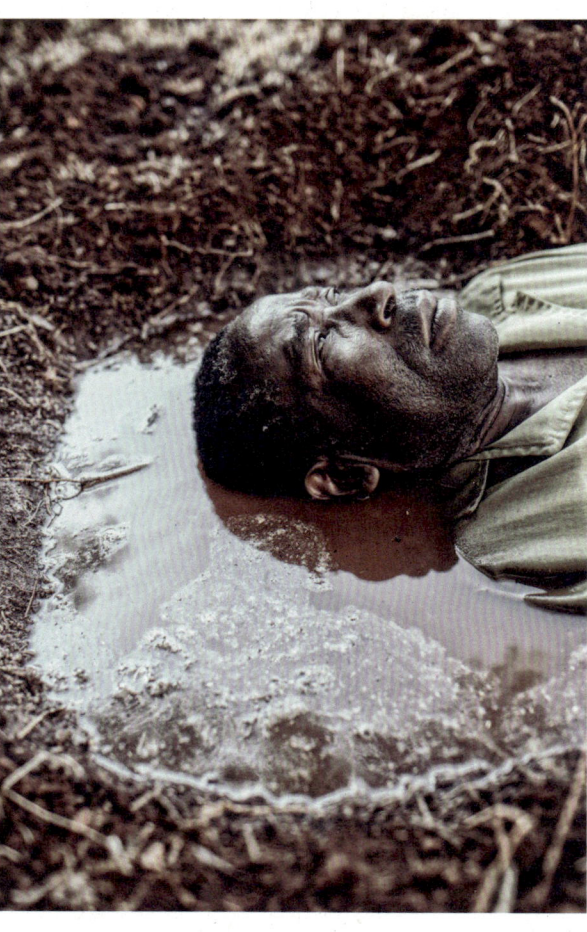

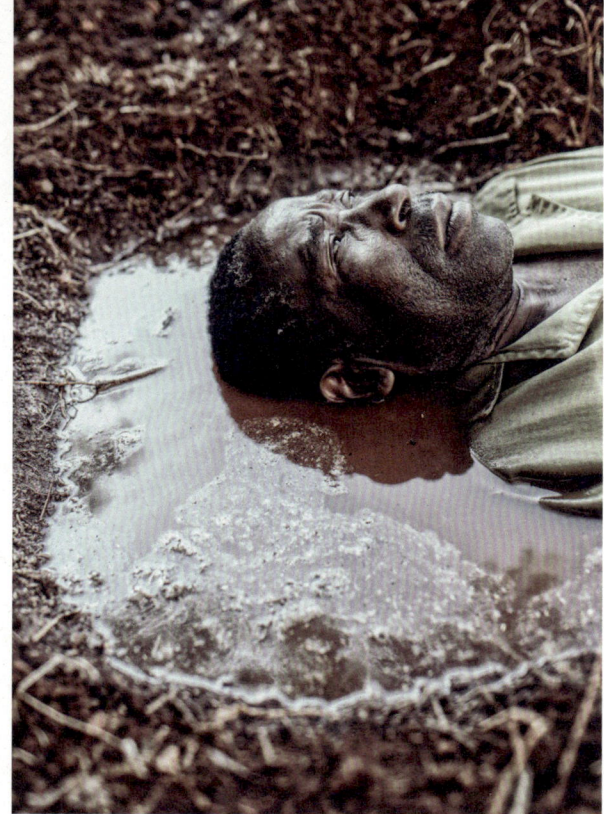

Muddy Pit, 2018
According to survivor testimonies, one way that the British military would torture Mau Mau suspects and prisoners was by forcing them to dig their own ditches, fill them with water, and lie in them for long periods of time.

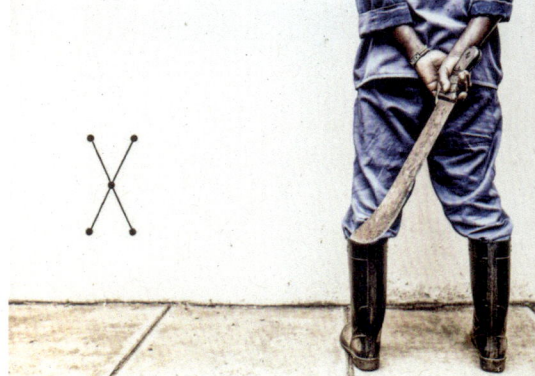

»I wanted to document the remaining resigned, yet spirited, men and women of this barely recorded conflict, the Mau Mau uprising. Were they living on the land they once fought for? I recorded some of the places and paths that soon will be forgotten and overgrown, along with the traces of how they were used. I set out to capture the spirit of these buried places and in the end imagined some of the stories that took place on them.« *Nura Qureshi*

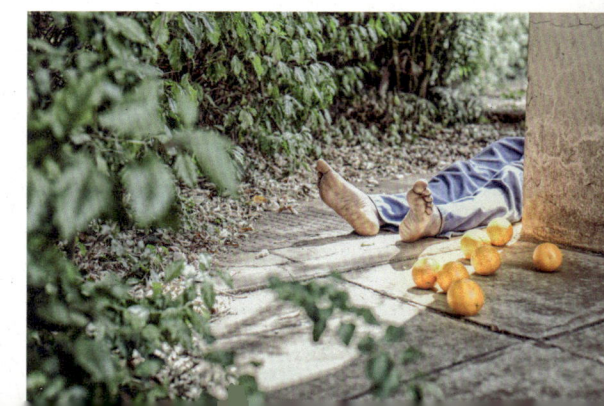

Kenya — 1952-1960
MAU MAU WAR

← Kipande, 2016
The Kipande identity document was a violent instrument of colonial control. Kept in a metal container on a chain around the neck at all times, it had to be worn by all adult males aged 16 and over. The Kipande contained information about basic personal details, the tribe to which a person belonged, and even their employment history with comments about their strengths and weaknesses.

Court Housing, Nyeri, 2016
Mau Mau fighters that surrendered would face a tribunal of judges, some of whom were housed in this now abandoned building in Nyeri, adjacent to the court house where Dedan Kimathi (1920–1957), a key leader of the Mau Mau rebellion, was eventually sentenced to death.

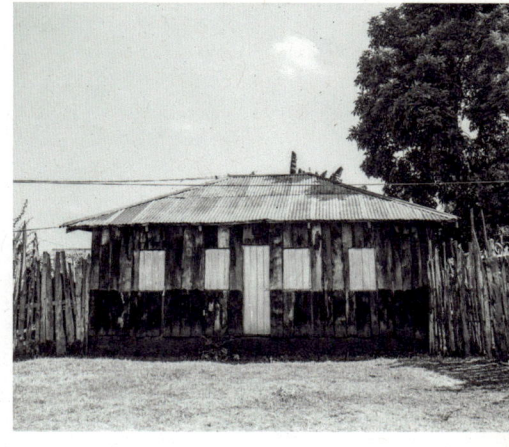

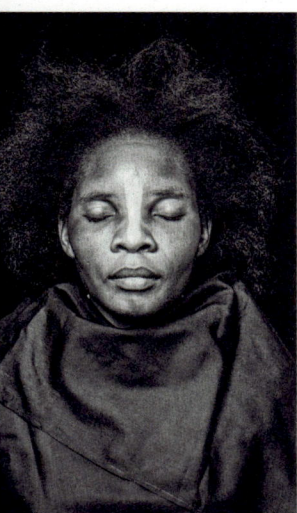

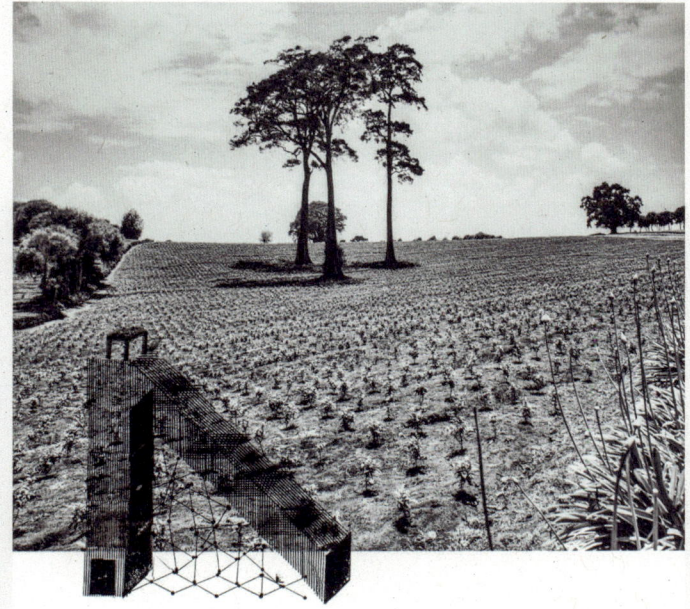

Moving Gallows, 2017
During the Kenya Emergency, the British Military introduced the more "efficient" moving gallows to hang Mau Mau suspects. A copy of a photograph is all that remains of this instrument of death.

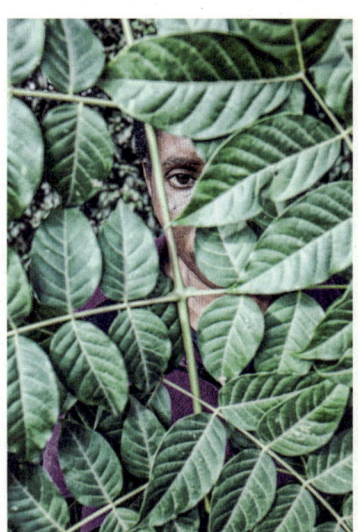

Surrender, 2017
Mau Mau fighters who chose to surrender identified themselves by carrying green branches in front of their faces.

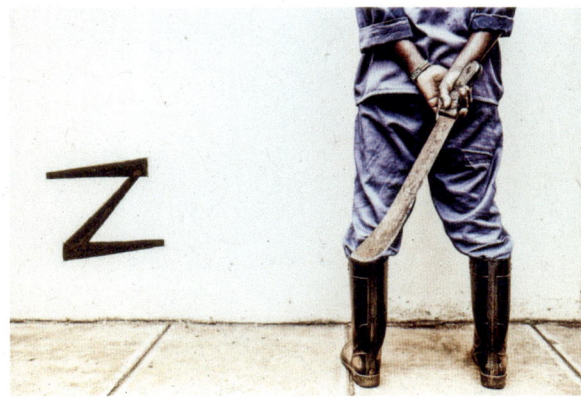

Confessed II, 2017
Mau Mau detainees were marked with a letter on their files: X: Confessed & Cooperative, Z: Hardcore

← Oranges, Nairobi 2018
The Mau Mau considered those who continued to work for white settlers to be traitors. Refusing to join the resistance was punishable by death.

Editions Mau Mau, Nyeri, 2016
Remnants of the Mau Mau movement are often hard to find. Many artefacts and records have been destroyed or are hidden, like this vinyl in a house in Nyeri.

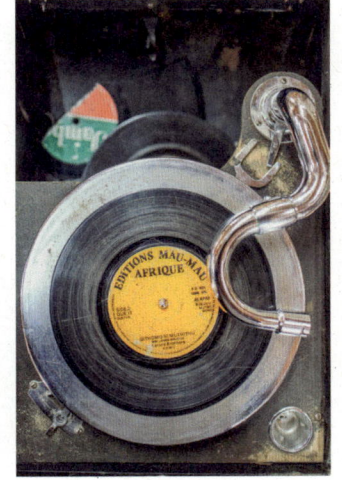

The Mau Mau movement emerged in Kenya in 1952 as a reaction to the cruel oppression and inequalities caused by decades of British colonial rule. The uprisings, led predominantly by members of the Kikuyu, resulted in a civil war-like guerrilla struggle in which some 7,800 resistance fighters were killed and 90,000 interned in concentration camps set up by the British. Lasting almost a decade, the conflict was the longest and most violent anti-colonial warfare in the former British colony of Kenya. While the Mau Mau rebellion officially ended in 1960, the movement had a profound impact on Kenya's fight for independence, which was achieved in 1963, and helped to inspire other anti-colonial movements throughout the African continent.

Now, almost sixty years later, the country's final liberation from its former colonial powers has still not occurred, as a large number of the colonial settlers have retained both their social status and the land. The traumatic traces of the violent conflict are still visible today, while the heroes of that period have long been forgotten.

In her photo essay *Are You Calling Me a Dog?*, Nura Qureshi searches for traces of the history of the Mau Mau resistance with the help of historical sources such as oral and military traditions, interviews with surviving Mau Mau fighters, and visits to historical sites. She refrains from graphic depictions of physical violence, instead focusing on Mau Mau rituals of initiation and surrender, as well as British symbols and infrastructures of oppression, in order to expose the brutality and dehumanisation of colonialism.

Courtesy of the Artist

»True resistance begins with people confronting pain ... and wanting to do something to change it«

bell hooks <small>Yearning: Race, Gender, and Cultural Politics, 1999</small>

Peter Magubane

Soweto, South Africa **16/06/1976**

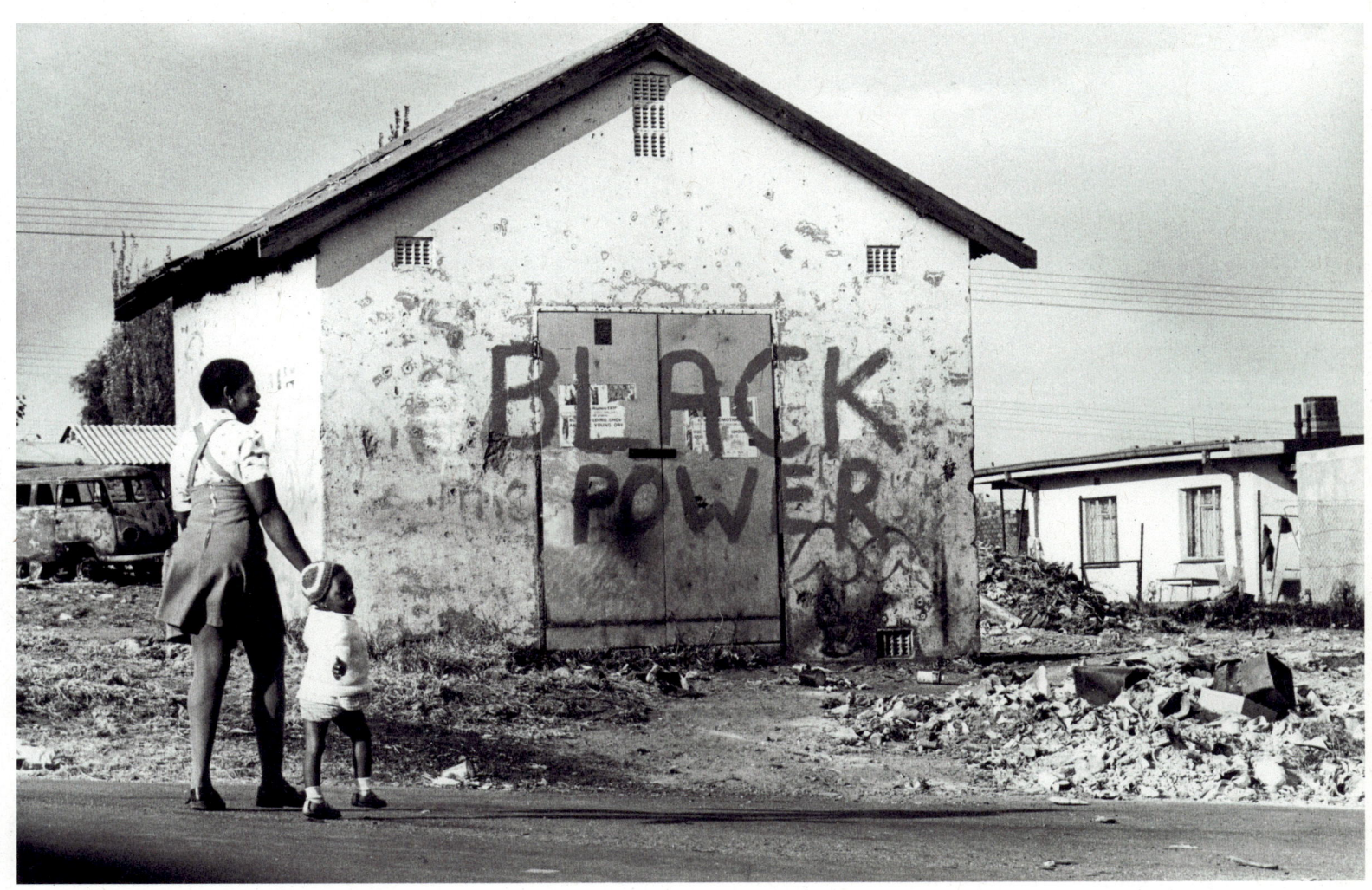

Black Power (South Africa, 1976)

»This is my country South Africa. My camera will give my country the freedom.« *Peter Magubane*

Peter Magubane

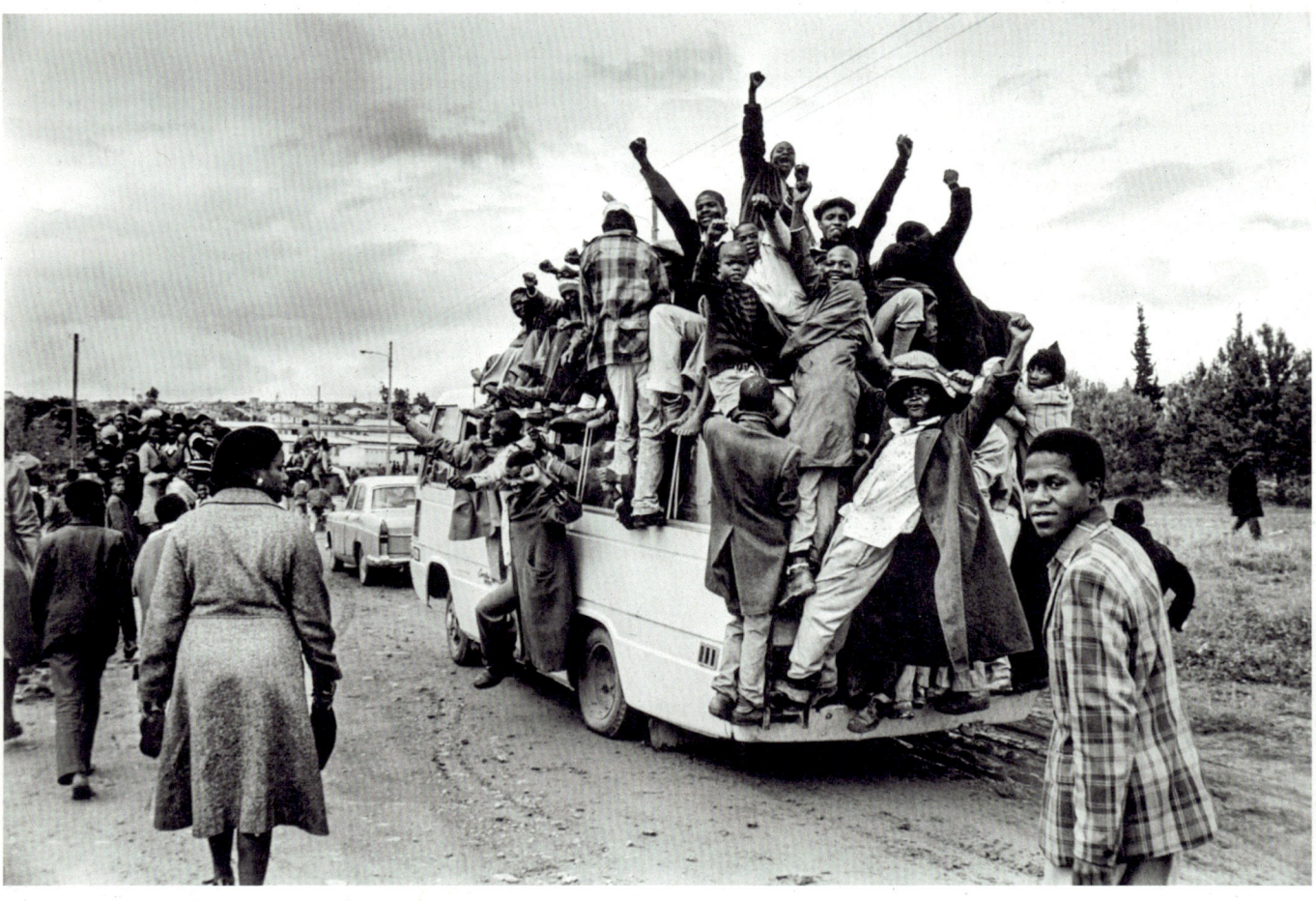

Defiant Protest (South Africa, 1976)
Mourners in defiant protest at a funeral in Eastern Cape, South Africa. The aftermath of the Soweto uprising as it spread throughout the country.

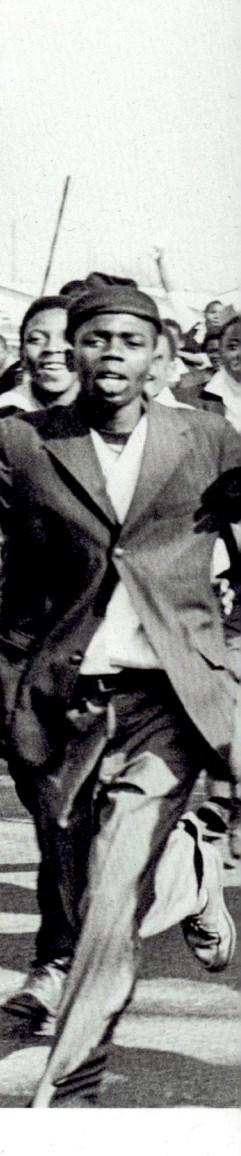

South African students were at the forefront of anti-apartheid campaigns. They raised money for South African liberation movements, fought against apartheid investments, and supported other liberation struggles in countries such as Mozambique, Angola, and Namibia. The uprising of June 16, 1976, which began in Soweto and spread nationwide, profoundly changed the sociopolitical landscape of South Africa. The causes of the uprising date back to the introduction of the Bantu Education Act of 1953, which stipulated that the education of the Black population should be inferior to white education and should only comprise training for unskilled work. When Afrikaans was made a compulsory medium of instruction in schools alongside English in 1974, between 3,000 and 10,000 students marched through Soweto on June 16, 1976. The peaceful demonstration ended in a violent confrontation with the police in which 400 to 700 marchers, many of them children, were killed. A great wave of protests swept the country as a result. Today, June 16 is commemorated in South Africa as Youth Day.

South African photographer Peter Magubane documented many pivotal and violent moments of the anti-apartheid struggle, including the signing of the Freedom Charter, the Rivonia Treason Trial, the 1976 riots, the states of emergency and the massacres at Sharpeville, Boipatong, Uitenhage, and King Williams Town, but also everyday situations in apartheid society. For Magubane, photography was a means of saving lives and showing the world what was happening in his country. Though he never received an official photography permit, his works were shown in many countries during apartheid. In 1990, Nelson Mandela appointed Magubane as his official photographer.

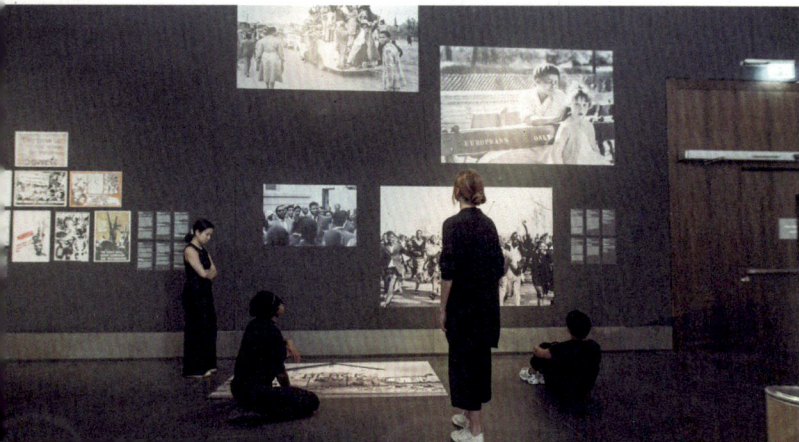

Chapter 1

South Africa 1976

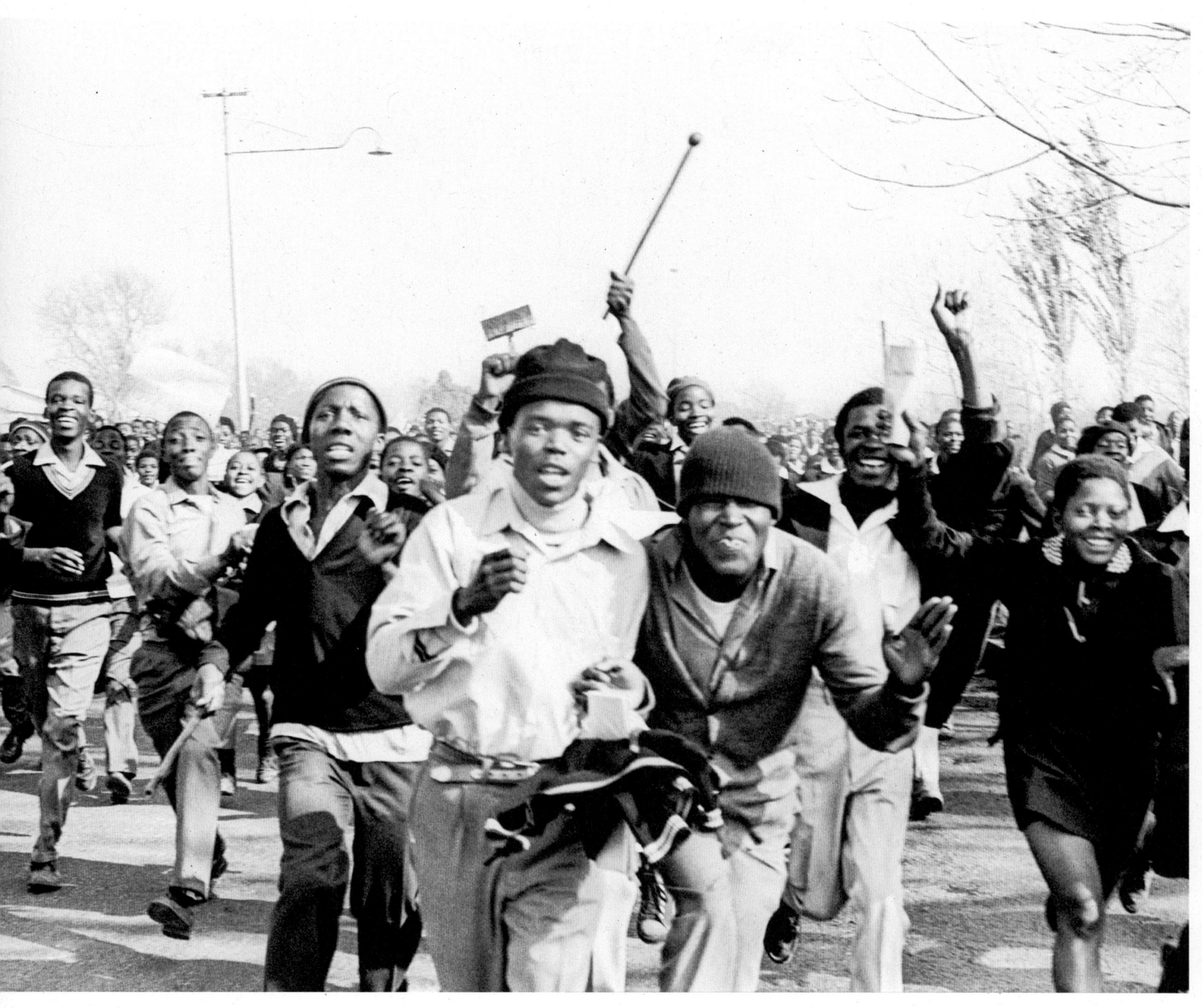

The Young Lions (South Africa, 1976)
"The Young Lions" students wanted to prevent Peter Magubane from taking photographs on the morning of June 16, 1976. Magubane explained to them, "A struggle without documentation is no struggle." They agreed and issued an order allowing photographers and journalists to document the march.

»I did not want to leave the country to find another life. I was going to stay and fight with my camera as my gun. I did not want to kill anyone, though. I wanted to kill apartheid.« *Peter Magubane*

Peter Magubane

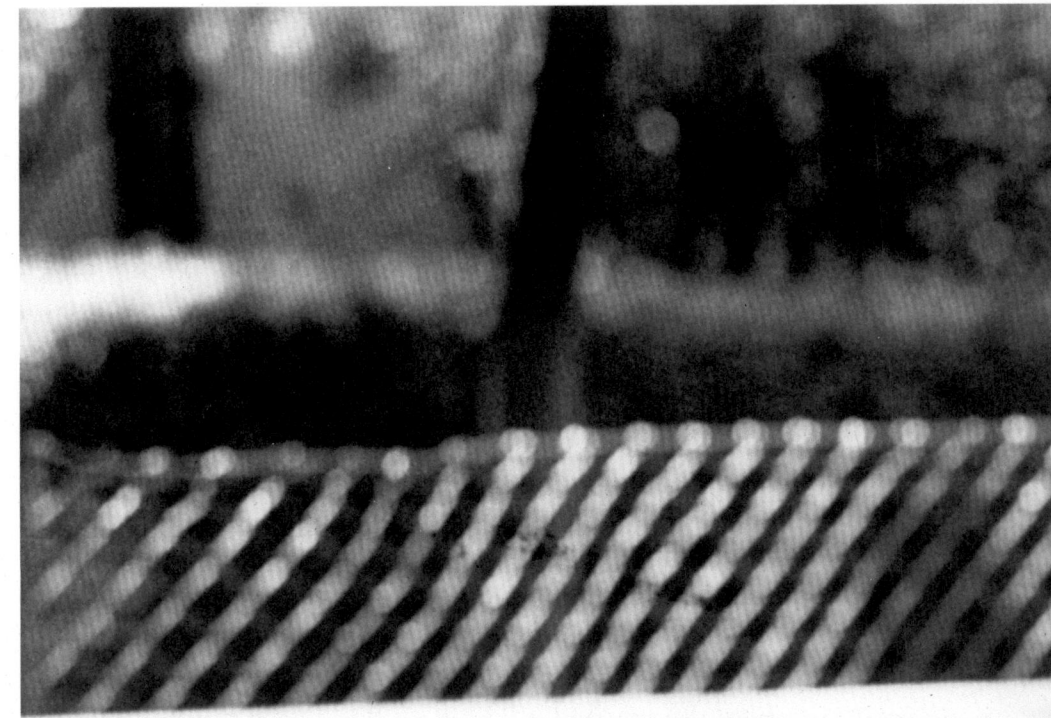
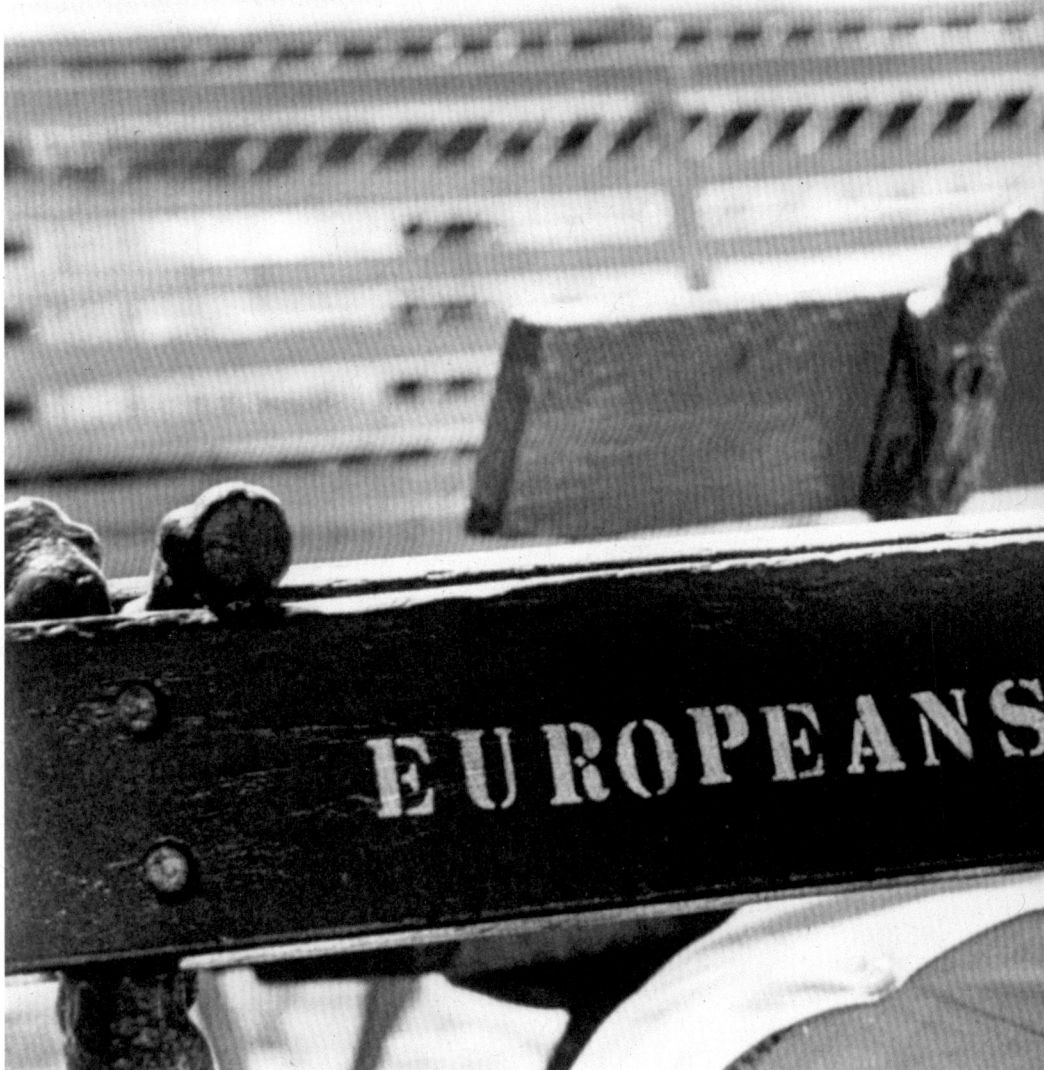

»This is one of my favourite pictures; it shows the world how apartheid operates. I never staged my pictures. They were moments I came across. I took this in 1956 while driving through a wealthy suburb in Johannesburg. I saw the girl on the bench and stopped. The woman worked for the child's parents, most likely a rich family. These labels – ›Europeans only‹, ›Coloureds only‹ – were on everything, by order of the apartheid government. When I saw Europeans only, I knew I would have to approach with caution. I did not have a long lens, just my 35mm, so I had to get close. I did not interact with the woman or the child, though. I never ask permission when taking photos. I have worked amid massacres, with hundreds of people being killed around me, and you cannot ask for permission. I apologise afterwards. When I showed it to my editor, he said it was wonderful. It was published worldwide: for many countries, apartheid was the news of the day. I have been trying to find this woman and child ever since. I have no leads, but I would love to say: ›Thank you for not interfering with me when I took this.‹« *Peter Magubane*

South Africa 1976

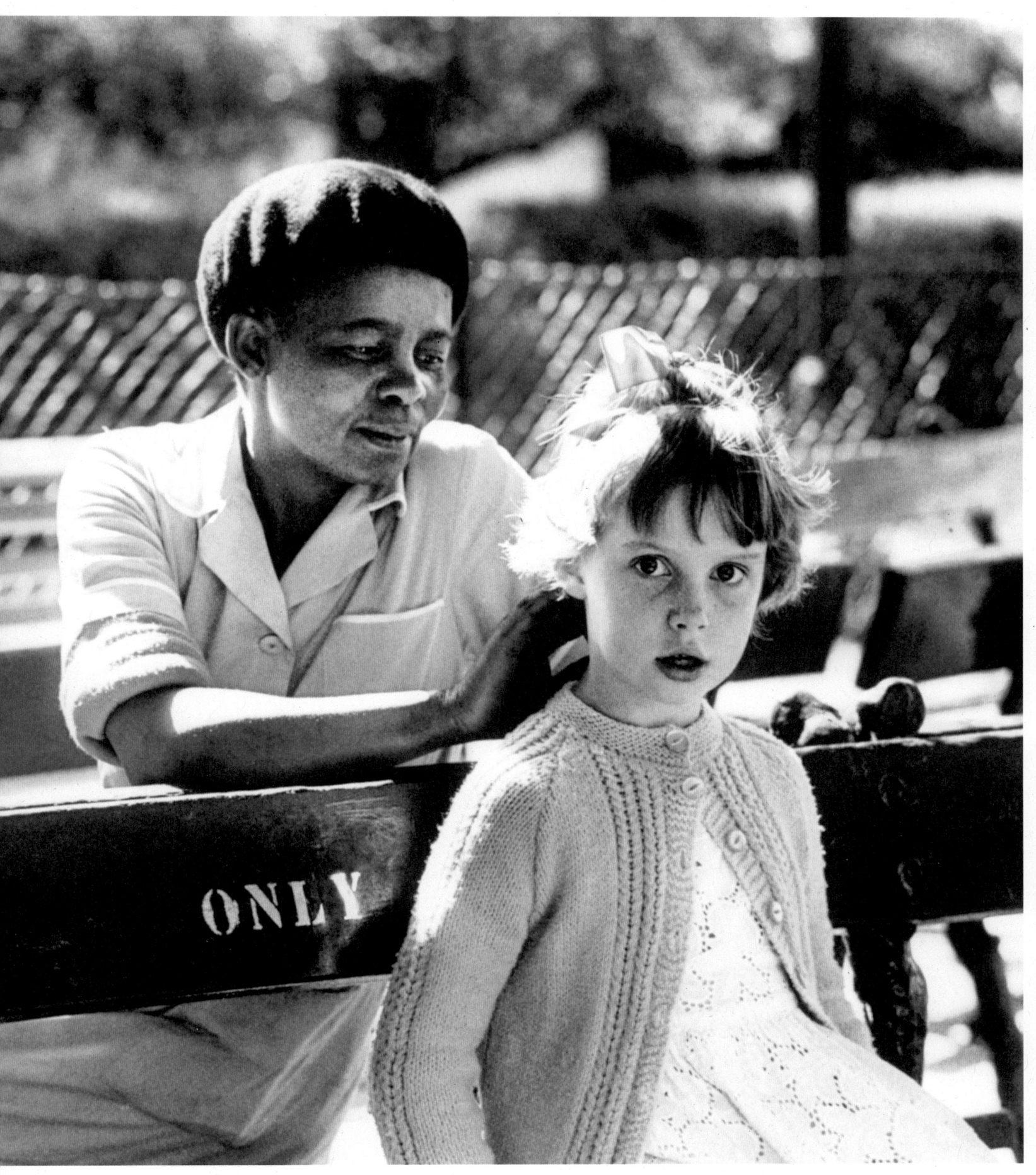

Nanny and Child (South Africa, 1956)

Medu Art Ensemble

Medu Art Ensemble / Judy A. Seidman
Don't Entertain Apartheid – Support the Cultural Boycott!, 1982

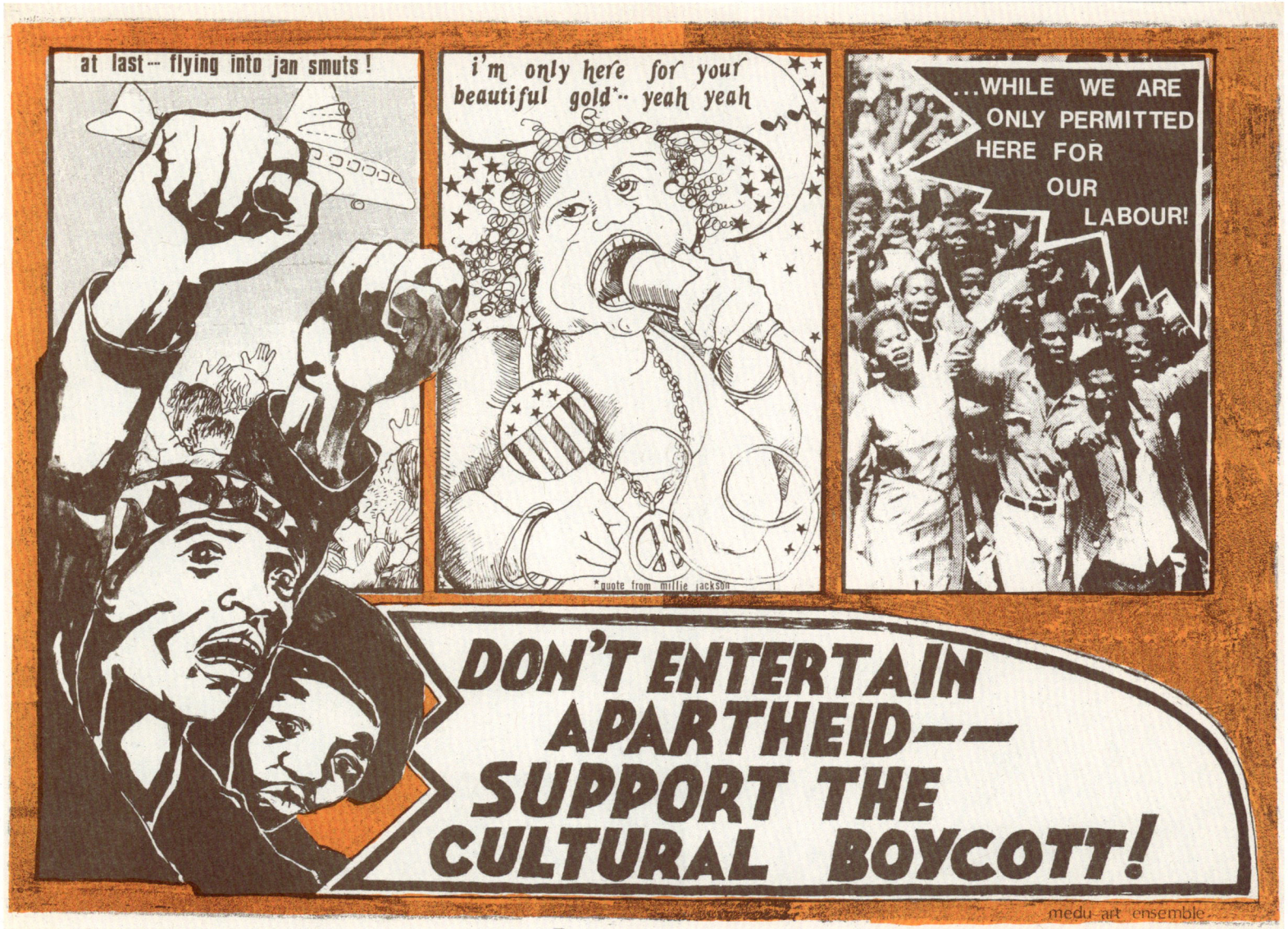

Medu Art Ensemble

The Medu Art Ensemble was a group of South African and international artists from the visual arts, theatre, music, and literature who came together in 1978 as a reaction to South Africa's apartheid policy. They called themselves "Medu", which means "roots" in the Sepedi language. As their name suggests, the collective operated underground. Many Medu members were politically persecuted. The group was founded by the famous poet Mongane Wally Serote (*1944) and the artist Thamsanqa "Thami" Mnyele (1948–1985). On June 14, 1985, Thami Mnyele was shot dead, along with six other members of the African National Congress, by South African Defence Force (SADF) soldiers. Mongane Wally Serote returned to South Africa after 18 years in exile. He became a Member of Parliament in South Africa in 1994, and was appointed as the country's Poet Laureate in 2018.

The six posters from the 1980s exhibited at *RESIST!* epitomise the Medu concept: silkscreen prints, resembling offset lithographs, with simple combinations of text and images and slogans such as "The People Shall Govern" or "Support the Cultural Boycott". The protest posters were designed for mass impact: they were easy to reproduce and distribute. "The act of creating art is not different from the act of building a bridge – it is the work of many hands," Mnyele once said.

In 1968, the United Nations General Assembly passed a resolution calling for the worldwide suspension of cultural and educational exchange with institutions that perpetuated apartheid. The United States rejected the resolution, and American companies profited from ignoring the boycott. Musicians like the Beach Boys, Cher, Curtis Mayfield, Queen, and Tina Turner made millions performing in South Africa.

In the run-up to Medu's 1982 Festival of Culture and Resistance, the group's members designed a poster to promote the cultural boycott as a key principle of the event. This poster is a response to the actions of American soul singer Millie Jackson, who performed in South Africa despite opposition from a Black Consciousness arts organisation.

South Africa 1981–1983

Medu Art Ensemble/Thamsanqa (Thami) Mnyele
Namibia. The Sun will Rise, 1981

Medu Art Ensemble/Judy A. Seidman *The People Shall Govern!*, 1982

Medu Art Ensemble/Thamsanqa (Thami) Mnyele & Judy A. Seidman *The People Shall Defeat Aggression and Destabilisation*, 1983

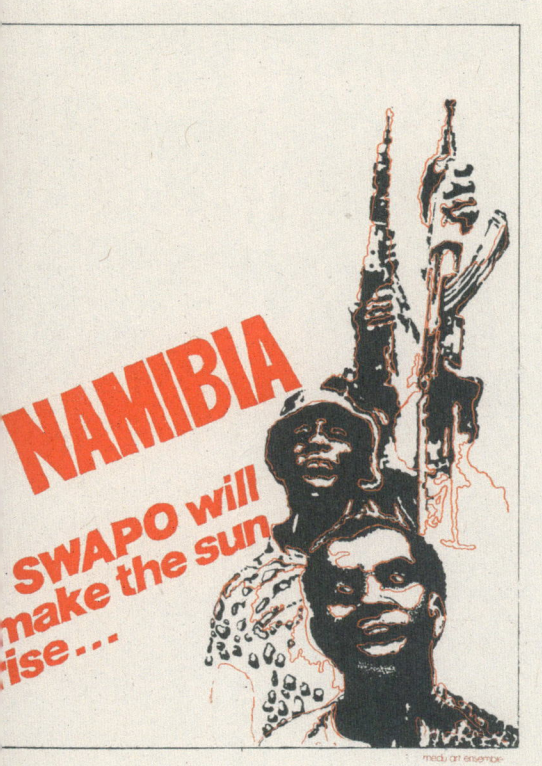

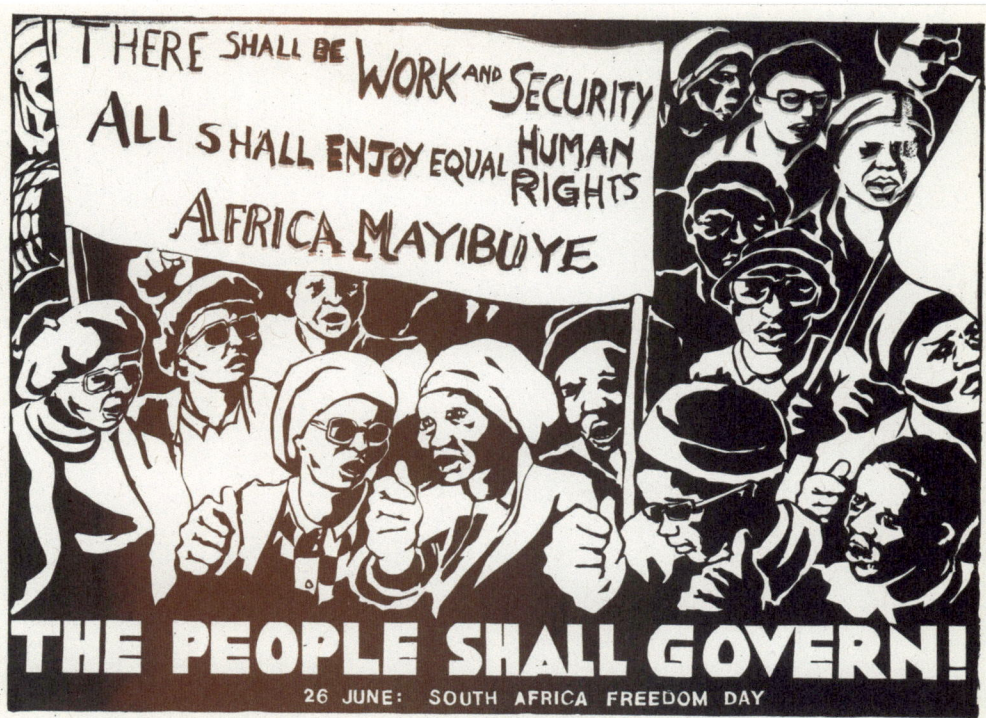

South Africa conquered Namibia from Germany during World War I and ruled the country as a province from 1915 to 1990. Under this occupation, Black Namibians were subjected to apartheid laws, denied political rights, economic opportunities, and social freedoms. This poster was created in support of the South West African People's Organisation (SWAPO), a Namibian political party that led the country to independence in 1990.

The bold slogans on this poster quote from the Freedom Charter of the African National Congress (ANC). This document outlined the core principles for creating a fair post-apartheid society. The drawing is based upon a photograph taken by Eli Weinberg – a member of the South African Communist Party and supporter of the anti-apartheid movement – during the public meeting at which the charter was formally ratified in 1955. The ANC drafted the charter by sending fifty thousand volunteers into townships to consult people about what changes would be necessary to realise such a society. They summarised these thousands of demands into ten key points, the most important being "The People Shall Govern!"

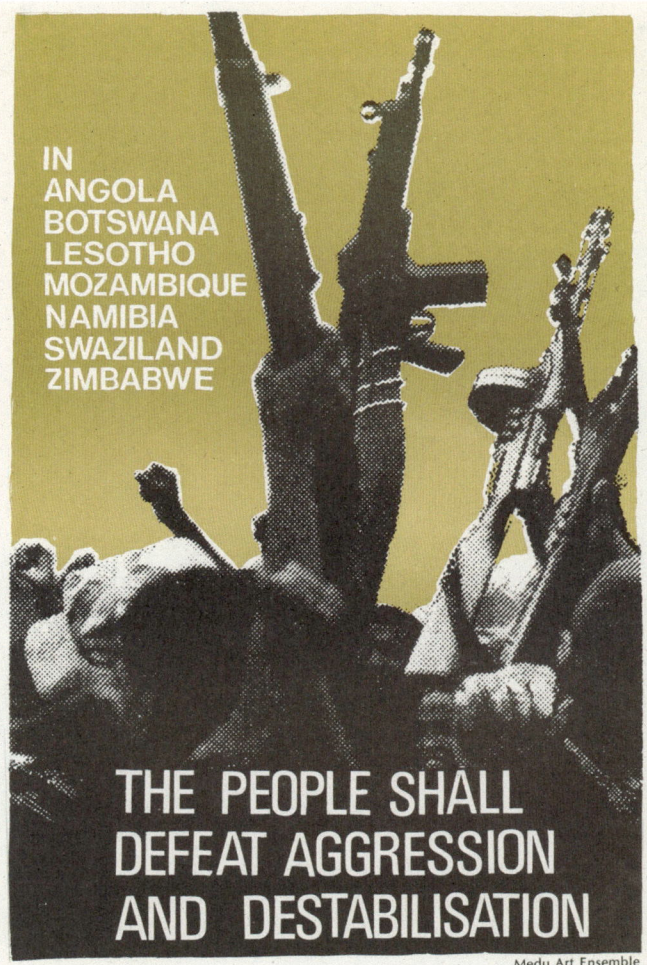

This poster opposes the continued attacks on Southern Africa's Frontline States. The image shows celebrations by the People's Armed Forces of Liberation of Angola (FAPLA).

Courtesy of The Art Institute of Chicago

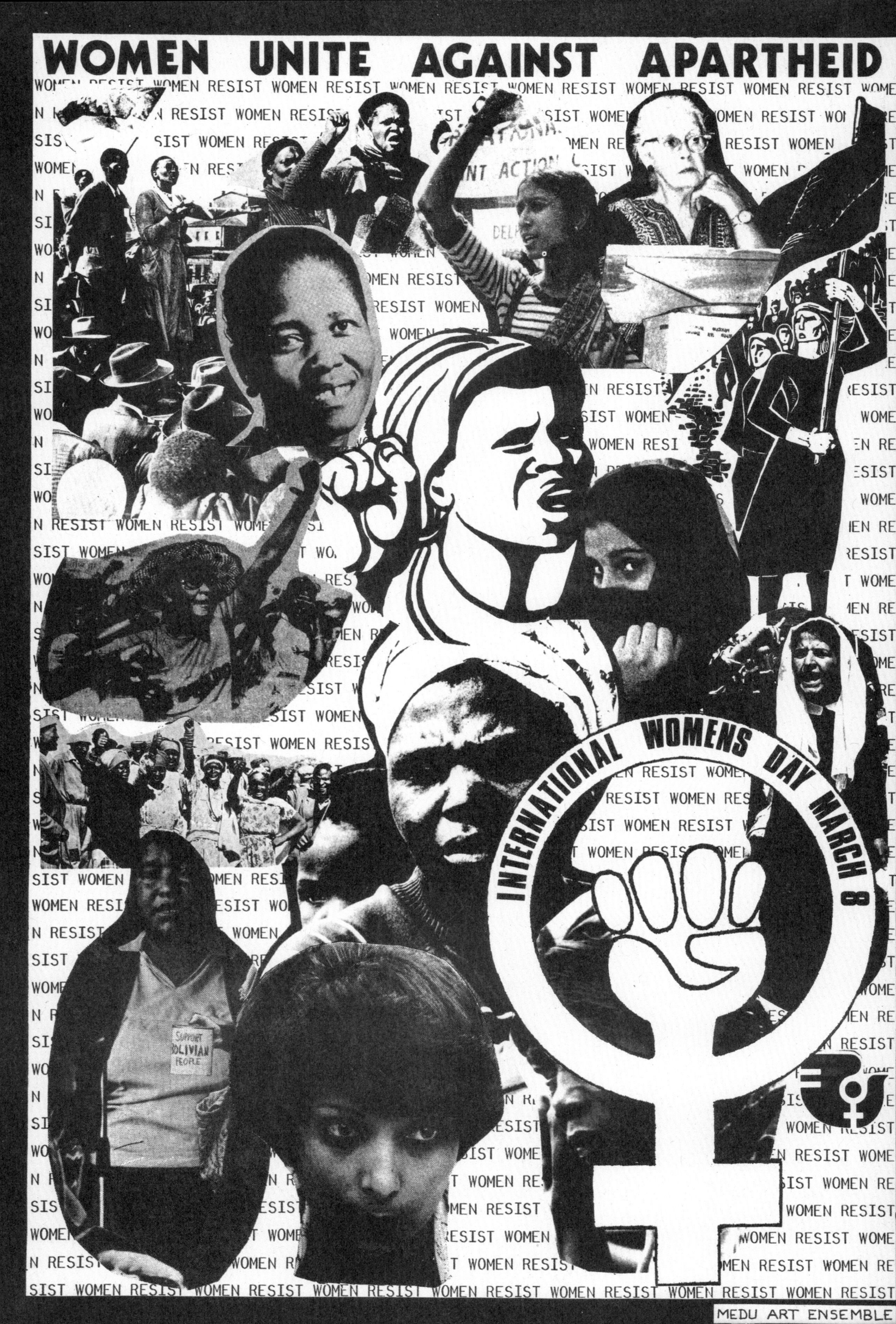

Medu Art Ensemble

South Africa 08/03/1981
03/09/1984

Medu Art Ensemble / Thamsanqa (Thami) Mnyele, Michael Kahn, Tim Williams *Women Unite Against Apartheid*, 1981

Medu Art Ensemble / Thamsanqa (Thami) Mnyele, Michael Kahn, Gordon Metz *This Is Our Land [Soweto]*, 1984

Women played a significant role in the anti-apartheid struggle in South Africa, and the Medu Art Ensemble set out to give them a stronger voice. One of the most important events took place on August 9, 1956, when 20,000 women from all over South Africa marched to the union buildings in the capital, Pretoria, in defiance of the passport laws that severely restricted the movement of Black women (and men) who wanted to commute to work or to travel within the country for any other reason. To this day, this protest march has great significance and is commemorated across the country as National Women's Day. However, women's activism has always been an international endeavour, as shown by this poster paying tribute to International Women's Day – a collage of female resistance fighters from all over the world.

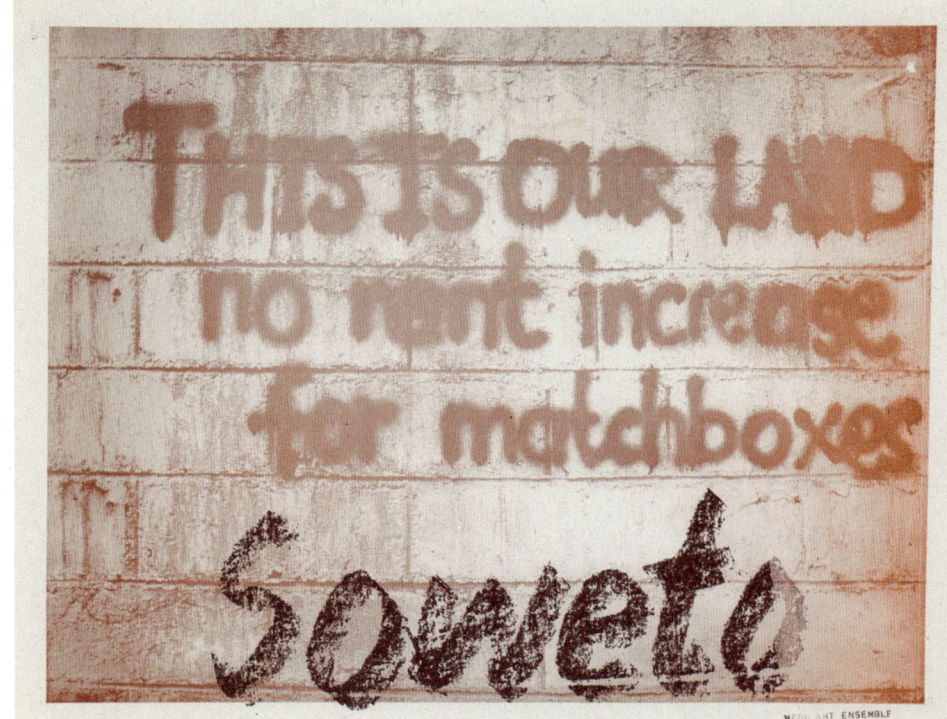

These posters were conceived in response to protests that erupted in South Africa's Vaal Triangle region on September 3, 1984 over rent increases proposed by local town councils. The protests ignited rent boycotts in predominantly Black townships such as Alexandria, Soweto, and Tembisa. By withholding rent, protestors refused to finance their own segregation from city centres and their relegation to the meagre "matchbox" homes imposed on them by the apartheid state. Medu printed the poster commercially as a template so that the names of specific townships could be inscribed through screen printing, as in this "Soweto" poster.

»The act of creating art is not different from the act of building a bridge – it is the work of many hands..« *Thami Mnyele*

Courtesy of The Art Institute of Chicago

Ernesto Yerena

El Centro, USA **2011–2017**

Akwesasne Notes (Hrsg.)

Akwesasne Mohawk Reserve **1970s**

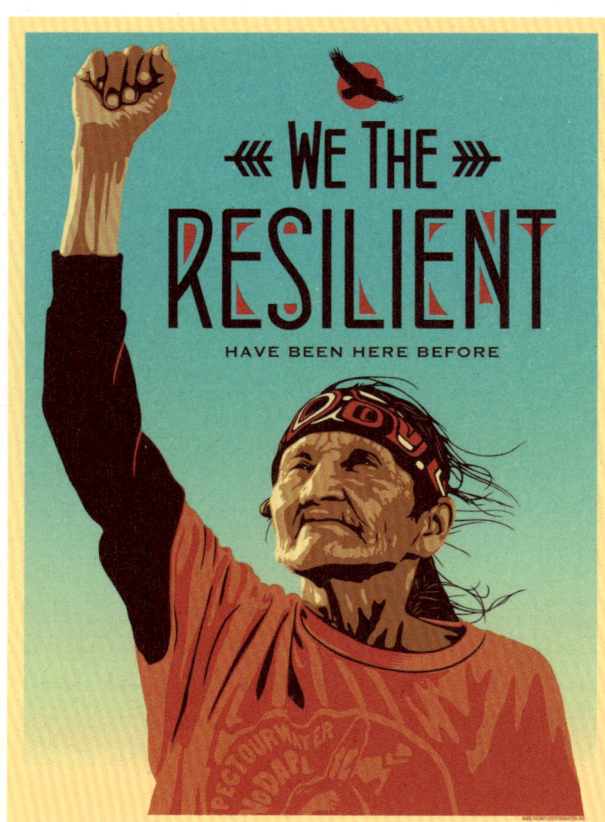

We the Resilient, 2017

The protests against the construction of the Dakota Access Pipeline (DAPL) were among the largest environmental movements of the 2000s in the USA. They led, among other things, to the largest gathering of Native Americans in history. The Dakota Access Pipeline was a 3.8 billion-dollar project to build an underground oil pipeline stretching 1,172 miles across the United States and crossing beneath the Standing Rock Reservation. The pipeline was proposed in 2014 and immediately met with opposition from resident groups and environmentalists due to the fact that it threatened culturally, spiritually, and ecologically significant areas, as well as waterways. On July 6, 2020, after multiple protests, a federal judge ruled to shut down the Dakota Access Pipeline and empty it of all oil pending an environmental review. Despite this, the pipeline is still in operation without a legal permit.

The poster shows Helen Red Feather, a veteran of the 1973 occupation of Wounded Knee, protesting the pipeline. She writes about herself on Facebook: "I'm a Lakota. I'm a freedom fighter. That's me. I've got history. I come from a warrior family that protect[s] the people ... I'm a warrior. I will fight for my grandkids till I leave this world."

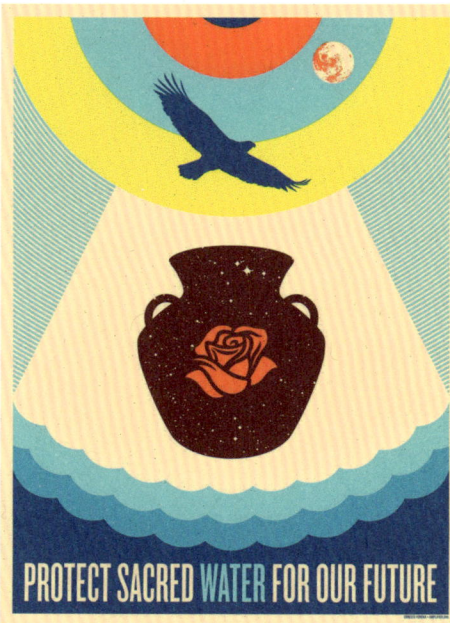

Protect Sacred Water, 2015

The poster was created in 2015 through a collaboration between the Lakota grassroots organisation Owe Aku and the artist Ernesto Yerena. Directed against the irresponsible exploitation of our most basic natural resource, it seeks to convey just how crucial water is for the survival of the Lakota. In the dry environment of the Great Plains, water takes on an almost spiritual role. The Lakota (or Blackfeet) living in the Great Plains of North America have developed their own methods of coping with the limited water supply over thousands of years.

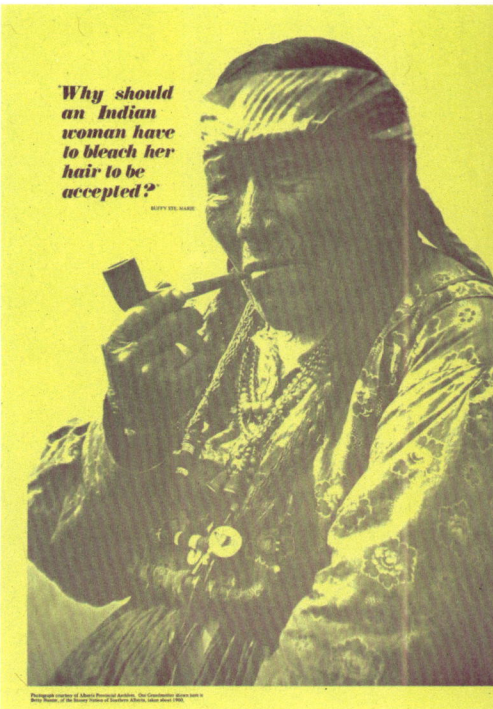

Why should an Indian woman have to bleach her hair to be accepted?,
1970s–1980s, Cornwall Island Reserve, NY, USA

In the title of her poster, Buffy-Sainte Marie (*1941) – a First Nations musician, composer, performing artist, teacher, and social activist – sums up the difficult living conditions for Native American women in the US today in a single sentence. They tend to be institutionally disadvantaged and are more likely to be violently assaulted than Euro-American women. The poster reproduces a photograph of Betty Hunter (Stoney Nakoda) taken around 1900.

Anthony Gauthier

Santa Fe, USA **1978**

Oglala Lakota College

Pine Ridge, USA **1979**

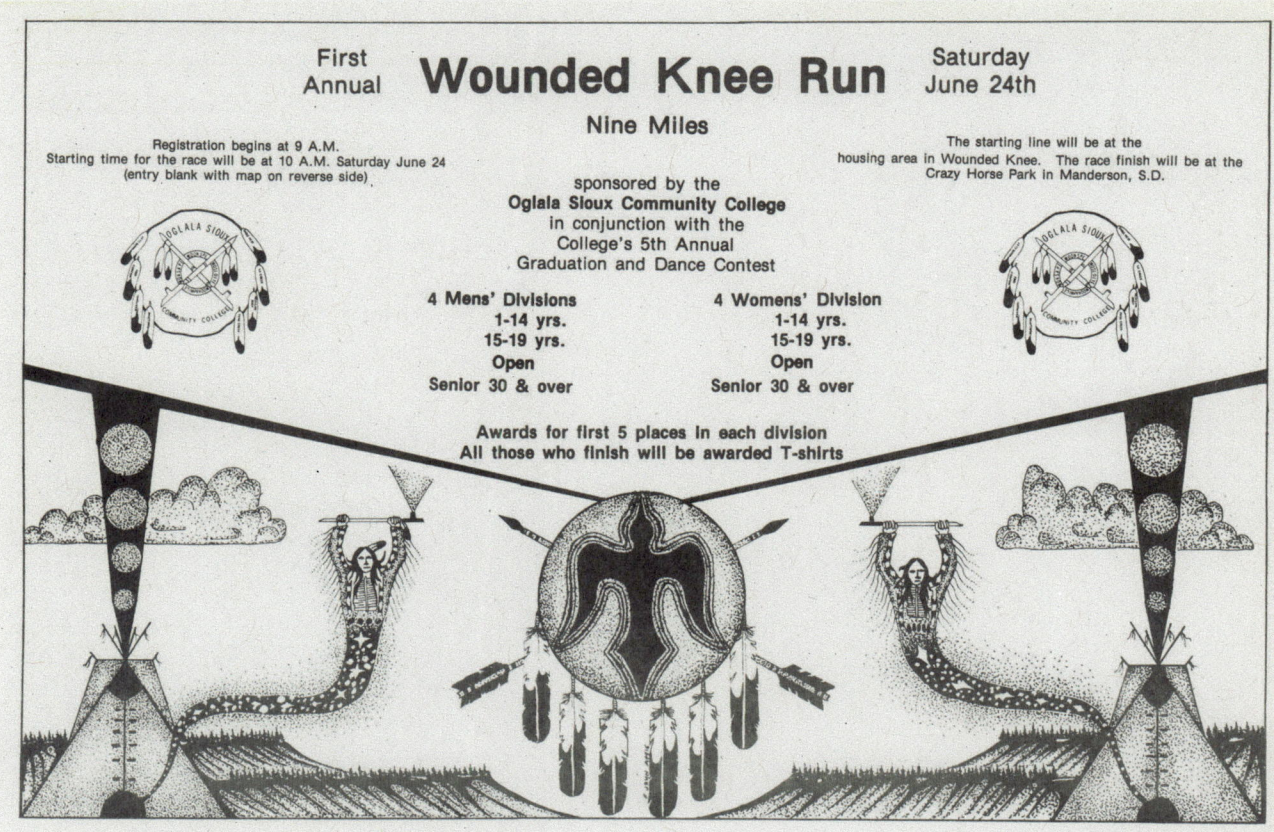

Wounded Knee Run, 1979,
Oglala Lakota College, Pine Ridge
Indian Reservation, SD, USA

On December 29, 1890, 150 to 300 Lakota were brutally gunned down by the US Army at Wounded Knee. This massacre was the culmination of the US Army's efforts to suppress the local population in the northern Plains. The background to this escalation was the death of the Sioux spiritual leader Thatȟáŋka Íyotake/Sitting Bull (ca. 1831–1890), coupled with the American desire to crack down on the emerging Ghost Dance movement. Today, the massacre still symbolises the end of the North American Native Americans armed struggle for freedom against the Euro-American settlers.

The poster was created in 1979 to mark the first Wounded Knee Run and the fifth anniversary of Oglala Lakota College, an accredited institute serving the Pine Ridge Reservation in South Dakota. The poster maps out the running route from the small town of Wounded Knee to the memorial stone. The Wounded Knee Run is a way of remembering the massacre, which remains a traumatic experience for the Lakota and has been commemorated in various forms since 1905.

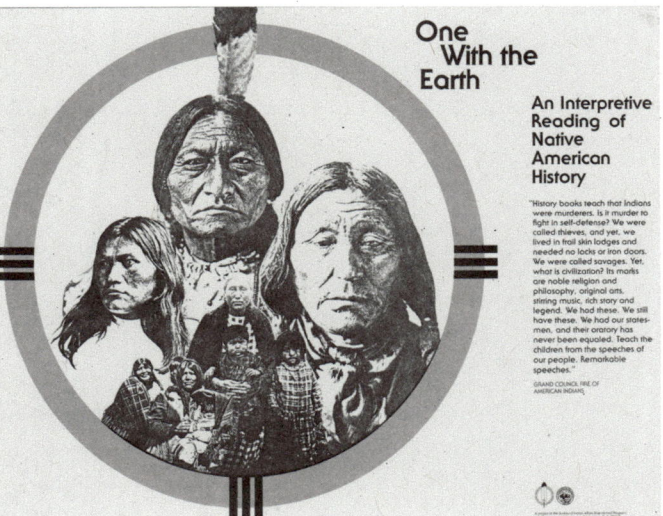

One With the Earth, 1978,
Institute for American Indian Art,
Santa Fe, NM, USA

Designed by the Menominee artist Anthony Gauthier (1942–2020), this 1978 poster refers to an open letter written by the Grand Council Fire of American Indians in 1927. It contains an excerpt of this letter to Chicago's then mayor William Hale Thompson, who campaigned as the Republican mayoral candidate in 1926 to remove all "British propaganda" from American schoolbooks so as to honour the heroes of the American Revolution as part of his "America First" movement. The members of the Grand Council Fire of America used Thompson's nationalist statements after his re-election in 1927 to point out the ignorance of US textbooks regarding Native Americans. This poster documents these political issues of the late 1920s. It shows how the members of the Grand Council Fire of American Indians saw themselves and their criticism of the country's nationalist policies.

REMEMBERING THE MASSACRE OF WOUNDED KNEE

Dakota, USA **29/12/1890**

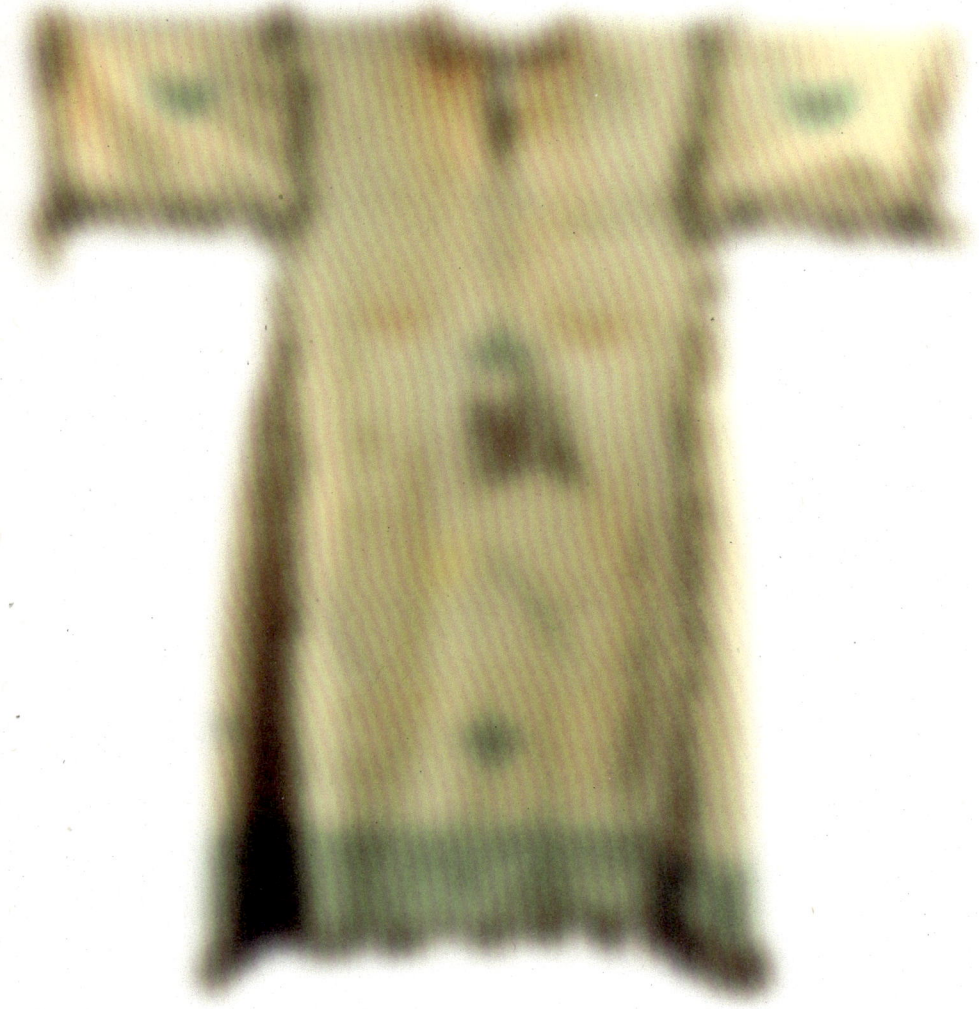

The Ghost Dance – Remembering Wounded Knee

In the late nineteenth century, the Indigenous population of North America, who were forbidden from practising their own religion and language, experienced a serious existential crisis. The almost complete extinction of the bison, their shrinking reservations due to the expansion of Euro-American settlers, and their dependence on food allocations from the US state as well as epidemics caused famine and resulted in numerous deaths. Thus, when the Paiute prophet Wovoka (ca. 1856–1932) started a largely peaceful political and religious movement, it spread rapidly among the reservations. This Ghost Dance movement promised the beginning of a new era and the restoration of the old way of life with the return of the bison, peace, and freedom.

A trance-like dance around a sacred tree or pole with chants was supposed to bring healing and establish a connection with the spirit world. The US government tried to suppress this movement in the Lakota reservations because it suspected that a mass uprising was imminent. After the killing of the leader Tȟatȟáŋka Íyotake/Sitting Bull (ca. 1831–1890), the US army pursued the fleeing members of the movement to Wounded Knee on the Pine Ridge Reservation in South Dakota, where it massacred about 150 to 300 men, women, and children on December 29, 1890. Following the massacre, the Ghost Dance was no longer practised by the Lakota, and it later disappeared on the other reservations, too. To this day, a memorial service is held every year with a march to Pine Ridge.

Ghost Dance Dress
Probably Northern Plains, North/South Dakota, USA, late nineteenth century, RJM Collection No. 49690

Ghost Dance dresses are rarely exhibited now because of the tragic circumstances associated with them. Out of respect for their societies of origin, they are only displayed with their consent. New findings in provenance research have led the Rautenstrauch-Joest-Museum to seek contact with possible descendants of their creators and to cover the glass box in which the dress was exhibited during the *RESIST!* exhibition. The dress entered the RJM collection in 1967. The previous owner was what is now known as the National Museum of the American Indian in New York, more specifically George Gustav Heye, who bought it from the collector and dealer Patrick Ryan in 1906.

»Our relatives were shot at very close range. They were so close that you could see the powder burn marks on the children and the women. There was no honour in these murders, and the Lakota live with these traumas to this day. Our lives are reminders of our courage, strength, and the will to survive in the twenty-first century. In the healing road that we have to all take, we are all human beings, and we need to work together.«
Iron Hawk, around 25/06/2019

Lawrence Paul Yuxweluptun
The Intellect, 1997

USA & Canada — 1890–2021

MEMORY IN SOLIDARITY

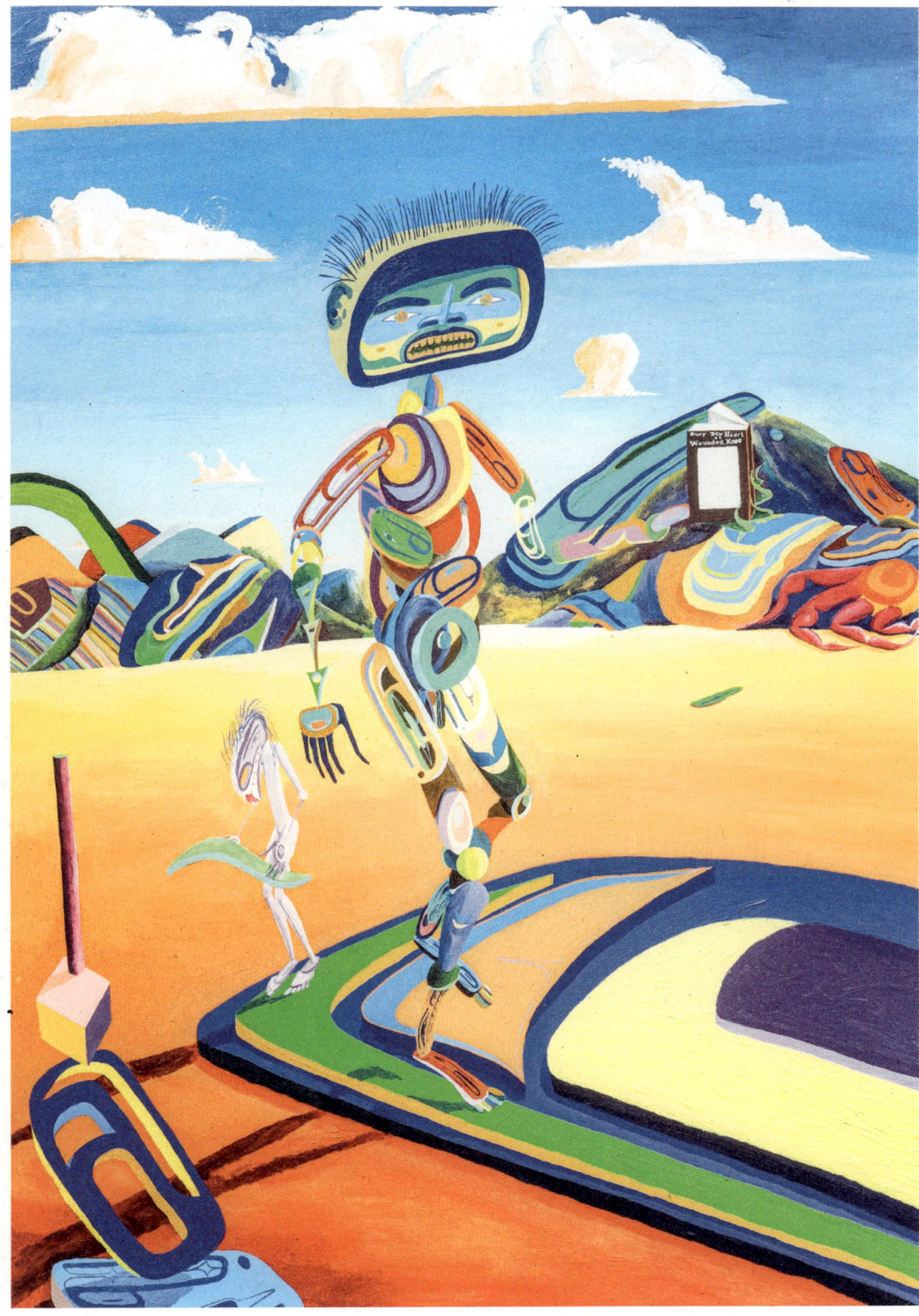

With *The Intellect*, Yuxweluptun shows his solidarity with resistance movements outside Canada. This image depicts a figure holding the book *Bury My Heart at Wounded Knee*, which chronicles the violent expansionism of the American West and the displacement of the First Nations, along with the traumas this caused, culminating with the massacre at Wounded Knee. Published in 1970 at the height of the American Indian Movement's activism, *Bury My Heart at Wounded Knee* had a profound impact on the awareness of the genocide against the First Nations.

The works of Lawrence Paul Yuxweluptun are visual protests that unequivocally criticise Canada's history and colonial continuities. In many of his works, the Coast Salish/Okanagan (Syilx) artist comes to terms with his own past as a student of a residential school – one of the Christian boarding schools established by the Canadian state. In spring 2021, the remains of 215 children were discovered at a former residential school in Kamloops (Yuxweluptun's hometown) in British Columbia. Yuxweluptun and the artist Tania Willard, who also featured in the exhibition *RESIST!* (see page 167), were child victims of the residential schools, where more than 150,000 First Nations children were re-educated, abused, and even several murdered up until 1996.

»If you allow only the colonialists to record history, they record it to their own glorification. I wanted to take that position of power, of historical painting, and put it into my own hands – take possession of history.
I'm just an Indian trying to emancipate myself, but I still will look at these things. I may be under colonial occupation, but I will think about these things.«
Lawrence Paul Yuxweluptun

Courtesy of private collection, Cologne

Patrice Lumumba
Declaration of the Congo's Independence

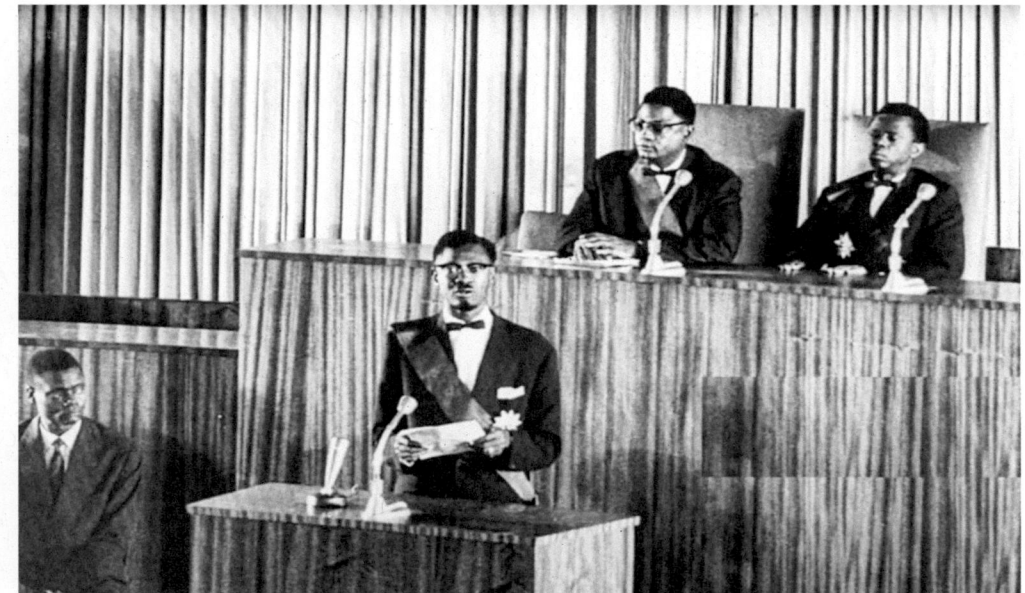

Speech by Patrice Lumumba at the Ceremony of the Proclamation of the Congo's independence, Kinshasa, 30/06/1960

On June 30, 1960, to celebrate the independence of what is now the Democratic Republic of Congo, the Belgian King Baudouin made a condescending speech praising the alleged good deeds of King Leopold II. Without being recorded in the minutes, Patrice Lumumba, the newly elected Prime Minister, took the floor and settled the score with Belgium. Lumumba's response was a blazing proclamation in which he accused the former colonial rulers of violent oppression and described the colonial system as slavery. Congolese and Belgian politicians attended the ceremony, as well as diplomatic representatives from many other countries. Six months after Lumumba made this historic and inspiring speech, the then Prime Minister and beacon of hope of the young independent country was assassinated on January 17, 1961 with the help of US intelligence and the Belgian government.

Men and women of the Congo,
Victorious independence fighters,
I salute you in the name
of the Congolese Government

I ask all of you, my friends, who tirelessly fought in our ranks, to mark this June 30, 1960, as an illustrious date that will be ever engraved in your hearts, a date whose meaning you will proudly explain to your children, so that they in turn might relate to their grandchildren and great-grandchildren the glorious history of our struggle for freedom.

Although this independence of the Congo is being proclaimed today by agreement with Belgium, an amicable country, with which we are on equal terms,

no Congolese will ever forget that independence was won in struggle, a persevering and inspired struggle carried on from day to day, a struggle, in which we were undaunted by privation or suffering and stinted neither strength nor blood.

It was filled with tears, fire and blood. We are deeply proud of our struggle, because it was just and noble and indispensable in putting an end to the humiliating bondage forced upon us. That was our lot for the eighty years of colonial rule and our wounds are too fresh and much too painful to be forgotten.
We have experienced forced labour in exchange for pay that did not allow us to satisfy our hunger, to clothe ourselves, to have decent lodgings or to bring up our children as dearly loved ones. Morning, noon and night we were subjected to jeers, insults and blows because we were "Negroes". Who will ever forget that the Black was addressed as "tu", not because he was a friend, but because the polite "vous" was reserved for the white man?

We have seen our lands seized in the name of ostensibly just laws, which gave recognition only to the right of might.

Kinshasa, DR Congo — **30/06/1960**

We have not forgotten that the law was never the same for the white and the Black, that it was lenient to the ones, and cruel and inhuman to the others.

We have experienced the atrocious sufferings, being persecuted for political convictions and religious beliefs, and exiled from our native land: our lot was worse than death itself.

We have not forgotten that in the cities the mansions were for the whites and the tumbledown huts for the Blacks; that a Black was not admitted to the cinemas, restaurants and shops set aside for "Europeans"; that a Black travelled in the holds, under the feet of the whites in their luxury cabins. Who will ever forget the shootings which killed so many of our brothers, or the cells into which were mercilessly thrown those who no longer wished to submit to the regime of injustice, oppression and exploitation used by the colonialists as a tool of their domination? All that, my brothers, brought us untold suffering.

But we, who were elected by the votes of your representatives, representatives of the people, to guide our native land, we, who have suffered in body and soul from the colonial oppression, we tell you that henceforth all that is finished with.

The Republic of the Congo has been proclaimed and our beloved country's future is now in the hands of its own people. Brothers, let us commence together a new struggle, a sublime struggle that will lead our country to peace, prosperity and greatness. Together we shall establish social justice and ensure for every man a fair remuneration for his labour. We shall show the world what the Black man can do when working in liberty, and we shall make the Congo the pride of Africa. We shall see to it that the lands of our native country truly benefit its children. We shall revise all the old laws and make them into new ones that will be just and noble.

We shall stop the persecution of free thought. We shall see to it that all citizens enjoy to the fullest extent the basic freedoms provided for by the Declaration of Human Rights.

We shall eradicate all discrimination, whatever its origin, and we shall ensure for everyone a station in life befitting his human dignity and worthy of his labour and his loyalty to the country. We shall institute in the country a peace resting not on guns and bayonets but on concord and goodwill. And in all this, my dear compatriots, we can rely not only on our own enormous forces and immense wealth, but also on the assistance of the numerous foreign states, whose cooperation we shall accept when it is not aimed at imposing upon us an alien policy, but is given in a spirit of friendship.

Even Belgium, which has finally learned the lesson of history and need no longer try to oppose our independence, is prepared to give us its aid and friendship; for that end an agreement has just been signed between our two equal and independent countries. I am sure that this cooperation will benefit both countries. For our part, we shall, while remaining vigilant, try to observe the engagements we have freely made. Thus, both in the internal and the external spheres, the new Congo being created by my government will be rich, free and prosperous. But to attain our goal without delay, I ask all of you, legislators and citizens of the Congo, to give us all the help you can.

I ask you all to sink your tribal quarrels: they weaken us and may cause us to be despised abroad. I ask you all not to shrink from any sacrifice for the sake of ensuring the success of our grand undertaking. Finally, I ask you unconditionally to respect the life and property of fellow-citizens and foreigners who have settled in our country; if the conduct of these foreigners leaves much to be desired, our Justice will promptly expel them from the territory of the republic; if, on the contrary, their conduct is good, they must be left in peace, for they, too, are working for our country's prosperity.

The Congo's independence is a decisive step towards the liberation of the whole African continent.

Our government, a government of national and popular unity, will serve its country. I call on all Congolese citizens, men, women and children, to set themselves resolutely to the task of creating a national economy and ensuring our economic independence.

Eternal glory to the fighters for national liberation! Long live independence and African unity! Long live the independent and sovereign Congo!

Tshibumba Kanda Matulu
Patrice Lumumba, 1973/74

DR Congo **1961–1964**

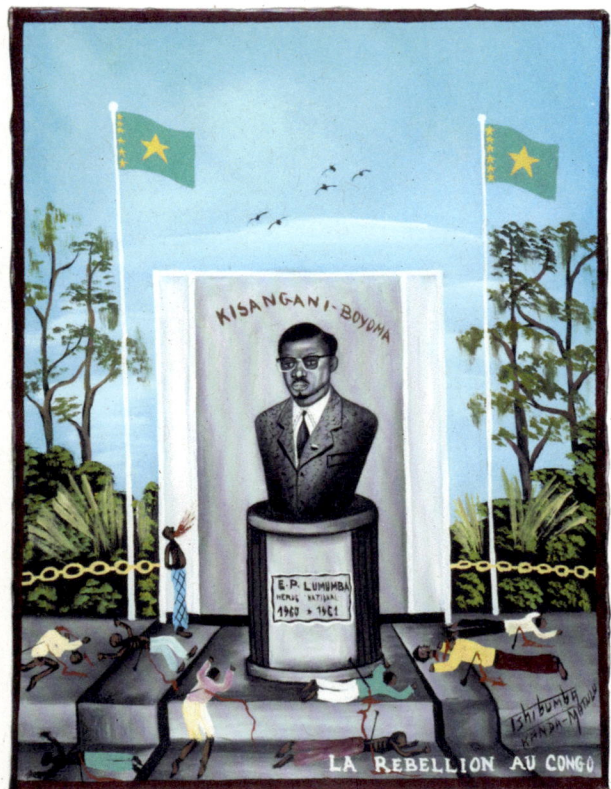

Tshibumba Kanda Matulu, 1973-74, *The bloody uprising in Kisangani on January 17, 1961, with numerous victims in front of a monument to Lumumba*

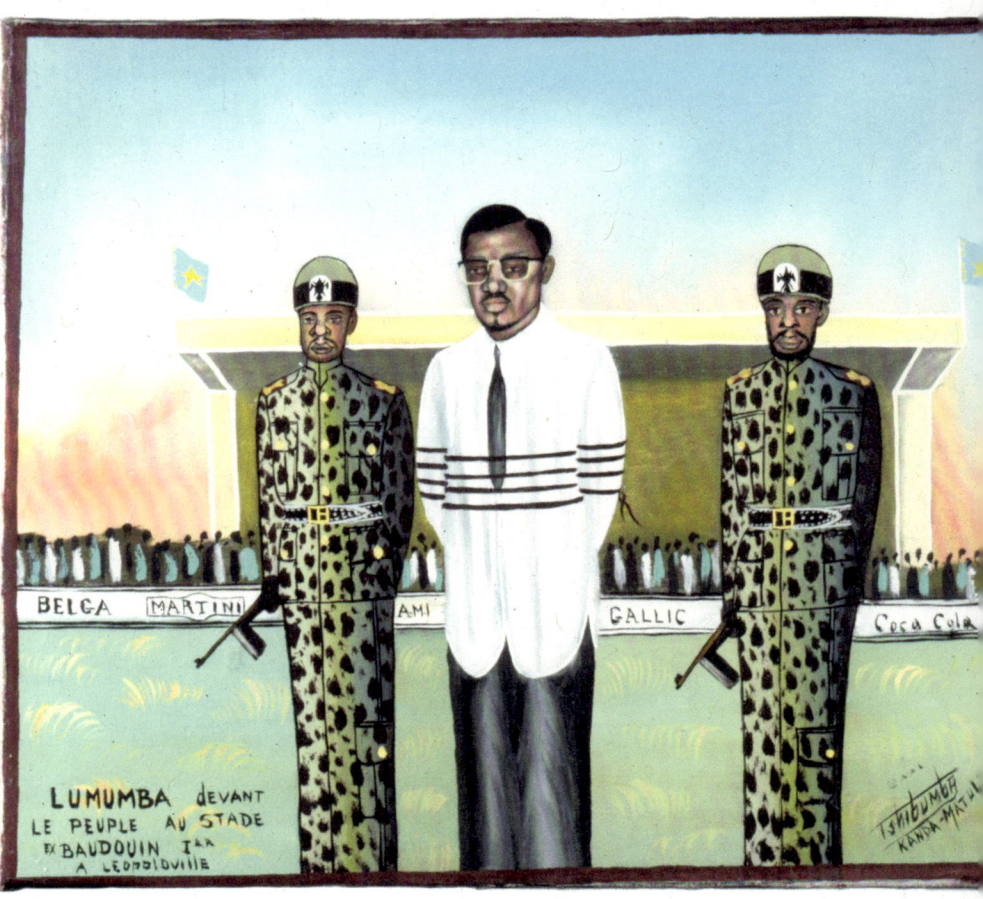

Tshibumba Kanda Matulu, 1973-74, *After his arrest, Lumumba is shown to the people at the King Baudouin Stadium*

European colonialism was arguably at its most atrocious in the Congo, which was ruled by the Belgian monarch King Leopold II. According to current estimates by historians, more than 10 million Congolese people died under the vicious colonial regime of the Congo Free State (1885–1908) – around half of the population at the time. After major international campaigns against Leopold II regarding the cruel conditions under which "red rubber" (Congo rubber came to be known as "red rubber", in reference to the blood of Africans killed during production) was extracted, the state became a Belgian colony in 1908. When pressure on the Belgian colonial government increased at the end of the 1950s and the mass demonstrations could no longer be prevented, Patrice Lumumba, a vehement opponent of colonial rule and a founder of the party Congolese National Movement (MNC), emerged as a beacon of hope for the Congolese people. He and his party won the parliamentary elections on May 25, 1960, and he served as the first Prime Minister of the independent Congo from June to September 1960. His assassination on January 17, 1961, which was assisted by US intelligence and the Belgian government, is still considered one of the biggest unsolved criminal cases in the history of postcolonial Africa. Upon his death, Patrice Lumumba became a political hero and an icon of resistance. On June 20, 2021, Belgian Prime Minister Alexander De Croo returned the only known remains of Patrice Lumumba – a tooth – to the Democratic Republic of Congo, after the Belgian parliament established the first commission in June 2020 to deal with Belgium's colonial past in the wake of the anti-racism and BLM movements. However, in December 2022, the commission failed to reach a consensus on a parliamentary resolution for the Belgian state to formally apologise and pay compensation for the atrocities committed.

The Congolese artist Tshibumba Kanda Matulu is one of the leading representatives of popular painting in Congo. In the 1970s, Matulu produced a series of paintings that told Congolese history from the people's perspective – in particular, the story of Patrice Lumumba. Matulu disappeared in 1981 and has not been found since.

Lapiztola
The Defence of the Maize, 2020

Oaxaca, Mexico   **2020**

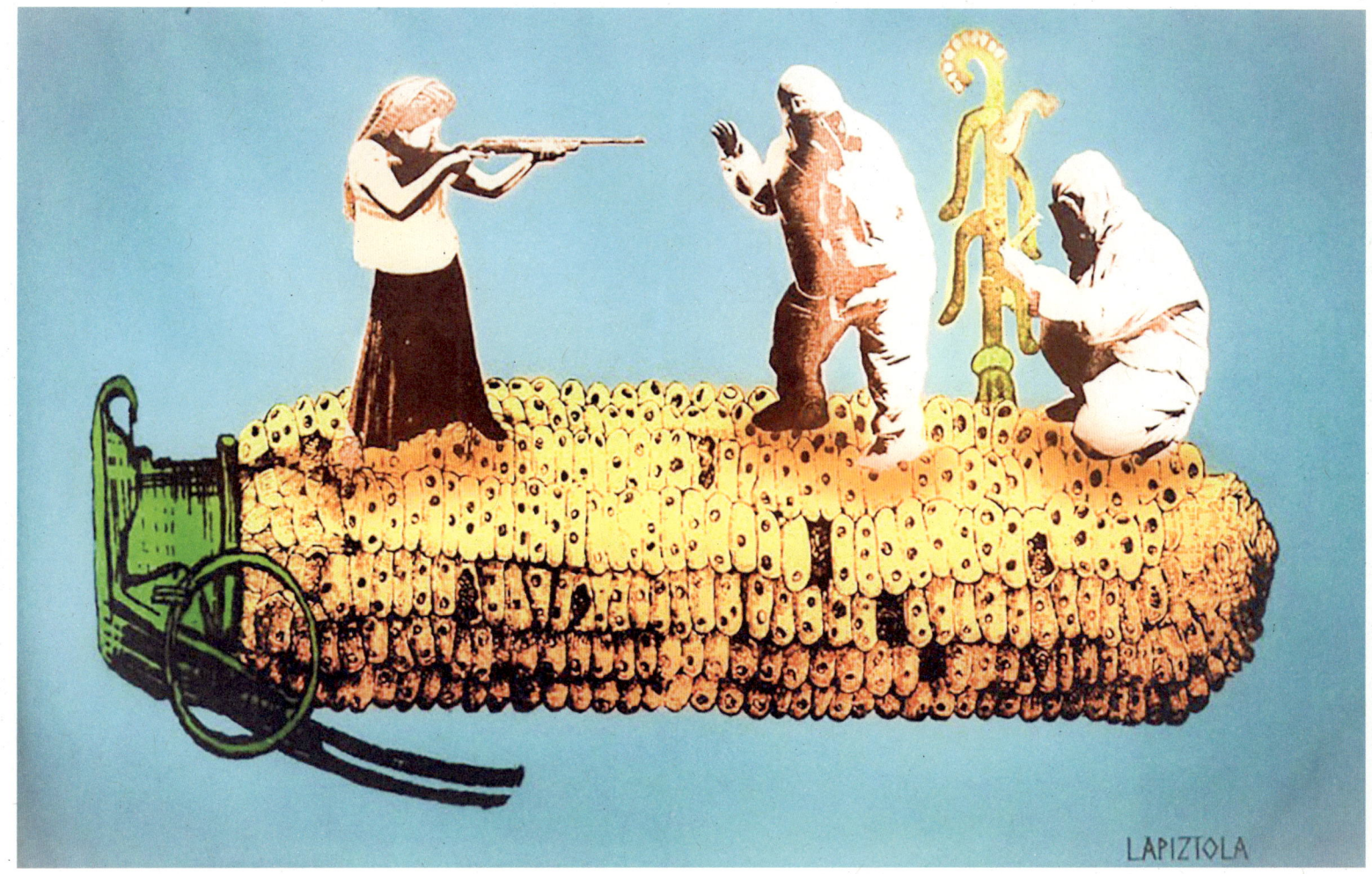

This graffiti installation by the artist collective Lapiztola from Oaxaca, Mexico combines the fight against genetically modified maize with the empowerment of diverse local communities. The stencil on a canvas shows a woman from Oaxaca pointing a rifle at researchers standing on a corncob in the shape of a grenade. They represent the government-sponsored genetic maize industry. These nutritionally poor varieties threaten traditional corn cultivation, the foundation of thousands of years of Central American civilisation, and consequently the economic basis of the Indigenous population.
The stencils were made in 2006 during the occupation of the city of Oaxaca by the Asociación Popular del Pueblo de Oaxaca (APPO). This conflict was triggered when the police opened fire on teachers who were participating in a peaceful protest against the low funding for rural schools. During the month-long occupation, artists sprayed graffiti on buildings to denounce neoliberal policies and the commercial appropriation of local cultures.

"Lapiz", the pencil, and "pistola", the gun: art as a more effective response to gun violence than ammunition is the idea behind the Mexican collective Lapiztola. However, the city of Oaxaca showed solidarity. Lapiztola carried their political agenda into the streets: the designer couple Rosario Martínez and Roberto Vega (both b. 1982) and architect Yankel Balderas have been protesting against grievances through their street art ever since. Their stencil and silk-screen works address global issues from a local perspective.

»No one colonises innocently, that no one colonises with impunity either; that a nation which colonises, that a civilisation which justifies colonisation – and therefore force – is already a sick civilisation.«
Aimé Césaire *Discourse on Colonialism, 1955*

Juan Manuel Sandoval Palacios, Diego Sandoval Ávila
Códice de Ayotzinapa, 2014

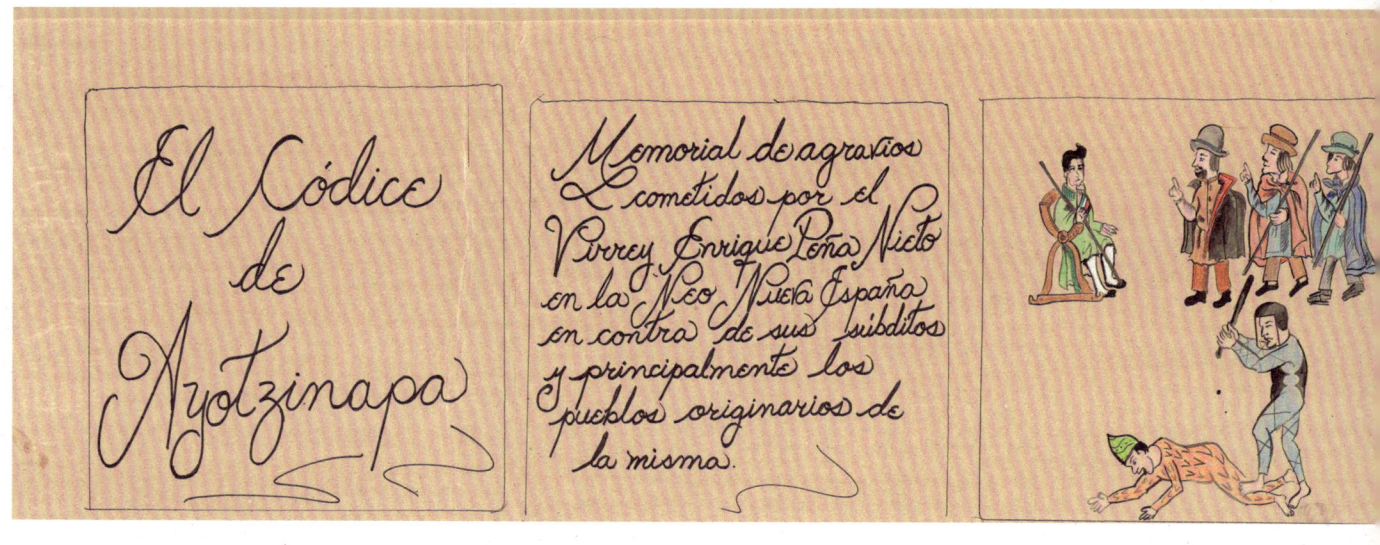

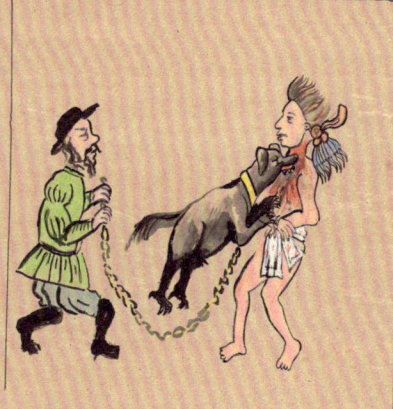

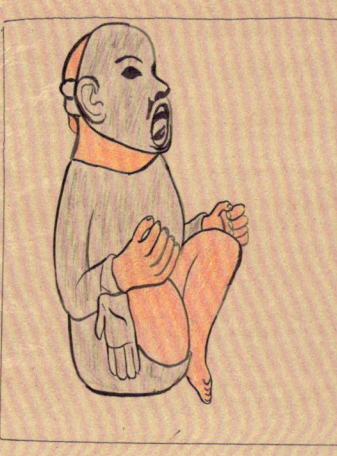

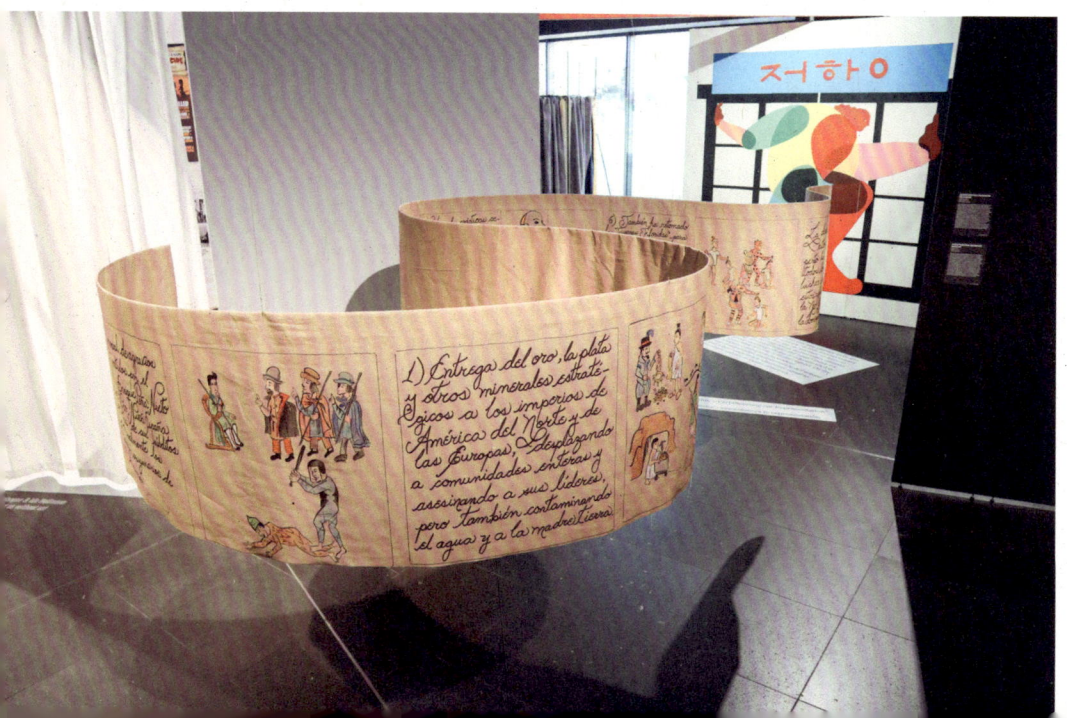

Mexico City, Mexico — 26–27/09/2014

1) Entrega del oro, la plata y otros minerales estratégicos a los imperios de América del Norte y de las Europas, desplazando a comunidades enteras y asesinando a sus líderes, pero también contaminando el agua y a la madre tierra.

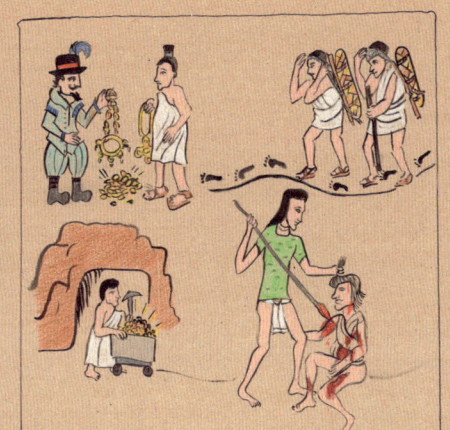

2) Restablecimiento de la esclavitud mediante una reforma laboral.

3) Entrega de los yacimientos de betún negro a intereses igualmente negros.

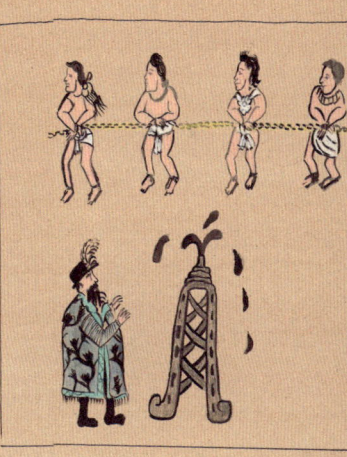

6) También ha retomado las "Guerras Floridas" para capturar prisioneros, como los 43 guerreros águilas y jaguares del Calmécac de Ayotzinapa, actualmente rehenes del déspota Virrey.

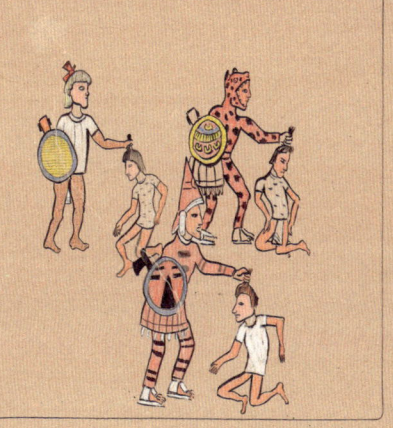

La desaparición de estos guerreros despertó la conciencia de todos los pueblos para luchar y resistir contra estos agravios y liberar a la Neo Nueva España de la dominación neocolonial.

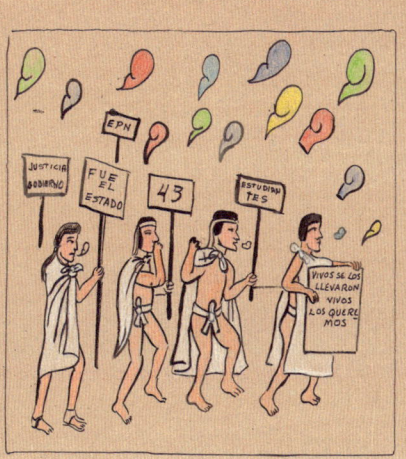

Pre-Hispanic symbols and visual forms of communication are still of great importance as strategies of resistance in Mexico today; the "speech scroll" (volute) motif, for example, signifies "powerful speech" in representations of deities. The anthropologist Juan Manuel Sandoval of the National Museum of Anthropology in Mexico City and his son Diego, a visual artist, drew the *Ayotzinapa Codex* together with children in the style of pre-Hispanic pictorial manuscripts. Since 2015 it has been exhibited once a month in the Mexican museum to commemorate the alleged murder of forty-three Indigenous students from Ayotzinapa by the police and drug cartels and to demand the investigation of this state-organised crime. On September 26/27, 2014, the students were on their way to Mexico City for a commemorative demonstration in memory of the brutal suppression of the 1968 student protests by the police and army. The narrative of the codex links the description of pre-Hispanic, colonial, and current cruel acts of injustice. The final image shows demonstrators protesting against neo-colonial conditions with their chants in the form of pre-Hispanic "speech scrolls" (volutes).

We first met Esther Utjiua Muinjangue at the Grassi Museum of Ethnology in Leipzig in 2017 (Nanette Snoep was director of the Grassi Museum of Ethnology from 2015 to 2019), when she was searching for the remains of her ancestors in museum collections. In 2018, she spoke at the Grassi Museum's conference, *Sensitive Heritage – Ethnographic Museums and Material/Immaterial Restitutions*, about her struggle for the recognition of the genocide against the Ovaherero and Nama. Later in 2019, when Nanette Snoep became director of the Rautenstrauch-Joest Museum in Cologne, she invited Esther Utjiua Muinjangue (and the Namibian activist Sima Luipert) to Cologne in December 2019 to talk about women's resistance and their role in the struggle to make the German Bundestag, the national parliament of the Federal Republic of Germany, acknowledge the genocide.

It's Yours! space: a space in a space

The exhibition *RESIST!* was an organic space of resonance and dissonance in a state of constant change. In the public, hegemonic space of the RJM, which, like other ethnological museums, is a place with highly asymmetrical power relations, *RESIST!* sought to make repressed and silenced stories and histories from the Global South as well as marginalised voices heard. With Esther Utjiua Muinjangue, Ida Hoffmann, Peju Layiwola, Tímea Junghaus, and In-Haus e.V with Elizaveta Khan, artists, curators, and activists who are directly affected by the topic of resistance were invited to create a non-hierarchical space in the museum to present conflicts, protests, and wounds, insofar as this is possible in a museum setting. Within the *RESIST!* exhibition space, they have taken the floor and curated their own autonomous *It's Yours!* spaces, places of agency and self-determination.

p. 064 Not about Us without Us
p. 094 Benin 1897
p. 138 Roma Resist!
p. 170 No Resistance Fits in a Box or a Museum

"It's Yours" Room

Esther Utjiua Muinjangue & Ida Hoffmann
Not about Us
Without Us

Germany's colonial genocide 1904-08 in what is today Namibia affected not only the resistant men but also women and children who died of thirst in the Omaheke/Kalahari region or were worked and tortured to death in concentration camps. The two Namibian activists Esther Utjiua Muinjangue and Ida Hoffmann speak in their It's Yours! room about their struggle for recognition of the genocide by the German Bundestag and explain why their communities demand an official apology and reparations from Germany.

We are the voices of people who died in 1904. We are speaking on behalf of those skulls, that are in Germany. And that is why we are saying: "it cannot be about us without us". Because the UN declaration on the rights of the indigenous people of 2007 it's very, very clear as to how the indigenous communities should be involved. Germany is a signatory to that and they cannot ignore that. We are saying "the pain that our people felt 117 years ago, we are still feeling that pain".

Esther Utjiua Muinjangue, Namibia, January 2021

Esther Utjiua Muinjangue

Esther Utjiua Muinjangue is a Namibian politician. She is the first woman to lead a political party (NUDO) in Namibia and the country's first female presidential candidate. For 15 years, she was the chairperson of the Ovaherero Genocide Foundation, a foundation that works to address the genocide of the Herero and Nama people.

Ida Hoffmann

Ida Hoffmann is a Namibian politician and activist. As chairperson of the Nama Genocide Technical Committee (NTLA), she is committed to the rights of the descendants of the victims of the Namibian genocide.

Windhoek, Namibia & Cologne, Germany — November 2020

Exhibition handout of the introductory text to the *It's Yours!* space
Not about Us without Us

A LUTA CONTINUA

Esther Utjiua Muinjangue and Ida Hoffmann, *It's Yours!* Curators

In recent years, scholars, researchers, and most importantly Indigenous communities have come to realise the importance of Germany's colonial history and the development of racism and total war practices in Africa, and especially in Namibia. Although German missionaries, explorers, and fortune-seekers began venturing into South West Africa (SWA; now Namibia) in the mid-nineteenth century, the territory did not become an official colonial possession of the German Empire until 1884. The Berlin Conference of 1884/85 played a major role in this; Namibia was Germany's largest colonial territory and became the main destination for German settlers. Today Namibia remains a prime attraction for tourists from Germany. The presence of the German missionaries, settlers, and soldiers brought about dramatic social, traditional, and structural changes in the Ovaherero community. The German Empire's increasingly authoritarian economic policies and violent punitive measures aggravated tense relations between the Germans and the Ovaherero leaders. German colonisers were intent on appropriating all natural resources, including land. They travelled thousands of kilometres to SWA to seize tens of thousands of hectares of land, drive the Ovaherero from their land, and confiscate their cattle. Why did all this happen? White supremacy, and the German conviction that the African natives were too primitive to make good use of the land. However, generations of Ovaherero people had been and are still successfully utilising the land as cattle farmers. Today they are living on what were formerly known as reserves and still desperately need the land to survive.

The Germans used various tactics to confiscate the land: one particularly destructive measure was the introduction of alcohol to the Africans. The Ovaherero refused to yield their land, and in instances where the German colonisers did not succeed in appropriating the land, they forced the Ovaherero off it by putting them into financial debt. Germans sold large quantities of alcohol to the Ovaherero on credit, who of course were unable to pay with cash. Consequently, this accumulated into unmanageable debts, an opportunity used by German traders and farmers to persecute entire tribes for the individual debts of its members, harassing them with the Schambock (whip) and taking their land and cattle as payment for the alcohol.

On January 12, 1904, an uprising began, so Kaiser Wilhelm approved large numbers of troop reinforcements. He forced out the relatively moderate governor of SWA, Theodore Leutwein, who wanted to avoid a costly war and sought peace through negotiations, and replaced him with the seasoned colonial warrior Lieutenant General Lothar von Trotha. In von Trotha's extermination order of October 2, 1904, he instructed his men to shoot all Ovaherero men, women, and children. The following year, on April 22, 1905 a similar order was issued regarding the Nama people. Kaiser Wilhelm ordered von Trotha to set up concentration camps with the help of missionaries, where the few survivors, who looked like walking skeletons, were detained. The concentration camps were disease-ridden; Ovaherero survivors were registered and labelled with metal tags, barred from owning land and cattle, and assigned hard labour.

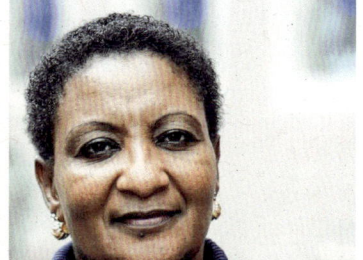

Esther Utjiua Muinjangue
*1962, Windhoek, Namibia

Ida Maria Magdalena Hoffmann
*1947, Karasburg, Namibia

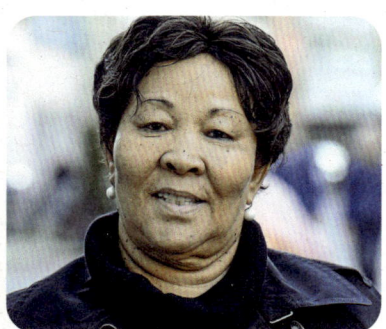

"Not without us about us!" – no debate about our history, our artefacts, our demands, without us having our say: this is one of the central concerns of Namibian politicians Esther Utjiua Muinjangue and Ida Hoffmann.

Esther Utjiua Muinjangue is a Namibian politician. She is the first woman to lead a political party (NUDO) in Namibia and the country's first female presidential candidate. For fifteen years, she was the chairperson of the Ovaherero Genocide Foundation, a foundation that works to address the genocide of the Herero and Nama people.

Ida Hoffmann is a Namibian politician and activist. As chairperson of the Nama Genocide Technical Committee (NTLA), she advocates for the rights of the descendants of the victims of the Namibian genocide.

> By 1908, the Germans had wiped out more than 80 per cent of the Ovaherero and 50 per cent of the Nama; the death rate for prisoners of war in the camps (among them women and children) was over 45 per cent. This dark past cannot and will never be addressed and discussed without the involvement of the Ovaherero and Nama people. Hence the slogan: It cannot be about us without us; anything about us without us is against us.

For the Ovaherero and Nama people, it is very important to make their concerns internationally visible and to continue seeking solidarity all over the world, thereby forcing the government of the Federal Republic of Germany to acknowledge its historical responsibility. The two governments have appointed special envoys to discuss how Germany can take responsibility for its "historical past". The negotiations started back in 2016 and have been conducted in private. The Ovaherero and Nama people see this as an attempt by the German government to avoid paying reparations.

The Ovaherero and Nama, in their progressive genocide and reparation movements (Ovaherero Genocide Foundation and Nama Genocide Technical Committee), have always been on record calling for a trialogue between:

Windhoek, Namibia — December 2020

1) the Ovaherero and Nama, including those in the diaspora, as direct victims of the genocide;
2) the government of the Federal Republic of Germany, as the successor to the government of Imperial Germany;
3) last but not the least, the Namibian government as a facilitator between the perpetrator and victims.

This trialogue has never been considered nor has it taken place. Thus, the Ovaherero and Nama cannot be said to have been included, because what is currently happening is purely bilateral negotiations between two sovereign states; more importantly, Dr Zedekia Ngavirue, the "Namibian negotiator", has been selected and appointed by the Namibian government and not by the Ovaherero and Nama people, meaning that he is paid by the Namibian government and works according to their Terms of Reference (TOR). It is not a matter of the Ovaherero and Nama joining the current bilateral talks, negotiations, or whatever you might want to call the ongoing overindulgences of the two governments.

> When the government of the Federal Republic of Germany one day awakens from its slumber, illusion, and self-delusion regarding genocide and reparations, the Ovaherero and Nama people are always ready to talk to the German government.

On January 5, 2017, the official representatives of the Ovaherero and Nama Indigenous peoples in Namibia and the worldwide diaspora – through their traditional leaders, Paramount Chief Advocate Vekuii Rukoro and Gaob Johannes Isaack – filed a federal class action lawsuit against Germany in the United States District Court for the Southern District of New York, seeking financial damages for the genocide and unlawful seizure of property in violation of international law during the German colonial occupation of South West Africa during the period from approximately 1884 to 1915. On March 13, 2018, Judge Laura Taylor Swain ruled in favour of the Germany's notice of motion to dismiss for lack of subject matter and personal jurisdiction, for failure to exhaust remedies in Germany, and under the doctrines of political question and forum non conveniens. However, on May 5, 2019, Kenneth McCallion, the lawyer acting on behalf of the Ovaherero and Nama, filed an appellate with the United States Court of Appeals for the Second Circuit. This appeal was also unsuccessful, but still:

> **A LUTA CONTINUA!**

> In conclusion, the Ovaherero and Nama people are direct victims of the 1904 genocide in Namibia and have the right to self-determination. They are not waiting for anyone to affirm their right on this issue. On their own initiative, they have stood up and started to affirm this right: the right to speak for themselves on the issue of genocide and reparation.

> Article 18 of the United Nations Declaration on the Rights of Indigenous Peoples states as follows: »Indigenous peoples have the right to participate in decision-making in matters which would affect their rights, through representatives chosen by themselves in accordance with their own procedures, as well as to maintain and develop their own indigenous decision-making institutions.«

Without question, the Nama and Ovaherero peoples have suffered incalculable cultural, intellectual, religious, and spiritual losses as a result of their mistreatment at the hands of the German colonial authorities, as well as the subsequent denials and rationalisations of those atrocities, which fall within the scope of Articles 11 (2) and 18 of the UN Declaration on the Rights of Indigenous Peoples.

Article 11 (2): "States shall provide redress through effective mechanisms, which may include restitution, developed in conjunction with indigenous peoples, with respect to their cultural, intellectual, religious and spiritual property taken without their free, prior and informed consent or in violation of their laws, traditions and customs."

The Ovaherero and Nama people are very much united in their demand for reparations from Germany.

> There is no ambiguity or compromise on the part of Ovaherero and Nama about their just cause. They believe that the German government must first admit to its crimes against humanity and then make amends for its transgressions in a fair and equitable manner. Only then can reconciliation be expected to take place.

THEY MARCH ON – FORWARD EVER – BACKWARDS NEVER!!!!!!

»›We are the voices of the people who died in 1904. We are speaking on behalf of the skulls that are in Germany. And that is why we are saying: ›It cannot be about us without us.‹ Because the UN Declaration on the Rights of Indigenous Peoples of 2007 is very clear as to how Indigenous communities should be involved. Germany has signed this declaration and they cannot ignore it. We are saying: ›The pain that our people felt 117 years ago, we are still feeling that pain.‹«
Esther Utjiua Muinjangue & Ida Hoffmann

"IT CANNOT BE ABOUT US WITHOUT US"

Conversation:

Not about Us without Us

A conversation between the Namibian politician and activist **Esther Utjiua Muinjangue** and Nanette Snoep about the German genocide of the Ovaherero and Nama. Muinjangue co-curated the *It's Yours!*-Raum *Not about Us without Us* with Nama activist Ida Hoffmann.

This conversation was part of the online programme *RESIST! DIGITAL*, which was launched due to Covid restrictions.

Nanette Snoep: Esther Utjiua Muinjangue, you have been cooperating with Ida Hoffmann, another Namibian politician, to address the German genocide of the Ovaherero and Nama from 1904 to 1908. What drives your work?

Esther Utjiua Muinjangue: As you said, my first names are Esther Utjiua, my surname Muinjangue. I always introduce myself with both of my first names, as they illustrate the colonial connection. My background as a social worker influences my activism in the community. After all, in social work, two values are crucial: treating people with dignity and kindness – and social justice, which is linked to human rights. As an Ovaherero woman, I have a direct connection to the genocide. **I see myself as a mouthpiece of all the women who were exposed to the brutality of the German Schutztruppe: the raping, the emotionally difficult labour – for instance, women were forced to clean the skulls that were later shipped to Germany and elsewhere.** I am the leader of a political party called NUDO, which is short for "National Unity Democratic Organisation". I was elected to this position two years ago, making history in Namibia: I was the first woman to lead a political party. Before that, I chaired the Ovaherero Genocide Foundation for fifteen years. Now I am participating in this exhibition as a community activist and a lobbyist on the issue of the genocide against the Ovaherero and Nama, demanding reparations. Ida Hoffmann is the chairwoman of the Nama Genocide Foundation. We first met in 2004, and since then, we've been working together, two women demanding attention for the first genocide of the twentieth century, a genocide very few people were aware of worldwide – including in Namibia. **We made this our duty because we felt we owed it to our ancestors who are no longer here to speak for themselves. And so Ida and I became the voices of the murdered Nama and Ovaherero.**

Snoep: When did you start negotiating with Germany directly?

Windhoek, Namibia & Cologne, Germany 23/01/2021

Muinjangue: In 2007, I was on an exchange programme at the University of Applied Sciences in Freiburg. This was an important time in my life. While I was there, I met Heiko Wegmann, the founder of the Freiburg Postkolonial project. He mentioned that there were Ovaherero skulls at the University of Freiburg. I was stunned to hear this. I approached the head of the university archive. I went up to him and said, "There are Ovaherero skulls in your archive; I want to see them." And he said they had almost 3,000 skulls from different parts of the world, all mixed up, so they didn't know exactly where the Ovaherero skulls were. I said, "Take me to the archive anyway, I want to see them."

Snoep: And then what happened?

Muinjangue: It was a very emotional moment. A chance to spiritually reconnect with the ancestors. Before we entered the archive, I said, "Give me a moment so I can talk to my ancestors." For Germans, these might be skulls, but for me, they were my people in that room. I said to my ancestors whose skulls I might encounter, "I'm here and I want to enter this room to be in contact with you again. Give me the strength to deliver a message back to Namibia: 'We can start negotiating the restitution of the human remains from Germany.'" Then the door opened, and we entered the archive. I can still see all the white boxes in front of me, stacked on top of each other. I said, "Can we open a box so that I can see what's inside?" And the head of the archive repeated that the skulls were all mixed up; sure, he could open any box, but there were not necessarily Ovaherero skulls inside. I said, "Never mind, I just want to know that there really are skulls in these boxes." Then he opened one of them – and "Herero" was written on the skull inside it. Next to it was a number that I can't remember any more. And I said, "This is an Ovaherero skull, after all." It was the skull of one of my people. I don't know if it was a coincidence that he opened a box that just happened to contain an Ovaherero skull. There was also a brown envelope in the box. We opened it, and the note inside said: "South West Africa, Swakopmund". And I said, "That's it." In Swakopmund was one of the biggest concentration camps where our people were killed. Their bodies were decapitated, their skulls taken to Germany. At that moment I was overwhelmed with emotion. I was looking at that skull and I saw an Ovaherero woman, an Ovaherero man, an Ovaherero child. For me, it confirmed the brutality to which my people had been subjected. Then we closed the box and left, and I thanked him.

Snoep: What happened after you returned?

Muinjangue: Through the traditional leaders, I let my community know what I had seen. It was around this point that Peter Hitjitevi Katjavivi, Namibia's ambassador to Germany at the time, also became aware of the skulls. We started speaking with the Namibian government about bringing them home. In 2011, a large Nama and Ovaherero delegation went to Berlin for the first time to bring around twenty Nama and Ovaherero skulls back to Namibia. All of a sudden, people were learning that what we were saying about the genocide was not just a story – we had proof. That was the moment that decided my involvement in the issue of genocide reparations and restitution.

Snoep: It was in this context that we met.

Muinjangue: I remember our meeting in Leipzig in 2017. I saw an Ovaherero skull there, too. But something struck me that day: the dignity granted to that skull in Leipzig. It was in a dark room, lying on a large piece of cloth. Not like the skulls that were being kept in boxes like eggs. In Leipzig, I found inner peace. I looked at that skull, and tears ran down my cheeks. I thought again of the violence that had been committed. I kept asking myself: what kind of person would decapitate a body and bring the skull to Germany, for whatever research? For them, they may have just been bones; for us, they are our people. That is why we will continue to lobby the German government to return all the human remains that were taken from Namibia to Germany.

Snoep: Now, in late January 2021, what is the current status of your struggle for the acknowledgement of the German genocide?

Muinjangue: As far as we are concerned, we are still right where we started fifteen years ago! The German government still refuses to include the Ovaherero and Nama communities. It is the same song they've always sung – the two governments only talk to each other. Our position is very clear: in 1904, when they committed this genocide, there was no Namibian government; instead, traditional leaders governed their communities. Moreover, our traditional leaders are legally acknowledged by the Namibian government; they form an extension of it. One excuse made by the German government is: "The Ovaherero are divided, whom should we talk to?" But Germany managed to listen to twenty-three groups representing the Jewish population all over the world. Now it is up to us Ovaherero and Nama to decide how many groups we want to send for talks with the German government! As far as the concrete negotiations between the two governments are concerned, I cannot comment on that; after all, we are not involved. From time to time, we hear something through the press, but there is no reliable information about the current state of affairs. While the governments were talking to each other, our traditional leaders also initiated a court case in New York, but there is no progress there, either. It was dismissed in court; an appeal has been filed. We have many other plans to get the German government to finally acknowledge the atrocities, apologise, and pay compensation to make up for the damage Germany has done to the Nama and Ovaherero communities. Let me say this: development aid is no substitute for reparations. Only reparations directly benefit those groups of people who have been wronged, who have suffered.

Snoep: The issue of reparations has other aspects, too. Because of the German colonial history in Namibia, there are so many human remains in German collections – but it seems that a change is taking place. Museums are not only willing to return objects and human remains; the mentality as such is changing. Especially since, in addition to human bones, artefacts have also been collected in the name of science: between 1904 and 1908 alone, thousands of objects that belonged to the Nama and Ovaherero were taken from Namibia. What is your position on the fact that many of them are in German museums, including the Rautenstrauch-Joest Museum?

Muinjangue: It's a question of knowledge. When does one become aware of that? When we started, we only thought about the genocide. We didn't know anything about the skulls or the human remains in German museums. It was only in the course of working on this topic that we learned about the other artefacts that had been looted and stolen. For two years now, we have also been fighting for the return of these objects. I remember asking: "If German museums had to return everything to their rightful owners, what would they still be able to exhibit?" These institutions have also made money from these artefacts – where does this profit end up? It does not go to the municipalities and states from which they were stolen. We are demanding what is rightfully ours. This is also now at the top of our agenda.

Snoep: The desire to have your say becomes very clear in the space you curated together as part of the *RESIST!* exhibition. It's called *Not About Us Without Us*. Could you explain the title?

Muinjangue: We say, »We are the voices of the people who died in 1904.« We are speaking on behalf of the skulls that are in Germany. And that is why we are saying: »Not About Us Without Us«.

The declaration on the Rights of Indigenous Peoples of 2007 is very, very clear as to how Indigenous communities should be involved. Germany has signed this declaration. The pain that our people felt 117 years ago, we still feel today. Because Germans took our land and cattle, we still live in poverty today. We are politically in the minority because our population is so small – as a result of the genocide. I remember reading a book about the psychological impact of the Shoah on Jewish communities: the author researched how trauma is passed on from generation to generation. We, too, still feel our trauma. It matters to us to be involved in this process. It would have a therapeutic effect. We would have the chance to heal our emotional wounds. Instead, the German government only talks about political and moral responsibility. That is precisely why it is crucial for us to sit at this table, to speak for ourselves when it comes to things that affect us. The outcome of the discussion has important implications for us. We want to steer this process. We are here and we can speak for ourselves, thank you very much..

Snoep: There are many pictures depicting genocide in the space you curated: hanged women and men, raped dead bodies. Some visitors were deeply shocked. Of course, you want people to be aware of this violence. But some people of colour, including the descendants of former colonised communities, were also very hurt by these images. They asked us, "Why are you showing this violence?"

Muinjangue: I am glad that people are shocked when they see this. That was my first reaction, too. I couldn't believe it. The victims looked like skeletons. Every time I saw one of these pictures, I had to cry – today, I don't cry any more; I have taken care of my trauma. Once, when I spoke in front of a German audience in Hamburg, we had social workers and psychologists on hand because we knew it could get very emotional. When I talk about all this, I often need someone to guide my thoughts afterwards, so that I can reframe them and come back to reality. There are still Germans who claim that we are lying, that there was no genocide, that we started it and so on. But how would that even be possible? We didn't go to Germany, or Berlin; we didn't start a war. The Germans came to Namibia and started taking away our land. And using us to take care of their sexual needs ... Our chiefs could not allow that. We had to fight back and protect what was ours. **Germans are good at keeping records. So what we did was use the same records – the pictures they took to humiliate and degrade my people. It was not us who took photographs of naked, hanged Ovaherero women. It was not us who took photographs of Ovaherero women forced to clean the skulls of their own people before they were shipped to Germany. It was Germans who did that. When you see what happened, the impact is greater than if you just read about it. That's why we show these pictures.**

Snoep: That's also why we have an awareness team for *RESIST!*, so that people can talk about the topics in the exhibition in a safer space. Our exhibition is also meant as a kind of therapy, including for the museum itself: it is about truth, reconciliation, and healing. This approach has become a worldwide issue in the wake of the Black Lives Matter movement. How does this movement manifest itself in Namibia? After all, the German colonial era is still present there: streets are named after German colonialists, and there are statues commemorating them.

Muinjangue: Yes, we have a lot of colonial statues. We also still have a Von Trotha Street. The municipalities have started to decolonise the street names. The statues are still standing. There have been heated debates about whether to remove them. Some say yes, others say they are part of history.

Snoep: What does it mean for you to walk along Von Trotha Street?

Muinjangue: **I will never set foot on Von Trotha Street, even if it's the shortest way. I will find another way to reach my destination – never via Von Trotha Street.** People are planning demonstrations to demand for it to be renamed. "Von Trotha" is a devil's name for us. We don't want to hear it. In 2019, I stood at his grave [in Bonn] and thought: I am standing here at the grave of the man who caused so much destruction in my community. What should I do? I was there with Mnyaka Sururu Mboro from Tanzania [founding board member of Berlin Postkolonial], who lives in Berlin. And I said, "I feel like throwing a stone or something." And he said, "Don't. We respect the dead, whether he was an enemy or not." And I said, "Okay, I agree." In Namibia, there are still many reminders of the historical connection to Germany. In the coastal town of Swakopmund, you get the feeling you're in a small town in Germany: the architecture of the buildings, the large German population there... The Black Lives Matter movement remains active. It is campaigning for the removal of all historical statues from the colonial era.

Snoep: What matters most to you when people visit your space at the *RESIST!* exhibition?

Muinjangue: I want them to be aware of the genocide against the Ovaherero and Nama. It is the first genocide of the twentieth century – but it is still not present enough, not talked about enough. Everyone who visits our *It's Yours!* space should learn what Germany did to our people in Namibia. I hope they'll talk about it when they sit together, when they're having a beer, say. It is an issue for all German men and women, not only for the government. The money for the special programme, for the development aid that Germany gives to Namibia through bilateral agreements, ultimately comes from the taxpayers, from the people of Germany. It is their money – and they should know how their money is being spent. We want to attract international attention to the genocide of the Ovaherero and Nama. That's why we build bridges of solidarity: without Berlin Postkolonial, I wouldn't have met you, Nanette, and many others. This way we can spread information so that the world becomes aware of the genocide and supports us. We need this moral support, we need to know that we are not alone in this struggle. Becoming aware of history is therefore the first step to making a change. Above all, we must look at the 1948 UN Genocide Convention: it provides a definition, condemns the atrocity, and contains a very important word – "prevention". We want to prevent what happened 100 years ago from happening again. We want to prevent human rights from being violated. **Whoever visits our space should say: »I've learned something« – and they should have something to think about over the next few days. The space tells people what happened, what we are doing, and what we want from the German government. It is a platform to speak up, to make our voices heard. And we appreciate that.**

Conversation:
Herero & Nama Voices from Namibia

Cologne, Germany 18/08/2021

"We've lost a great deal." Five Herero and Nama activists discussed the reconciliation agreement between Germany and Namibia regarding the German genocide of the Herero and Nama, which was announced in May 2021. It provides development and reconstruction aid of 1.1 billion euros over thirty years as reparations for the German colonial crimes in present-day Namibia. The agreement recognises the German crimes against the Herero and Nama as genocide in the historical sense, but not in the sense of international law.

What does this agreement mean for the descendants of the Herero and Nama? Why is the agreement criticised by many victims' associations? Esther Utjiua Muinjangue and Ida Hoffmann invited important Herero and Nama activists to join this discussion.

coversation:

Esther Utjiua Muinjangue, *It's Yours* curator *RESIST!*

Sam Geiseb, **member of the Nama Genocide Technical Committee, consultant and director of Integrated Social Development Services in Windhoek.**

Kambanda Nokokure Veii, **former board member of the Ovaherero/Ovambanderu Genocide Foundation and director of the Riruako Centre for Genocide and Memory Studies in Windhoek since 2018.**

Mbakumua Hengari, **member of the Ovaherero/Ovambanderu Genocide Foundation.**

Israel Kaunatjike, **Ovaherero activist from the Völkermord verjährt nicht (»Genocide has no statute of limitations«) alliance. Born in Namibia, he has lived in Berlin for over thirty years, where he works as an educational consultant with a focus on German colonial history.**

Moderated by political scientist and human rights activist Joshua Kwesi Aikins.

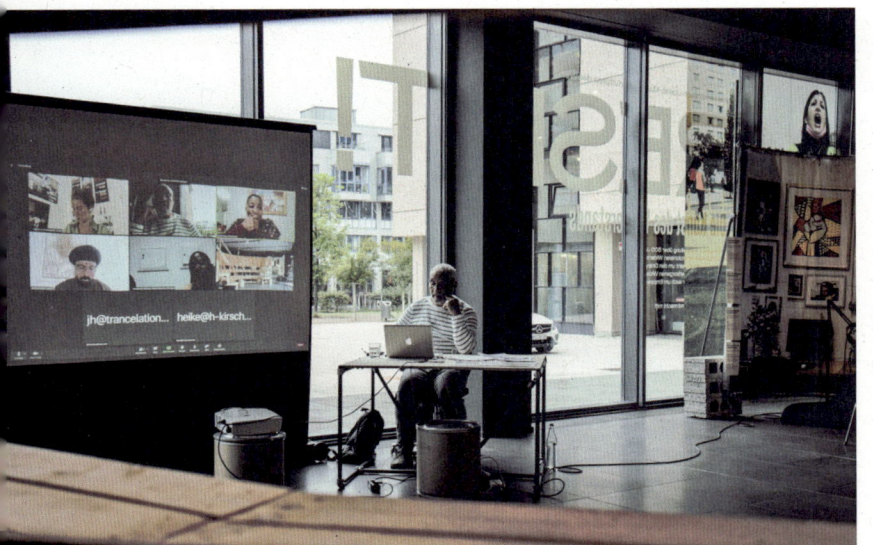

Israel Kaunatjike in the exhibition *RESIST!* in online conversation with the other participants on 18/08/2021

Aikins: The historical injustices of colonialism still have an impact today. In the context of the 1904–1908 German genocide of the Ovaherero and Nama, we are talking to Esther Utjiua Muinjangue, Sam Geiseb, Kambanda Nokokure Veii, Mbakumua Hengari, and Israel Kaunatjike about the responsibility for history and memory. Esther Utjiua Muinjangue, you curated an autonomous space entitled *Not About Us Without Us* as part of *RESIST!* together with another Namibian politician and activist, Ida Hofmann. The space addresses Namibian–German history, the genocide committed, and its historical context from a Namibian perspective – in particular, from the perspective of the Ovaherero and Nama descendants. What made the two of you accept the invitation to do this work in Germany?

Muinjangue: I grew up with my great-grandmother; she was born in 1911, three years after the end of the war. Her parents had survived the genocide. The stories she used to tell us at bedtime were about the "German–Herero War", as she called it. My paternal great-grandfather was half-German: the product of rape committed by Germans. He never knew his biological father. There is thus a gap in my family tree, a space that will never be filled because I will never know who my great-great-grandfather was. I am a social worker, a profession committed to social justice and human rights – this is how I got involved in the issues of genocide and reparations. For fifteen years, I chaired the Ovaherero/Ovambanderu Genocide Foundation. As you can see, these issues occupied a significant space in my heart during much of my youth and adult life. I travelled extensively around the world, visiting international capital cities and advocating for the heritage of my people. **When the RJM invited me, I knew I should seize this opportunity with both hands. I saw this exhibition as the right platform to advance the struggle for the recognition of the genocide committed by Germans against the Ovaherero and Nama. My main intention was to make society at large – in Germany and internationally – aware of the genocide that has been committed. Since we are living in the digital age, our space is not only accessible to people in Cologne; no, everyone can see this exhibition. I didn't want to miss such a chance.**

The mass murder of the Ovaherero and Nama is considered the first genocide of the twentieth century. Even so, it is still relatively unknown to the general public and is not recognised as a genocide by many countries, including Germany. To compare: in 2013, sixty-seven museums and exhibitions worldwide, temporary and permanent, were dedicated to the Holocaust. This shows that exhibitions matter greatly; they provide continuous education and awareness. They are also an instrument for change; they can be used to highlight what happened to the Ovaherero and Nama in the years from 1904 to 1908. With our Not About Us Without Us space, we make the voices of Nama and Ovaherero descendants heard and help share memories with our neighbours, such as Peju Layiwola, who curated an autonomous space at *RESIST!* to commemorate the looting committed in the Kingdom of Benin. However painful the subject matter, I enjoyed the project. I've never curated an exhibition before. Right away, I said to myself, "I want to do this." I am deeply moved by what I see here. And I'm very proud of our space, it looks really impressive. **After all, who should talk about the genocide if not ourselves?**

Aikins: As deputy minister, you are a key figure in Namibia's national politics, and you advocate for the recognition of the genocide. How do you currently evaluate Germany's offer to Namibia and the idea of reconciliation?

Muinjangue: At the beginning of this year, when we officially opened the exhibition, I said that we are the voices of the Nama and Ovaherero. **We are the voices of the human remains and skulls that are still in Germany.**

It is painful that essential key figures in the struggle for reparation were lost to Covid. But this encouraged us even more to become the voices of the murdered. The 2007 UN Convention on the Rights of Indigenous Peoples clearly describes the role, participation, and involvement of affected communities – and Germany has signed it. On the basis of this convention, we are saying: "It can never be about us without us!" I want to be very clear: the genocide of the Ovaherero and Nama is no different from the Holocaust. Both involve negotiations with the government of the Federal Republic of Germany. We are talking about the same issues. Genocide, apology, and reparations. There should be no difference in the

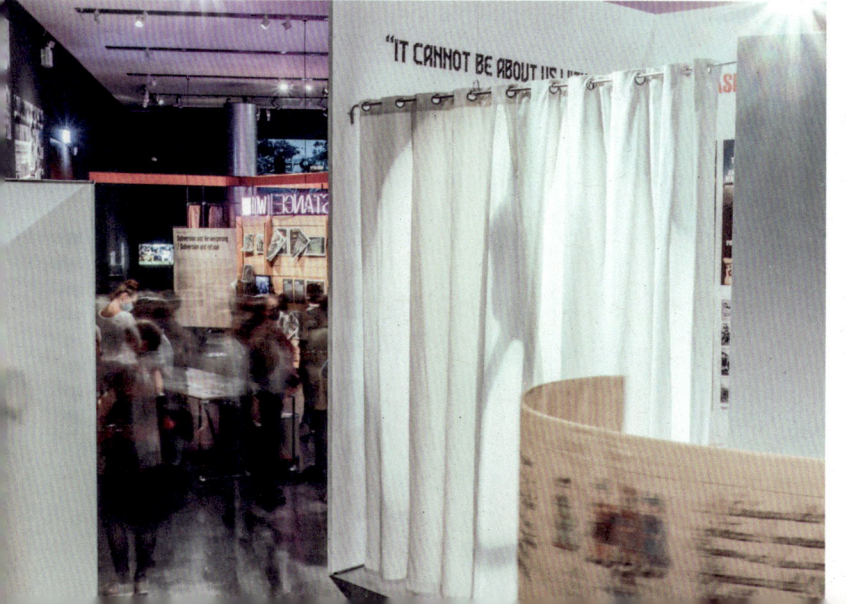

View on the closed curtains of the *It's Yours!* room *Not about Us without Us* onto which a gallows was projected

It's Yours!

way the German government deals with the victims today. I can assure you that the agreement currently being negotiated by the Federal Republic of Germany with the Namibian government has no significance for us, the descendants of the Nama and Ovaherero. The fundamental question is: what is the basis of these negotiations? Well, Germany proceeds on the basis of the Bundestag resolutions of 1989 and 2004, which stress three points. The first is: Germany's special historical and moral responsibility. But what does "special" mean? There is no precise definition, no explanation why Germany has a special historical relationship with Namibia, of all places. Second, the Federal Republic of Germany has given high priority to building bilateral relations with Namibia since the country gained independence in 1990. Again, this is about bilateral relations between governments. And third, these resolutions state that the German Investment Corporation has given priority support to Namibia since 1990. Well, we in Namibia adopted our own resolution in October 2006: Germany should acknowledge that it committed genocide against the Ovaherero and Nama, issue an unequivocal apology, and pay reparations to the affected communities. Now compare the German resolutions of 1989 and 2004 with the Namibian resolution of 2006: they have nothing in common. One talks of bilateral relations; the other of genocide, apologies, and reparations. We will not accept an agreement that speaks of reconciliation, reconstruction, development aid and projects without ever directly mentioning the words "genocide" and "reparations". Clause ten of the agreement mentions "events" that "took place in 1904 and would, from today's perspective, be described as genocide". It was genocide! In 1868, the Swiss lawyer Johann Caspar Bluntschli wrote that "wars of extermination and elimination against peoples and tribes capable of life and culture" were "contrary to international law". It is therefore quite clear that Germany was already violating international law at this point. The Namibian resolution from 2006 suggests a trialogue between the Namibian government, the German government, and representatives of the Ovaherero and Nama descendants. Until now, all we have seen are bilateral relations between governments. The descendants of the two communities have not been involved.

Posters by Asser Karita presented in the *It's Yours!* room

Aikins: Sam Geiseb, in light of your work with the Nama Genocide Technical Committee, how do you assess the developments of the past months and weeks?

Geiseb: It is crucial to understand that bilateral negotiations have never represented what we would consider an ideal approach to discussing the genocide. We have not deviated from what we originally called for as due process – a process including representatives of the affected communities. Over the past two decades, we have never stopped emphasising this, but to no avail. We not only hold the German government responsible but also the Namibian one. It, too, conducted these bilateral negotiations without the participation of the affected communities – who absolutely must be part of the discussion on the key issues of apology and recognition. We know that people in Germany know little about these mass murders.

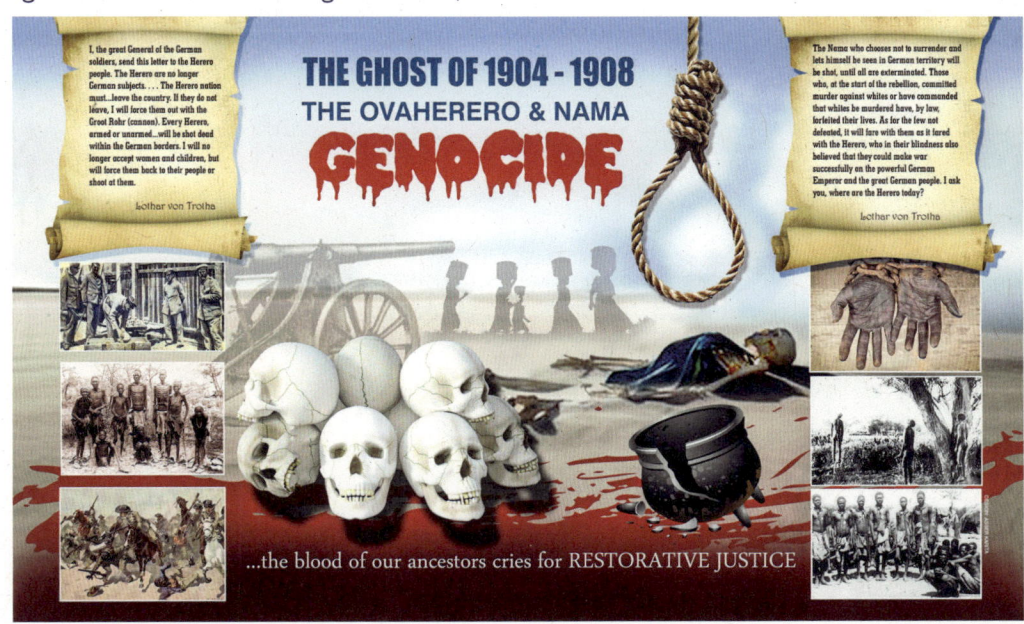

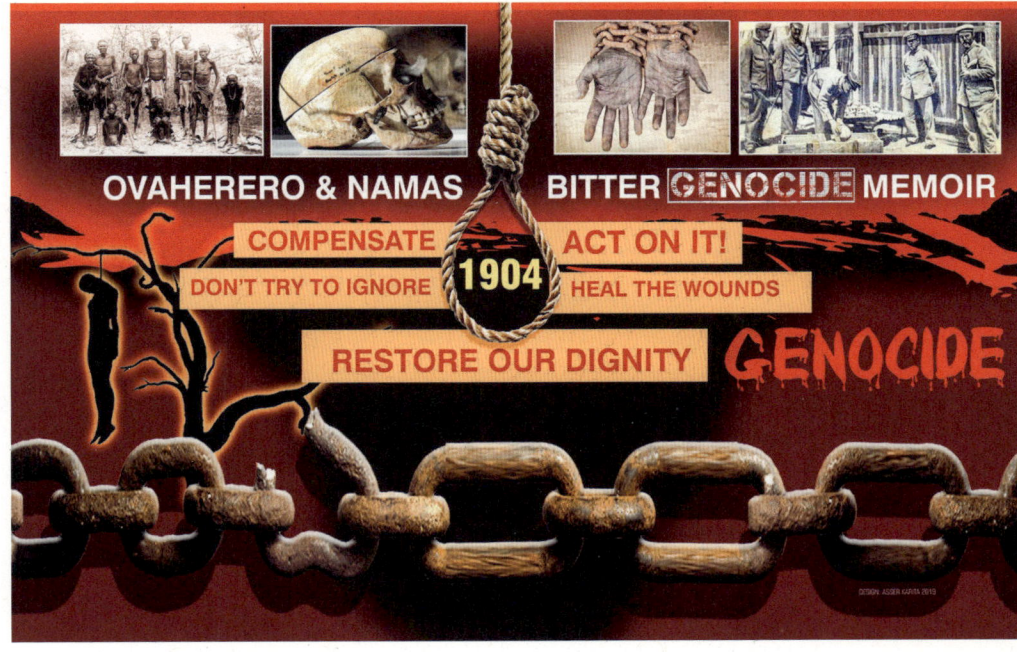

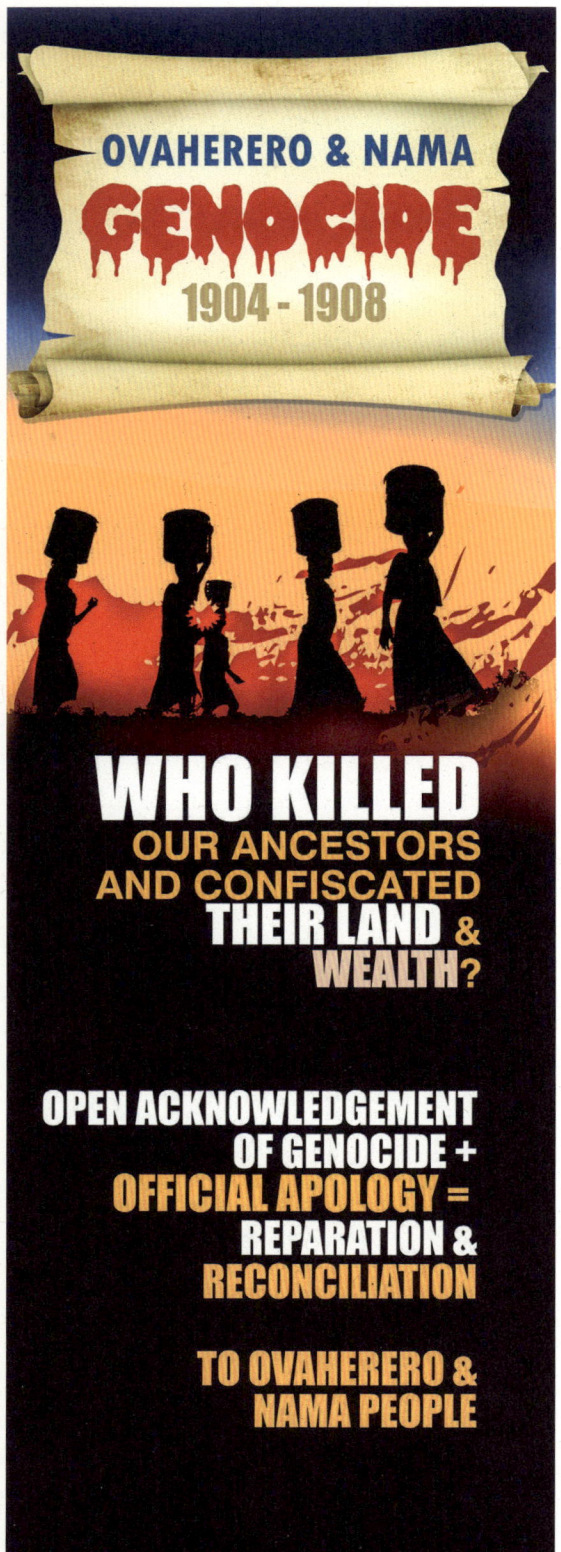

Posters by Asser Karita presented in the *It's Yours!* room

What does Germany recognise as genocide? We must have this discussion: it is not just a matter of them saying, "Yes, we killed a lot of Nama, a lot of people", the word "genocide" matters. There has to be a genuine acknowledgement, in that the government must name and admit what happened to our people. **The record of atrocities committed must be disclosed so that present-day Germany knows the facts. Yes, we are talking about something that happened over 100 years ago – but we still feel the effects today. We are landless; we are still dispossessed. This is why we consider it fundamentally justified to demand reparations. How else are we to address these injustices?** At this point, I am only speaking about what we have lost materially, not about the human losses. To be honest, these government negotiations changed nothing for the descendants. We are still discussing the same issue, we are still making the same demands, and we are not prepared to deviate from what we think is the right procedure. The end result that we want to see is restorative justice.

Aikins: Right, so you are demanding a justice that rectifies imbalances. Israel Kaunatjike, you've been fighting for decades to have the genocide recognised in Germany. Recently, Heiko Maas, Federal Minister for Foreign Affairs, said that the agreement is not the end of the historical debate. Do you think that, despite this statement, it is actually trying to draw a line, to preclude further claims and legal obligations?

Kaunatjike: I would like to start with my biography. I left my country in 1964 when I was seventeen. I joined the liberation movement and have been a member of SWANU (South-West African National Union party) ever since. So when I came to Germany, I knew about the historical background of apartheid – but even I was not really aware of the genocide. Second, my grandmother, too, had been raped by German soldiers, which is why my skin colour is a bit lighter than the others in this room. For me, it was a challenge to talk about what had happened to my grandmother. When I first came to West Berlin, I became active in the anti-apartheid movement; soon, Namibia gained its independence. Now the question was: what would happen to my people, to my ancestors in German South West Africa? Since then, I've been committed to demanding apologies and reparations for the genocide. My activism began with my first documentary about the war against the Ovaherero [*White Ghosts – The Colonial War against the Ovaherero*]. We have lost our land, the land of our ancestors; our cultural artefacts are here in Germany. As Esther said, museums all over Germany harbour the bones of our forefathers. This is very painful for us. Against this background, we cannot accept the deal between Germany and the puppet government in Namibia; it has no legitimacy to represent us. Moreover, as my friends said, we were not invited to participate in this agreement in the first place. So how could we possibly accept it? I've been active in Germany since 2004, working in various ways in schools and in the media. The time to act is now – and has been for quite a while **The younger generation does not have the patience that we have; they are becoming more radical because our country is still occupied by Germans. We are doing our best to have streets renamed, especially in Germany.**

But our main demands are apology, recognition, and reparations – for the Damara, Ovaherero and Nama. We stand united. The extermination order was directed against the Ovaherero and Nama, but Damara and San people were killed by Germans, too. We will never accept an agreement that was negotiated exclusively between the two governments. We don't want development aid. We will fight until we get our land back. The Namibian government can do whatever it wants with the 1.1 billion euros in aid; it is not our business. We do not trust this government. How could we do so when it is now fracking in the Okavango? They are drilling for oil and gas, destroying our paradise. What will happen to the people who live along the Okavango? This government is not working in the interests of the Namibian people. I remain on the front line in Berlin and will give everything I can until I leave this world.

Aikins: The imbalance in land ownership continues from colonial times through apartheid to the present day. Mbakumua Hengari, you are, among other things, a farmer. How does land matter to the affected communities – and what is the extent of the imbalance?

Hengari: Let me first give an overview of land expropriation in Namibia and its causes. After Germany officially became a colonial power in 1884, it turned to the locals, trying to acquire land. But traditionally, land was not a commodity that could be sold. It was part of one's heritage, one's livelihood, culture, and ancestry – especially among the Ovaherero/Ovambanderu.

Last weekend, we buried my niece, my brother's daughter. She had been a deputy minister. We had the honour of the President leading the funeral in the cemetery of the community where we now live. As we sat there, I noticed that the oldest member of our family buried there was my grandfather. You see, the concentration camps were closed in 1908, and in 1923, people retreated to where they had lived after the war. In 1923, the South African regime, which succeeded Germany in 1915, essentially continued the Reservation Proclamation declared by Germany in 1896. And so my grandfather was one of those who had settled in the village where we buried my brother's daughter. As I said, to us, the land is a part of our ancestry: in our cultural tradition or religion, people do not disappear when they die, they leave this life and pass on to the spiritual realm. Thus, their bones must stay in a place that you can relate to. **Colonial land confiscation cut this link between us and our ancestors. When my grandfather died in 1968, he did not return to his forefathers.** Instead, he ended up in a place that felt alien to him. Still, he had to be buried there; he could not return to the resting place of his father and grandfather. To this day, we have no access to that place. For the Ovaherero and the Ovambanderu, what defines us is the land and the place where we live; our cattle, too, contribute to a sense of identity – you can hear this in our folk songs. Our cattle and land are deeply connected to each other and to us, because cattle live and thrive on the land. To us, land means not only a livelihood but also an identity. When talking about a group of our people, people would associate them with a certain area in Namibia, and also with a certain kind of cattle: black and white, red, black, or brownish, with long or short horns ... The land as the Ovaherero and Nama people know it today is the result of German expropriation. In the middle of the war, in 1906, there was a decree: all Ovaherero/Ovambanderu land was confiscated and declared "Crown land". The authorities reallocated it to German settlers. It was also considered a capital offence to own an animal, whether it was a goat, a sheep, or other livestock, or even a dog. All that we had was now German property. All our fertile land was gone.

Aikins: You've mentioned how history is intertwined with your personal biographies. This helps us to better understand your criticism of the current German offer. Since our audience is predominantly German, I'd like to ask – what do you expect from German civil society regarding this issue?

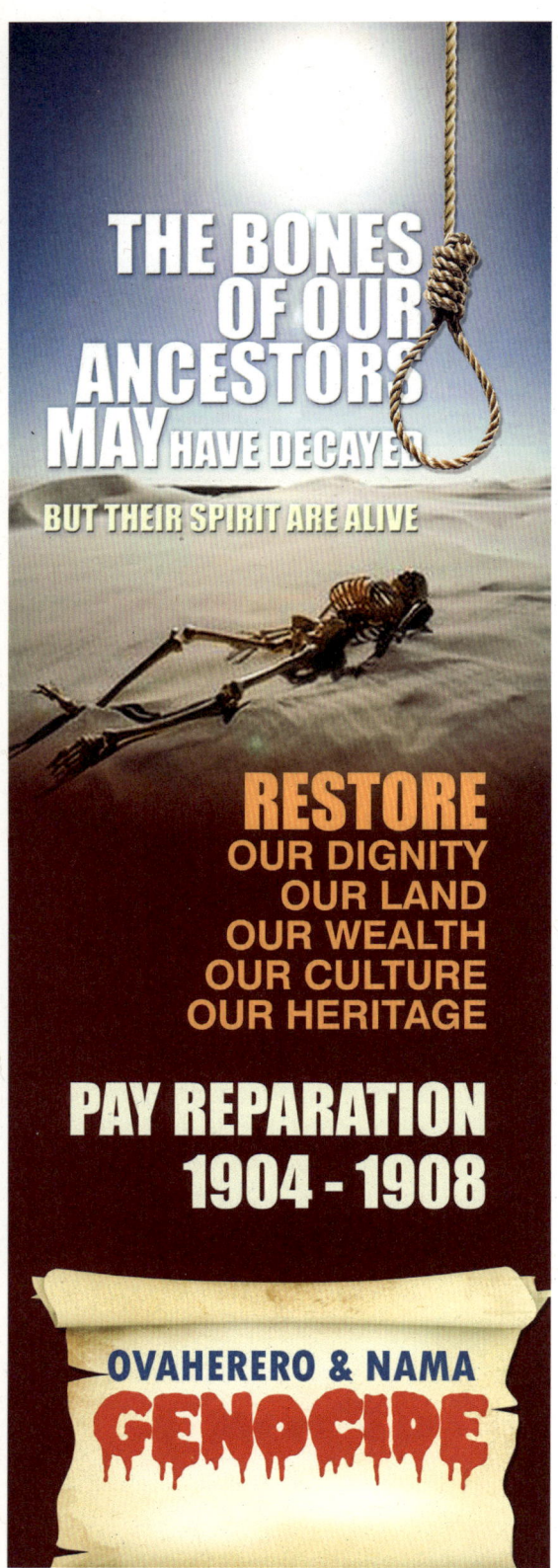

Posters by Asser Karita presented in the *It's Yours!* room

Geiseb: Since the parliamentary resolution of 2006 and the return of the skulls and some artefacts, we have seen that German civil society is bringing the genocide to the fore. I think it could be the voice of reason, the voice to ensure that all of Germany knows about the genocide. Commentators keep mentioning how the wider public hardly knows anything about the genocide of the Nama and Ovaherero. Of course, civil society also plays a crucial role in advocacy. It could make the powerful do the right thing – provide what we call restorative justice – by ensuring that the process is participatory, that descendants of the victims are involved. Mbakumua spoke about our country. Now, there are 14 regions in Namibia; one of them is the Habab region, home to over 4,000 commercial farms. In the last 30 years, as far as I know, the government of Namibia has only been able to buy back 66 farms for resettlement purposes. One of the reasons why we reject the agreement and, well, its price tag, is simply this: this money cannot buy back even half of the region or the farms. **This is why we talk about restorative justice. To what extent would the current offer actually help us address the problems of land expropriation? It is therefore crucial that civil society becomes more involved and helps us engage with the German population at large on issues of victim-centred justice.**

Aikins: The issue of land is urgent, the scale of injustice great. Israel Kaunatjike mentioned that younger generations have a different approach. Kambanda Nokokure Veii, you work with young people. How is this generation in Namibia dealing with the issue?

Veii: For some of us, genocide is a very, very personal issue. Like Esther, I grew up with my great-grandmother, a survivor of the genocide. She was always a quiet woman; often she'd sit outside the house and cry. As a little child, I never understood what it was all about. And whenever I went to her and asked why she was crying, she would just shoo me away and tell me to go and play – until I grew up, until I had learned about the genocide and could understand her. **So many of us grew up with people who were traumatised by what had happened to their families back then. We lost a lot. We lost lives. We lost land. We lost an identity. We lost our culture, our language, especially those who live in the diaspora.** As Sam put it, you can't put monetary value on that, can you? It is priceless. But this doesn't mean that money doesn't matter. To rebuild a people, you need money. This agreement between the two governments is a slap in the face, both to us and our ancestors. As Esther said, this document doesn't speak to the descendants at all. It uses a different language. It names things differently: the extermination order is merely called an "order". Genocide is referred to only as "atrocities". Instead of reparations, it speaks of "development aid" or whatever. From the beginning, the two governments were doing everything wrong – because they didn't include the descendants. They went on negotiating, and half the time we didn't even know what was going on. I remember the late Namibian envoy telling us about a year ago that they were trying to decide what term to use for these atrocities. That was shocking: this was where we stood after five, six years of negotiations? **Now, on top of everything we have lost, we are being denied the chance to negotiate with Germany and** therefore heal some wounds. We are being denied the chance to draw a line under all the suffering. As Mbakumua said, many of our ancestors, many of our great-grandfathers and great-grandmothers lie in anonymous graves. We don't know where they are buried – and this knowledge matters immensely in our culture. Many of them are buried on farms owned by white people, which you have to ask permission to enter. And this permission may well be denied. All the cultural rituals that we normally perform when a person passes away are denied to us. What have we done that is so bad to be treated like this? I get very emotional when I talk about this, I'm sorry …

To come back to the issue of land and the youth: Israel was right in saying that the youth are more radical. They want action. They know what happened. They want their land back. To remind you, we are talking about our land, our heritage that was taken from us. We are talking about the white people here in Namibia who are enriching themselves on the land that their ancestors stole from us. I might tell my daughter or my son: this is where our grandparents lived, but we are not allowed to enter the farm because it belongs to someone else. And then we start talking about the history of how the land was expropriated in the first place. A young person gets angry about that; angrier, I think, than the older generation. They have a different energy. Israel also said that he will continue to fight – but the difference is that our younger generations are more radical, more aggressive. They say: the land you Germans took from us is not in Berlin but here in Namibia. They have an utterly different approach. They want things to change – and change quickly.

Aikins: Thank you for this conversation about lived realities, collective experiences, and an intergenerational struggle that continues to this day. Now we open the discussion to questions from the audience.

Andreoletti (RJM): In Germany, the agreement became public at the end of May this year, but nothing more has been heard about it since. What is the current status?

Muinjangue: It is very interesting to learn that there isn't much talk about the agreement in Germany. This is rather strange, considering that it was composed here. I'd like to quote something that the Minister of Foreign Affairs, Heiko Maas, said on May 28. He said that the agreement is a gesture recognising the immeasurable suffering that has been inflicted on us. But we are not asking for a gesture. We are asking for justice. Germany has committed genocide. Germany is not doing us any favours with a gesture of 1.1 billion euros. As it happens, the German government recently renovated a castle where the emperor responsible for this genocide once lived. This refurbishment cost almost 700 million euros. This shows a willingness to spend a lot of money. Even if we ignore the time value of money, Germany's offer comes down to about 36.7 million euros per year since Namibia's independence in 1990. I don't know if this is by coincidence or design, but this sum is roughly equivalent to the amount of annual development aid that Germany has paid to Namibia since the independence. There is a snake in the grass here, so to speak. To our knowledge, the Namibian government originally put a demand of about 75 billion euros on the table. The German government counter-offered 300 million euros. If we look at the 1.1 billion euros in the current agreement, this means that Germany only increased its offer 3.7-fold, while Namibia has lowered its demand by a factor of 68.2. These are very one-sided negotiations. We have said from the start that they are neither realistic nor transparent. I am glad that Minister Heiko Maas acknowledges the immeasurable suffering of our people. But immeasurable means massive: very, very large. And thus, the German government has to understand. **We are not asking for a gesture. We are not asking for a favour. We demand restorative justice.** After the Second World War, Nahum Goldmann negotiated with Adenauer about reparations for Israel, Jewish Holocaust survivors, and the descendants of victims, including on behalf of Israel. So it is feasible. This is what we are asking

Posters by Asser Karita presented in the *It's Yours!* room

for: to sit at the table and speak for ourselves. This would also be a chance to alleviate our emotional pain. Many books about the Holocaust talk of transgenerational trauma. We, too, suffer from this. In the case of the Shoah, Konrad Adenauer made a public statement in the Bundestag, saying that Germany would take full responsibility and pay reparations. In our case, however, the agreement is to be first submitted to the Namibian parliament for ratification. We hear nothing about it being submitted to the Bundestag. What makes it binding for the German government if it is not ratified by the Bundestag? I'd better stop now, otherwise I'll get angry.

Veii: The title of the declaration is problematic for many of us. It says »united in remembrance of our colonial past«. Who is united here? And how exactly are we united in remembering »our« colonial past? What is Germany doing to remember it? I've been to Berlin many times and have never seen monuments or memorials to the genocide committed against the Ovaherero and Nama. And the title goes on to say: »united in our will to reconcile«. Whose will? Who are we talking about here? Are we only talking about the Namibian and German governments, or also about the descendants of the victims? The last part of the title reads: "united in our vision of the future". What kind of vision is that? Does "vision" only stand for the 1.1 billion euros to be paid out over thirty years? Germany is really not being fair here; we are being disadvantaged. What I don't understand is why our government is allowing this. I can hardly imagine that there were descendants of the Ovaherero and Nama in the negotiating team. And as Esther just said, why is this agreement being discussed and ratified in our parliament – and not in the Bundestag? It's best to just tear it up and flush it down the toilet.

Geiseb: I would like to add another dimension. I think it is futile to discuss this agreement in which we were not involved. We did not write it; we did not contribute in any way to its intention and content. Therefore, the agreement is meaningless for many descendants of the victims. What is crucial is how we proceed now. This agreement is not even a matter of discussion among the descendants of the victims in Namibia. It does not address the issues that prompted us to raise and represent our cause in the first place. Our country is littered with the bones of this genocide's victims. We do not know where many of our ancestors rest. What we do know is that some of them lie on farms to which we have no access, these links having been destroyed long ago. The land we are talking about is land that made generations of Germans powerful and successful; they still benefit from it today. As a result of the genocide over 100 years ago, they have our economy in their hands. Their children keep flying from Namibia to Germany and back – and the trips are paid for using money generated on this land. I'd like to give you an example: if you drive seventy kilometres southeast from where I live, you will find about twenty commercial farms owned by twenty families. These farms are so big that I can't even see cattle from the road when I'm driving past. To compare, in an enclave of less than 600 hectares of land, there are about 120 households trying to farm – I belong to one of them. We are trying to eke out all the grazing we can from

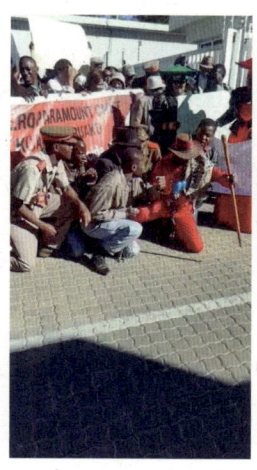 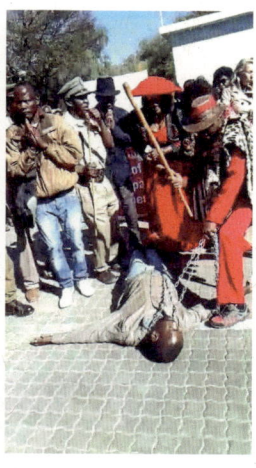 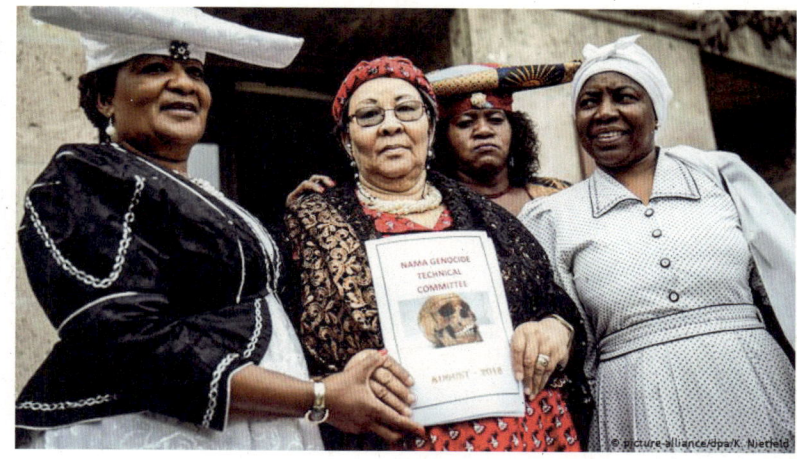

Screenshots from videos in the *It's Yours!* space

our 600 hectares. This is what we are talking about here. **We are talking about most Namibians having no access to land. Land that would give them economic opportunities, land that has been used by Germans for generations – the descendants of the very people who betrayed us.** We live this scenario every day. These people say we are inciting conflict. But we are not inciting anyone. We are just saying that these are the harsh realities faced by the Namibian youth and that they are getting impatient. How long will this go on? This agreement has done absolutely nothing to solve these problems. **For many Germans today, the genocide may be in the distant past, but for us it is our present reality: we have no access to land in the country of our birth.** It is shocking to us that the Namibian government would even think of accepting such an agreement. What our government now intends to sign wouldn't solve 1 per cent of the problems that need to be solved in the name of justice and reparations.

Hengari: The agreement has divided our people even more. As part of the ruling political elite, our young politicians are trying to convince their own parents, their own communities, of positions that are unacceptable. This undermines the basis for any semblance of the restorative justice we have been yearning for. For some twenty years, the Namibian government has been utterly indifferent to our fate as descendants of the victims. A political and ethnic minority in a largely ethnocratic society, we have been neglected. In the thirty years since independence, there has not been a single attempt to commemorate the genocide of the Nama and Ovaherero. There is no memorial. No day of mourning. No school textbook in Namibia contains a single chapter on this genocide. So why should we believe that the government is the best advocate for our cause? Instead of speaking for us, it has exploited the role of the victims. German colonialism and genocide wiped out our culture, our social fabric. All this still reverberates today. We, as victims or descendants of victims, continue to suffer from this trauma.

Kaunatjike: We have to move forward and continue with our strategy. That's all. We don't want to waste time discussing the negotiations between the German and Namibian governments – the Namibian government behaves as if it is part of Germany. Our ancestral land is very, very important to us. As long as I'm here in Germany, I will do my best and fight for our cause.

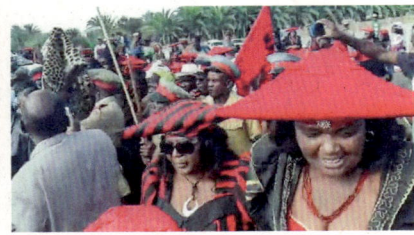
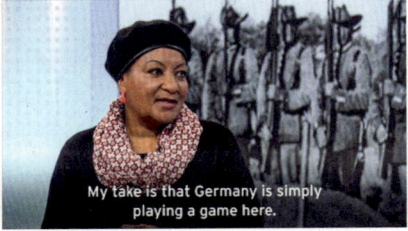
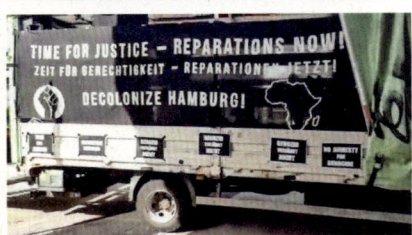
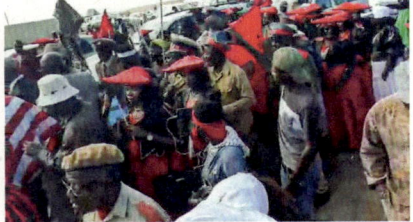
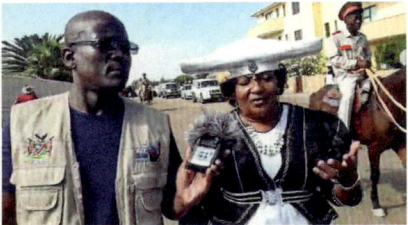
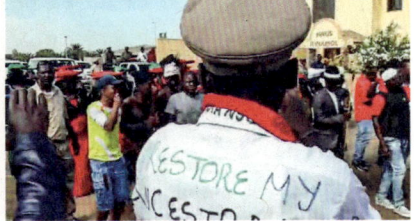
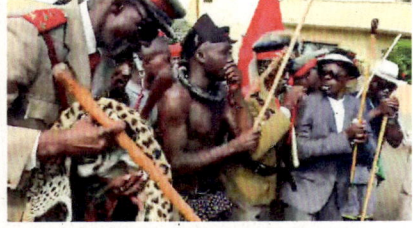
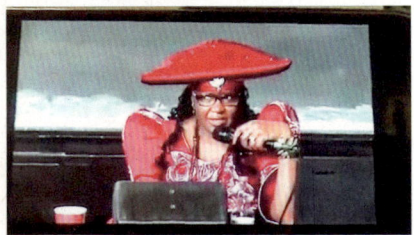

Screenshots from videos in the *It's Yours!* space

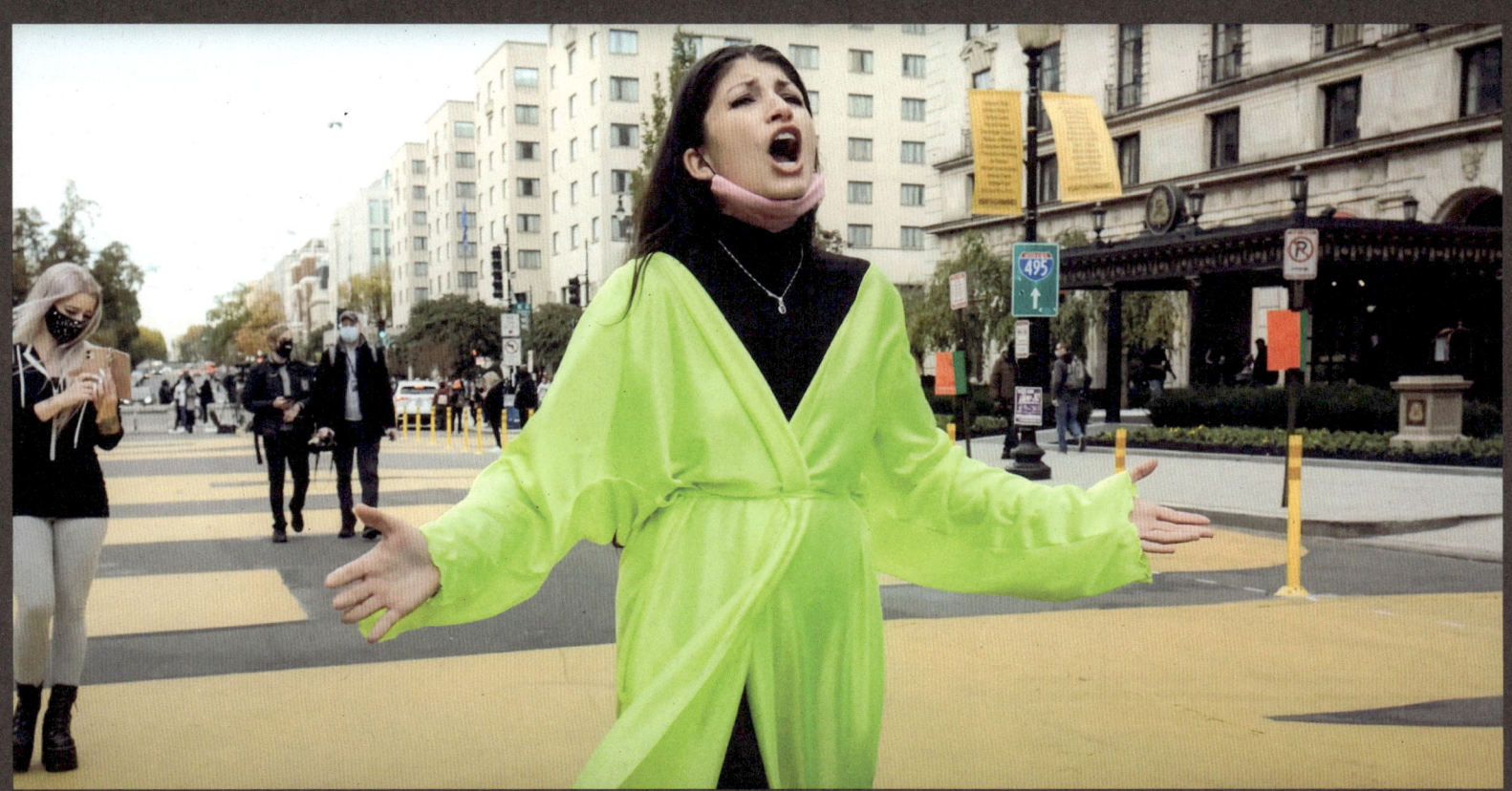

Selma Selman: *You Have No Idea*
3/11/2020, US Presidential Election Day, performance between BLM Plaza and the White House, Washington, DC, video, 5 min.

Washington, USA 03/11/2020

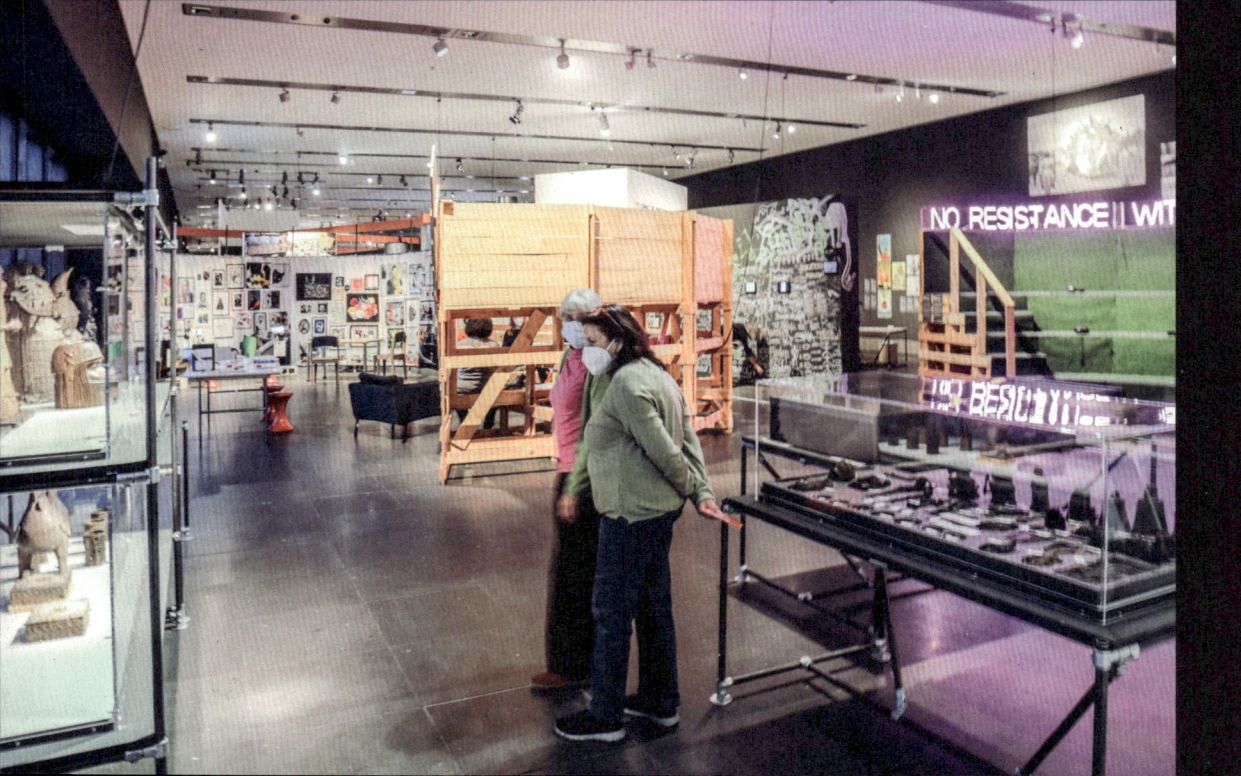

Subversion and Refusal

In addition to overt physical violence and clamorous protests, the repertoire of resistance also features forms of expression that are silent and not immediately perceptible. It is these covert but ongoing, daily forms of resistance, often ignored or derided by historiography, that have contributed in significant ways to the failure of colonial authority, the end of slavery, the independence of the colonies and the end of the apartheid regime.

When forcibly imposed colonial norms and interventions cause the destruction of local structures, practices and ways of life, subversion can become the only survival strategy. Rituals and customs were often carried out in secret, or their performance was altered in a way that rendered them unintelligible to the colonisers and thus unsanctionable. These forms of resistance included subversive anti-colonial messages in music, dance and song, codes concealed in language and clothing, secret signs and objects, but also humour, especially mockery of the white colonial population. Even "gaze strategies" were arguably an act of resistance: after all, merely meeting the eyes of the slave owner could result in punishment. Still, gaze could be employed even amidst the most severe oppression, which introduced opportunities for action. This interplay of hidden and visible protocols created a crucial window for action in anti-colonial resistance.

Forms of non-violent action and evasion strategies such as sabotage, theft, and the refusal to work or pay the imposed taxes were also meaningful methods of resistance. Despite forced Christianisation, strategies were developed to continue living one's faith or to reinterpret religious symbols.

In many cases, however, resistance was achieved through the colonised or enslaved people's withdrawal from the physical and social relationship of violence. Some managed to achieve this through physical escape from the occupied territories or slave plantations. For others, abortion, infanticide or suicide were the only way out of an unbearable and inhuman existence.

Theater Company GAKOEKOE
"Les Racontottes" – Humour as a Subversive Act of Resistance

Video stills of Les Racontottes, Lomé, 2020

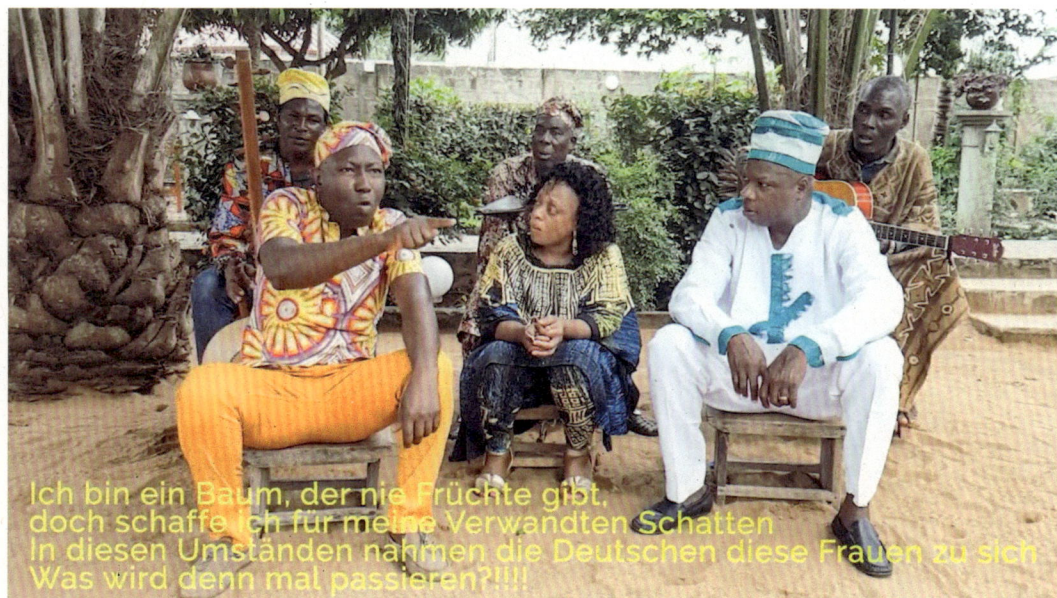

I am a tree that never bears fruit, but I create shade for my relatives. In these circumstances, the Germans took these women in. What will happen?!

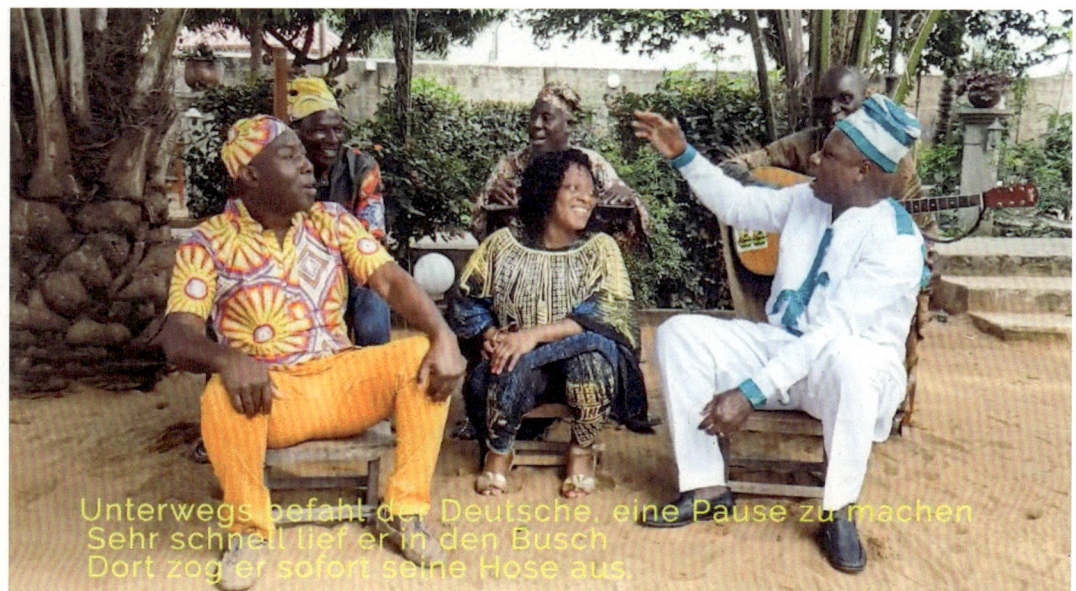

On the way, the German ordered him to take a break. Very quickly he ran into the bush. There he immediately took off his pants.

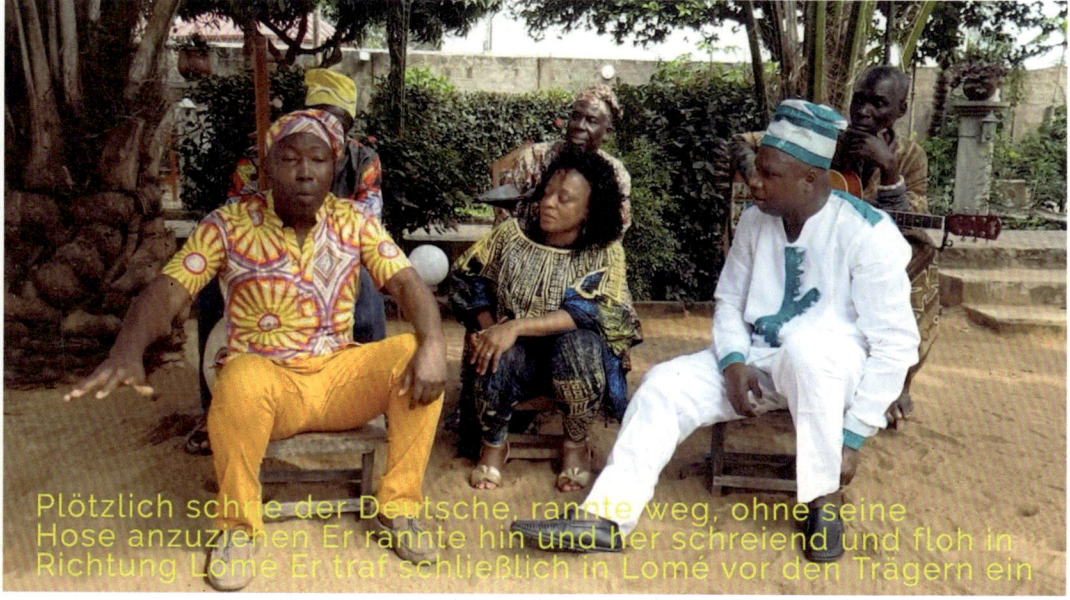

Suddenly the German screamed and ran away without putting on his pants. He ran back and forth screaming and fled in the direction of Lomé. He finally arrived in Lomé before the porters.

Lomé, Togo — 2020
GERMAN COLONIAL RULE 1884–1916

The Demystification of the German Colonist

narrated by Marcel Djondo, 9:26 min.

»What does a white man's excrement look like? That's what people are interested in.«
A story about a "big fat German" and his excrement, and how the villagers no longer had a complex about white people after seeing their faeces.

Narrator: Listen to the story.

Listener: With pleasure!

All: This tale goes round and round, jumps back and forth, and lands on the Germans.

Narrator: When the Germans arrived in the village, they liked it very much. According to a saying of the elders, people like to create descendants in a place if they want to leave their name there forever. That is why the Germans once sent for all the women in the village, wives and unmarried women alike. The Germans then chose the ones they wanted. Husbands who opposed their wives being selected were beaten up – oh, that's a bit much, letting women cheat. In the village they used to sing a song: »I am a tree that never gives fruit, yet I create shade for my relatives.« It was in these circumstances that the Germans took these women. What do you think happened next?! Nine months later, these women gave birth to very beautiful children. The children looked very beautiful. That is why nowadays in our country there are German names like Gruner, Buckner, Schneider, Otto, even Hamburger. Another time, a ship full of Germans landed at the jetty. They brought with them small plants from Europe. When they planted them, they grew and produced nuts. The villagers tasted these sweet nuts and liked them; they called them »European nuts«. Other plants yielded big round coconuts, which were very sweet and known as »European coconuts«, while another plant produced small slimy fruits called »yovo missi«. There was also »European papaya« and so on. The locals said to themselves that the Europeans only had good things. This made them wonder what their excrement looked like. Each time a German came out of the toilet, they secretly tried to check what kind of faeces they produced. But they couldn't see anything, because it had fallen into a deep hole. So they thought that the white man's excrement must be valuable if they hid it in a deep hole. The excrement was like gold to them. This is why the locals were eager to find out more about this excrement.

Listener: So they thought the white man was God?

Narrator: Yes, exactly! This went on until one day, a physically large German official arrived by ship – he was so big and fat. At that time, white people were carried in hammocks by locals. Two people would carry the hammock poles from the front and two more would carry them on their shoulders from behind. They were carried like kings. Now, when the time came for the fat German man to be carried, the hammock bearers ran away. The Germans searched for them, caught them, and had them thoroughly beaten up. Eventually, the hammock bearers were forced to carry the large German man. They obeyed this order with helpless frustration. Finally, there was an opportunity to see what a white man's excrement looked like. They were sure that the German would have to go to the toilet at some point en route. While they were on their way, the German ordered them to take a break. He dashed into the bushes and immediately took off his trousers. The hammock bearers hid and watched him. As soon as the German relieved himself, they noticed a terrible smell. They realised that the German was like them – he had similar organs to theirs. Suddenly, they felt capable of dealing with him. When the German had finished, he searched in vain for toilet paper. He looked everywhere, but found nothing suitable. However, he could not put his trousers back on just yet. Then he saw a leaf nearby. He went to take the leaf. All the hammock bearers knew that this leaf was not appropriate for this task: it causes irritation when it comes into contact with the skin. The leaf is known as »azra«. Everyone knew about its negative effects – except the German. He took the leaf and cleaned his bottom with it. All of a sudden, he screamed and ran away without putting his trousers back on. He ran back and forth, screaming, and fled in the direction of Lomé. He ended up arriving in Lomé before the hammock bearers.

This is how the tale was told to me and how I've told it to you. Ever since then, the villagers have no longer had a complex about white people.

More filmed *racontottes* produced in Lomé and shown in the exhibition *RESIST!*:

The Protectorate Treaty and the Resistance of Agotimé Batoumé

German Colonisation and the Resistance of the Vodu Priestess

The Resistance of the Konkomba and the Cut Thumbs

Why Does the Railway Stop at Blitta?

"Racontottes" are little stories told at evening gatherings around the fire or under the palaver tree. The six storytellers from the Togolese theater company GAKOEKOE bring stories to life. Twisting and turning, jumping back and forth, these stories chronicle the German invasion of Togo in 1884. In these tales, history becomes a jumble of anecdotes and jokes. The storytellers narrate the many forms of resistance to the Germans: mental, physical, and moral. Some anecdotes come from the narrators' families, while others were inspired by history books. In this production, a still shot was chosen to symbolise the gaze of the wise man who sits at a distance and watches the "little" people debate. The story of the Germans' arrival in Togo begins with a protectorate treaty signed with a village unknown to the Togolese people. This treaty signalled the beginning of the invasion, along with its punishments and forced labour. "Togoland" was born. People resisted using any means possible. But how could the invaders be defeated when the locals had never seen firearms before? These stories find the humorous side of terrible situations, forming an amusing yet tragic portrayal of colonial life as well as a disturbing contrast to the official historiography.

Courtesy of the Theater Company Gakoekoe

MUSIC AND DANCE AS A SECRET WEAPON

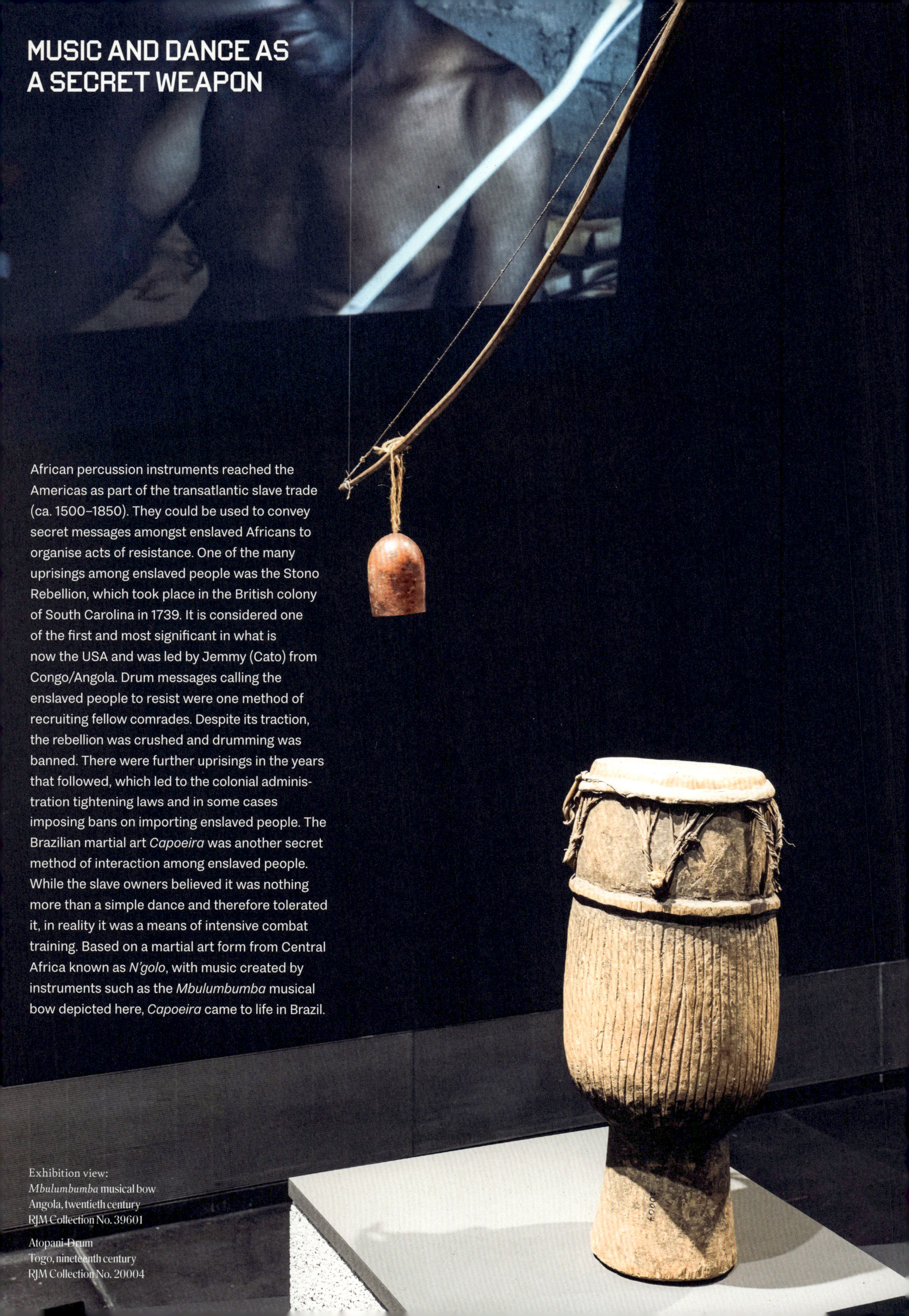

African percussion instruments reached the Americas as part of the transatlantic slave trade (ca. 1500–1850). They could be used to convey secret messages amongst enslaved Africans to organise acts of resistance. One of the many uprisings among enslaved people was the Stono Rebellion, which took place in the British colony of South Carolina in 1739. It is considered one of the first and most significant in what is now the USA and was led by Jemmy (Cato) from Congo/Angola. Drum messages calling the enslaved people to resist were one method of recruiting fellow comrades. Despite its traction, the rebellion was crushed and drumming was banned. There were further uprisings in the years that followed, which led to the colonial administration tightening laws and in some cases imposing bans on importing enslaved people. The Brazilian martial art *Capoeira* was another secret method of interaction among enslaved people. While the slave owners believed it was nothing more than a simple dance and therefore tolerated it, in reality it was a means of intensive combat training. Based on a martial art form from Central Africa known as *N'golo*, with music created by instruments such as the *Mbulumbumba* musical bow depicted here, *Capoeira* came to life in Brazil.

Exhibition view:
Mbulumbumba musical bow
Angola, twentieth century
RJM Collection No. 39601

Atopani-Drum
Togo, nineteenth century
RJM Collection No. 20004

Richard Pakleppa, Matthias Röhrig Assunção, Christine Dettmann
Body Games – Capoeira and Ancestry
Documentation, 87:00 Min.

Brazil & Angola — 2014

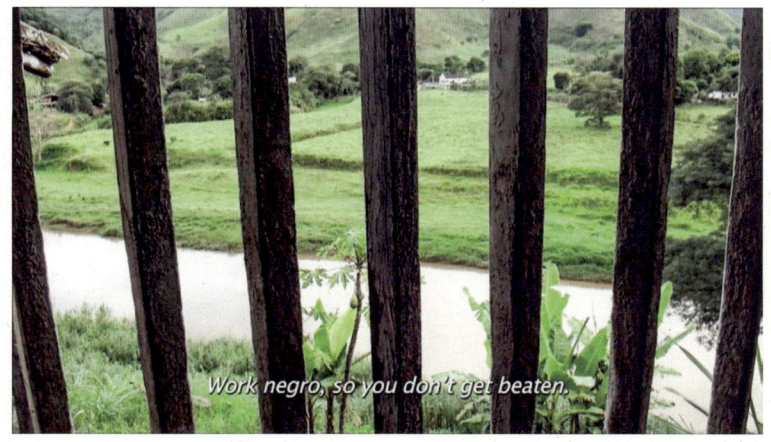

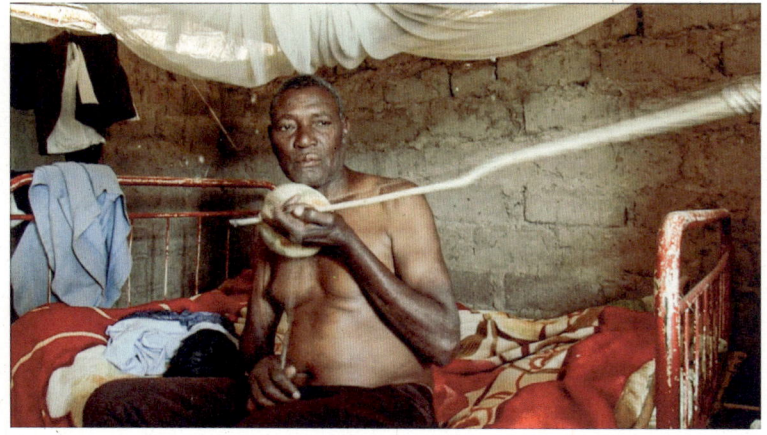

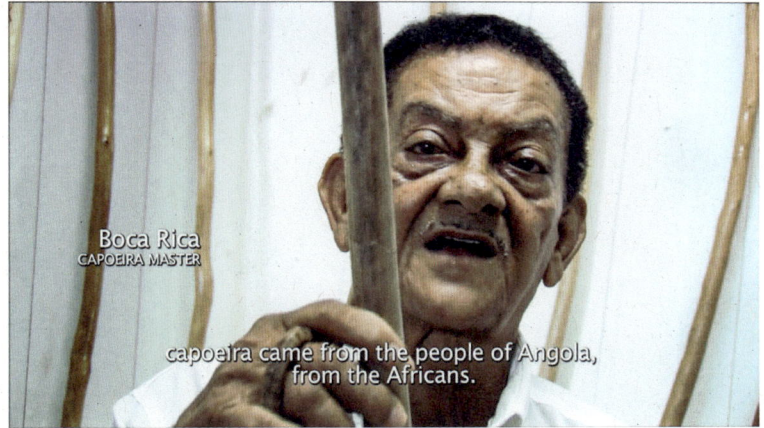

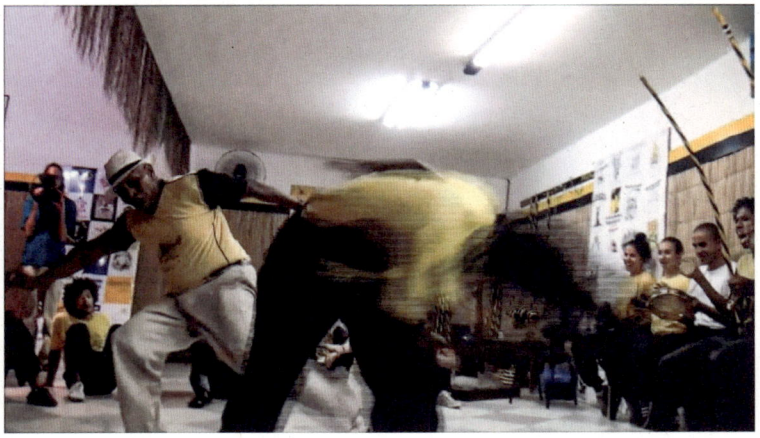

»I imagine my ancestors. I imagine that their little moments of rest must have felt like eternal freedom in a slave house. Everyone is together, playing, exchanging physical memories with each other. The body games, the dancing, the rhythm, the toques, the songs and movements they brought from Africa to Brazil.«
Mestre Cobra Mansa

The film follows *Capoeira* master "Mestre" Cobra Mansa and his friends on their search for the African roots of the Brazilian martial art *Capoeira*. A powerful myth connects *Capoeira* with a legendary Angolan game called *N'golo* – also known as the Zebra dance. In the film, *N'golo* as well as other fighting games, dances, and the music of the Nyaneka-Humbi people in southern Angola are documented for the first time. The exchange between *Capoeira* and *N'golo* in Angolan villages and the glimpses from the streets of Rio and Bahia highlight the similarities and differences between martial arts and musical bows on both sides of the Atlantic.

NO RESISTANCE WITHOUT MUSIC
Artist & DJ in Residence: Rokia Bamba

A sound experience composed by Rokia Bamba which visitors could hear everywhere in the first two chapters of the exhibition.

#1 My Strange Fruit

1. Slam Poetry „White Privilege", *Kyla Jenée Lacey*
2. *Maya Angelou* singing a song for the Antioch College, Yellow Springs, Ohio (Greene County Public Library)
3. „Click Song (Qongqothwane)" (Live), *Miriam Makeba*
4. Meet the Vodou Priestess Summoning Healing Spirits in Post-Earthquake Haiti (Vice)
5. „Strange Fruit", *Billie Holiday*
6. Slam Poetry „Black Privilege", *Crystal Valentine*

#2 My Fruit Strange

1. „Sink Em Low", *Bessie Jones & The Georgia Sea Island Singers*
2. „Your silence will not protect you", *Audre Lorde*
3. Black Nationalist Sonic Weaponry „The Man-Not" and „Black Industrial Complex" – Automation Repress Revolution in the Process of Production and Intercontinental Missiles Represent a Revolution in the Process of Warfare, *Speaker Music*
4. „Summertime", *Jeanne Lee & Ran Blake*

»When you asked how I began writing, I told you how poetry functioned specifically for me from the time I was very young. When someone said to me, ›How do you feel?‹ or ›What do you think?‹ or asked another direct question, I would recite a poem, and somewhere in that poem would be the feeling, the vital piece of information. It might be a line. It might be an image. The poem was my response.«
(An Interview: Audre Lorde and Adrienne Rich, in: Audre Lorde, *Sister Outsider*, 2019, p. 72)

"Inspired by my reading of Audre Lorde, I realised that I needed to compose sound journeys in order to let my emotions out. My need to say things is expressed through sounds, noises, voices, music … Enter one of my bubbles: *I'm a woman, I'm Black. I'm Belgian-Malian and Ivorian! My name is Rokia Assah Bamba, daughter of Fatoumata Sylla and Youssouf Bamba. I come from my father's line. I am a Samoghos, granddaughter of Kader Bamba, descendant of a long line of farmers.* Faced with our multiple identities, we have to learn to deal with others and what they see in us … without silencing any of these multiple facets. For me, the desire for change is an act of resistance, having the privilege to speak and express myself is an act of resistance, and not being silenced or remaining silenced in the face of these changes is an act of resistance. Let's transform our silences into words and actions! Our silence will not protect us!" Rokia Bamba

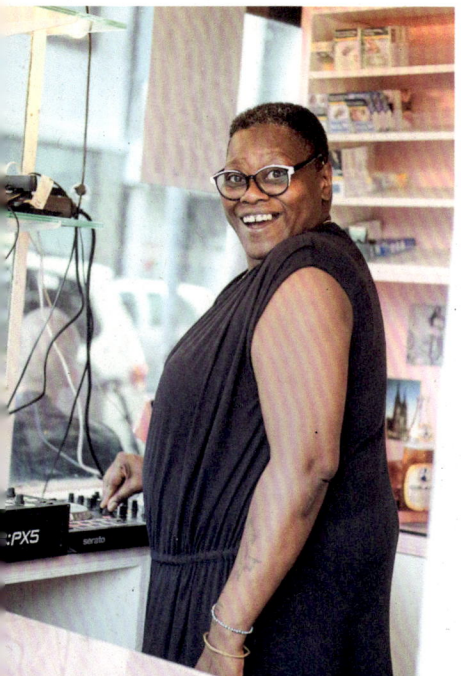

»Music is a weapon. Because if you study the history of music from the beginning of slavery to the end, and the Black liberation movements, music is a constant, it's very strong. Music has always heralded the transition to a new movement; something always follows behind it.« *Rokia Bamba*

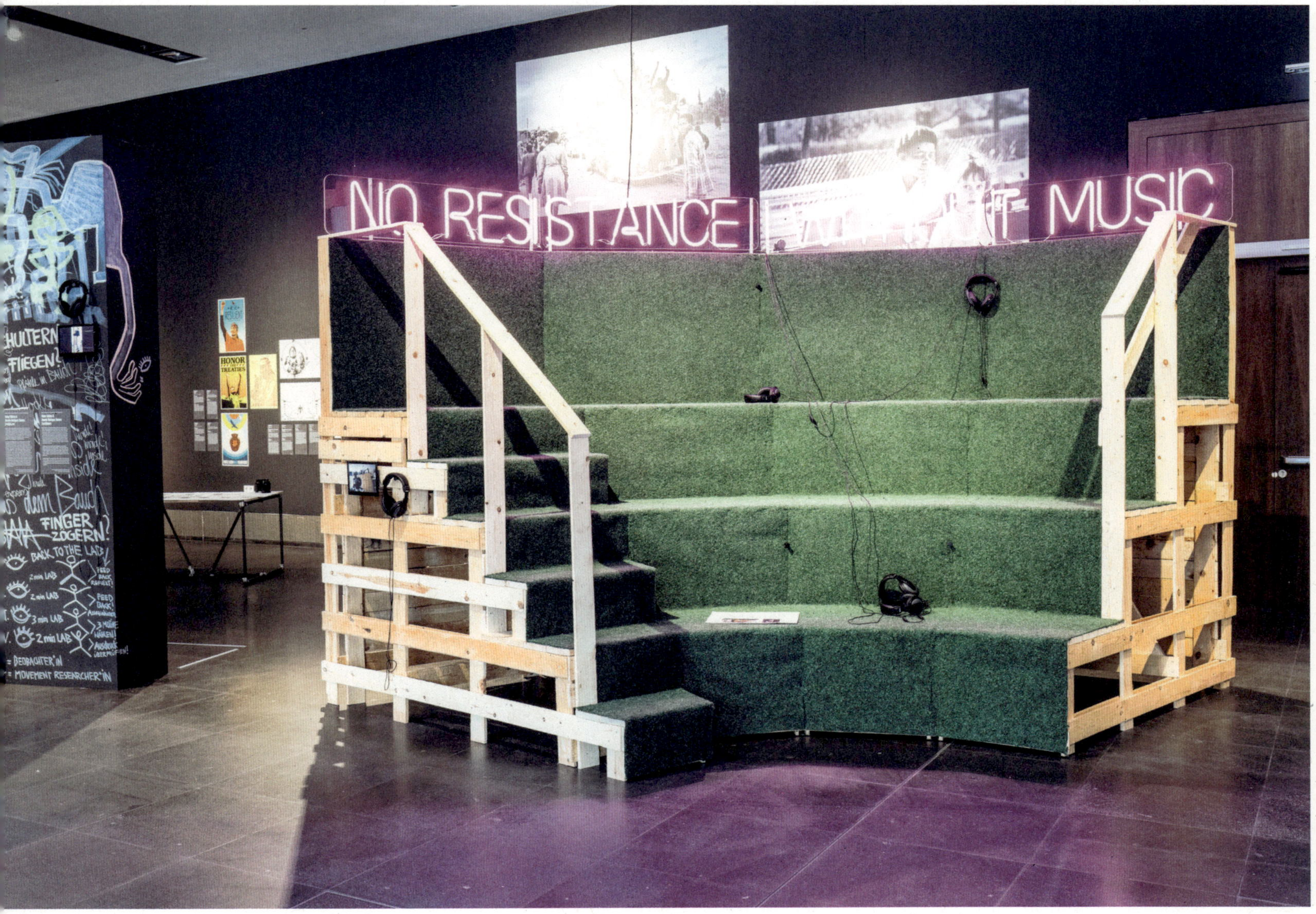

"I'm really sick of being asked, where are you from, where are your parents from? I'm here in front of you, don't ask me that. Change the way you speak to me, change the way you get to know me. I am an artist. Ask me what I'm going to do, what I do for a living. But don't keep asking me over and over again where I'm from and where my people are from. I prefer to decide when I'm going to say that."

"For me, it's important to say 'I'm proud'. Normally I don't know how to do that – how to be proud of me, proud of being Black, proud of being a woman. For me, it's my new way of life – to be proud, to be Black, and to tell everybody: 'I'm not only a Black woman, I'm not only a woman – I'm both and I'm more besides.' Don't tell me again where I'm from – I'm sick of it."

"The Rautenstrauch-Joest Museum is the perfect place to be heard by everyone. It's a form of resistance to say: 'It's a colonial museum. What am I going to say there?' It's important for us to be a part of the museum."

"It's more than a collaboration, it's more than an artist doing something for the museum. It's a new way of thinking about the future of this museum. And everything is going to change. I'm sure that the museum of today will definitely not be this kind of museum tomorrow."

RESIST! Just Ask #2:
Live speaker Fatima Remli in conversation with Rokia Bamba

Peju Layiwola's struggle for the restitution of the artworks looted from the court of the Kingdom of Benin by British soldiers in 1897 and subsequently scattered all over the world began more than two decades ago – when their restitution seemed a distant vision of the future. Peju Layiwola and RJM Director Nanette Snoep first met in Paris in early 2000 as part of the *Broken Memory* project led by Bernard Müller. *Broken Memory* was an international platform that examined the theft of cultural objects from the Global South and how they were remembered. Over twenty years later, following decades of professional exchange and friendship, Nanette Snoep invited Peju Layiwola to become an *It's Yours!* curator and to present her perspective on the Benin court artworks in *RESIST!*

It's Yours! space: a space in a space

The exhibition *RESIST!* was an organic space of resonance and dissonance in a state of constant change. In the public, hegemonic space of the RJM, which, like other ethnological museums, is a place with highly asymmetrical power relations, *RESIST!* sought to make repressed and silenced stories and histories from the Global South as well as marginalised voices heard. With Esther Utjiua Muinjangue, Ida Hoffmann, Peju Layiwola, Tímea Junghaus, and In-Haus e.V with Elizaveta Khan, artists, curators, and activists who are directly affected by the topic of resistance were invited to create a non-hierarchical space in the museum to present conflicts, protests, and wounds, insofar as this is possible in a museum setting. Within the *RESIST!* exhibition space, they have taken the floor and curated their own autonomous *It's Yours!* spaces, places of agency and self-determination.

p. 064 Not about Us without Us
p. 094 Benin 1897
p. 138 Roma Resist!
p. 170 No Resistance Fits in a Box or a Museum

"It's Yours" Room

Peju Layiwola
Benin 1897

There is no better description of what resistance means than the recent global protests against police brutality and racism. In these protests is a renewed quest for the return of plundered objects from Africa. The same paternalism that undergirds police actions against helpless people is akin to the idea of cultural superiority that enabled a group to plunder the artefacts of another group and continue to keep them. Museum and galleries, like other public spaces and institutions, are also yearning for decolonisation. They must now be tired of rehashing histories and stories of imperial violence in a world supposedly governed by reason, justice and equality.

The 96 Benin objects in this room originate from a violent incident in history perpetrated by British soldiers in Benin City, Nigeria in 1897. Contemporary artists like Osaze Amadasun, Alao Lukman, Monday Midnite, Jimoh Ganiyu, Nwakuso Edozien and Christie Akumabor bring in private experiences and stories about Benin art and culture to compete with the narrative of conquest symbolised by the experience of 1897. There are some hangovers of that overwhelming cultural erasure till date. Other works are a response to the general call for resistance and have been made by artists committed to this cause.

The 1897 video by Monday Midnite, a Belgian-based Edo musician, cartoons by Jimoh Ganiyu, and the images of an installation from my solo exhibition, Benin 1897.com: Art and the Restitution Question (which held in Lagos and Ibadan in 2010) portray strong messages and responses to colonial injustices in Benin. So also does the collaborative public art project, Whose Centenary? The project highlights 1914 as the year of the passing of Oba Ovoranmwen, and therefore subordinates the British amalgamation of Nigeria that also took place in 1914 to the death of the exiled king of Benin. Photography, site-specific installations, video art, performances, poetry, and drawings are featured in the format of a visual diary.

I find a correlation between the concept of "RESIST!" in my recent body of works referencing Yoruba indigo dyeing (àdìrẹ) and "Resistance". In fabric designing, the starch or wax builds a wall of resistance against the dye in forming a design. In certain social and political contexts of today, 'resist' and 'resistance' imply putting a guard in place to stem injustice. The voice of the colonised or the oppressed becomes the resistance, breaking down frameworks of subjugation and control to enable desired and desirable patterns to emerge, whether on cloth or the body politic.

Peju Layiwola, Arkansas, 2020

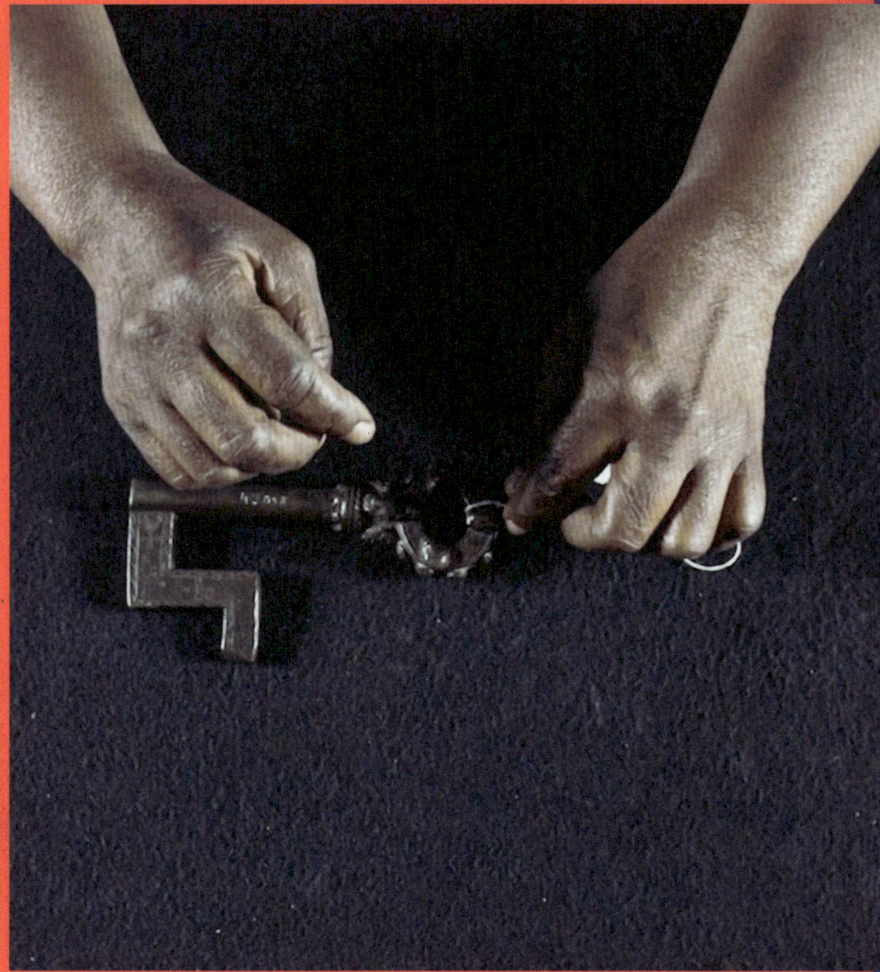

Untangle the Threads. Video featuring Peju Layiwola, 09:00 min., directed by Salman Alkhir Abdo & Fadi Elias, April 2022.

Video of Peju Layiwola preparing the installation *I MISS YOU* (opened April 2022) as part of the continuation of *RESIST!* and the *It's Yours!* space Benin 1897. In a kind of reactivation or purification ritual, Peju Layiwola removes the inventory numbers from the RJM's ninety-two Benin artworks with great tenderness and concentration in an act of liberation and resacralisation. This carved key from one of the Palace doors, from which Peju Layiwola removes the label, was one of the first three objects from the RJM collection to be physically returned to Nigeria in December 2022.

CLAIMS FOR RESTITUTION OF THE BENIN COURT ARTWORKS

Cologne, Germany — 16/12/2021

Peju Layiwola's demand for the restitution of the Benin court artworks when she was able to visit the museum in Cologne in person for the first time.

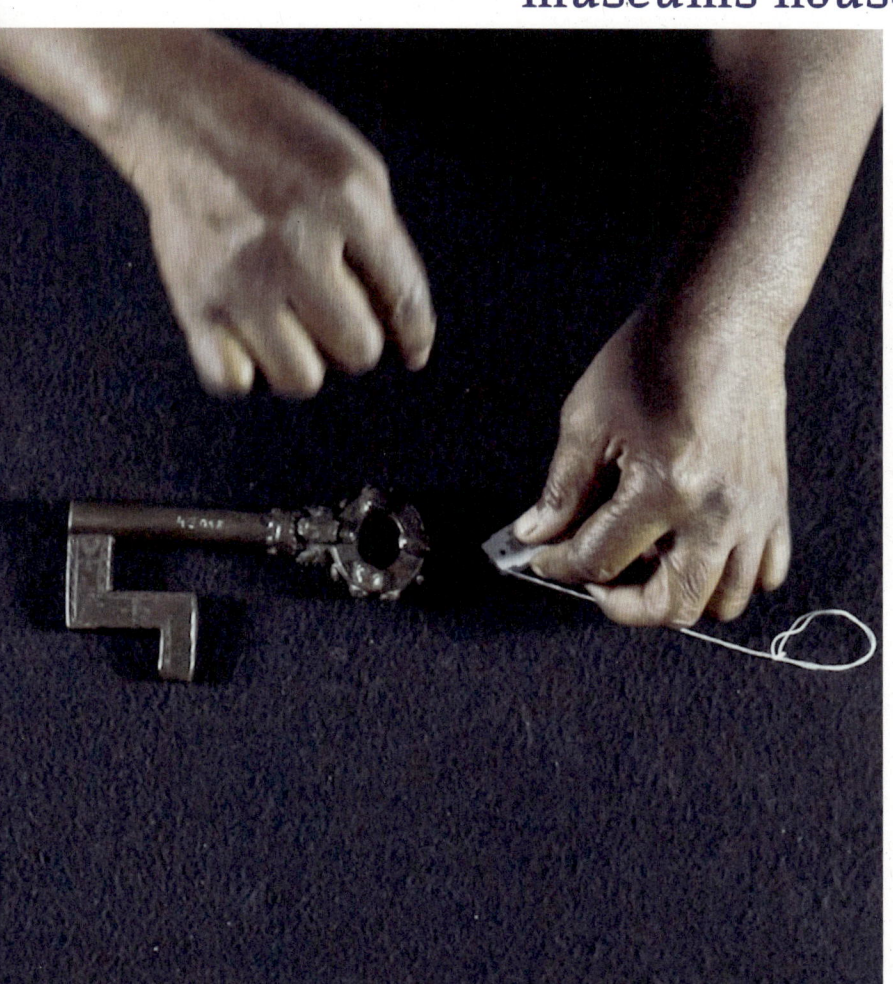

»Resistance is an instinctive reaction to oppression and humiliation. In Africa, resistance has continued long after the end of colonial oppression. It has persisted and morphed into demands for compensation for the atrocities and injustices committed during that inglorious era. Ethnographic museums house many collections from the former colonies and seem to address the epistemic violence of colonialism. I think that such creative intervention serves history and the colonised people of Africa better when it is done in their own spaces and on their own terms.«

Peju Layiwola

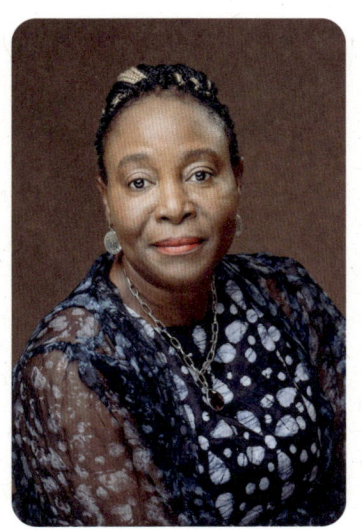

Peju Layiwola
*1967, Benin City, Nigeria

A glimpse at Layiwola's family history reveals the origins of her versatility as an artist as well as her historical and personal connection to the court artworks from the Kingdom of Benin held in various European and North American museum collections. Her mother, Princess Elizabeth Olowu, daughter of the Benin King Oba Akenzua II, is a renowned artist; she was the first woman to graduate with a degree in art history after Nigeria's independence, as well as the first woman to be admitted to the Benin guild of brass casters. Layiwola's work addresses personal histories on the ground, colonial memory, and the question of restitution, focusing on Benin City as both an ancient kingdom and a contemporary city. Layiwola received a BA in metal design from the University of Benin (Benin City) in 1988 and an MA and a PhD in art history from the University of Ibadan, Nigeria in 1991 and 2004 respectively. Peju Layiwola is an artist and professor of art history in the Department of Creative Arts at the University of Lagos. Layiwola's book about the restitution of the Benin artworks, named after her exhibition *Benin 1897.com*, was published in 2010.

Benin Court Artworks

owned by the RJM, donated or acquired between 1899 and 1967 and restituted in December 2022

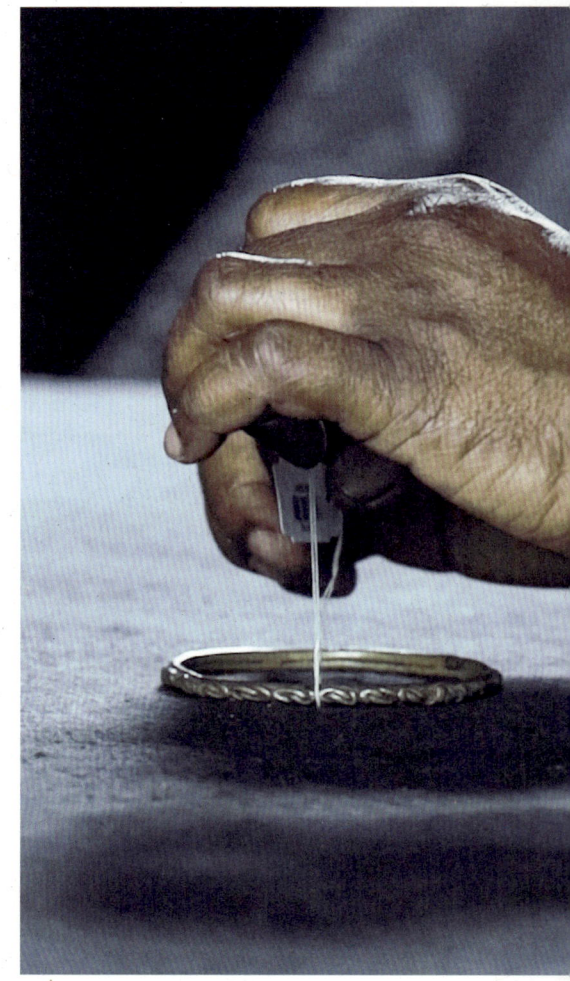

Cologne, Germany 1899–2022

Context of The Restitution Debates in Germany in Recent Years

»Any decision that is made about our heritage, about our lives, has to involve us [...]. We want to be able to tell our own stories.«

Peju Layiwola, *It's Yours!* curator, *RESIST!* January 2021

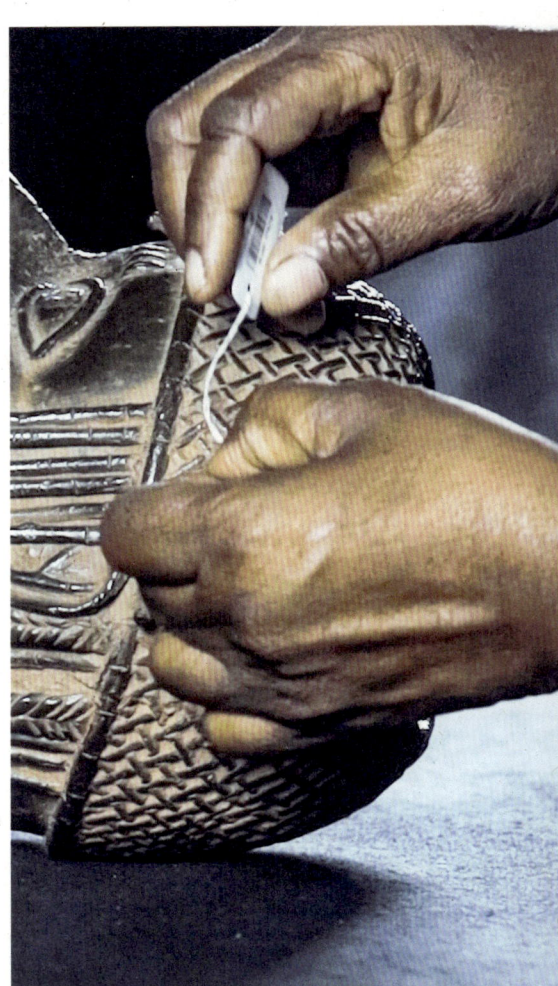

»The Kingdom of Benin first demanded restitution of the so-called ›Benin Bronzes‹ shortly after the massacre of 1897. The new Nigerian state began to demand the same immediately after independence in 1960 [...]. The importance of these cultural assets for our still young postcolonial national consciousness is high, especially in view of the fact that our country has a young population that has hardly any or no opportunity to visit European museums.«

H. E. Yusuf. M. Tuggar, Ambassador of Nigeria to Germany, April 2021

> »How can it be that I have to fly all the way to London to look at something that belongs to my culture that was stolen from us?«
>
> Adekunle Gold, Nigerian singer, June 2018

Since French President Emmanuel Macron made his famous speech at the University of Ouagadougou in Burkina Faso in November 2017, in which he laid out the prerequisites for the restitution of African cultural artefacts within five years, the debate surrounding the restitution of African artefacts looted in a colonial context has taken on a new dimension. Following Macron's speech, he commissioned the report *Restoring African Heritage: Toward a New Relational Ethics*, which was written by Senegalese author and economist Felwine Sarr and French art historian Bénédicte Savoy. Published one year later, this report had a decisive impact on the whole restitution debate and changed the position of museums once and for all. What seemed almost inconceivable ten years ago suddenly became museum practice. With Dan Hicks' book *The Brutish Museums: The Benin Bronzes, Colonial Violence and Cultural Restitution*, published in 2020, and the opening of the Humboldt Forum in Berlin in 2021, the debate around the restitution of cultural artefacts collected during the colonial era was definitely reaching a climax in Germany.

Benin artworks from the Kingdom of Benin in Nigeria

However, the controversies surrounding the restitution of cultural artefacts collected during the colonial era go back decades. As early as the 1960s, the former African colonies, freshly independent, began to fight for the return of their heritage stolen by European colonial rulers, which Bénédicte Savoy describes in her book *Africa's Struggle for Its Art: History of a Postcolonial Defeat* (2022). The most prominent objects in the restitution debate are the so-called "Benin Bronzes" from the Kingdom of Benin, located in present-day Edo State in Nigeria.

The Benin Kingdom dates back to the twelfth century and is one of the most important kingdoms in the history of the African continent. From at least the sixteenth century, the royal art of Benin was created by specialist guilds working for the royal court of the King in Benin City, the historic capital of the Kingdom of Benin. While the kingdom resisted its colonial conquest, it ultimately became part of the British Empire (1897–1960) after a massacre in which the royal palace along with other monuments and palaces were sacked, looted, and burned to the ground by British troops in February 1897. The king, Oba Ovonramwen Nogbaisi, was exiled and thousands of objects of ceremonial and ritual value – many dating back to the sixteenth century – were looted and brought to Europe as so-called spoils of war. Many of the works were sold by London auction houses and thus entered museum collections around the world, most of them before the First World War, which was also the case for the RJM.

The theft of Benin court artworks – a lingering colonial trauma?

The Benin kingship, its traditional ruling structures, and its cultural heritage still play an important role in Nigeria today, both politically and spiritually. For centuries, the Edo recorded pivotal events in each king's reign through their court artworks: wars and warlords, the merits and deeds of kings, successions to the throne, and significant rituals. The court artworks tell dynastic and social histories, but they also had an important sacred function: they honoured ancestors, past Kings and Queen Mothers. In 1897, the British looted almost the entire material archive of the kingdom and therefore the memory of the population.

Benin artworks at the RJM

With a total of 92 court artworks from the Benin Kingdom, the RJM's collection the fourth largest in Germany after Berlin, Saxony, and Hamburg. The oldest Benin works, which were part of the RJM collection until December 2022, date back to the sixteenth and seventeenth centuries, although most were produced from the mid-eighteenth century to 1897. It is certain that all of them were looted during the Benin massacre in February 1897. The 92 royal artworks entered

> »A sincere approach to colonial history also includes the question of the restitution of cultural assets [...]. This is a question of justice.«
>
> Heiko Maas, Federal Minister of Foreign Affairs, March 2021

> »No Nigerian will get a visa if they state that they want to visit a museum in London, New York, or Berlin to look at his country's cultural assets.«
>
> Victor Ehikhamenor,
Nigerian artist, June 2018

the RJM collection as donations or acquisitions between 1899 and 1967. 75 of them were acquired before 1907 by the Rautenstrauch family – the eponym of the museum and a major patron – from auction houses in London and donated to the city of Cologne. In the past decades, only a few of the 92 artworks have been exhibited, most recently three in the RJM's permanent exhibition that was inaugurated in 2010. The Benin collection was shown to the public in its entirety for the first time in 2021, in the *It's Yours!* space Benin 1897.

Finally, on December 8, 2022, Cologne City Council approved the transfer of ownership of the RJM's 92 Benin royal artworks to the Federal Republic of Nigeria. On December 15, 2022, the Mayor of the City of Cologne, Henriette Reker, and the Director General of the National Commission for Museums and Monuments in Nigeria, Abba Isa Tijani, signed an agreement regarding the transfer of ownership. Five days later, on December 20, 2022, in Nigeria's capital Abuja, the first three works from Cologne – a key, a commemorative head, and an altar stool – were officially handed over to Nigeria by the Minister of Foreign Affairs Annalena Baerbock and the Minister of State for Culture Claudia Roth.

"There is one artefact […] that I find particularly fascinating. It is a very small object: a key that we have brought with us today. It is a unique piece, beautifully decorated with leopards and human faces. Its creator must have been a great artist.

We are not quite sure what the key was used for. Perhaps to open a shrine, a palace door, or even a treasure chest. But we do know that after it was stolen from Benin, it was brought to the United Kingdom. It was sold there and then travelled to Cologne via Ireland and France. Today the key is back. It is back where it belongs. I am moved to see the love with which you have received this key and the other bronzes here in Abuja today. This key is a symbol. It can help us open a new chapter in the friendship between our two peoples."

From a speech by German Minister of Foreign Affairs Annalena Baerbock about the Benin key (see key on page 96) from the RJM's collection at the handover of the Benin court artworks in Abuja, Nigeria on 20/12/2022

> »What are they doing in the depot when they serve a different purpose in Nigeria and could inspire a new generation of artists, a new generation of younger Nigerians who, as you know, will have a lot of connections to these works? So I think that these works don't have as much meaning in the West as they do with the people who created them.«
>
> Peju Layiwola, It's Yours! curator RESIST!, May 2021

BENIN CITY, NIGERIA, 29/04/2022:
Prince Aghatise Erediauwa, brother of the Oba of Benin, in a video message broadcast at the opening of the exhibition *I Miss You: About Missing, Giving Back and Remembering* at the RJM.

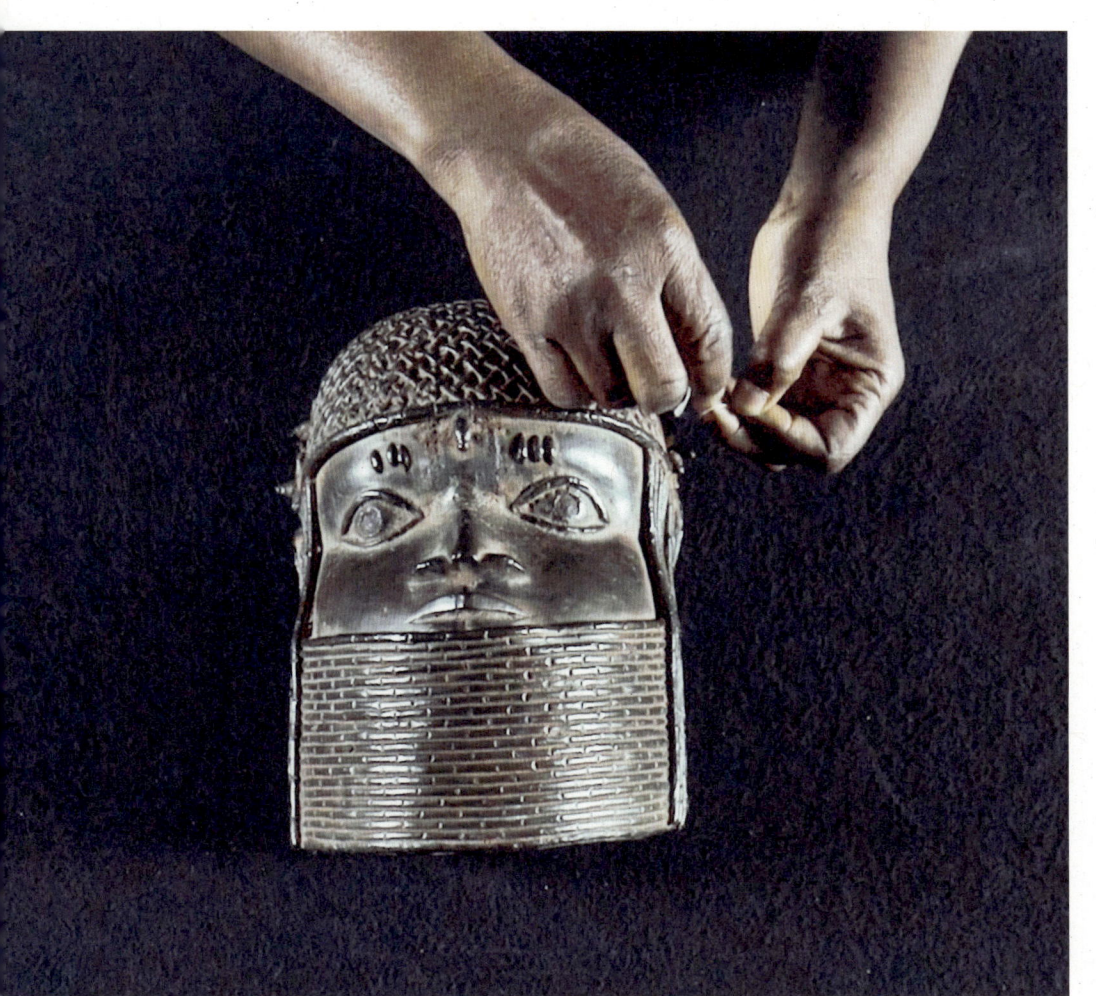

»They are symbols of our identity. We are still trying to get them back, 100 years after they were snatched from us with terrible violence. What happened in 1897 traumatised our whole nation. It was a shock. Don't forget that Benin was once a world power«

Godwin Nogheghase Obaseki, Prime Minister of Edo State in Nigeria, Summer 2018

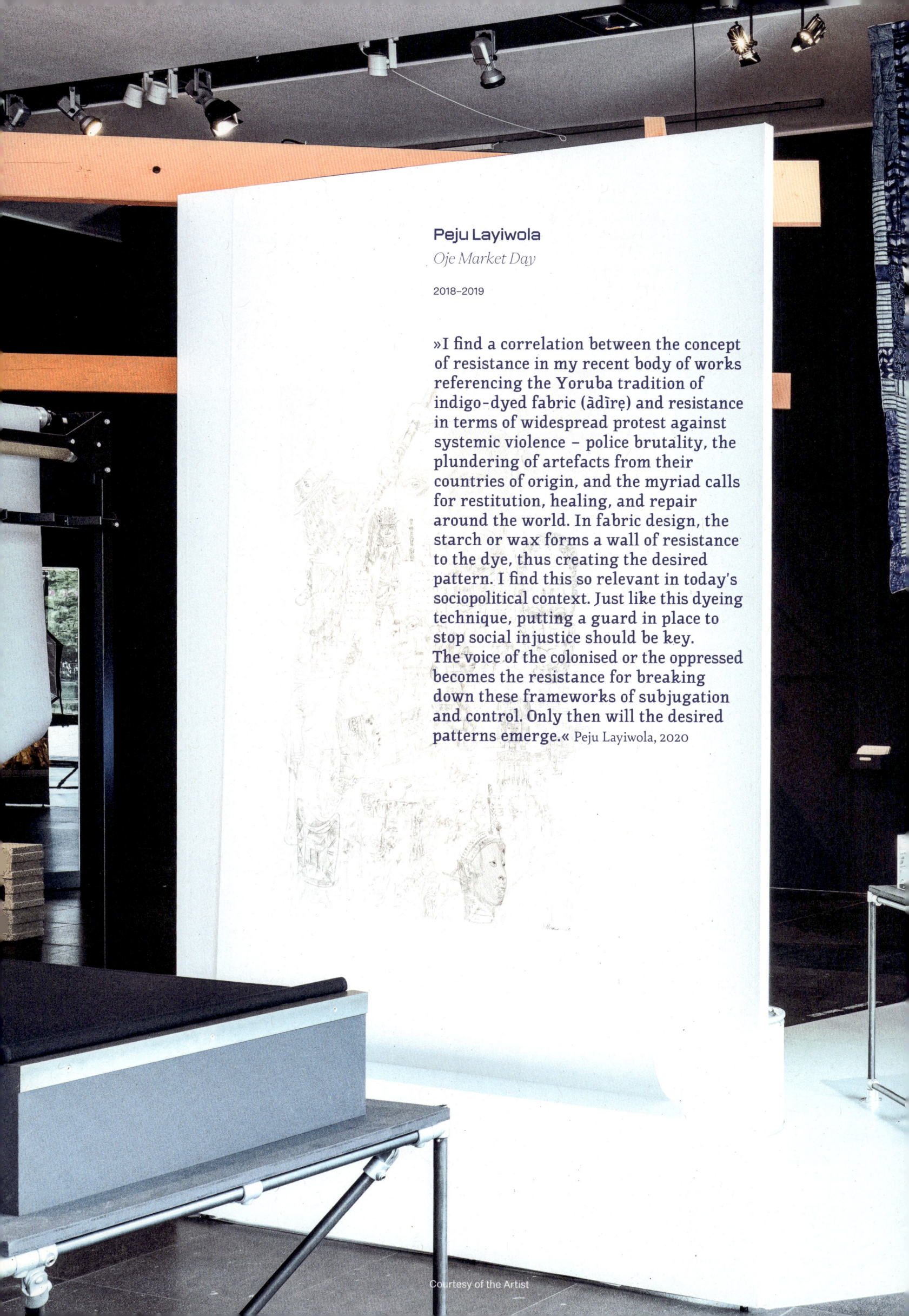

Peju Layiwola
Oje Market Day

2018–2019

»I find a correlation between the concept of resistance in my recent body of works referencing the Yoruba tradition of indigo-dyed fabric (àdìrẹ) and resistance in terms of widespread protest against systemic violence – police brutality, the plundering of artefacts from their countries of origin, and the myriad calls for restitution, healing, and repair around the world. In fabric design, the starch or wax forms a wall of resistance to the dye, thus creating the desired pattern. I find this so relevant in today's sociopolitical context. Just like this dyeing technique, putting a guard in place to stop social injustice should be key. The voice of the colonised or the oppressed becomes the resistance for breaking down these frameworks of subjugation and control. Only then will the desired patterns emerge.« Peju Layiwola, 2020

Courtesy of the Artist

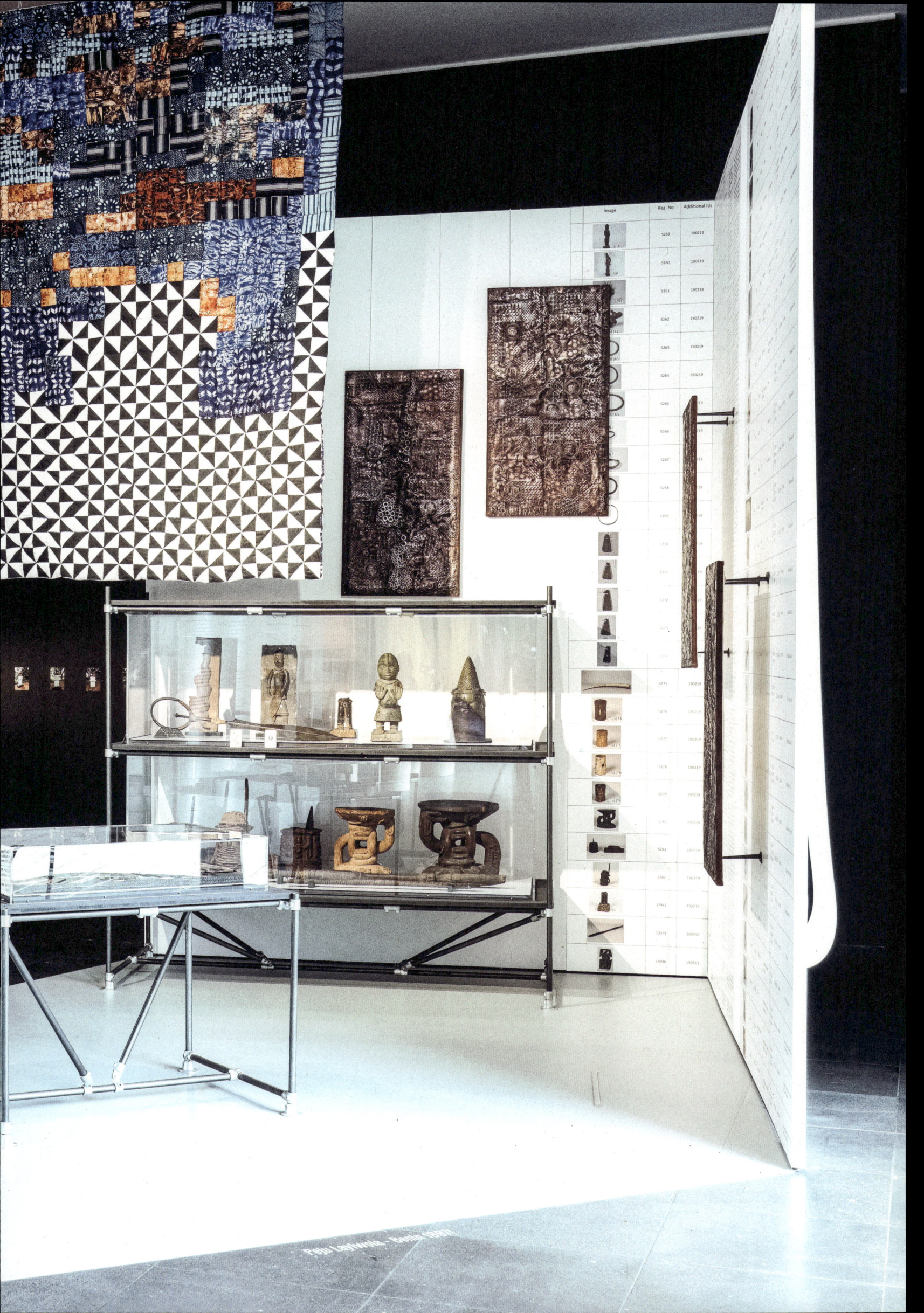

Nwakuso Edozien
The Close Relationship between Past and Present

2019

This piece is part of the artist's ongoing project called the *Traditional Modernity Series*. Through linework, illustration and layering, the series aims to highlight the strong relationship between past, present, and future in Nigeria. In the middle is the mask of Queen Idia from the British Museum, which has become an icon for restitution claims.

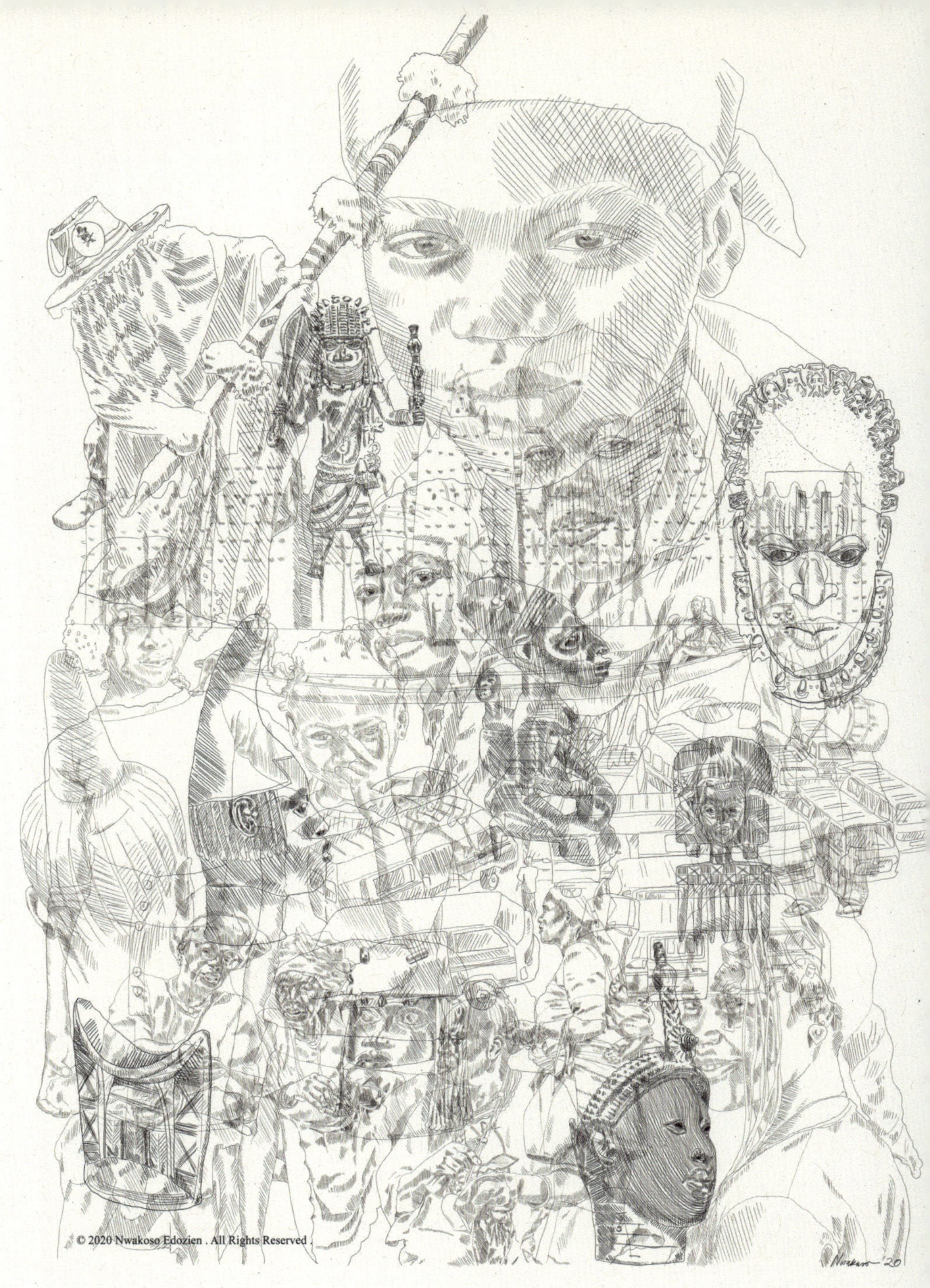

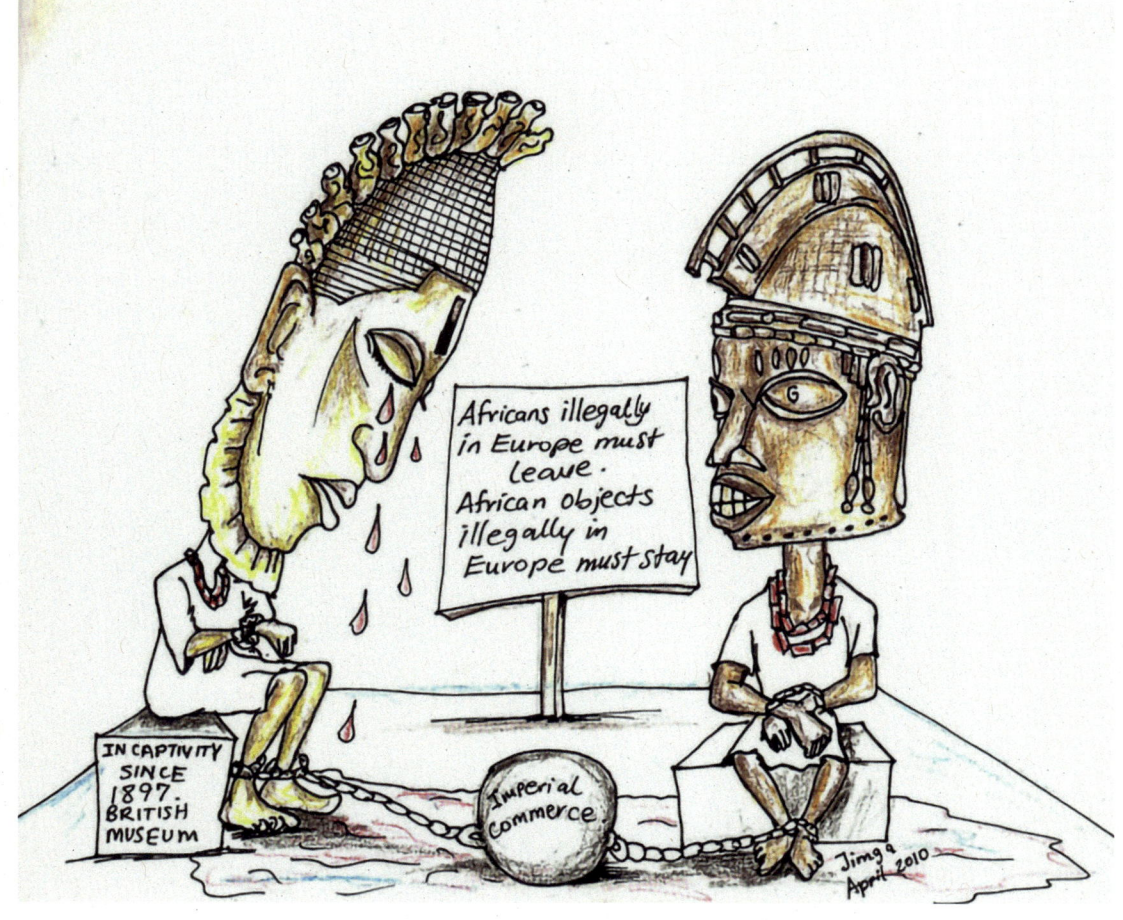

Jimoh Ganiyu
Double Standard

2010

Jimoh Ganiyu is a cartoonist, activist, and digital artist from Lagos. In his works, Jimoh Ganiyu (Jimga) speaks about social and socio-political issues. One of his particular concerns is addressing the issue of looted art and highlighting postcolonial practices. He thus represents a significant voice in the restitution debate. His work Double Standard denounces the double standard of Western policies regarding African migrants and African cultural assets.

It's Yours!

Monday Midnite
1897
2009

With the single *1897*, which was first released in 2009 and is part of Midnite's personal campaign for the restitution of all artworks that the British invaders looted from his homeland of Benin in 1897, the musician and activist makes an important contribution to the restitution debate. The song deals with the most tragic event in the history of his people and is an anthem to officially launch a campaign for the return of traditional and historical artefacts.

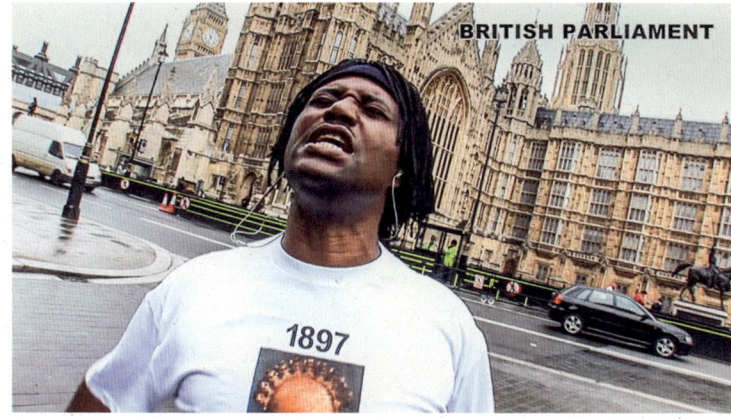

BRITISH PARLIAMENT

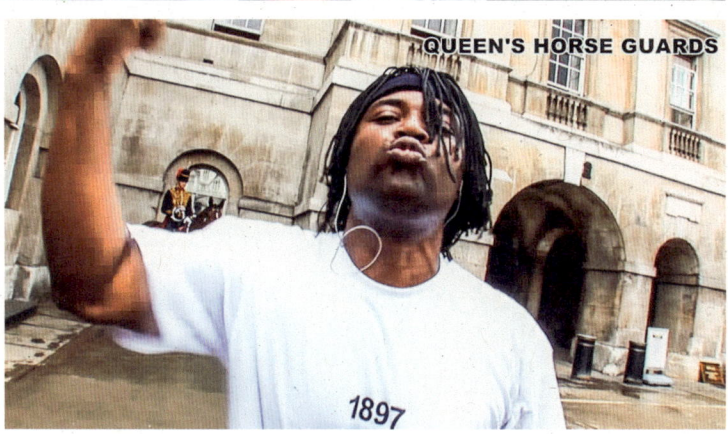

QUEEN'S HORSE GUARDS

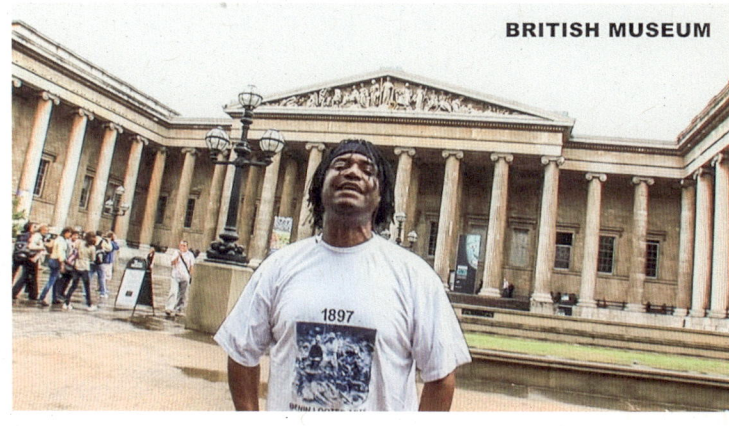

BRITISH MUSEUM

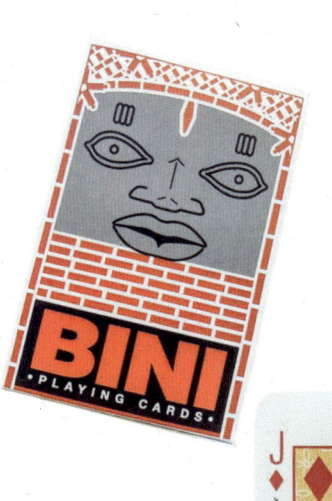
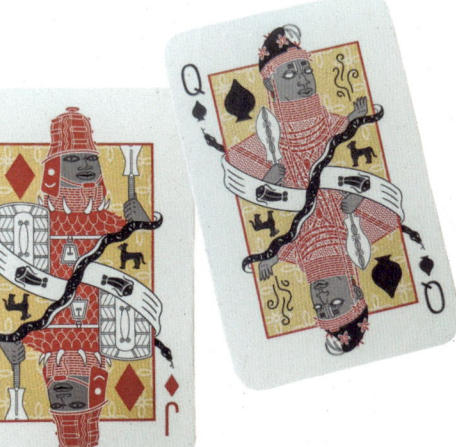
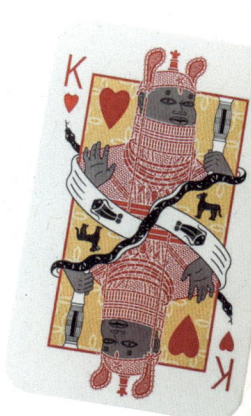
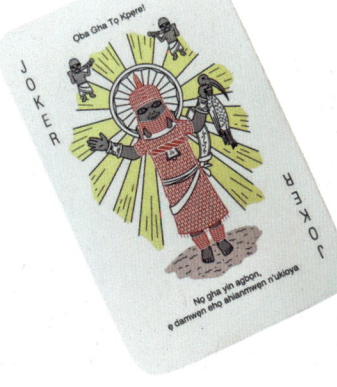
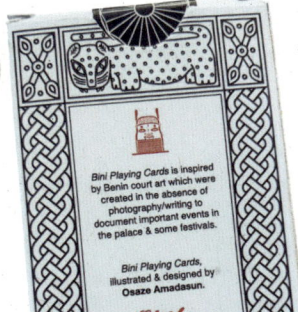

Osaze Amadasun
Bini Playing Cards
2018

Inspired by Benin culture, these playing cards pay homage to the ancient kingdom of Benin and its classical artworks. The *Bini Playing Cards* serve as a fun introduction to the Kingdom of Benin and its art, while also seeking to spark debates about the return of stolen artefacts from Western museums.

Courtesy of the Artists

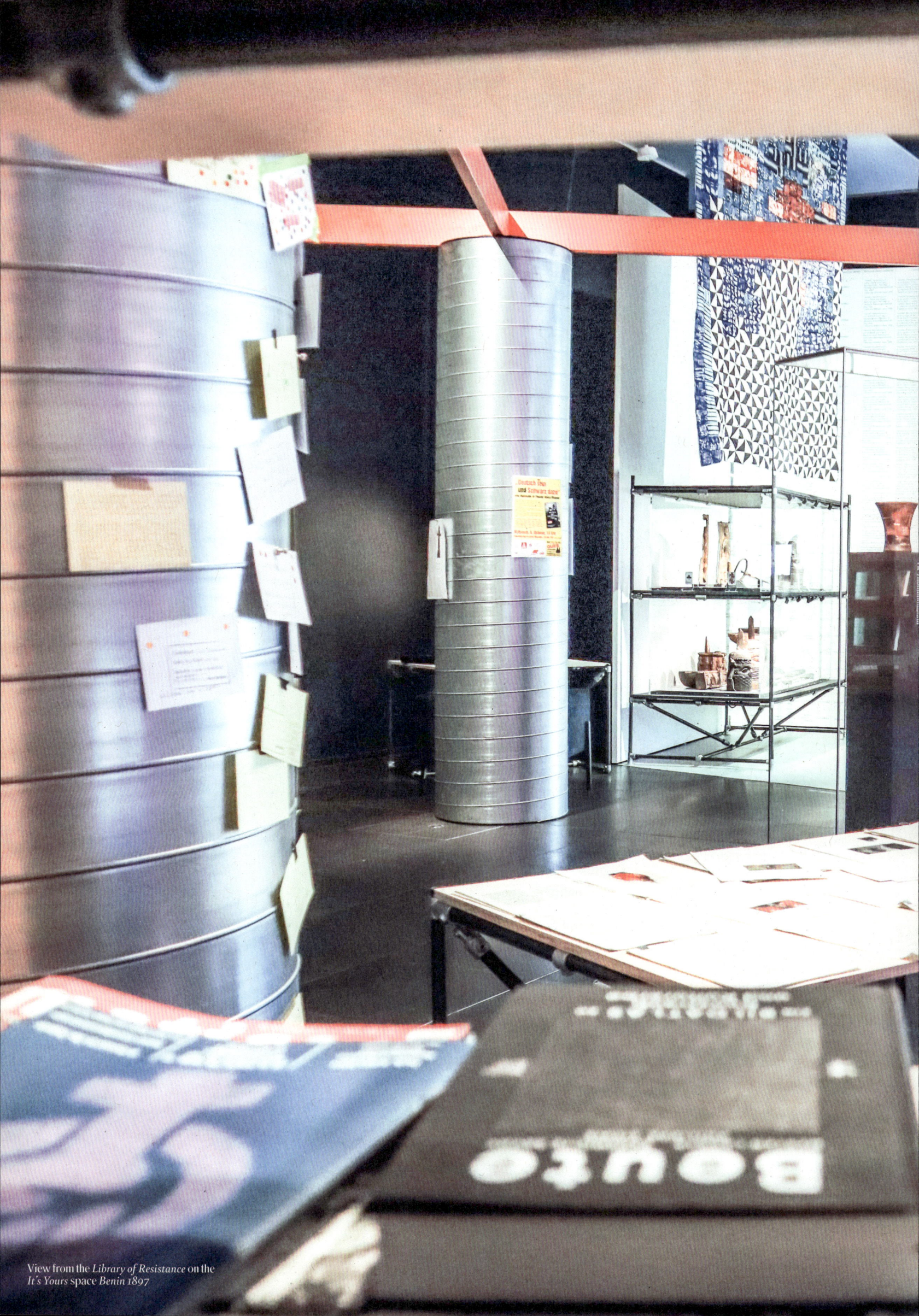

View from the *Library of Resistance* on the *It's Yours* space Benin 1897

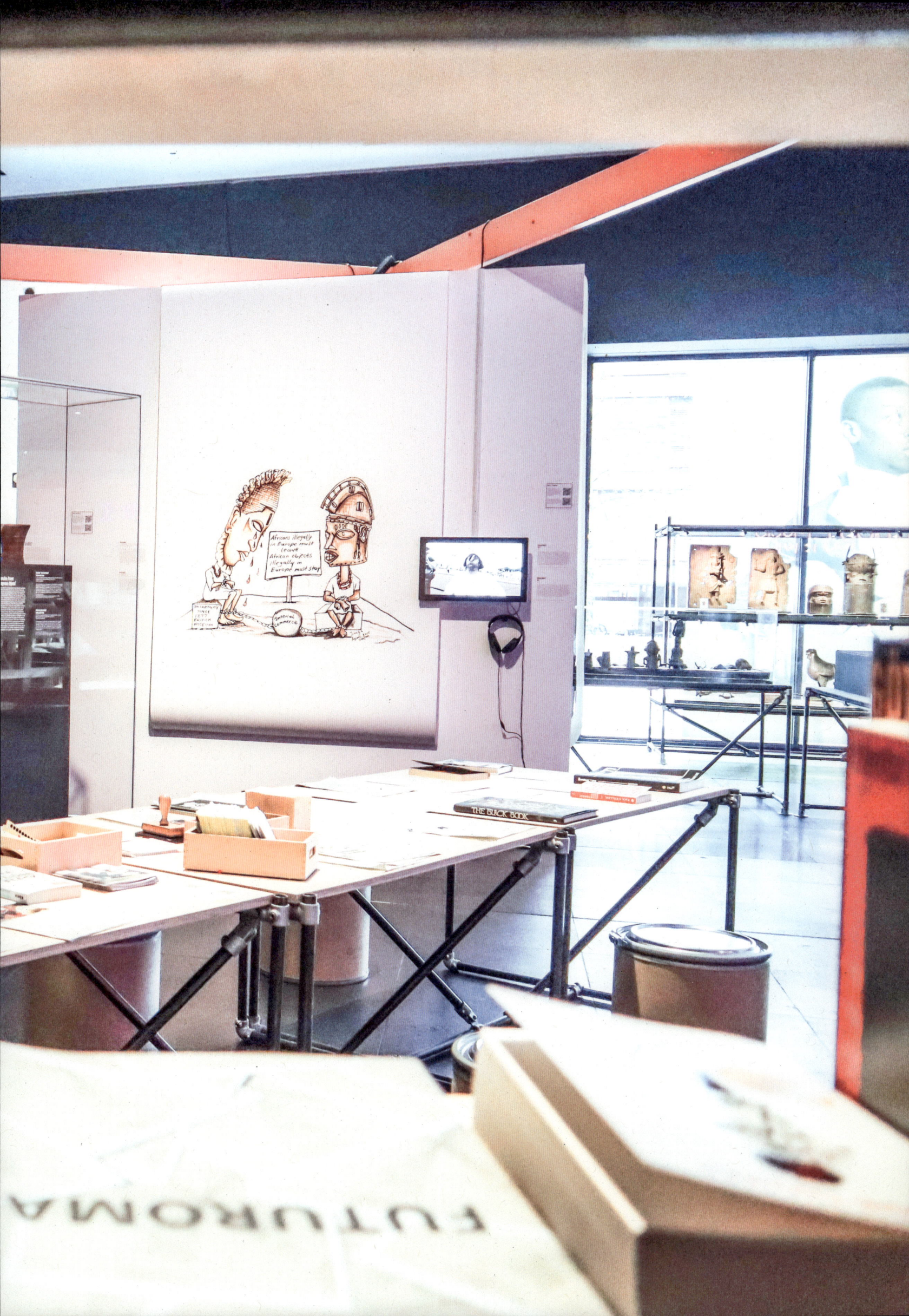

Conversation:
Benin 1897

Peju Layiwola is an artist, lecturer, and the granddaughter of Oba Akenzua II, King of the Kingdom of Benin. In conversation with Nanette Snoep, she spoke about the autonomous *It's Yours!* space she curated for *RESIST!*, *Benin 1897*, the return of the Benin court artworks, and the gap left by looted cultural heritage. At the time of this conversation, we did not know that in less than two years the "Benin Bronzes" would be returned to Nigeria.

This conversation was part of the online programme *RESIST! DIGITAL*, which was launched due to Covid restrictions.

Nanette Snoep: The *It's Yours!* space you curated is dedicated to the so-called "Benin Bronzes", which were looted from the palace of the Kingdom of Benin by British soldiers in 1897 as part of a punitive expedition. The British took them to London, where, a few months after the looting, the Rautenstrauch family bought the first Benin artworks. They were one of the first collections at the Rautenstrauch-Joest Museum and are thus crucial to its history. What is your personal connection to the Benin Kingdom and the looted artworks?

Peju Layiwola: I grew up in this wonderful city, Benin City. It is in the south of Nigeria. Benin City was the capital of the old Mid-Western region of Nigeria and is currently the capital of Edo State. It is not to be confused with the country of Benin, the former Kingdom of Dahomey.

Snoep: Everyone gets that wrong, don't they?
Layiwola: Always.
Snoep: It really is confusing, though!

Layiwola: It certainly is. The former Kingdom of Dahomey is to the west of Nigeria in Francophone Africa; it gave rise to the Republic of Benin, a neighbouring country. I hope our listeners and readers will now be able to keep them apart. Benin in Nigeria is a city of art and culture. The whole of Benin seems to me like an artist's studio; it's full of galleries and other art spaces. As a young girl, I often watched the carvers working with ebony, the brass casters remodelling their houses, turning their properties into foundries. Like many other artists who grew up in this city, I remain inspired by the performances, street processions, festivals, beautiful dances and songs. And also by the colourful and truly regal robes of the king, his courtiers and chiefs, the women's regalia and hairstyles. This piqued my interest in the rich cultural heritage of the Edo people of Benin City. I studied fine art at the University of Benin, specialising in metalsmithing and metal casting. I had the rare privilege of working

Ibadan, Nigeria & Cologne, Germany 26/02/2021

closely with some of these new traditional artists. Moreover, my mother is Princess Elizabeth Olowu, daughter of His Royal Majesty Oba Akenzua II. She is also an artist – and was the first woman to cast bronze in Benin City. She was very interested in her cultural heritage and told stories about her lineage. **So when I was growing up, the story of the plunder of Benin was very present: at home, on the street, at school, in public.** Joseph Nevadomsky described the 1897 event as a "terminus ad quem". It was a defining moment in the history of Benin: ultimately, everything comes back to that event. I have a personal connection to the royal family of Benin through my mother, but others, too, are reacting to the violence of 1897: artists and activists, and, more recently, museum curators, academics, and scholars from all over the world. At university, our teachers wanted us to draw from the rich trove of Benin art. Early on, my work referenced its iconography, but the crucial moment came in 2003, when I was invited to participate in a research project by the Franco-German anthropologist Bernard Müller. The project engaged with stories about looting and what the loss of African objects meant to the people and communities they originally came from. My task was to conduct surveys and work with the bronze casters from Igun Street in Benin City. In order to learn about the works of their predecessors, most of these artists were reduced to looking at catalogues, pictures, postcards, and publications from the West. They had no other access to the sculptures created by their ancestors. This is really a shame!

Snoep: How have you responded to this in your work?

Layiwola: My first solo exhibition in Nigeria – in Lagos and Ibadan in 2010 – was called *Benin 1897.com: Art and the Restitution Question*. I wanted to confront the public with all these open questions: the ownership of these objects, copyright and reproduction rights, how these objects are exhibited in Western museums, and who benefits from the entrance fees. I mean, all this is happening at the expense of the Nigerian government, at the expense of the royal family in Benin. And I'm not just saying this because I'm connected to the royal family through my mother. Above all, I am interested in how this history is presented as an artist and art historian – and I want to change its representation. For instance, when the catalogue for my exhibition was published, we focused on texts by African scholars and other African voices. We wanted to respond to the descendants of the colonisers, to those who brought us into this situation.

Snoep: What was it like for you to physically come into contact with artworks from Benin in European museums for the first time?

Layiwola: I think the first time was at the *Benin – Kings and Rituals exhibition* in Vienna in 2007. I had mixed feelings. About 320 works were on display from various Western museums that had held these objects for decades. In addition, there were works in possession of the royal family of Benin made available by them. **You look at these artefacts and, on the one hand, you feel nostalgia, a deep sense of loss. It is overwhelming that these things belong to you and yet you don't have them. You have no access to them, no control over them, you know?** And at the same time, you are struck by their beauty and depth. My only other experience was at the British Museum in London in 2009. I was preparing my exhibition for the following year there – and I left the museum utterly dejected. It was very painful to see these looted objects outside their place of origin. When I see these artworks in display cases, it creates distance – I have no access, I can't touch them. Seeing them in storage feels completely different. In 2015 or thereabouts, at the Museum of Ethnology in Dresden, I could hold these objects in my hand and feel them. Despite all the mixed emotions, I'm excited about what you are doing here at the RJM, and I'm really looking forward to seeing your huge collection. I have the entire list and photos of the works. For me, this is a paradigm shift.

Snoep: In what way?

Layiwola: As recently as 2010, when I had my solo show, it was difficult to openly discuss the role of institutions, never mind organising an exhibition focusing exclusively on the return of the artworks from Benin. But now museum curators and directors are opening up their collections. We keep pointing out that the exact number of objects taken from Benin is not known. Some say 1,000, others 3,000, 4,000. It's a shame that to this day (February 26, 2021) we have no accurate record of what the museum archives really contain. To have access to the images, the numbers, the provenance of the objects at the RJM and to be able to work with them is very satisfying for me. And I'm really looking forward to seeing the objects in the physical space, in my space. This approach serves as an inspiration for all museum directors to be transparent, to open up their collections, and to deal with these objects as if they had a soul. Because they do. The RJM project shows that there are different sides to the story. It represents a sincere effort to create a multivocal platform for talking about these works.

Snoep: Yes, as museum workers, we must learn to consider these aspects: the soul of the objects, but also how display cases can symbolise violence. As far as restitution is concerned, what is the status quo in the struggle for the return of the "Benin Bronzes"? Just a few weeks ago – and a few days before the opening of the Humboldt Forum in Berlin in mid-December 2020 – the Nigerian ambassador submitted another restitution request to Germany.

Layiwola: He has written to those in charge at the Humboldt Forum, demanding to bring the objects back to Benin. That is a step in the right direction. **But as with many official requests from Nigerian cultural institutions, one can predict that it will be ignored. The list of requests for the return of Benin objects is long. As early as 1935, His Royal Majesty Akenzua II asked for the return of thrones that were kept at the Ethnological Museum in Berlin – they are still there. Or perhaps they have now moved to the Humboldt Forum. At the time, it took two years for plastic replicas to be made – and the king was asked to pay for the transport of these copies to Benin City.** Now that is really despicable behaviour. In 1976, Nigeria asked the British Museum in London to loan a carved ivory mask of Queen Idia for the FESTAC festival in Lagos: when the British soldiers ransacked the palace in 1897, they stole valuable objects from the king's bedchamber, including a mask of Queen Idia, the mother of Oba Esigie who ruled in the sixteenth century. The British government refused to return the mask, even on loan. On the list of requests for restitution is also one by Prince Edun Akenzua – the Enogie[3] of Obazuwa – who presented Benin's case to the British Parliament in March 2000. In 2008, Prince Adetokunbo Kayode, then Nigerian Minister of Culture, travelled to Berlin to deliver the "Berlin Plea" for the return of the Benin objects. In 2007, Tunde Babawale, director of the Centre for Black African Arts and Civilization, wrote to the British Museum demanding the return of the Benin objects. But there was no reply. There were requests from the Oba of Benin, His Royal Majesty Oba Erediauwa, as well as the king's brothers, to institutions holding looted art from Benin: nothing has been done so far; it is really shameful. We are being treated shabbily. It is unlikely that the request submitted by the Nigerian ambassador to Germany will be fulfilled. My latest update is that Berlin is now proposing a different form of restitution: the objects that were looted from Benin City are now to be loaned to us, the owners.

3   a title, sometimes translated as "duke"

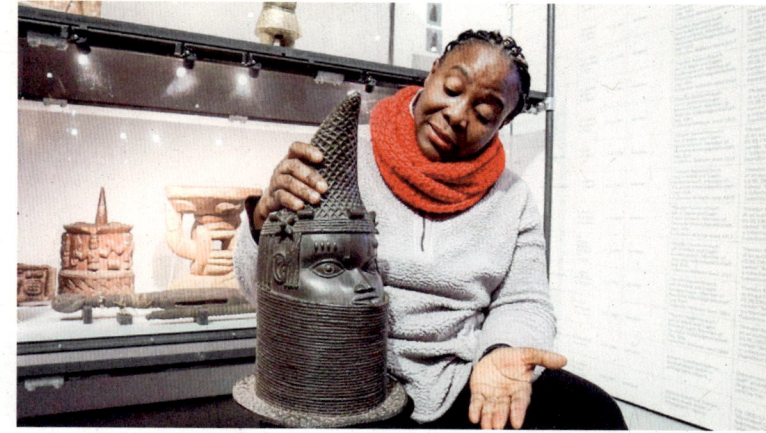

Peju Layiwola in the *It's Yours!* space she curated, with a Benin memorial head on her lap.

> Children, women and men were killed. The king's palace was burned down; the king, the supreme ruler, was put on trial and exiled, where he died in 1914. People were robbed of their art; museums then kept this art for over a century. It is one of the best-documented cases of looting in Africa. And now these works are to be returned »temporarily« – on loan. This is an insult to all Africans. It is unacceptable.

Snoep: The Benin artworks have become the icons of the restitution debate in Europe. But how is the debate proceeding in Nigeria?

Layiwola: I showed my exhibition *Benin1897.com* at the universities in Lagos and Ibadan over a lengthy period in 2010. It was crucial for me to get people engaged with this contested patrimony and the question of restitution. We achieved that. I am glad that discussions about the repatriation of looted colonial property are continuing all over the world. But it is an ethical problem that Europe must solve. A problem created by your ancestors. That is why the discussions are taking place mainly in Europe. But of course, all the petitions and demands for restitution, the Benin Action Plan, the Benin Dialogue Group – it is all documented in the Nigerian media, and the discussions are ongoing on our side as well.

Snoep: Could you elaborate on your view of the current proposal being considered by the Benin Dialogue Group involving loaning some of the Benin artworks from European museums to Nigeria?

4 Edo Museum of West African Art in Benin City

Layiwola: We should refrain from a loan as proposed by the Benin Dialogue Group. Instead of pushing for speed, I think it is crucial that the works come back in the right context, that they are not only taken to Nigeria in order to return to Europe. Especially since it's also a business matter, as becomes apparent with the Humboldt Forum: more visitors will come to Berlin to see these objects, which means more money. This is what the title of my 2010 exhibition refers to: ".com" stands for "commercial". I'm delighted that the Royal Museum[4] is finally being built. And I think that the choice of David Adjaye as architect is great. He built the Smithsonian Museum of African American History and Culture in Washington, DC, a phenomenal building. He will certainly succeed in incorporating Edo cultural heritage. For instance, he's using laterite earth, which Benin is known for; it is used in the beautiful walls of the palace and the furniture – all this comes together in his architecture. It is crucial to preserve this heritage for future generations.

Snoep: The *RESIST!* exhibition also features four *It's Yours!* spaces, where we gave free range to external curators. The Namibian politicians Esther Utjiua Muinjangue and Ida Hoffmann titled their room *Not About Us Without Us*. What does this slogan mean to you?

Layiwola: It reminds me of a Yoruba proverb: »**You can't shave a man's head if he's not there.**« It means that we must be consulted. Any decision that affects our heritage, our lives, must include us. We don't want to be merely spoken to; we want to be part of a dialogue. We want to tell our stories. The RJM enables us to do that: in these independent spaces, we can present our own ideas, stories, and perspectives.

Snoep: Which Benin artworks from the museum's collection mean the most to you?

Layiwola: All the works speak to me. They represent the history of fragmentation: the way the artefacts were ripped out of the sacred shrines and stacked in the palace courtyards like commodities shows the utter disrespect for art as well as the religious and cultural significance of these objects for our people. Thus, any Benin collection – not just the one at the RJM, but anywhere in Europe or the Americas – is incomplete. They are fragmented representations of our cultural heritage. But there are some objects that I really contemplate every time – the bells. I have a personal relationship with them: my mother, Princess Elizabeth Olowu, told me a story about her childhood in the palace in Benin. Each new king built a shrine in honour of his deceased predecessor, a shrine with beautiful tusks, the staffs of office, the "Ukhurhe" – the sacred staff, and the bells, too. My mother and her siblings liked to play with them. This made the king rather nervous. He'd tell the children, "No, no, no, put the bells down!" – for him, their sound was the call to prayer. **The shrines were not only religious sites but also places of remembrance. They were the archives of the palace, which documented the cultural history of the people.**

Another object in your collection that means a lot to me is the key. It has a strong symbolic power for me because it tells my own story. At the beginning of the Nigerian civil war, the king called his children back to the palace from all over Nigeria so that they would be safe. My mother was heavily pregnant and when she arrived with my grandmother, they found themselves standing in front of the doors of the harem that led to the king's quarters – great big wooden doors with many hinges, latches, and locks. That's when my mother went into labour. My grandmother banged the metal door knocker until the king came out. When the sword bearers finally opened the heavy door, I was born in the entrance of the palace. The king said, »I think she brought her own name with her« – my real first name is Peju, but he used to call me Uroga, which means »born at the entrance of the palace«.

Snoep: Thank you for this story! A key to a very heavy door – that fits with the idea of opening the doors of our museum. When you designed the *It's Yours!* space for *RESIST!*, you were in the USA, experiencing the Black Lives Matter movement first hand. Is there a connection for you between that movement and the restitution debate?

Layiwola: Certainly: both are directed against oppression of all kinds, slavery, colonialism, racism. In Washington, DC, I photographed many protest posters. Reparations were at the top of the agenda; there was a call for the return of the Benin objects and other works from different parts of the world. We also saw statues being toppled. In this way, people are tearing down the violent colonial structures that are still present in public spaces and in museums, too.

Snoep: You invited other Nigerian artists to your *It's Yours!* space. Who did you choose – and why?

Layiwola: Rather than just exhibiting my own work, I wanted to give a platform to artists who are less visible, so that the voices for restitution add up. Alao Luqman combines different techniques in his work; for example, he has mastered repoussé, a framing technique in which shapes are beaten out of flat sheets of metal. Christie Akumabor, a poet and doctor in the UK, has written a poem about being inspired by her origins, the beauty of Benin, the bronze works. Jimoh Ganiyu's cartoons were a response to my 2010 exhibition *Benin 1897.com*, and Osaze Amadasun has replaced English kings and queens on playing cards with kings and queens from Benin, thus commenting on Benin as a playground for colonial powers. Nwakuso Edozien is an architect: using beautiful, very intricate lines and illustrations, her work combines past, present, and future.

Snoep: And your own work?

Layiwola: One of my works in the space is titled *Dialoguing Sarahs*: it frames the history of Benin in a larger context, showing how other regions of Africa were also plundered. The title refers to the story of Sarah Baartman and thus to the genocide of the Ovaherero and Nama people. My work is a demand for an apology and for the skulls of their ancestors to be returned. Another looting I mention took place during and after the Battle of Magdala, when thousands of Ethiopian artefacts were stolen; it is said that the British needed 15 elephants and 200 mules to cart away the Ethiopian treasures. A more recent work I'm showing considers fabric culture as a response to colonialism. Creating patterns with wax is also an act of resistance: a surface that is covered with wax does not allow dye to penetrate.

Opportunities like *RESIST!* are crucial. It is vital that decision-makers like you, who are trapped in hegemonic spaces, create a platform to come to terms with the evils of the past.

I MISS YOU: About Missing, Giving Back and Remembering

Cologne, Germany **since 29/04/2022**

The aim of the RJM series *I MISS YOU: About Missing, Giving Back and Remembering*, which was initiated in 2022, was to create a space in the permanent exhibition that highlights objects from the RJM's collection that are under scrutiny because of their origins: whether because there is an official restitution claim for them, because they have already been restituted, or because it is certain that they originate from a context of colonial injustice. After the *RESIST!* exhibition ended on January 9, 2022, we decided not to put these works back into storage, because they needed to remain accessible to visitors in their entirety until a possible transfer of ownership and their physical return to Nigeria. We started *I MISS YOU* together with Peju Layiwola by presenting the 92 court artworks in a new setting. This new installation is not a historical survey exhibition about the Kingdom of Benin, but rather a place for debate, sharing and mourning, as well as a collaboration with Nigerian experts and the local Nigerian diaspora so that they can be an active part of this debate.

The presentation of the Benin court artworks, which opened on April 29, 2022, has become historically obsolete: on December 15, 2022, in front of the gallery where all of the Benin works were exhibited, the agreement for the transfer of ownership of these 92 works to the Republic of Nigeria was signed by Mayor Henriette Reker and Abba Isa Tijani, Director General of the National Commission for Museums and Monuments of Nigeria. It was also agreed that three works would return to Nigeria in the days after the agreement, followed by the gradual return of a further 52 works from 2023 onwards, and that 37 of the works would remain at the RJM on loan until 2033.

The remaining Benin artworks on view at the RJM are now in a state of transit, awaiting their return, and are on loan from Nigeria to the city of Cologne. The form in which these works will be shown in the museum in the future is to be discussed with representatives of the current owners in Nigeria.

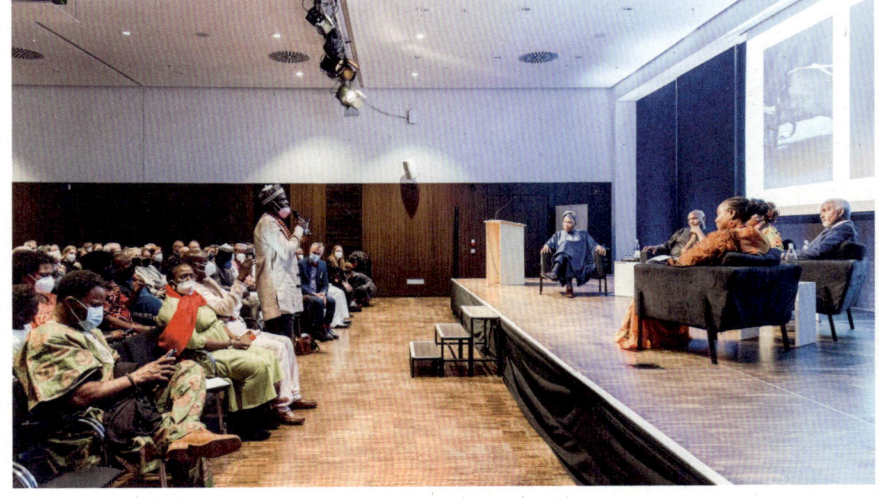

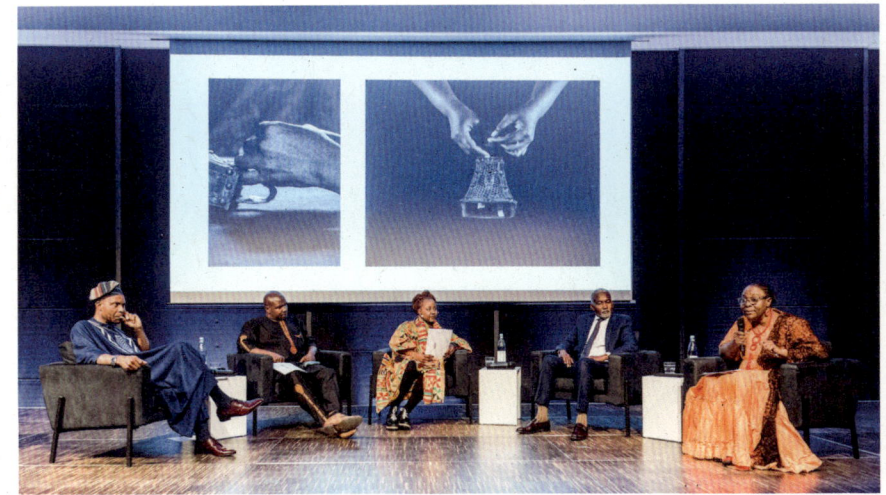

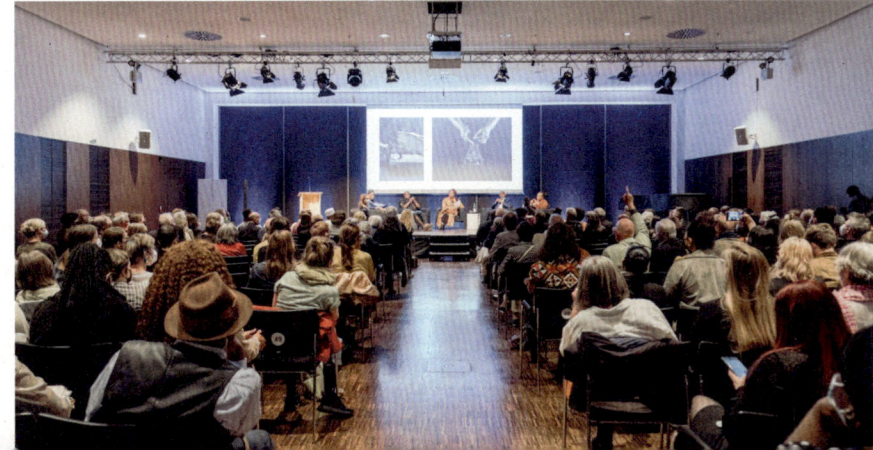

At the opening of the exhibition *I MISS YOU* on 29/04/2022. With contributions from Andreas Wolter, Deputy Mayor of the City of Cologne; Nanette Snoep, Director of the RJM; Yusuf Maitama Tuggar, Ambassador of the Republic of Nigeria.

Centre photograph, from left to right: Eli Abeke, Chairman of Bündnis14 Afrika e.V., Cologne, Samuel Egharevba, Chairman of Edo United Cologne; Rahab Njeri, Historian and Desk Officer for Gender Equality and Diversity, University of Cologne; Yussuf Maitama Tuggar, Nigerian Ambassador to the Federal Republic of Germany; Peju Layiwola, *It's Yours!* Curator for *RESIST!* and Co-curator of the exhibition *I MISS YOU: About Missing, Giving Back and Remembering*.

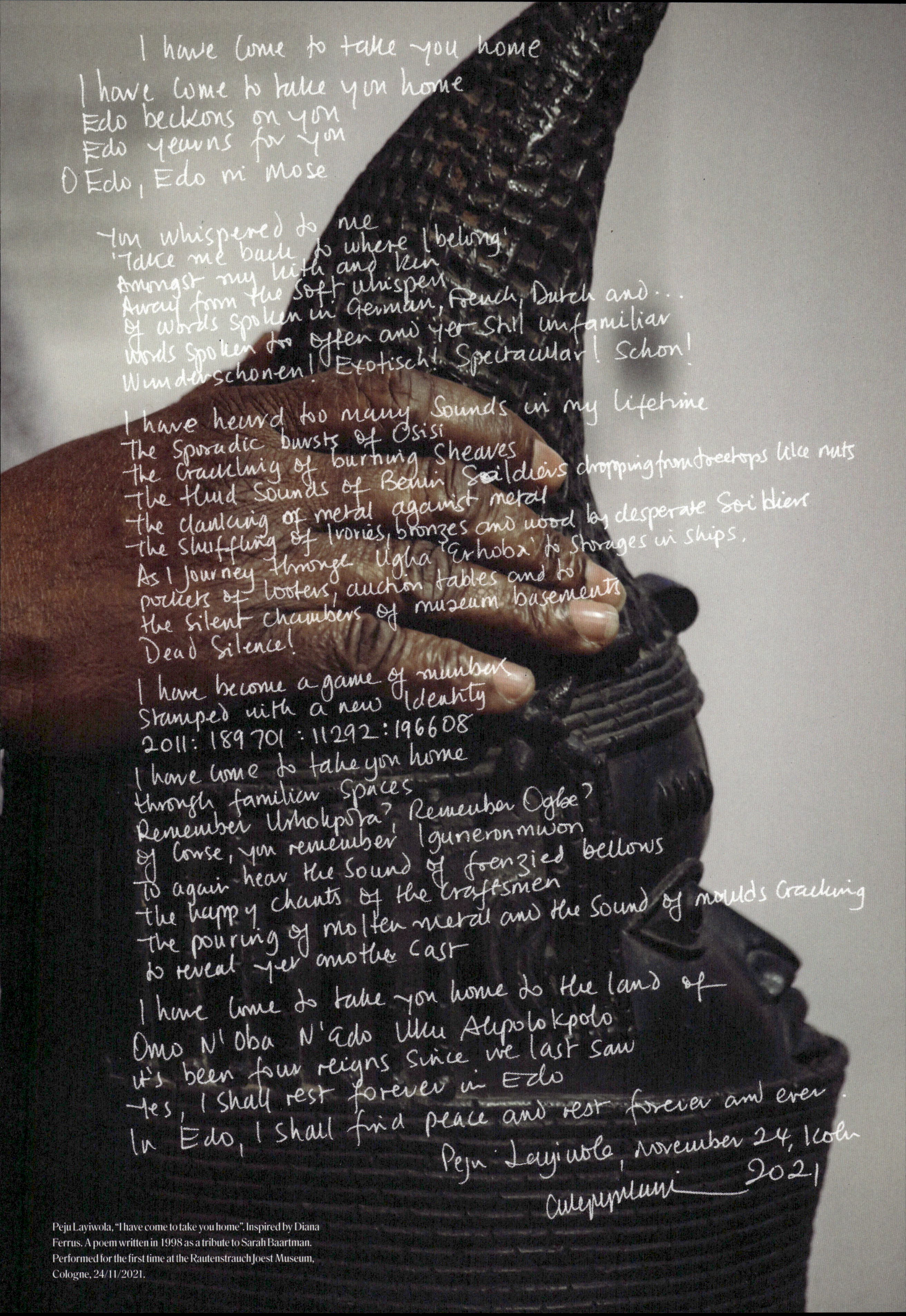

I have come to take you home
I have come to take you home
Edo beckons on you
Edo yearns for you
O Edo, Edo mi mose

You whispered to me
'Take me back to where I belong'
Amongst my kith and kin
Away from the soft whispers
Of words spoken in German, French, Dutch and...
Words spoken too often and yet still unfamiliar
Wunderschönen! Exotisch! Spectacular! Schön!

I have heard too many sounds in my lifetime
The sporadic bursts of Osisi
The crackling of burning sheaves
The thud sounds of Benin Soldiers dropping from treetops like nuts
The clanking of metal against metal
The shuffling of ivories, bronzes and wood by desperate Soldiers
As I journey through Ugha 'Erhoba' to storages in ships,
pockets of looters, auction tables and to
the silent chambers of museum basements
Dead Silence!

I have become a game of number
Stamped with a new identity
2011: 189 701 : 11292 : 196608
I have come to take you home
through familiar spaces
Remember Urhokpora? Remember Ogbe?
Of course, you remember Iguneronmwon
To again hear the sound of frenzied bellows
the happy chants of the craftsmen
the pouring of molten metal and the sound of moulds cracking
to reveal yet another cast

I have come to take you home to the land of
Omo N'Oba N'edo Uku Akpolokpolo
It's been four reigns since we last saw
Yes, I shall rest forever in Edo
In Edo, I shall find peace and rest forever and ever.

Peju Layiwola, November 24, Koln
2021

Peju Layiwola, "I have come to take you home". Inspired by Diana Ferrus. A poem written in 1998 as a tribute to Sarah Baartman. Performed for the first time at the Rautenstrauch Joest Museum, Cologne, 24/11/2021.

Back to Benin-City!
Agreement of the Transfer of Ownership of 92 Benin Court Artworks

Agreement on the Return of Benin Bronzes

between

Stadt Koeln

and

The Federal Republic of Nigeria

The following Agreement is concluded between

The Stadt Koeln (City of Cologne) represented by the Mayor of the City of Cologne, Mrs. **Henriette Reker**, Historisches Rathaus, 50667 Cologne, Germany

(hereinafter referred to as the City of Cologne)

and

The **Federal Republic of Nigeria**, acting through the Director General, National Commission for Museums and Monuments, Professor Abba Isa Tijani, Head of Service Building, 1st Floor, Block C, Shehu Shagari Way, Abuja, Nigeria

(hereinafter referred to as Nigeria),

The two sides hereinafter being collectively referred to as the "Parties":

Preamble

Convinced that the return of the Benin Bronzes to Nigeria is an important element of addressing the colonial past and strengthening the future cooperation between German museums and the relevant stakeholders in Nigeria,

Acknowledging the importance of the Benin Bronzes to the people of Nigeria, particularly for the Edo people, and their universal importance for humankind,

Considering that German museums and institutions hold significant collections of Benin Bronzes looted from the former Kingdom of Benin after its colonial occupation and acquired in the aftermath mainly through colonial trading networks,

Underlining the importance of sharing related documentation such as reports, archive material, inventories, historical loan reports and photographs,

Considering the need to continue museum exchanges and to establish future cooperation, including contemporary and future productions of works of art,

Reaffirming the Joint Declaration on the Return of Benin Bronzes and Bilateral Museum Cooperation, signed on 01.07.2022,

Recalling the Report of the German-Nigerian Bi-National Commission, signed on 3 November 2021 as well as the Bilateral Agreement between both governments on Cultural Cooperation, signed on 17 December 1999,

Emphasising the spirit of the German Framework Principle for dealing with collections from colonial contexts adopted on 13 March 2019 and the Statement on the handling of the Benin Bronzes in German museums and institutions adopted on 29 April 2021,

Noting that this Agreement consists of two parts, the first part containing the transfer of ownership and return (I.) and the second part containing provisions on transit and loan covering Benin Bronzes (II.).

The parties agree as follows:

I. Transfer of ownership

1. Subject Matter

(1) The City of Cologne and Nigeria agree that the ownership of all Benin Bronzes listed in the Appendices 1, 2 and 3 is transferred to Nigeria. In this Agreement, the expression "Benin Bronzes" encompasses not only bronzes but all artefacts from Benin, i.e. also those made of e.g. wood, ivory, coral and iron, looted from the former Kingdom of Benin after its colonial occupation and acquired in the aftermath mainly through colonial trading networks.

(2) The transfer of ownership is unconditional. In particular, no payment is required for the transfer of title.

(3) Nigeria declares that it accepts the objects in their current physical condition and state of preservation.

2. Performance

Title to the objects passes from the City of Cologne to Nigeria upon the signing of this Agreement. From this time, the museum will hold the objects in accordance with part II of this Agreement.

3. Liability Clauses

(1) In consideration of the City of Cologne's transfer of ownership of the objects to Nigeria, Nigeria hereby releases, acquits and forever discharges the City of Cologne and the Federal Republic of Germany from any and all liability for all claims, demands, damages, actions, causes of action, or suits at law or in equity, of whatsoever kind or nature, which Nigeria had, has or may in the future have arising from or relating to the City of Cologne's possession of the objects prior to the date of this Agreement and the return of the objects to Nigeria pursuant to this Agreement.

(2) In addition, Nigeria shall not hold the City of Cologne and the Federal Republic of Germany liable for any third party claims involving the objects, especially claims based on ownership or possession as well as corresponding claims for damages.

II. Transit and Loan

1. Subject Matter

(1) Upon the passing of title to the objects, Nigeria shall grant the City of Cologne the possession and use of the objects listed in Appendix 1 (objects to be returned to Nigeria in the short term) and Appendix 2 (objects which will remain on loan) free of charge.

(2) The objects listed in Appendix 1 of the Agreement shall remain in the possession of the City of Cologne only until the return to Nigeria can be effected. Both parties agree that three of these objects, listed in Appendix 3, shall be physically returned to Nigeria before the end of 2022.

(3) The Parties have reached an Agreement that the objects listed in Appendix 2 shall remain on loan with the City of Cologne for the duration of 10 years. The parties aim to collaborate on the curation of the presentation of these examples of Benin court art in the museum.

2. Loan Conditions

(1) The City of Cologne will afford to the objects on loan the same care as to its own collections in accordance with international museum standards and will make every effort to safeguard them. Damage arising during the term of the loan will be repaired by the City of Cologne within the scope of what is possible in terms of restoration. The City of Cologne shall not be liable for damage caused by force majeure.

(2) The City of Cologne will make the loaned objects accessible to the public under the same conditions that apply to its own collections. The Parties aim to liaise on the presentation of the works.

(3) The Parties will share with each other any results of research conducted with reference to the objects on loan. The Parties aim to work together on researching the objects.

(4) The City of Cologne may make individual objects available to other public institutions as sub-loans. The City of Cologne will ensure that the same conditions that apply to this loan also apply to the sub-loan. In each case, Nigeria must be informed of the loan.

(5) The City of Cologne may produce images and other reproductions of the objects and make use of these images and other reproductions non-commercially in the same way that it makes use of images of its own collections, i.e. for purposes of education, research, promoting exhibitions, exhibition catalogues etc. free of charge. Insofar as images of the objects already exist, it may continue to use these images in the same way. On request, the City of Cologne will make images of the objects that it has produced available to Nigeria free of charge.

(6) The City of Cologne should disclose digital assets and share them. They shall share with the National Commission for Museums and Monuments all profits derived from these if commercially used.

(7) Whenever the objects are displayed or published, the City of Cologne shall use the following credit line:

German: Diese Ausstellung zeigt Leihgaben der National Commission for Museums and Monuments Nigeria.

English: This exhibition displays loans from the National Commission for Museums and Monuments Nigeria.

3. Duration and Termination

(1) The parties shall begin immediately to organise the return of the objects listed in Appendix 1 to Nigeria.

(2) For the purposes of the timely physical return of the objects listed in Appendix 1, Nigeria will inform the City of Cologne at its convenience when it is ready to receive the objects back to Nigeria or whether they will be included in a travelling exhibition. From the date of this notification, the Parties will work diligently together to ensure the timely and efficient return of the objects.

(3) The loan period for the objects that remain on loan to the City of Cologne (Appendix 2) shall be ten years from the signing of this agreement. Before the expiration of this term, the loan may only be terminated for good cause. The loan is automatically renewed for successive periods of ten years unless one of the Parties terminates the loan by giving written notice of at least twelve months prior to the end of the period.

(4) Both Parties may terminate the loan for good cause at any time. For the purposes of this Agreement, good cause shall include:

- Any material breach of the obligations imposed in this Agreement which is not remedied within four weeks upon notification.

- The application for or opening of insolvency proceedings against the City of Cologne.

(5) The termination of a loan concerning one or more individual objects will not affect the loan agreement as a whole. Notice of termination must be given in writing.

III. Final Provisions

(1) This Agreement is governed by German law. All disputes arising out of or relating to this Agreement, or in breach thereof, shall be determined by arbitration administered by the ICOM-WIPO Art and Cultural Heritage Mediation.

(2) No collateral oral agreements to this Agreement have been made. Any amendments or additions to this Agreement must be made in writing in order to be valid. This also applies to any renunciation of the written form.

(3) The City of Cologne shall bear the cost of packing and shipping the objects to a location within Nigeria indicated by Nigeria. The transfer of risk takes place when the objects are handed over to the transport company at the seat of the City of Cologne. The City of Cologne shall not be liable for loss or damage to the objects incurred during transportation. Nigeria confirms that the entry of the objects into Nigeria shall not be liable to customs duty. In the case that (Nigeria) decides that the objects should not be transported directly to Nigeria but to another location (e.g. travelling exhibitions), the City of Cologne shall not bear the cost of packing and shipping unless the City of Cologne is part of the travelling exhibition arrangement.

(4) If any provision of this Agreement is invalid, the validity of the remaining provisions shall remain unaffected. The Parties undertake to replace the invalid provision with valid wording

Cologne, Germany **15/12/2022**
Abuja, Nigeria **20/12/2022**

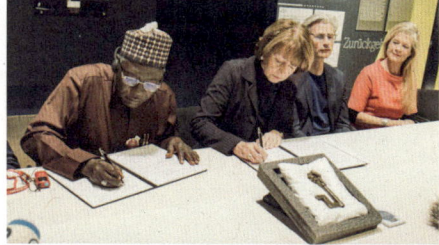
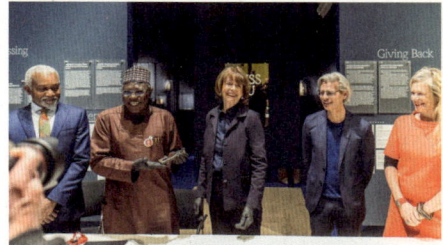
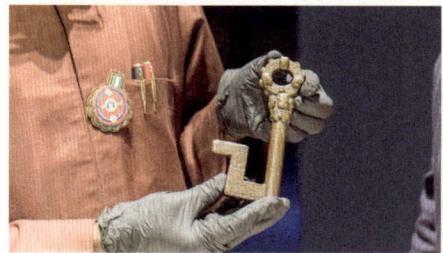
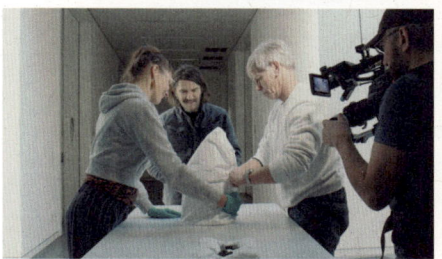
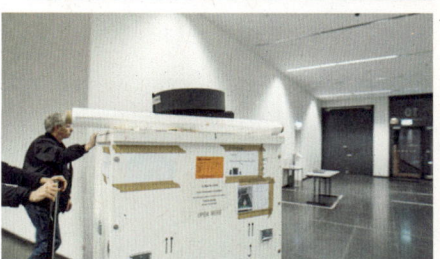
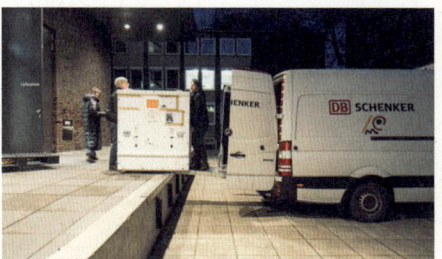
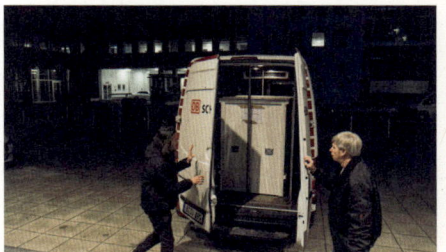
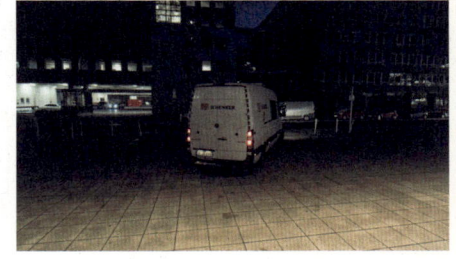

that best reflects the object and purpose of the invalid provision. The same applies to any omissions in the Agreement.

(5) The Appendices 1-3 constitute an integral part of this Agreement.

Abuja, date   Cologne, date

Prof. Abba Isa Tijani   Frau Henriette Reker
Director-General   Mayor of the City of Cologne
National Commission for Museums and   Stadt Koeln
Monuments

Appendix 1
Objects to be returned according to sections II, 3 (1) and (2)

Appendix 2
Objects which will remain on loan to Rautenstrauch-Joest-Museum according to sections II, 3 (3)

Appendix 3
Objects which shall be physically returned to Nigeria before the end of 2022 according to section II, 1 (2)

---

(2) Es wurden keine mündlichen Nebenabreden zu dieser Vereinbarung getroffen. Alle Änderungen oder Ergänzungen dieser Vereinbarung bedürfen der Schriftform, um gültig zu sein. Dies gilt auch für jeglichen Verzicht auf das Schriftformerfordernis.

(3) Die Stadt Köln trägt die Kosten für Verpackung und Versand der Objekte an einen Ort innerhalb Nigerias, der von Nigeria genannt wird. Der Gefahrenübergang erfolgt mit der Übergabe der Objekte an das Transportunternehmen am Sitz der Stadt Köln. Die Stadt Köln haftet nicht für Verluste oder Schäden an den Objekten, die während des Transports entstehen. Nigeria bestätigt, dass die Einfuhr der Objekte nach Nigeria nicht zollpflichtig ist. Für den Fall, dass (Nigeria) beschließt, dass die Objekte nicht direkt nach Nigeria transportiert werden sollen, sondern an einen anderen Ort (z. B. Wanderausstellungen), trägt die Stadt Köln nicht die Kosten für die Verpackung und den Versand, es sei denn, die Stadt Köln ist Teil des Arrangements der Wanderausstellung.

(4) Wenn eine der Bestimmungen dieser Vereinbarung ungültig ist, bleibt die Gültigkeit der übrigen Bestimmungen davon unberührt. Die Parteien verpflichten sich, die ungültige Bestimmung durch einen gültigen Wortlaut zu ersetzen, der den Gegenstand und den Zweck der ungültigen Bestimmungen am besten wiedergibt. Das Gleiche gilt für alle Auslassungen in der Vereinbarung.

(5) Die Anhänge 1-3 stellen einen integralen Bestandteil dieser Vereinbarung dar.

Abuja, Datum 15th December 2022   Köln, Datum 15.12.2022

Prof. Abba Isa Tijani   Frau Henriette Reker
Generaldirektor   Oberbürgermeisterin der Stadt Köln
National Commission for Museums and   Stadt Köln
Monuments

Anhang 1
Objekte, die gemäß Abschnitt II Paragraf 3 Absatz (1) und (2) zurückgegeben werden müssen

Anhang 2
Objekte, die gemäß Abschnitt II Paragraf 3 Absatz (3) als Leihgabe beim Rautenstrauch-Joest-Museum verbleiben

Anhang 3
Objekte, die gemäß Abschnitt II Paragraf 1 Absatz (2) vor Ende 2022 physisch an Nigeria zurückgegeben werden

Since only the German agreement was signed, the last page (no. 5) is shown here in both languages.

On December 8, 2022, Cologne City Council decided to transfer ownership of 92 court artworks from the Kingdom of Benin to the Federal Republic of Nigeria. The transfer of ownership agreement was signed at the RJM on December 15, 2022 and three works were returned promptly: an altar stool, a memorial head, and a key.

Timeline
of the Restitution of the Benin Court Artworks at the RJM

February 1897
Benin massacre. Thousands of looted works from the Benin Royal Palace are brought to London by British soldiers and sold worldwide. More than 1,300 works end up in German museum collections.

1914
Oba Ovonramwen Nogbaisi dies in exile.

1935
First restitution claims submitted to Great Britain and Germany by Oba Akenzua II (1899–1978), including for a throne stool in the Museum of Ethnology in Berlin. The museum refuses both the restitution and the resale. Oba Akenzua II receives a replica instead, which he must pay for himself.

1938
Return of royal coral insignia to the Benin Kingdom by the son of a military man involved in the 1897 massacre. They are still used in Oba ceremonies today.

1949–53
After unsuccessful restitution claims by Oba Akenzua II against the British Museum, the museum sells 10 duplicates of 200 relief plates to the National Museum in Lagos.

1960
Nigeria gains independence.

1965
Worldwide public call for the general restitution of cultural property to Africa by the pan-African magazine *Bingo*.

1970
UNESCO adopts the "Convention on the Means of Prohibiting and Preventing the Illicit Import, Export and Transfer of Ownership of Cultural Property".

1971
Premiere of *You Hide Me* by the Ghanaian director Nii Kwate Owoo. The documentary shows the British Museum's repositories and ends with the demand that the Benin artworks should be restituted.

1973
The new National Museum in Benin City opens with approximately 100 objects, including copies. The resolution submitted to the International Council of Museums (ICOM) in Grenoble/France by a Nigerian delegation calling for donations to the new museum remains unanswered.

1974
For the Second World Black and African Festival of Arts and Culture (FESTAC), scheduled to take place in Lagos in 1977, the planning committee submits its first loan request for the ivory mask of Queen Idia to the British Foreign Office and the British Museum.

1977
The British Museum rejects the loan request. The mask of Queen Idia becomes the political symbol of the restitution claims and the FESTAC logo.

2002
Prince Edun Akenzua, successor to Oba Akenzua II, demands the restitution of the "Benin Bronzes" from the British Parliament.

2010
Foundation of the Benin Dialogue Group, in which museums from Germany, Great Britain, the Netherlands, Austria, and Sweden meet with Nigerian partners and representatives of the royal court of Benin to jointly develop new perspectives on dealing with the Benin artworks.

2014
Adrian Mark Walker returns a privately owned Benin artwork to the royal household that was taken by his grandfather, Captain Herbert Sutherland Walker, during the 1897 massacre at the palace.

2015
The student Chumani Maxwele protests against the bronze statue of Cecil Rhodes – one of the most prominent representatives of British colonial power and a proponent of apartheid ideas – situated on the University of Cape Town campus. This leads to the Rhodes Must Fall movement (RMF), which results in the emergence of a broad movement at other universities in South Africa, the UK, and the USA, and eventually to the toppling of colonial monuments worldwide in the following years.

2017
Speech by French President Emmanuel Macron at the University of Ouagadougou in Burkina Faso announcing the restitution of looted African cultural treasures from French museums.

2018
Felwine Sarr and Bénédicte Savoy publish their report on the restitution of African cultural objects from French museums.

2018
The German Museums Association (DMB) publishes their first guidelines on "Dealing with Collections from Colonial Contexts".

2019
The Federal Government of Germany, the Federal States, and leading municipal organisations adopt the first key points on dealing with collections from colonial contexts.

August 2019
The RJM, with the fourth-largest collection of Benin court artworks in Germany, becomes a member of the Benin Dialogue Group.

2019
The German Minister of State for Culture, Monika Grütters, announces the possible restitution of Benin works in a newspaper interview.

Early December 2020
The Nigerian ambassador to Germany, Yusuf Maitama Tuggar, announces that the Nigerian government has officially demanded the restitution of the Benin Court Artworks from Berlin.

16/12/2020
In the context of the partial digital opening of the Humboldt Forum in Berlin, the critical debate intensifies, especially with regard to African artefacts.

29/01/2021
Launch of the digital programme for *RESIST! The Art of Resistance*, as the exhibition itself cannot be opened due to Covid restrictions.

March 2021
The University of Aberdeen and Jesus College, Cambridge each return a Benin work looted in 1897 to the royal court in Benin City. Other institutions announce restitutions, including the Smithsonian in Washington, DC and the Weltmuseum in Vienna.

01/04/2021
Opening of the exhibition *RESIST! The Art of Resistance*, where the 92 Benin artworks in the RJM collection are shown for the first time in their entirety.

April 2021
Online meeting between the Federal Commissioner for Culture and Media, the director of the Department of Culture and Communication at the Federal Foreign Office, and German museum experts, including the director of the RJM and local politicians responsible for culture: there is a reaffirmation of the fundamental willingness to return Benin works and an agreement to jointly develop concrete steps for the preparation of restitutions over the course of 2022.

23/04/2021
RESIST! Conversation: Discussion with Bénédicte Savoy about her new book, *Africa's Struggle for Its Art: History of a Postcolonial Defeat*.

29/04/2021
The German Minister of State for Culture, Monika Grütters, initiates an online discussion regarding the further handling of the "Benin Bronzes" held in German museums and institutions. In a joint declaration, the participants reaffirm their fundamental willingness to "substantially" return them

14/05/2021
International online discussion *Benin 1897–Cologne 2021* as part of *RESIST!*, with speakers from Nigeria, Great-Britain, South Africa, and Germany.

February 1897 – 20/12/2022

25/10/2021
Professor Abba Isa Tijani, Director General of the National Commission for Museums and Monuments in Nigeria, submits a restitution claim to the British Museum for the Benin works

Oktober 2021
Signing of a "Memorandum of Understanding" between the National Commission for Museums and Monuments of Nigeria and the Federal Foreign Office of the Federal Republic of Germany, declaring the "intention to transfer ownership of the Benin Bronzes".

29/04/2022
After the closure of the *RESIST!* exhibition, the 92 Benin artworks are exhibited in a new installation, *I MISS YOU: About Missing, Giving Back and Remembering*, co-curated by Peju Layiwola.

01/07/2022
A joint political declaration regarding the return of the Benin artworks is signed in Berlin by the Federal Republic of Germany and the Federal Republic of Nigeria. The RJM and Peju Layiwola are among the guests.

15/12/2022
Lord Mayor Henriette Reker and Professor Abba Isa Tijani, Director General of the National Commission for Museums and Monuments in Nigeria, sign an agreement at the RJM regarding the transfer of ownership of the RJM's Benin collection to the Federal Republic of Nigeria. This legally completes the transfer of ownership.

20/12/2022
German Foreign Minister Annalena Baerbock and Minister of State for Culture Claudia Roth hand over the first three Benin court artworks from Cologne to Abuja, Nigeria, as well as 22 additional Benin artworks from collections in Berlin, Leipzig, Dresden, Hamburg, and Stuttgart.

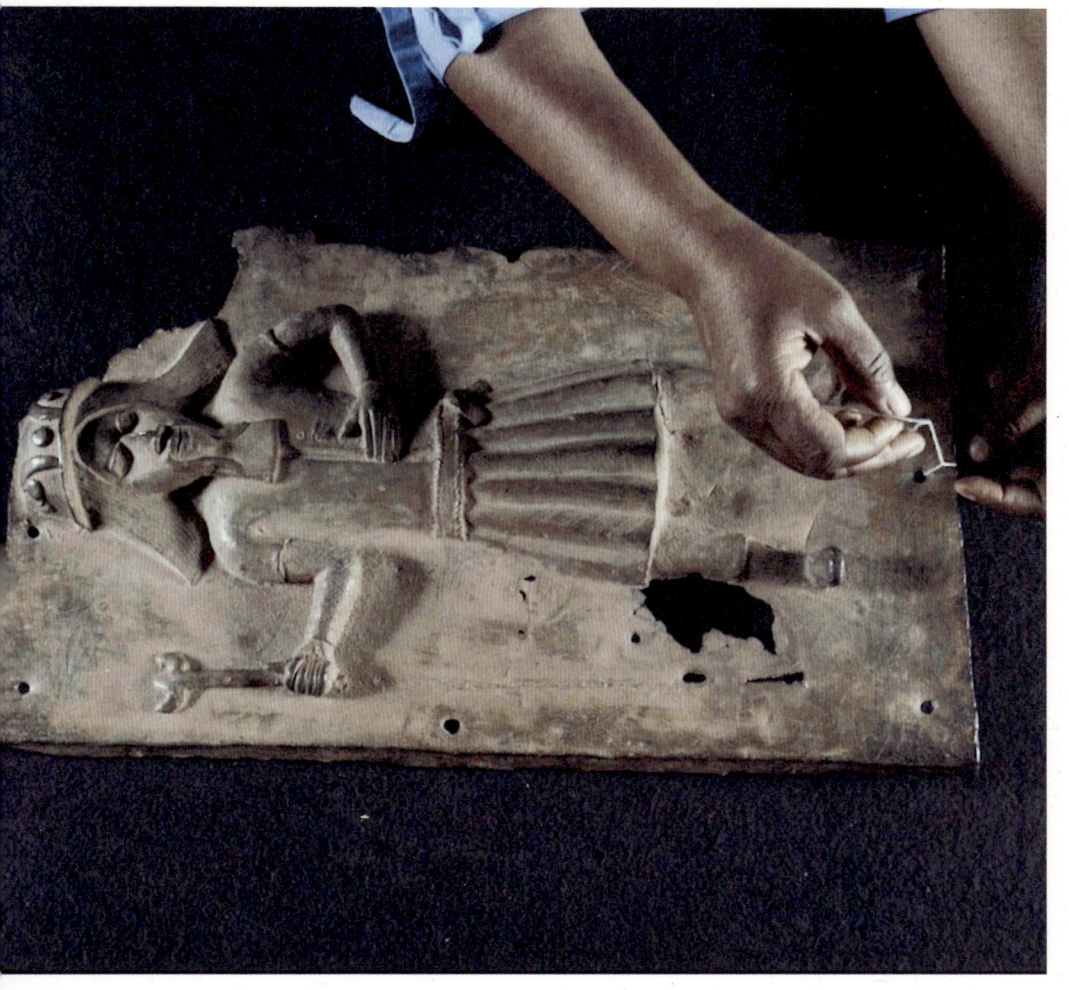

03/12/2021
RJM & online panel discussion, *RESIST! Conversations – All in One*, with Felwine Sarr, Ciraj Rassool, Nana Oforiatta Ayim, Bénédicte Savoy, Andreas Görgen, Peju Layiwola, Elizaveta Khan, Rahab Njeri.

09/01/2022
Last day of the exhibition *RESIST! The Art of Resistance*.

Februar 2022
Cologne City Council instructs the administration to prepare the return of the 92 Benin works from the RJM.

09/07/2022
Panel discussion at the RJM, *Why Restitution Matters*, with H.M. Asabaton Fontem Njifua, King of Fontem/Bangwa (Cameroon).

17/09/2022
Last major partial opening at the Humboldt Forum, including the "Benin Bronzes" gallery.

08/12/2022
Cologne City Council approves the transfer of ownership of 92 Benin artworks from the RJM to the Federal Republic of Nigeria. This entails the physical return of three works of art by the end of 2022 and a further 52 works from 2023 onwards, as well as the retention of 37 works at the RJM on loan from Nigeria for an initial period of ten years.

Conversation: AFRIKA'S STRUGGLE FOR ITS ART

Bénédicte Savoy

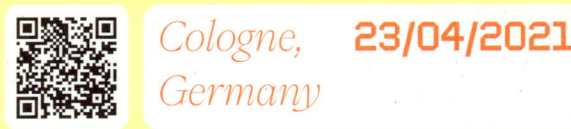

Cologne, Germany   23/04/2021

Bénédicte Savoy in an online conversation with Nanette Snoep, drawing on her latest book *Africa's Struggle for Its Art: History of a Postcolonial Defeat*. Her book describes in meticulous detail every event in the fifty-year struggle for the restitution of African cultural artefacts captured by former colonial empires. Documented by various official papers, letters held in the archives of ethnological museums, newspapers, news broadcasts, talk shows, documentaries, and films, Savoy demonstrates how this fifty-year struggle, mostly by African intellectuals, politicians, and curators, has been silenced in the current restitution debate. She reconstructs decades of a coordinated "defensive battle" by European museum directors, whose patterns are still being repeated today. Savoy calls for an end to this obstructionist attitude and for change that will finally make restitution possible as a gesture of fairness and solidarity.

Conversation: Benin 1897 – Cologne 2021

Peju Layiwola
Andreas Görgen
Dan Hicks
Nanette Snoep
Ciraj Rassool

Cologne, Germany   14/05/2021

»We are brave enough to dare to think and act differently. It is truly moving that art can inspire us to take new paths, that it inspires us to meet each other as friends without the need for resistance.«
Video message by Mayor Henriette Reker

Benin 1897–Cologne 2021 took place online due to Covid.
The topic of this conversation was what happens when we reconsider restitution – given the fact that it is often seen as a final act, as an definitive end point that can even threaten the existence of museums – as part of the work of an ethnological museum. What can we gain if we understand restitution as an integral dimension of the museum, as a process through which artefacts held in museums can be reconnected with their societies of origin?

This online conversation as part of *RESIST!* was the first international panel discussion after the meeting on April 29, 2021, chaired by the German Minister of Culture, together with the Ministry of Foreign Affairs, as well as the five German museums with the largest Benin collections and their representatives. In this political meeting, restitution was agreed upon as a priority and the first planned returns were scheduled for as early as 2022 …

Peju Layiwola, Artist and Professor of Art History (Head of Department of Creative Arts) at the University of Lagos, Nigeria

Andreas Görgen, Head of the Department of Culture and Communication at the Federal Foreign Office

Dan Hicks, Head of Contemporary Archaeology at the University of Oxford and Curator of World Archaeology at the University's Pitt Rivers Museum

Nanette Snoep, Director at the RJM

Moderation:
Ciraj Rassool, Professor of History at the University of the Western Cape in South Africa, Head of the African Program for Museum and Cultural Heritage Research, Associate Member of the Global South Studies Center at the University of Cologne

Conversation: RESIST! All in One

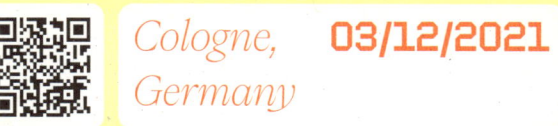

Cologne, Germany 03/12/2021

Hybrid event with **Felwine Sarr, Ciraj Rassool, Nana Oforiatta Ayim, Bénédicte Savoy, Andreas Görgen, Peju Layiwola, Elizaveta Khan,** moderated by **Rahab Njeri**, with an introduction by the Lord Mayor Henriette Reker and Nanette Snoep, director of the RJM

»Resistance means that something is in front of you and you are standing against a force, something in front of you. The idea is to go beyond this resistance and create a new space, a space of creativity – not just to face up to something that wants to suppress you or restrict you, but to create a new space, a new universe, a new world.« *Felwine Sarr*

»I've heard a lot about ›being on an equal footing‹ and for me this phrase is an empty one, because the only way in which we can have real equality is if we have equality with the people present, if we have equal resonance, if our voices are just as important as everyone else's, and we don't have that at the moment in this restitution debate.« *Nana Oforiatta Ayim*

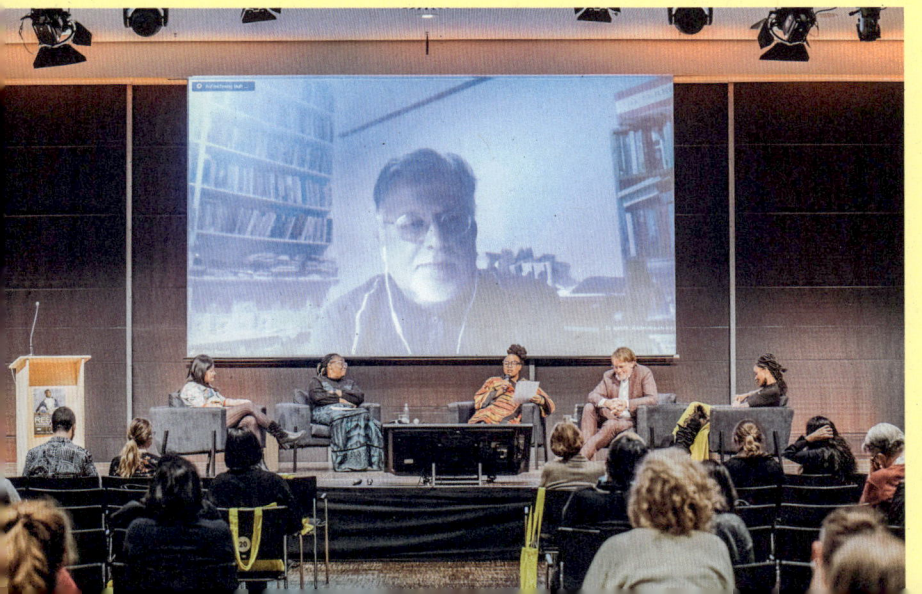

RESIST! All in One, 03/12/2021. From left to right: Elizaveta Khan, Peju Layiwola, Rahab Njeri, Andreas Görgen, Nana Oforiatta Ayim and on screen Ciraj Rassool from Cape Town

»Restitution is not an event that takes place [...], we have to understand restitution as a long-term project, as reconstruction, as healing, it involves restitution, it involves the restoration of the relationship between museums and people. For us this is an opportunity to rethink the whole concept of a modern museum.«
Ciraj Rassool

»The world is calling for empathy, for reconciliation, for reparation, and I believe that we are going in the right direction.«
Peju Layiwola

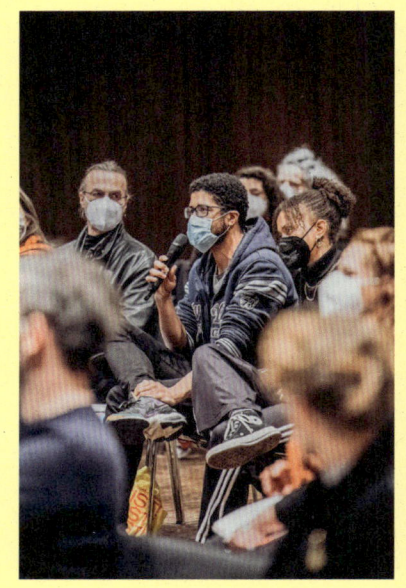

»The European arrogance towards the legitimate desire of Africans to recover their artistic, cultural, and historical heritage belongs to the past. [...] The time of denial is over.« *Bénédicte Savoy*

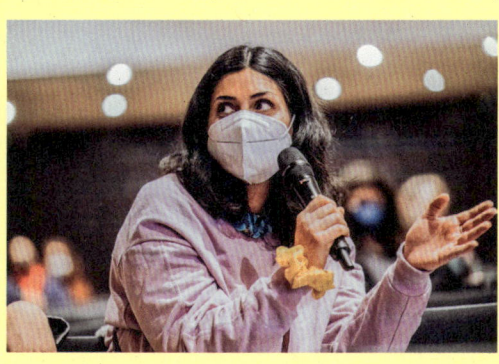

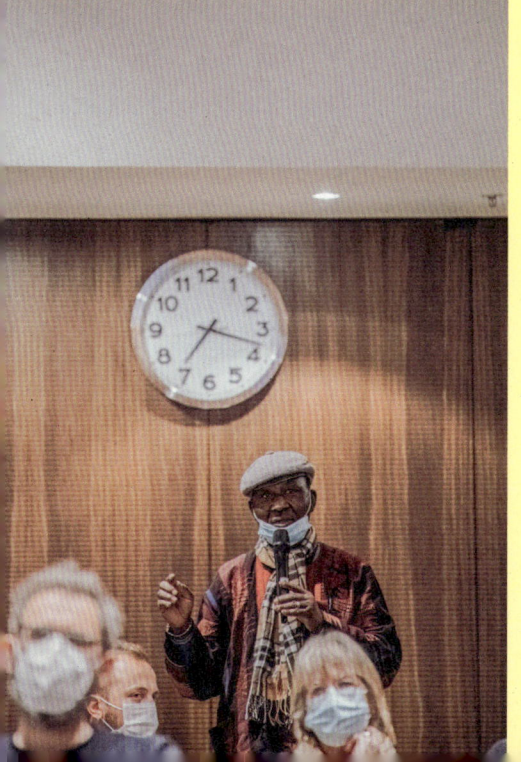

»For me, restitution means daily work. [...] For us, restitution means restoring something as a form of solidarity, a sense of belonging, empowerment, and power sharing – it's about humanity and dignity.«
Elizaveta Khan

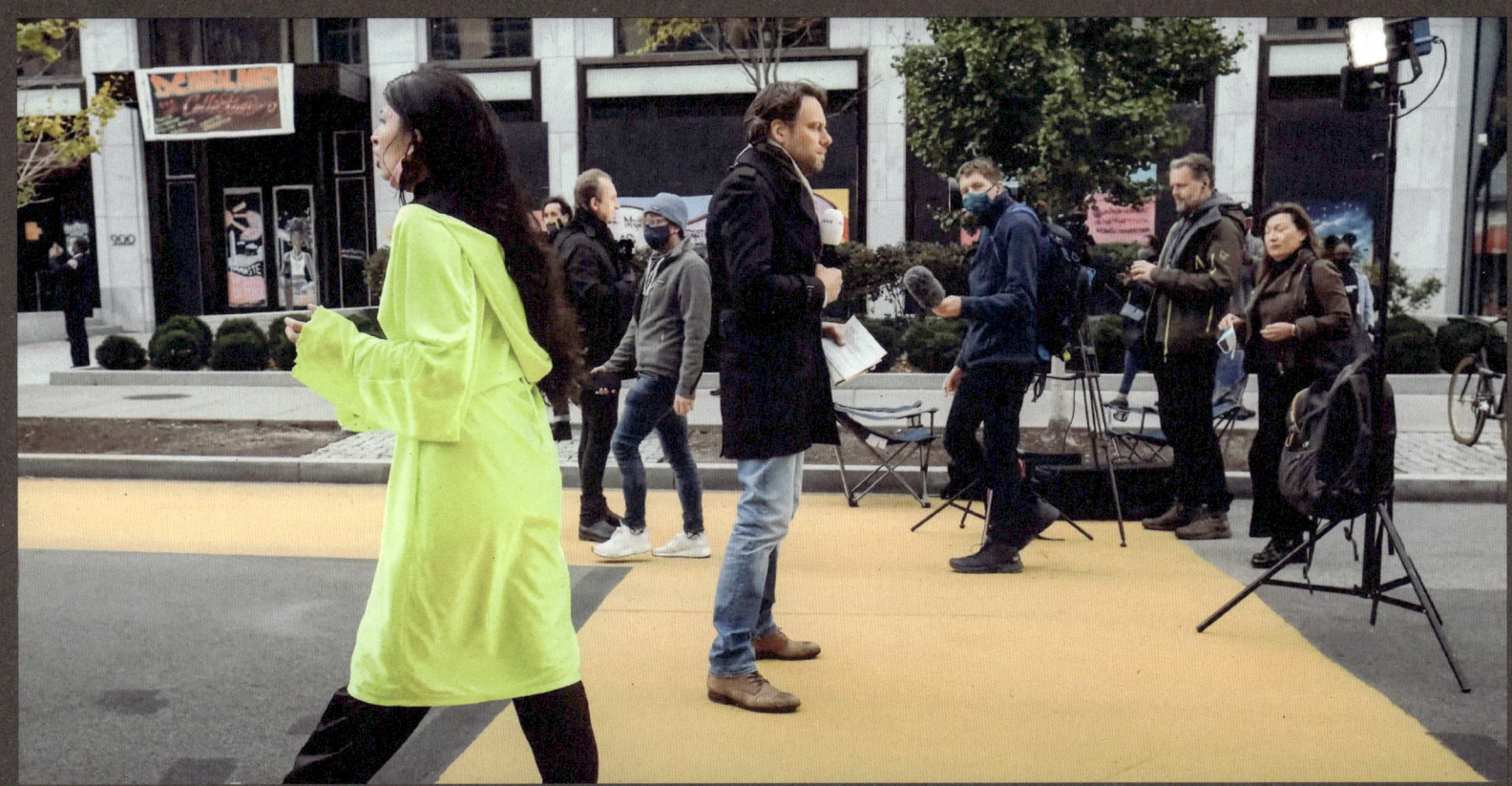

Selma Selman: *You Have No Idea*
3/11/2020, US Presidential Election Day, performance between BLM Plaza and the White House, Washington, DC, video, 5 min.

Washington, USA 03/11/2020

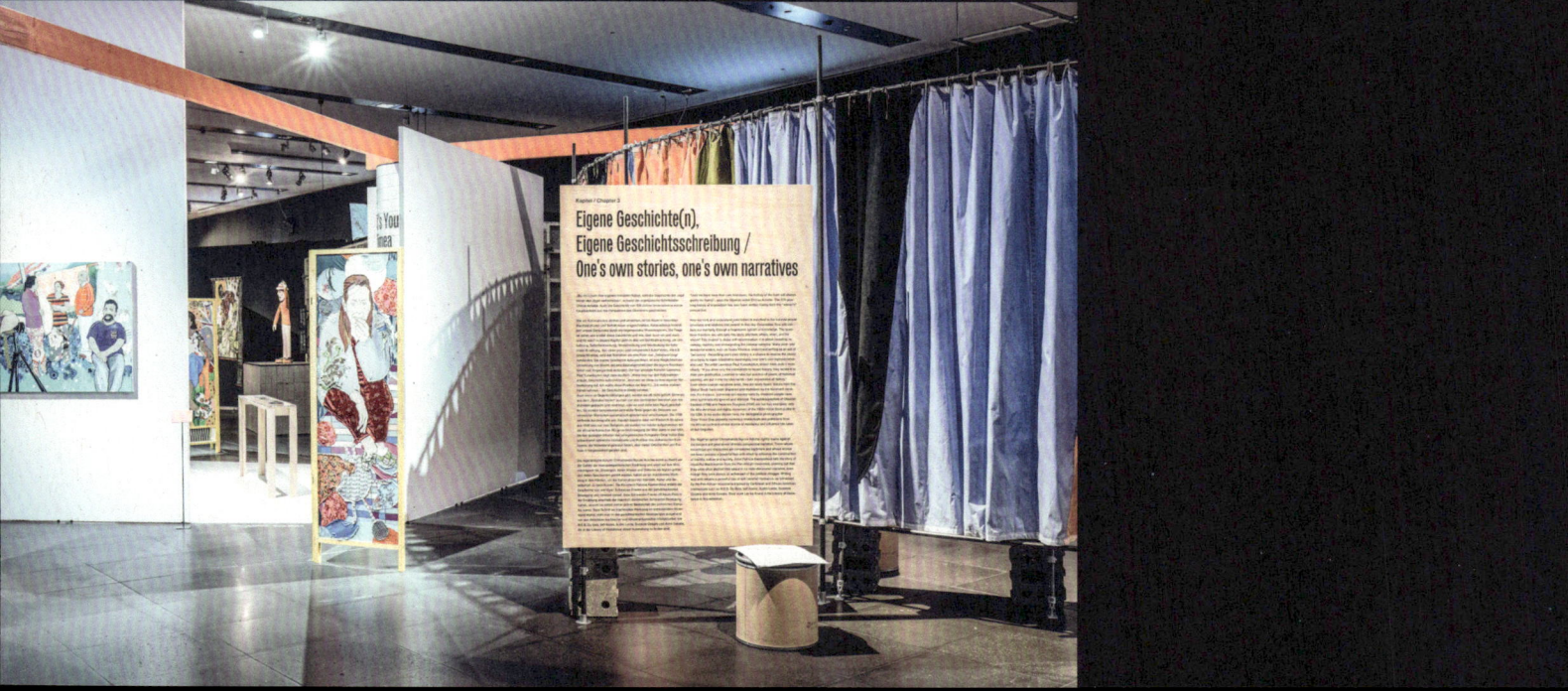

One's own stories, one's own narratives

"Until the lions have their own historians, the history of the hunt will always glorify the hunter", says the Nigerian writer Chinua Achebe. The 500-year-long history of imperialism has also been written mainly from the "winner's" perspective.

How we think and understand colonialism is inscribed in the colonial power structures and relations that persist to this day. Colonialism thus still controls our mentality through a hegemonic system of knowledge. The questions therefore are: who tells this story, and how, where, when, and for whom? This chapter is about self-determination; it is about revealing, reversing, rewriting and reinterpreting the colonial narrative. Many post- and decolonial writers, such as Grada Kilomba, understand writing as an act of "becoming". Recording one's own history is a chance to reverse the power structures, to claim interpretive sovereignty over one's own representation and past. The artist Lawrence Paul Yuxweluptun, shown here, puts it most clearly: *"If you allow only the colonialists to record history, they record it to their own glorification. I wanted to take that position of power, of historical painting, and put it into my own hands – take possession of history."*

Even where counter-narratives exist, they are rarely heard. Voices from the Global South have been displaced and repressed by the dominant narrative. For instance, numerous anti-slavery texts by enslaved people have been systematically ignored and silenced. The autobiographies of Olaudah Equiano (1789) and Frederick Douglas (1846) are but two examples: only the Afro-American civil rights movement of the 1960s made them public in the USA. In his works shown here, the Senegalese photographer Omar Victor Diop presents numerous intellectuals and politicians from the African continent whose stories of resistance and influence has been all but forgotten.

The Nigerian author Chimamanda Ngozie Adichie rightly warns against the dangers and great power of mono-perspectival narration. Those whose knowledge and discourses are considered legitimate and whose stories are heard possess a powerful tool with which to influence the construction of identity, culture and society. Artist Patricia Kaersenhout tells the story of impactful Black women from the Pan-African movement, pointing out that they were often allotted little space in its male-dominated narrative, even though they were always an active part of the political struggle. Writing was and remains a powerful tool of anti-colonial resistance, as witnessed by the Pan-African movements inspired by Caribbean and African-American intellectuals such as W.E.B. Du Bois, bell hooks, Audre Lorde, Suzanne Césaire and Aimé Césaire. Their work can be found in the Library of Resistance in this exhibition.

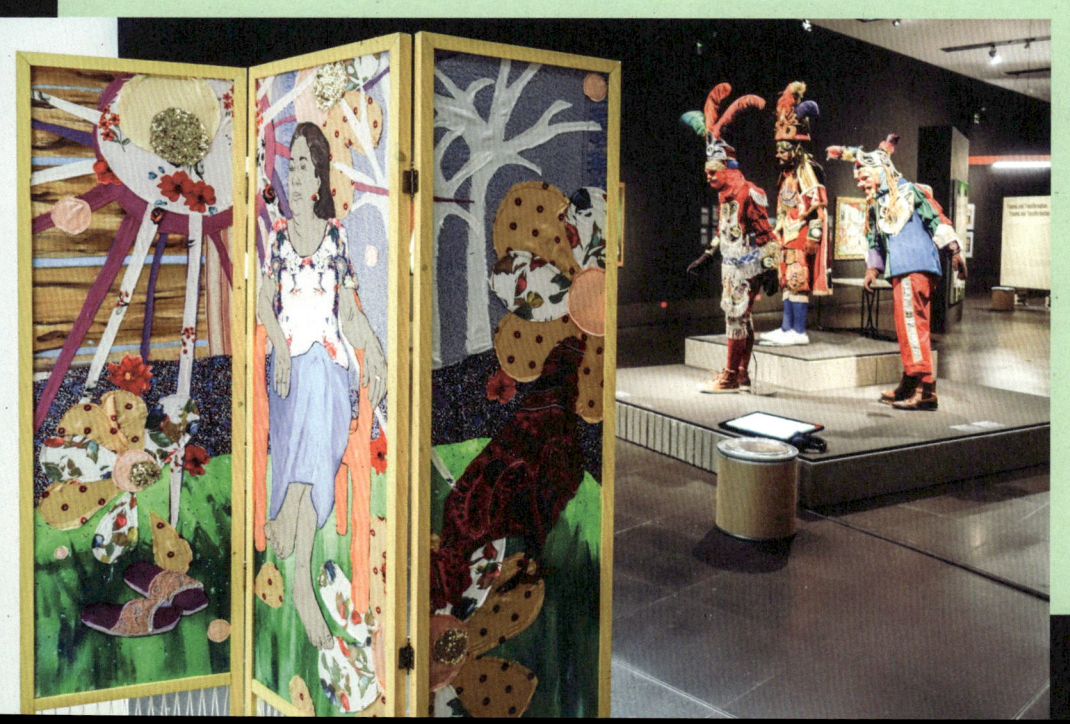

Omar Victor Diop
Project Diaspora, 2015

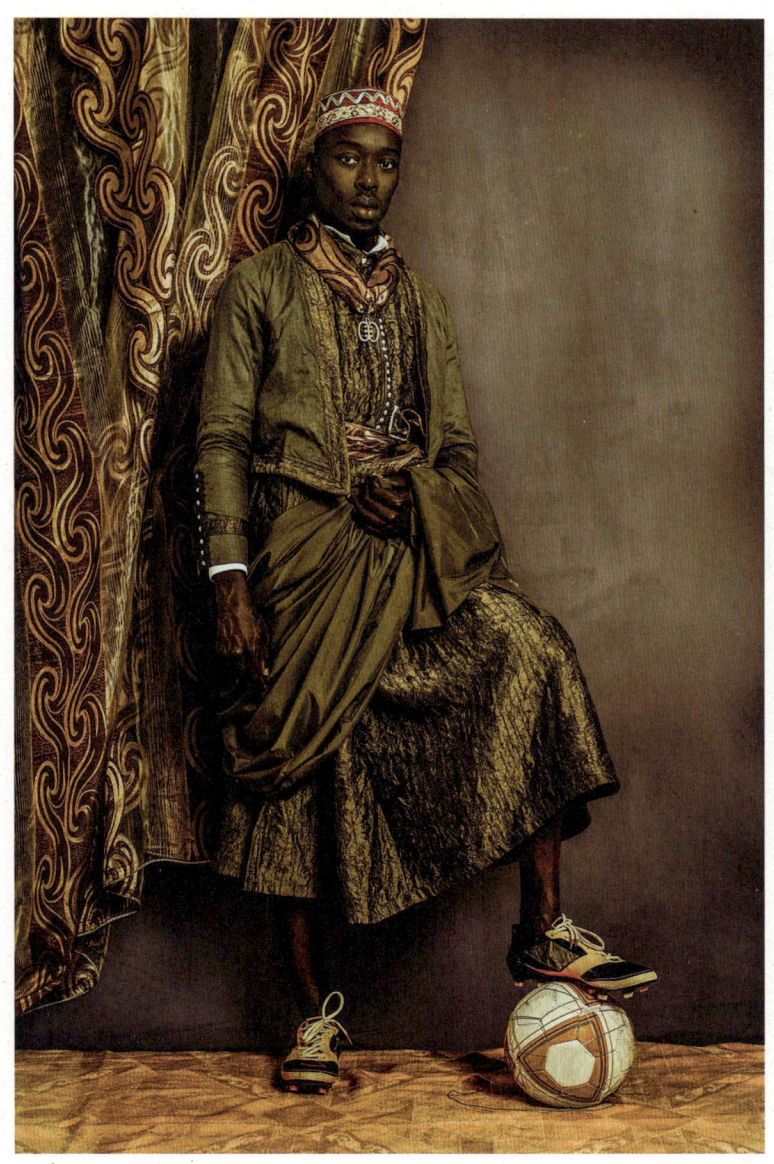

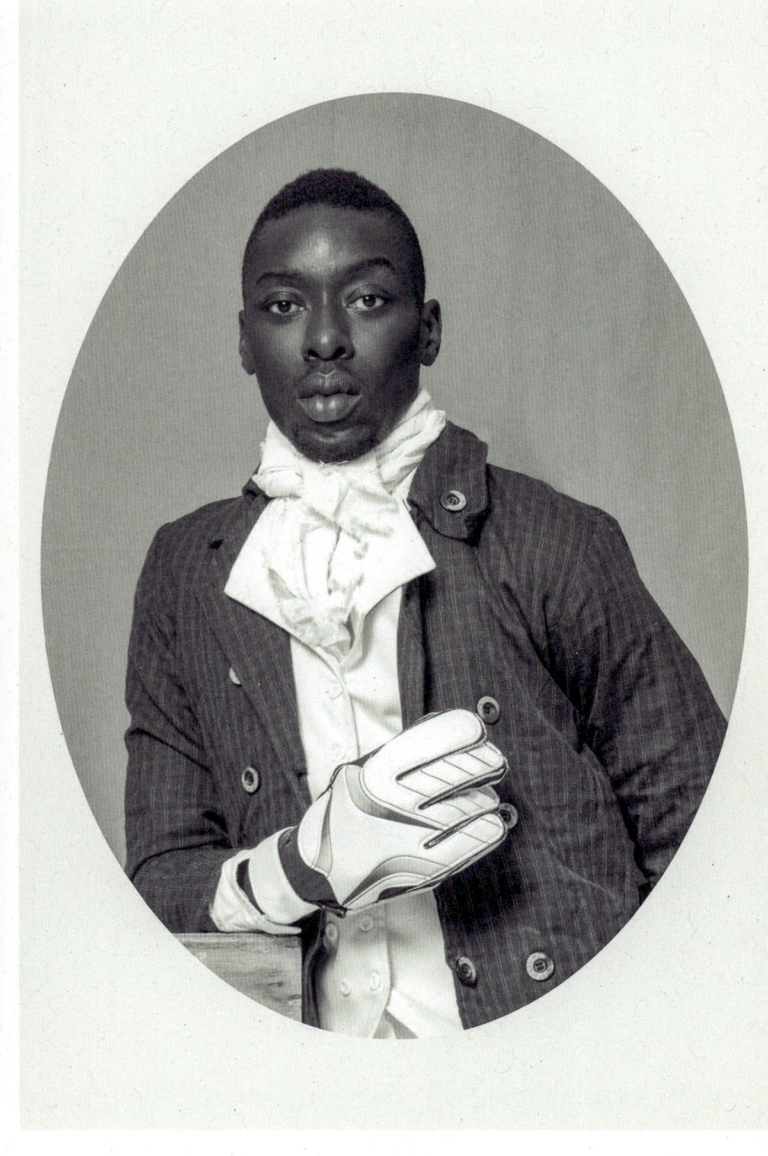

Dom Nicolau (ca. 1830–1860)

When the slave trade in former Portuguese Angola, the first European colony on the African continent (1655–1975), was abolished in 1836, Portugal attempted to replace its income from the slave trade with increased commercial, political, and military expansion. In this context, Dom Nicolau, Prince of Kongo (Angola), wrote an official letter objecting to Portuguese commercial and military activities in Angola. This letter was published in a Lisbon newspaper in December 1859. Nicolau's protest letter is perhaps the first written opposition to the Portuguese colonisers since the famous letters sent by the kings of Kongo to Lisbon and the Vatican in the sixteenth century.

Olaudah Equiano (1745–1797)

Born in Nigeria, Olaudah Equiano was enslaved as a child and taken to the West Indies, Virginia, and Georgia. He was finally able to purchase his freedom when he was 21 years old. He then travelled to London, where he supported the British abolitionist movement and became a leading figure in the fight against the slave trade. His autobiography, T*he Interesting Narrative of the Life of Olaudah Equiano, or, Gustavus Vassa, the African, Written by Himself* (1789), narrating his life in slavery, attracted much attention. It was considered highly influential in the passage of the Slave Trade Act 1807, which prohibited the slave trade in the British Empire.

»It started with me wanting to look at these historical Black figures who did not fulfil the usual expectations of the African diaspora insofar as they were educated, stylish, and confident, even if some of them were owned by white people and treated as the exotic other. I wanted to bring these rich historical characters into the current conversation about the African diaspora and contemporary issues around immigration, integration, and acceptance.« *Omar Victor Diop*

Courtesy of Galerie Magnin-A

Omar Victor Diop
Project Diaspora, 2015

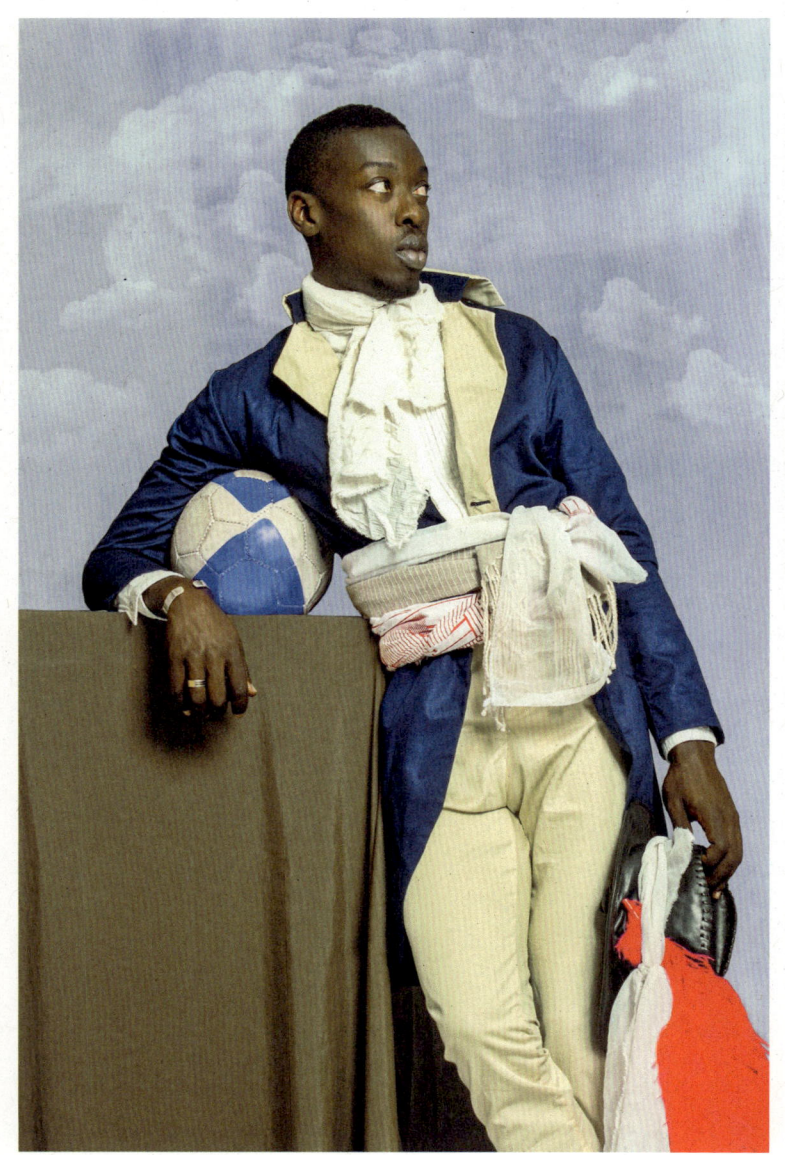

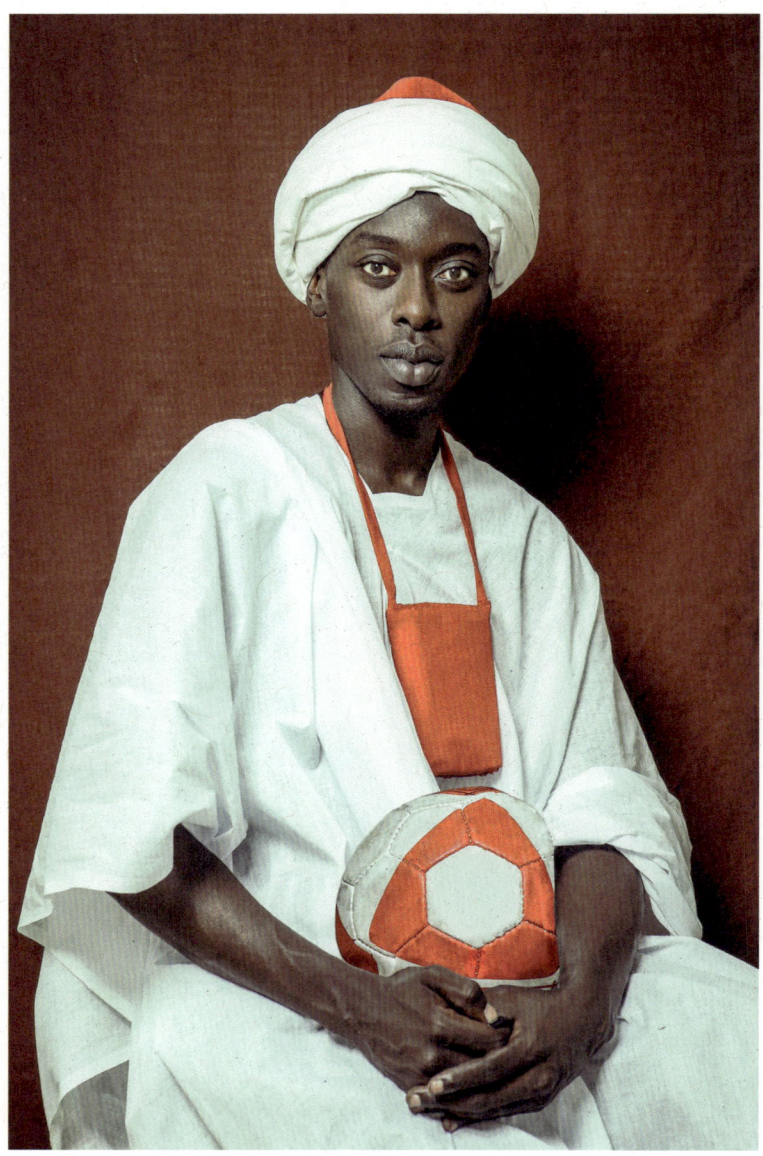

Jean-Baptiste Belley (1746–1805)

Jean-Baptiste Belley was a native of Senegal (island of Gorée) who was enslaved in Saint-Domingue (now Haiti) and bought his freedom with his savings. In 1791, the enslaved people of Saint-Domingue, under the direction of Toussaint Louverture – who was formerly enslaved himself – started the Haitian Revolution (1791–1804). In 1793, Belley fought against the white colonists of Saint-Domingue as an infantry captain. On September 24, 1793, he was elected to the National Convention in Paris, becoming its first Black deputy. On February 3, 1794, he spoke in a debate in the Convention when it decided unanimously to abolish slavery. In 1802 Napoleon Bonaparte restored slavery and the slave trade in France and its colonies.

Ayuba Suleiman Diallo (1701–1773)

Ayuba Suleiman Diallo, also known as Job Ben Solomon, was born into a prominent family of Muslim clerics in the kingdom of Bundu (part of modern-day Senegal). In 1730 he was captured and enslaved in Maryland for around two years; he was then taken to England. After five years of enslavement, he finally became free and managed to return to his homeland in 1734. His memoir, published in London in 1734, was one of the earliest first-hand accounts of the slave trade.

In the photo essay *Project Diaspora,* Senegalese photographer Omar Victor Diop brings together forgotten figures of the Black Diaspora who lived between the fifteenth and the nineteenth centuries. The staged studio portraits in this eighteen-part series allude to famous historical depictions. The protagonists that Diop selected for his portraits are all liberated, formerly enslaved men who achieved renown as diplomats, thinkers, politicians, artists, and warriors. Their extraordinary biographies point to crucial episodes of Black resistance that have received too little attention in the official historiography.

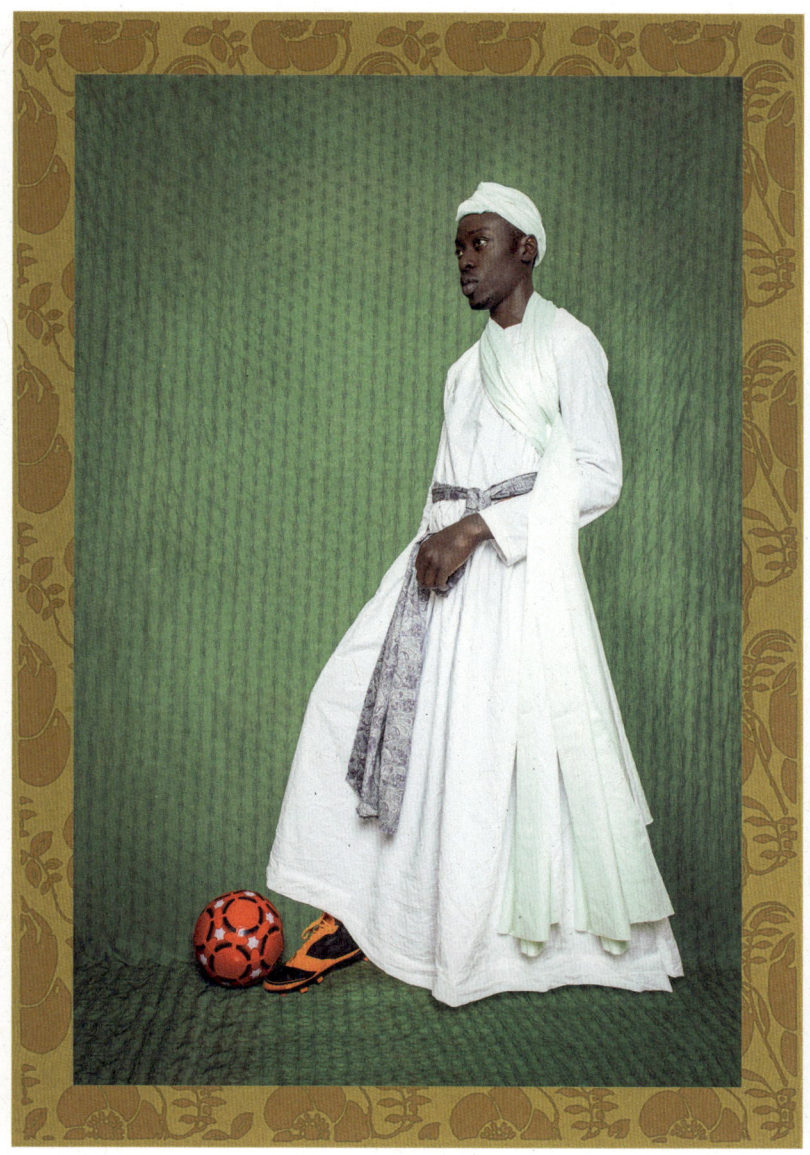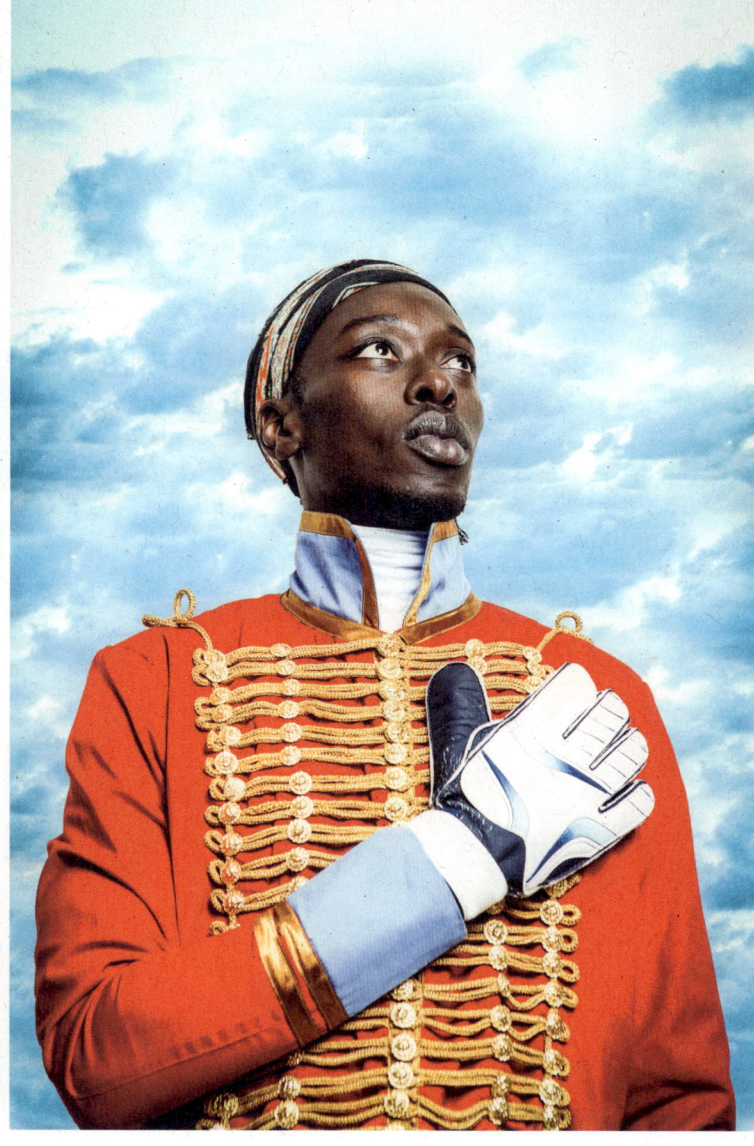

Malik Ambar (1548–1626)

Malik Ambar was an Ethiopian citizen born in Harar whose destitute parents were forced to sell him into slavery. He was taken across the Red Sea to Yemen, where he was re-sold and sent to Baghdad. He received an education there before being sent to India, where he finally became Prime Minister of the Ahmednagar Sultanate. By 1600, Ambar emerged as the leading figure in the resistance movement against the expansion of the Mughal Empire. Around 1619 Ambar founded the city of Khadki (the future site of Aurangabad), where he built several palaces, developed an irrigation system, and was a patron of many Hindu and Muslim craftsmen and artists. When he died in 1625, he was known as one of the greatest leaders of the region.

Pedro Camejo (1790–1821)

Pedro Camejo was born into slavery. He fought as a cavalry lieutenant in the independence army during the Venezuelan War of Independence against the Spanish (1810–1823). During this war, he was nicknamed "El Negro Primero" ("Black man at the fore"), being the only Afro-descendant officer in the Venezuelan independence forces led by Simón Bolívar. Rising out of slavery to the rank of cavalry officer, Camejo is a symbol of upward mobility and a figure with whom the many Black people who fought in Venezuela's War of Independence for their own freedom and that of the colony could identify. In 2011, Venezuela's National Assembly passed the "Law against Racial Discrimination", which legally requires the recognition of the country's Afro-descendant population in the construction of the Venezuelan nation.

Through idiosyncratic references to football culture, Diop transports the significance of these iconic images into the present. In doing so, he refers to the stereotypical representation of Black men in popular media, which is associated, as he puts it, with "a very interesting blend of glory, hero-worship, and exclusion". Although Diop appears in the photographs, they are not self-portraits in the traditional sense. Rather, the artist and fashion photographer uses himself as an object in front of his lens while retaining control over the image – a level of agency that was only partially granted to the subjects in their historical context.

Courtesy of Galerie Magnin-A

Patricia Kaersenhout
Objects of Love and Desire, 2019

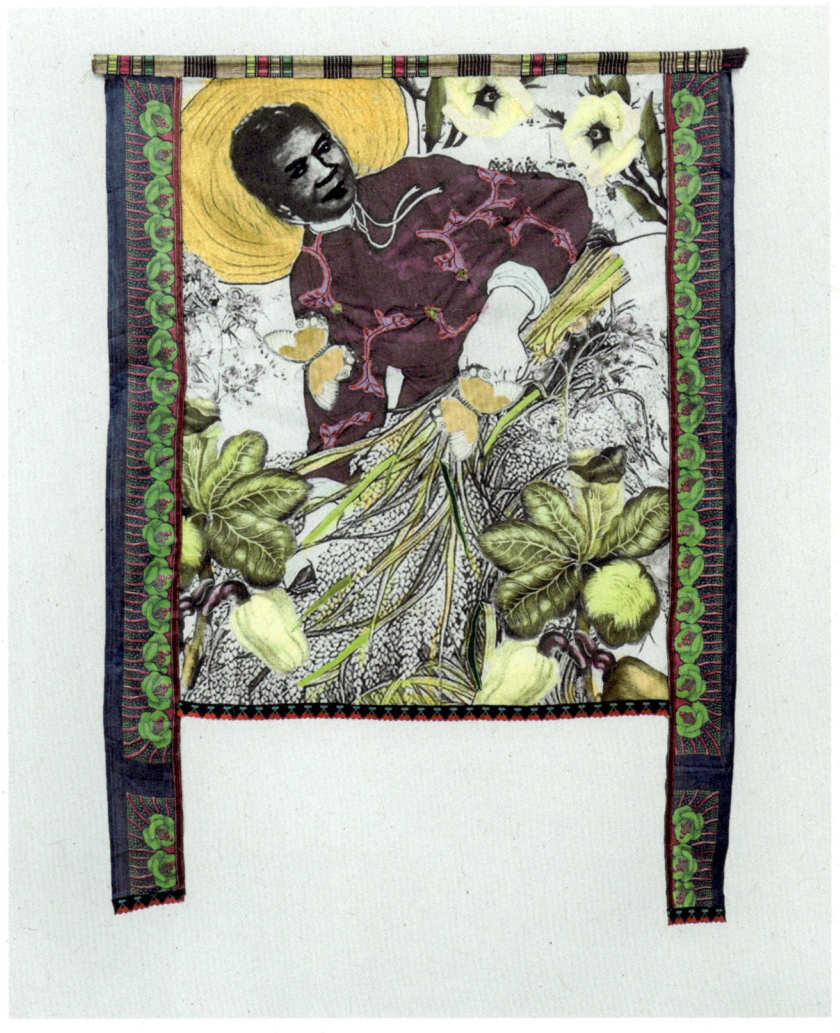

»Especially for young Black women it is important to know their history, to know that their past is filled not only with oppression and suffering, but also with resistance.«
Patricia Kaersenhout

Amy Jacques-Garvey (1895–1973)

The Jamaican editor, feminist, and activist Amy Jacques Garvey emigrated to the United States in 1917. Her husband was Marcus Garvey, founder of the Universal Negro Improvement Association (UNIA), which campaigned for all Black people to return to Africa. After his arrest, she became the unofficial leader of the UNIA and made crucial contributions to Pan-Africanism. As co-editor of the *Negro World* magazine, she was responsible for the "Our Women and What They Think" page. She argued that Black women's experiences of multiple forms of oppression had equipped them to lead a global movement for the liberation of all Black people.

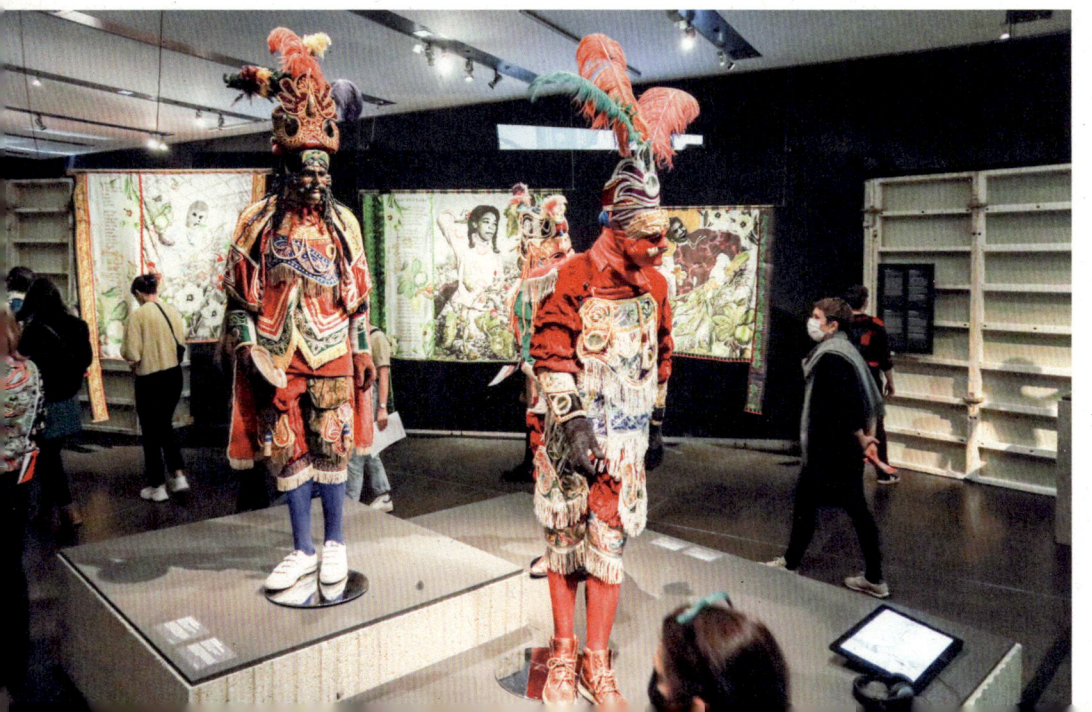

Chapter 3

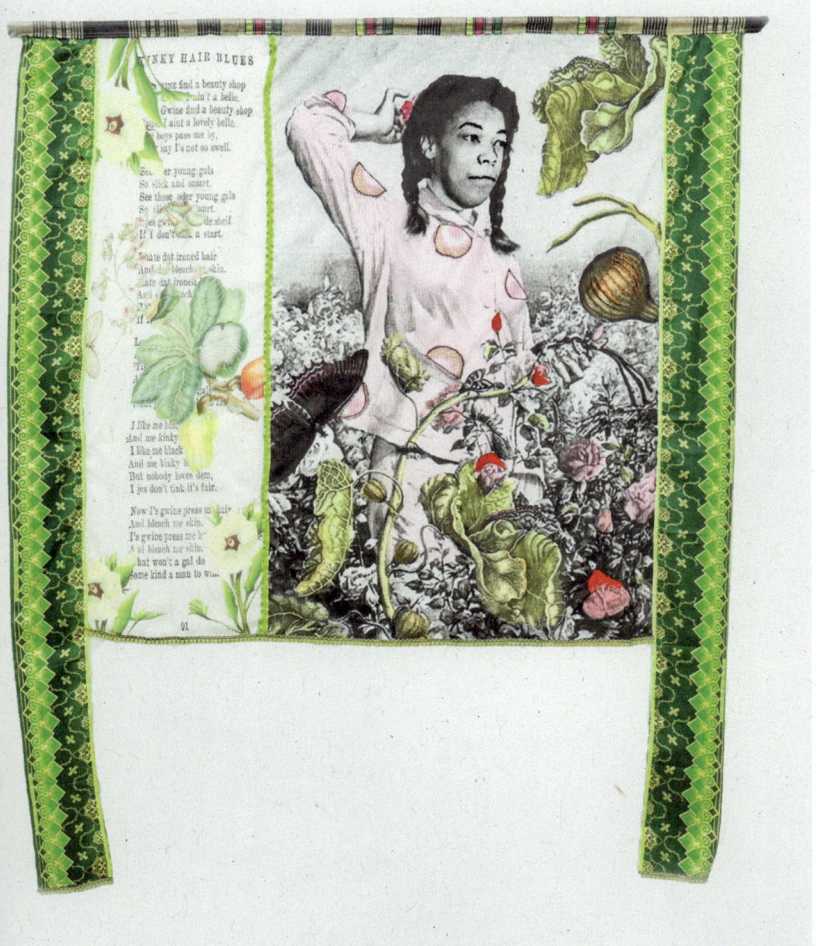
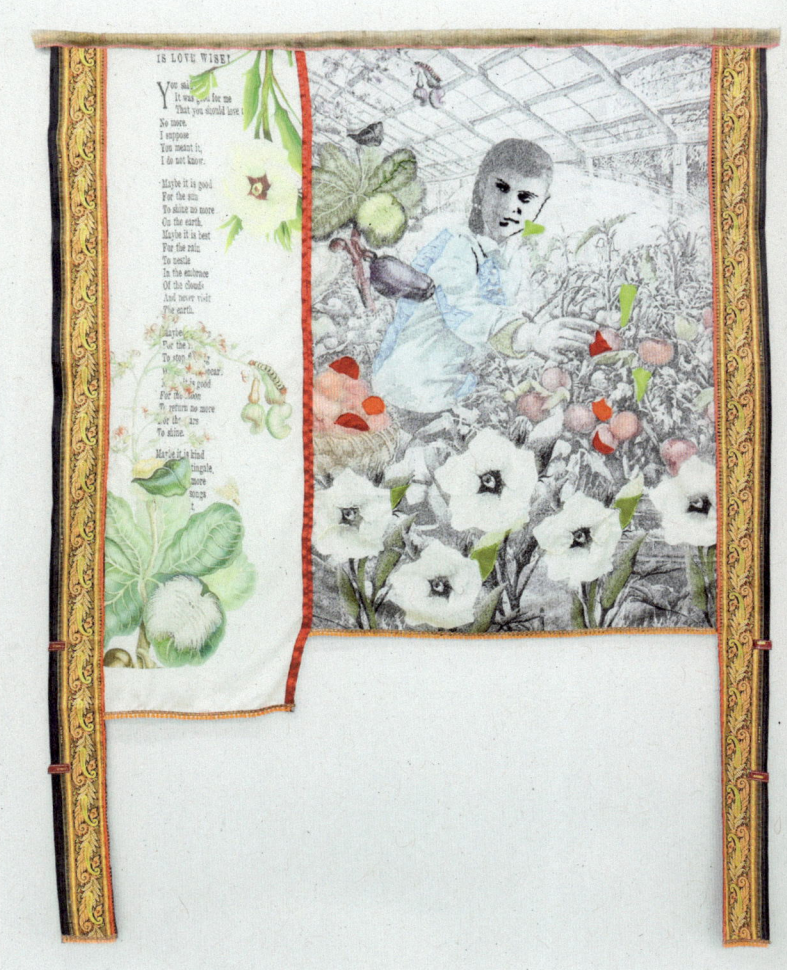

Una Marson (1905–1965)

Today, Una Marson is recognised as the first major woman poet of the Caribbean and is known for her outspoken ideals about empowering Black women. Marson wrote poetry, plays, and radio features. In 1932 she moved to London as part of the Pan-African movement. One of her poems, "Kinky Hair Blues", is an ode to Black beauty written in a Jamaican dialect. Marson became a member of the League of Coloured Peoples, where she advocated for radical feminism and spoke about the role of women in anti-colonial struggles. During the Second World War, she became the BBC's first ever Black producer.

Eslanda Robeson (1895–1965)

"International affairs are merely an extension of domestic affairs, which in turn are merely an extension of community affairs, family affairs, and relations with the neighbours." These were the words of Eslanda Robeson in a 1957 interview for the magazine of the Women's International Democratic Federation. Robeson was an American anthropologist, author, actor, feminist, and civil rights activist who fought against colonialism, racism, and traditional gender roles in America, Africa, and Europe. Together with her husband Paul Robeson and W. E. B. Du Bois, they founded the Council on African Affairs, an African-American organisation that supported African struggles against colonialism and apartheid. In her political writings Robeson stressed the crucial role of women in Black self-determination movements.

Black women have often been repressed and forgotten in official, male-dominated historiographies. The Black feminist writer Audre Lorde coined the term "sister outsider" to refer to this erasure from mainstream feminist and Black American thought.

The Surinamese-Dutch artist Patricia Kaersenhout has long been inspired by Black activism and considers her art as a form of activism, too. The three textile banners from her *Objects of Love and Desire* series portray three heroines of the Pan-African movement. All three are Black female thinkers, poets, and activists who advocated for the perspective of Black women, defying conventions with their way of life.

Though they are not well known today, their struggle against racism, sexism, and inequality had a great impact on the Black movement in different parts of the world in the second half of the twentieth century.

Kaersenhout's works are influenced by the life of the German-Dutch naturalist Maria Sibylla Merian (1647–1717), whose research was enabled by one of her assistants, an Indigenous woman from Suriname, who is never mentioned in her books and remains invisible. Kaersenhout addresses the hegemonic logic of historiography, urgently calling for the role of Black women and people of colour not to be forgotten.

Courtesy of private collections, Netherlands

Franky Mindja
Rudolf Duala Manga Bell and His Anti-Colonial Petition

Resistance: Three Generations of Anti-Colonial Protest in Cameroon, 2019; Comic book, illustrations by Franky Mindja and Daniel Assako; Texts: Hilaire Djoko, Katharina Lipowsky and Bathilde Maestracci

Yaoundé, Cameroon   2019

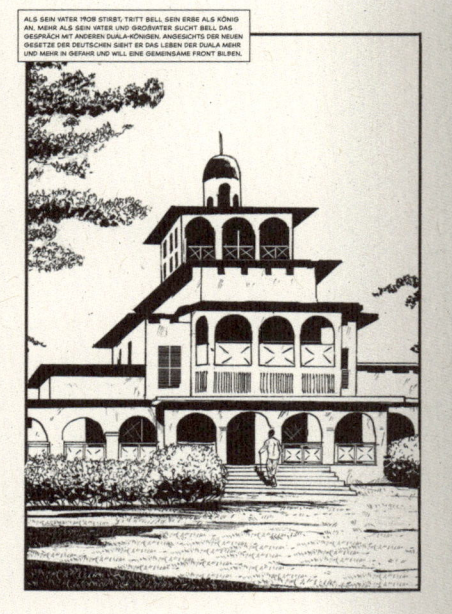
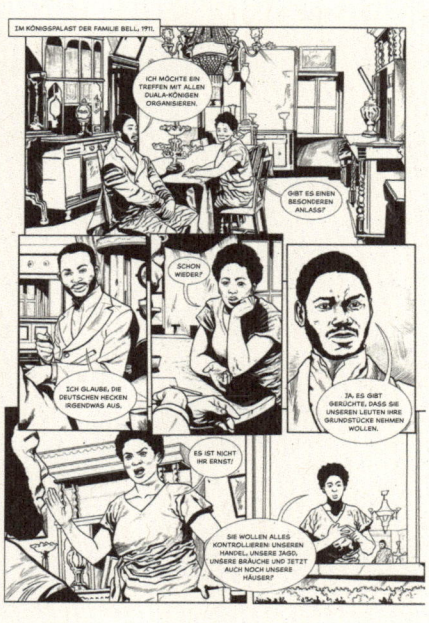
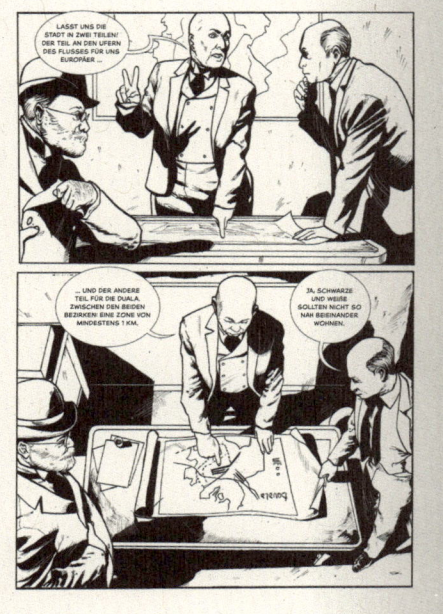
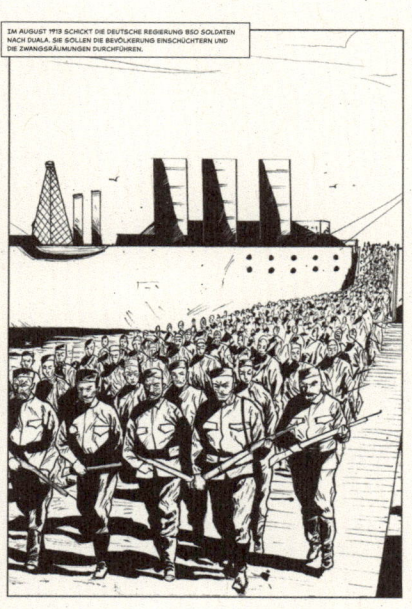
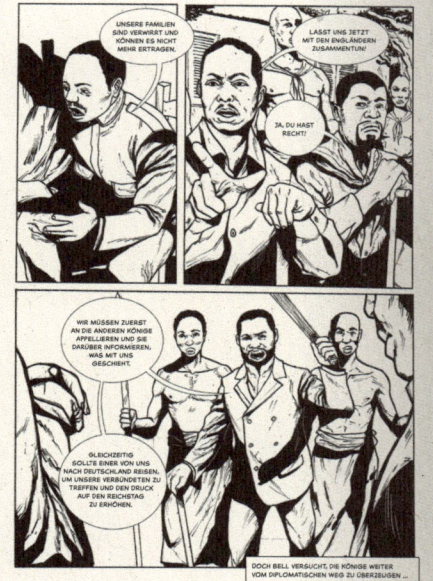
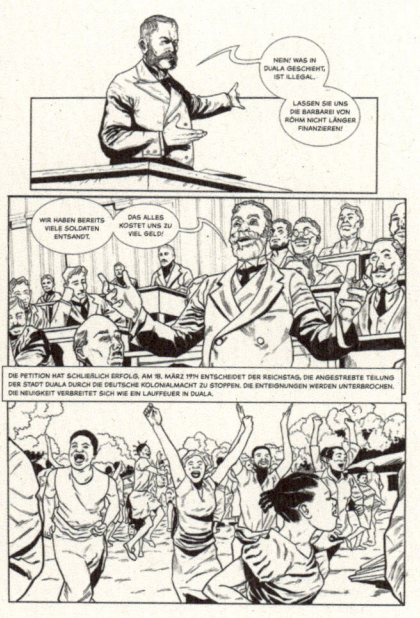

In 1884, local Duala kings signed a so-called treaty of protection with representatives of the German Empire that promised the Duala would retain their land and trading rights. The Germans, however, had never intended to honour this agreement. Under the first German governor, Jesko von Puttkamer (1855–1917), Rudolf Duala Manga Bell (1873–1914) – to use his full name – soon experienced how the German colonial administration gradually broke all the promises of the protection treaty and exercised brutal violence and tyranny against the population. His grandfather, Ndumb'a Lobe Bell (1839–1897), who co-signed the so-called protection treaty in 1884, and his father, August Manga Ndumbe Bell (1851–1908), had already resisted this authoritarianism as kings of the Duala people. Manga Bell spoke fluent German and was familiar with German culture and the German legal system because he had spent several years studying there. In 1912, together with other Cameroonian kings, he sent an extensive petition to the German Reichstag in Berlin. As this and other acts of resistance remained ineffective, and Manga Bell and his allies were prevented from leaving the country by the German colonial administration, Manga Bell's secretary, Ngoso Din, managed to make his way to Germany on Manga Bell's behalf in order to inform the politicians in Berlin about the breach of the treaty, the violent attacks on the local population, and the unlawful expropriations by colonial officials, hoping to mobilise their support. Instead of responding to the peaceful demands to comply with the protection treaty made by Manga Bell and his fellow comrades, the German colonial administration sentenced Manga Bell and Ngoso Din to death in 1914 for alleged high treason in a summary trial without observing the minimum legal standards applicable at the time. They were executed on August 8, 1914. In March 2022, Manga Bell's great-granddaughter, Princess Marilyn Douala Manga Bell, and other initiators launched a petition for Manga Bell and Ngoso Din to be acquitted.

Courtesy: Initiative Perspektivwechsel e.V.

Njoya, King of Bamum
A Survival Strategy?

Cameroon & Germany
1884–1916
GERMAN COLONIAL ERA

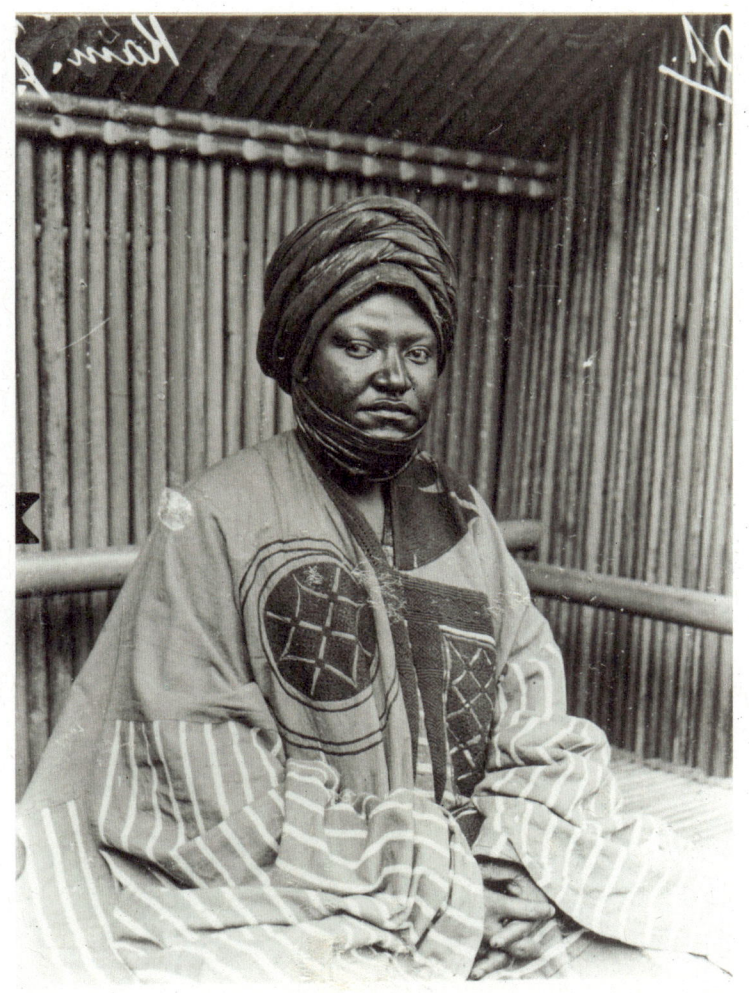

King Ibrahim Njoya (ca. 1872–1933) of the Kingdom of Bamum played an ambivalent role in Cameroon during the German colonial period (1884–1916) and at the beginning of the French Mandate (1919–1959). Unlike Manga Bell, Njoya did not fight against the colonisers, opting instead for a policy of accommodation, because he felt that opposition to the Germans could have negative consequences. Njoya sought a partnership on an equal footing with the German colonisers without having to relinquish his own position of power. The donation of valuable Bamum artworks to the German colonial elite, which were highly sought after by German ethnographic museums, was a diplomatic strategy that Njoya deployed very skilfully. Njoya was very aware of the brutality of the colonisers and tried to spare his subjects the fate suffered by many neighbouring kingdoms. Njoya also invented his own writing system to record the history and culture of his kingdom and thus gain authority over his own historiography. These extraordinary chronicles depict the history of the Bamum kings and events from the founding of the Kingdom of Bamum to the German and French colonial periods.

Under French colonial occupation, the French – unlike the Germans – saw Njoya as a ruler with too much influence and consequently tried to progressively limit his power. The French administration terminated his reign by deporting him to Yaoundé, where he died on May 30, 1933, after spending three years under house arrest.

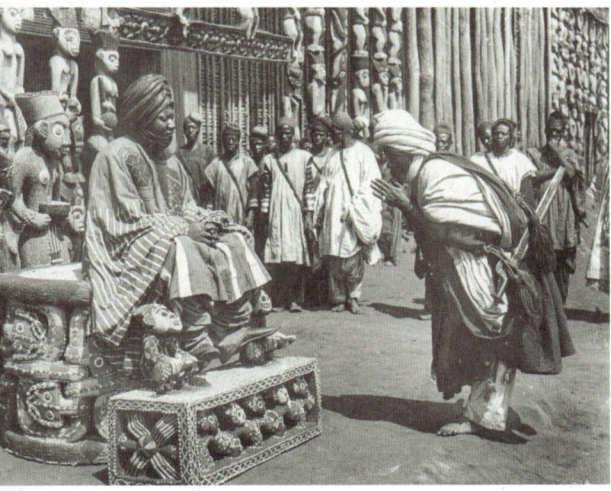

Portraits of King Ibrahim Njoya of Bamum (1894–1924). Photographs by Marie Pauline Thorbecke, January 1912, RJM Collection No. 19333 and 19336

Throne, Bamum, Cameroon, late nineteenth century, RJM Collection No. 43576

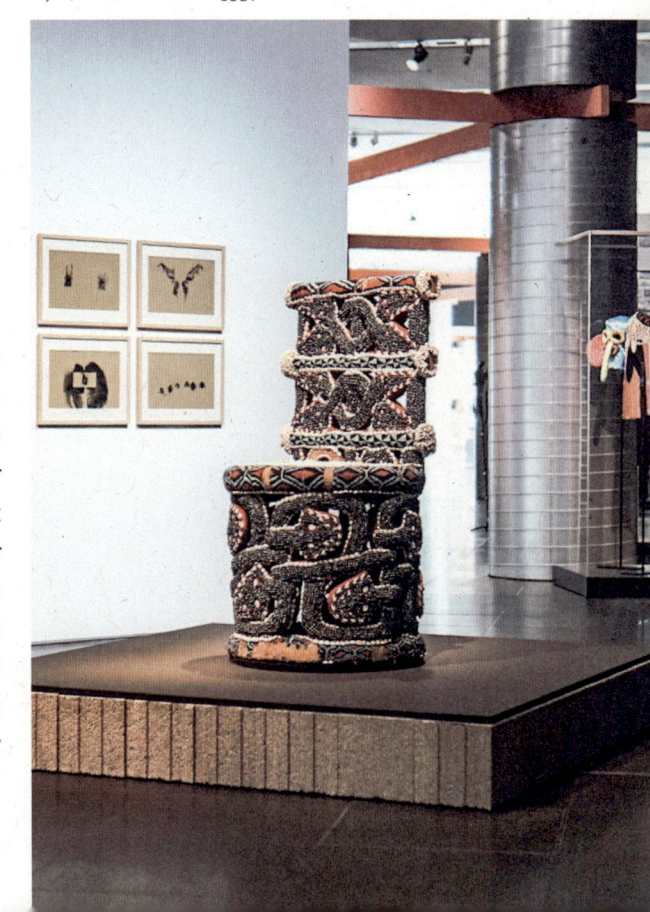

Are diplomatic gifts under colonial rule really gifts?

The RJM collection contains more than 1,000 historical photographs from the German colonial period (1884–1916) in Cameroon. Most of them were taken by Marie Pauline Thorbecke as part of a so-called research expedition to Cameroon (1911–1913), during which she traveled with her husband on behalf of the German Colonial Society. The photo above left shows King Njoya sitting on his throne, which he "presented" to Kaiser Wilhelm II for his 50th birthday in 1908. It is now in the Humboldt Forum in Berlin. As for the throne in the Cologne collection – see the photo on the right – King Njoya presumably "gifted" it to the then German colonial governor in Cameroon, Theodor Seitz (1863–1949), in 1908, who is said to have passed it on to the Grand Duke of Baden until the throne finally entered the RJM collections in 1953.

indieguerillas
This Hegemony Life, 2012

Java War   1825–1830

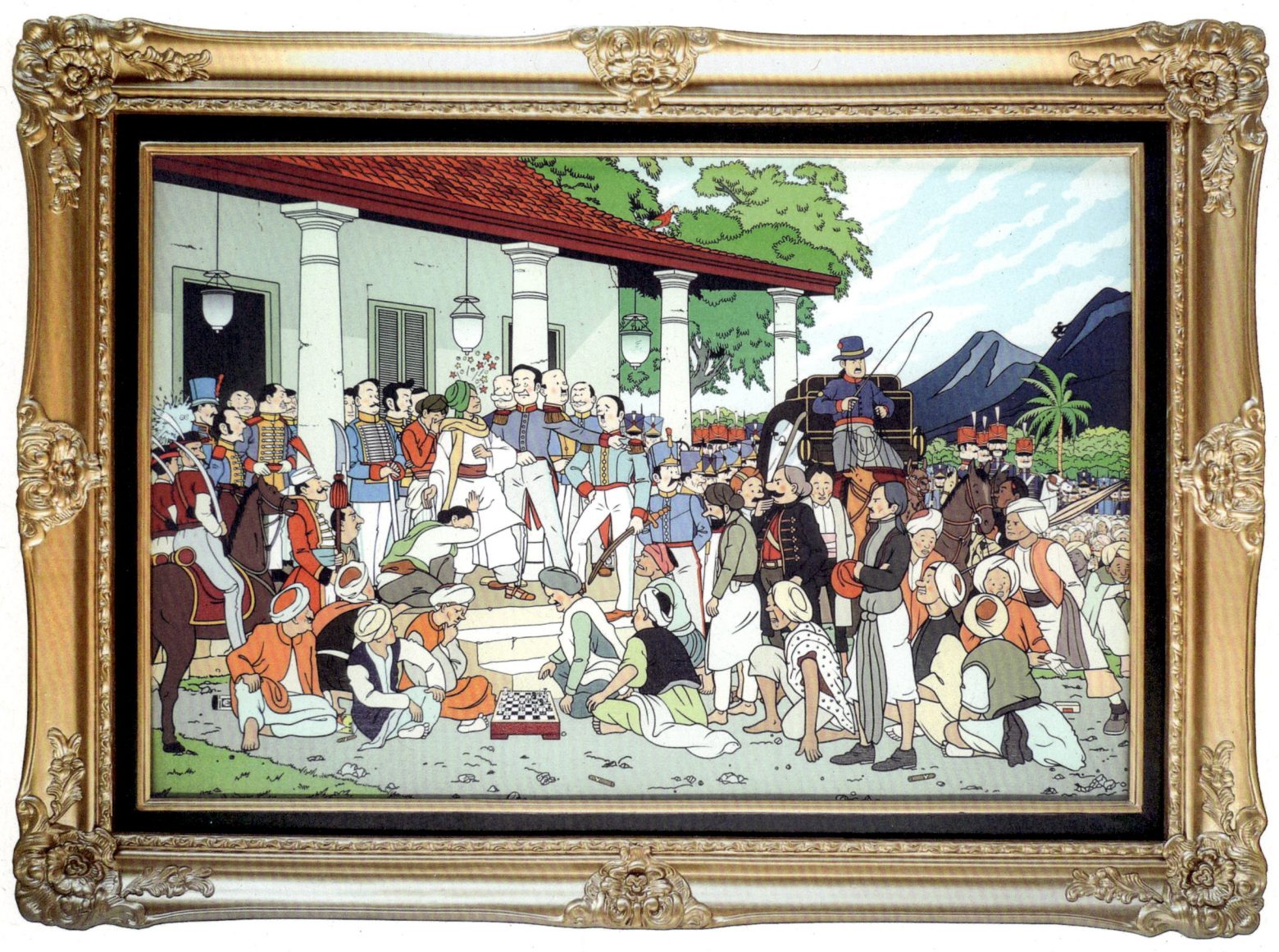

The arrest of the Javanese resistance fighter Pangeran Diponegoro

Trade and profit maximisation were central concerns during the approximately 350 years of Dutch rule and colonisation of what is now Indonesia. Even before the national independence movement, there was repeated resistance to the Dutch occupation. The last major armed conflict in this center of colonial power was the Java War (1825–1830), led by resistance fighter Pangeran Diponegoro (1785–1855), a son of the Sultan of Yogyakarta. The war lasted five years and cost the lives of around 200,000 Javanese, 8,000 Dutch Soldiers and 7,000 native soldiers of the Dutch colonial army. 1829 saw a victory for the Netherlands. In 1830, Diponegoro was invited to Magelang on Java for peace negotiations. However, his unconditional surrender was the only acceptable course of action to the Dutch governor general. After twenty days of negotiations, Diponegoro was arrested and taken to the island of Sulawesi, where he died in 1855 after twenty-five years in exile. His arrest signalled the end of this significant war of resistance. Indonesia officially gained its independence in 1949. In 1973, the Indonesian government awarded Diponegoro the title *Pahlawan Nasional Indonesia* – National Hero of Indonesia.

This Hegemony Life is an interpretation of a painting by the Indonesian artist Raden Saleh (ca. 1811–1880), which shows the arrest of Pangeran Diponegoro. With their interpretation of his painting in the style of the comic series Tintin, the Indonesian artist duo indieguerillas wants to bring Indonesian history to a younger audience.

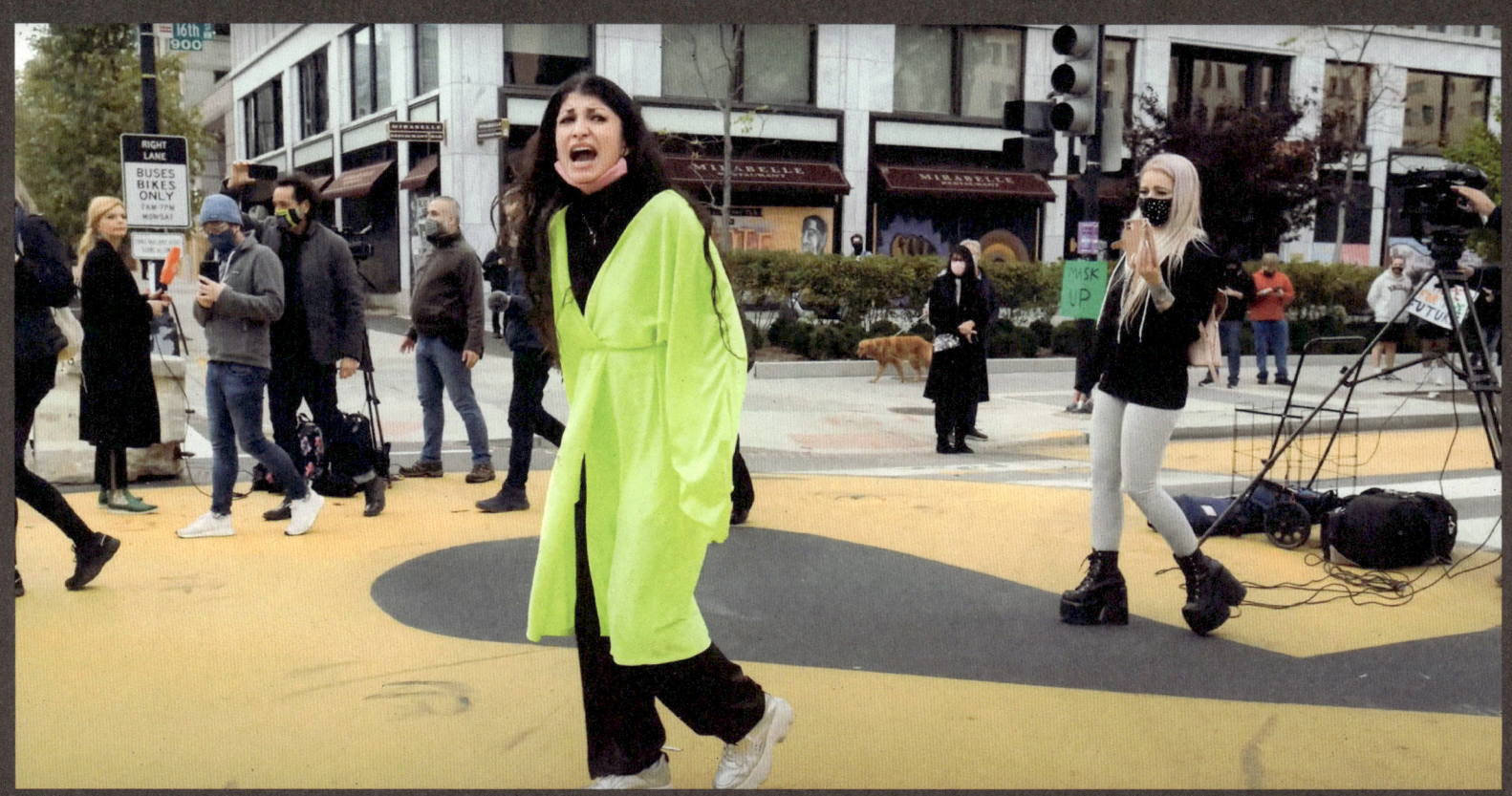

Selma Selman: *You Have No Idea*
3/11/2020, US Presidential Election Day, performance between BLM Plaza and the White House, Washington, DC, video, 5 min.

Washington, USA 03/11/2020

We first got to know Tímea Junghaus's struggle for the self-determination of Sinti and Roma people at the *RomAmor* festival in Dresden in 2016. This tribute to Roma and Sinti cultures at Hellerau European Centre for the Arts was curated by Vera Marušić. Junghaus's exhibition *(Re-)Conceptualizing Roma Resistance* presented the ways in which the Sinti and Roma have fought and continue to fight against all the forms of forced rule they have been subjected to over the centuries. Tímea Junghaus decolonises supposed knowledge about Sinti and Roma and campaigns for the return of their cultural heritage, because there are still over 33,000 artefacts created and owned by Sinti and Roma people in European museum collections today.

It's Yours! space: a space in a space

The exhibition *RESIST!* was an organic space of resonance and dissonance in a state of constant change. In the public, hegemonic space of the RJM, which, like other ethnological museums, is a place with highly asymmetrical power relations, *RESIST!* sought to make repressed and silenced stories and histories from the Global South as well as marginalised voices heard. With Esther Utjiua Muinjangue, Ida Hoffmann, Peju Layiwola, Tímea Junghaus, and In-Haus e.V with Elizaveta Khan, artists, curators, and activists who are directly affected by the topic of resistance were invited to create a non-hierarchical space in the museum to present conflicts, protests, and wounds, insofar as this is possible in a museum setting. Within the *RESIST!* exhibition space, they have taken the floor and curated their own autonomous *It's Yours!* spaces, places of agency and self-determination.

p. 064 Not about Us without Us
p. 094 Benin 1897
p. 138 Roma Resist!
p. 170 No Resistance Fits in a Box or a Museum

"It's Yours" Room

Tímea Junghaus
Roma Resist!

Roma Resist! takes its departure from the series of photographs documenting the research by anthropologists and racial scientists, Robert Ritter, Eva Justin, with Sophie Ehrhardt recording the making and collection of masks with original human remains during the National Socialist Regime.

Roma subalternity, as Gayatri Chakravorty Spivak condensed in her philosophy: "this burden of being the 'other', and the physical, symbolic, epistemic – violence", i.e., the colonising act of European majorities toward the Roma, is most visible and evident in the visual field. Thus, exploring the desires of Roma subjectivity through the visual has transformative power, and any intervention by the Roma into the conflicting history of Roma representation operates as an act of resistance.

As a counterpoint to the horror of anthropological photos, and also to the false romanticised, sexualised and criminalised image of the Roma in the history of western art, Roma art is a movement for self-determination.

The exhibited artists emphasise the embodiments and narratives of Sinti and Roma resistance as a central aspect of their own experience. Sinti and Roma art itself is seen as a measured and creative method of Sinti and Roma resilience, a well-established form of cultural survival, and a demonstration of ethical and political commitment to the future of the Sinti and Roma community.

The works by Robert Gabris, Małgorzata Mirga-Tas Emilia Rigova, Selma Selman and Alfred Ulrich contain the imaginings of the Sinti and Roma transformative subject, the prospects of new historical and political tectonics for our common prosperity, building on the power of assembly and the alliances we establish for the self-determination of all minorities.

Tímea Junghaus, 2020

Cologne, Germany — November 2020

Tímea Junghaus
Roma Resist!

ERIAC
EUROPEAN ROMA INSTITUTE FOR ARTS AND CULTURE

The Roma contribution to this exhibition was supported by ERIAC. (www.eriac.org)

The Sinti and Roma are Europe's largest internal colony. The majority of the 12 million members of the Sinti and Roma population live in Central, Eastern and Southern Europe, but every European state has a significant Roma minority. Sinti and Roma have been present and contributing to European history, culture, and life for over 600 years. The history of the Roma and Sinti within Europe is one of persecutions, expulsions, slavery, violent events, and genocides. The Roma Holocaust had over 500,000 victims, and was only publicly recognised for the first time in 1982. The 500 years of Roma slavery remains a hidden element of Europe's history.

In the case of the Sinti and Roma, we must understand colonialism as a strategy deployed by the majority in order to maintain asymmetrical economic and political power relations (in the same way that Edward Said speaks of »Orientalism« as the application of different strategies that generally result in the superior position of the »West« in relation to the »East«). The unequal structures of colonial power can be easily identified: the way knowledge is collected about the Roma without their own contribution, for example, as well as the way this knowledge is disseminated without their involvement, are both ideological manifestations of colonial power. The civilising efforts of majority societies towards the Roma stretch throughout European history up to the present day, when a neo-colonialist attitude towards the Roma is widespread in the political landscape: the political discourse of contemporary integration politics is the »Gypsy problem«, which frames the issues that Roma face – such as housing, segregated education, health, and employment – as inevitable by-products of Roma and Sinti culture.

»The history of the Roma is not a story of victimisation, but one of survival, resilience, and true resistance.« *Tímea Junghaus*

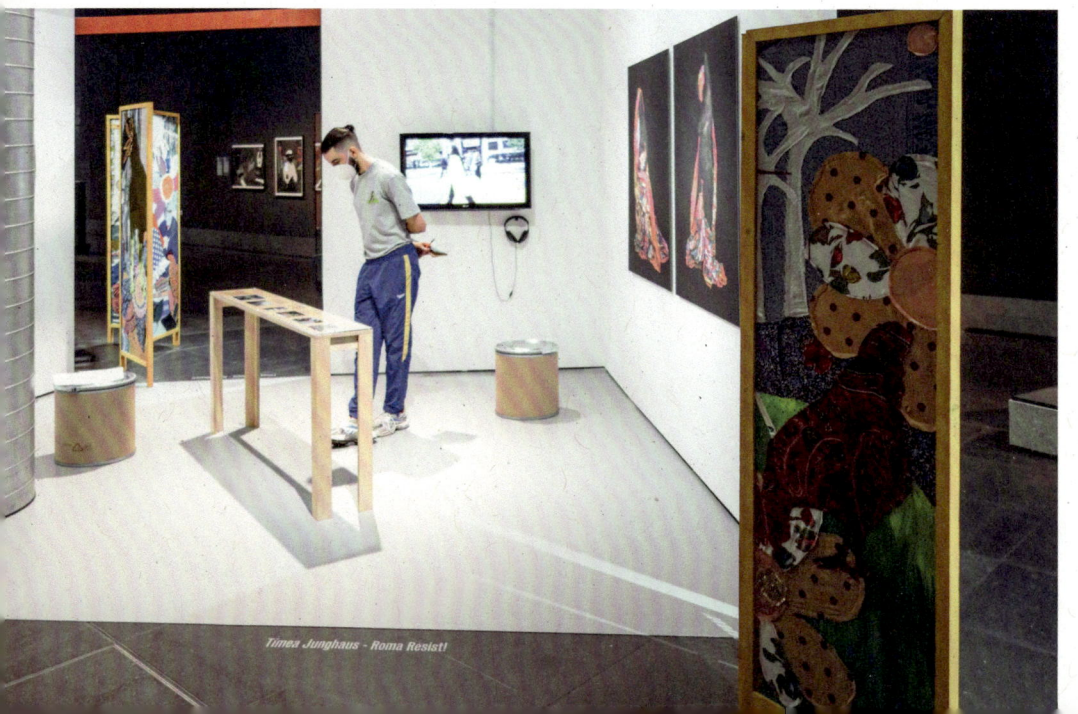

It's Yours!

Berlin, Germany — December 2020

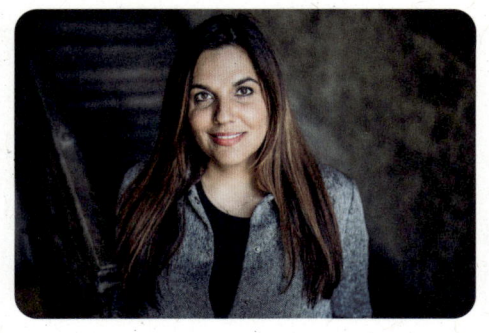

Tímea Junghaus
*1975, Budapest, Ungarn

Combining activism and contemporary art practice is how the Hungarian Romni Tímea Junghaus describes her task. Junghaus is an art historian and contemporary art curator of Roma/Sinti origin. She has researched and published extensively on the conjunctions of modern and contemporary art with critical theory, with particular reference to issues of Roma cultural oppression, colonialism, and minority representation. Her curatorial work catalysed the recognition and inclusion of Roma/Sinti artists into the contemporary art scene and unveiled the hidden genealogy of the contributions made by diverse minorities to what we call Europe today. She is also the executive director of the European Roma Institute for Arts and Culture (ERIAC), which acts as an international creative hub to support the exchange of creative ideas across borders, cultural domains, and Romani identities. She lives and works in Berlin.

1 Peggy Piesche et.al., "Museum. Space. History: New Sites of Political Tectonics; A virtual exchange between Belinda Kazeem, Nicola Lauré al-Samarai, and Peggy Piesche", trans. Tim Sharp, Transversal, June 2008, https://transversal.at/transversal/0708/kazeem-piesche/en (accessed November 25, 2020).

The (re-)exploration of the forgotten and unwritten history of the Sinti and Roma clearly shows that the Sinti and Roma had the power to resist oppression and to take part in different forms of resistance – and therefore have the capacity to take on a role other than that of the victim. In this immersive unlearning and rewriting of Sinti and Roma history, a history of oppression is replaced by a history of resistance.

New research proves that the Sinti and Roma have always taken an active and conscious role in shaping their lives and defining their own beliefs. Roma history is a story of flight, uprisings, heroes, active participation in the partisan movements … In this process of re-learning, Sinti and Roma resistance emerges as an inspiring model for knowledge and agency.

Ethnographic museums have vastly contributed to the social assignment of Roma bodies to an underclass, and were historically instrumental in shaping both slavery and mass media. Today the role of the ethnographic museum must be – as this museum demonstrates – to theoretically analyse and explore how race is constructed through the gaze, as well as how this spectatorial surveillance complicates social relations because of the way in which it is historically and inextricably woven into the European collective consciousness and cultural ethos through popular media.

Our objective is the liberation of Roma subjectivity – and therefore the liberation of the Roma people. In this special exhibition, Roma bodies are not presented in a way to objectify, re-shape or dis-figure them. Instead, the Roma body is the vehicle for finding specific practices »to re/configurate diasporic gazes into subjects, and to invite ourselves to be viewers; […] to uncover the colonial discourse inscribed in us and to depict it in exhibitions so that it is quasi disenchanted, […] to unmask the Western master-discourse as historical legend.«¹

»Roma subalternity, as Gayatri Chakravorty Spivak summarised in her philosophy, ›this burden of being the »other«, and the physical, symbolic, epistemic – violence‹, in other words, the colonising act of European majorities toward the Roma, is most visible and evident in the visual field. Thus, exploring the desires of Roma subjectivity through a visual lens has transformative power, and any intervention by the Roma into the conflicting history of Roma representation operates as an act of resistance.« *Tímea Junghaus*

Malgorzata Mirga-Tas
Romni Kali Daj [Roma Madonna]

2019/2020

This series of patchwork screens portrays women who are important to Mirga-Tas – her mother, grandmother, aunts, and extended family members; women who represent strength and resilience and who often transcend traditional gender roles. Mirga-Tas incorporates fabric from clothing worn by them as well as other personal objects, such as jewellery or scarves. The women are depicted in intimate moments of reflection, alone or with other family members – they are witnesses to history and become the link between the past and the present.

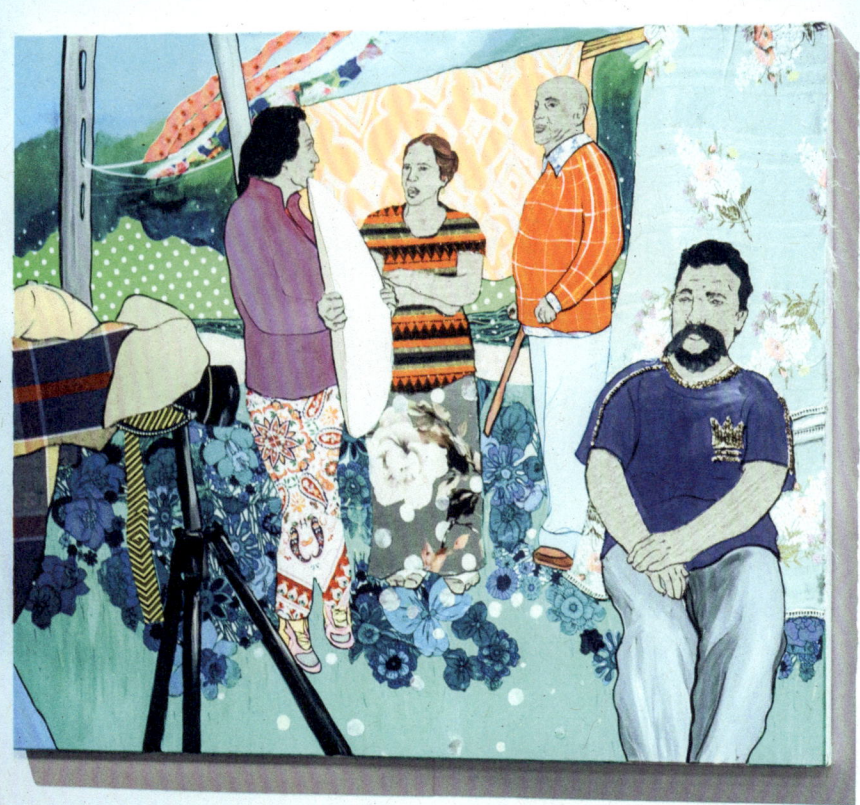

Courtesy of the Artist and Galeria Szydłowski

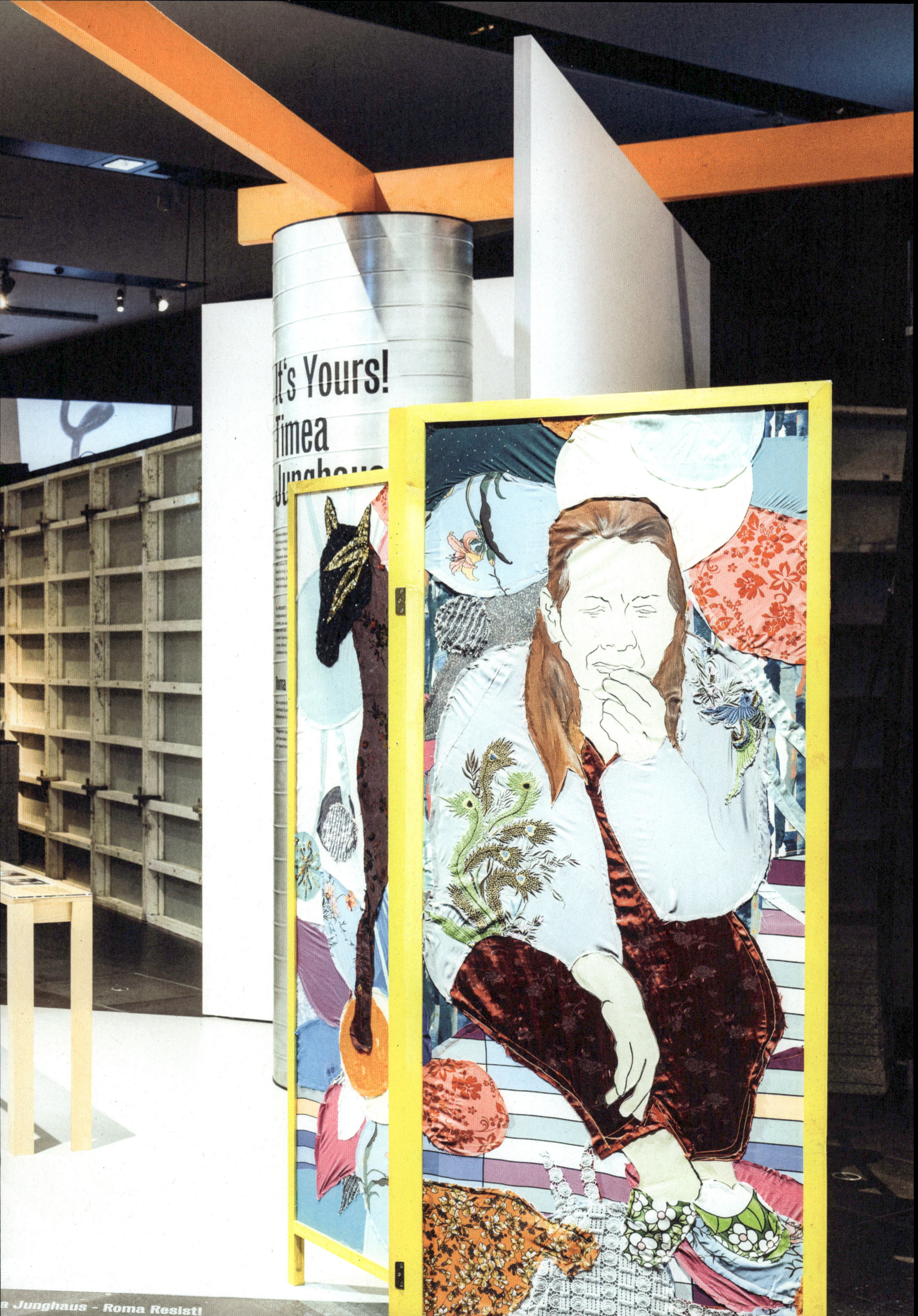

Alfred Ullrich
Casting Pearls before Swine

2020

»I suddenly thought of this proverb ›casting pearls before swine‹. It was a desperate move for me, because I thought: ›The pigs certainly don't realise that they're being thrown pearls instead of accusations.‹« *Alfred Ullrich*

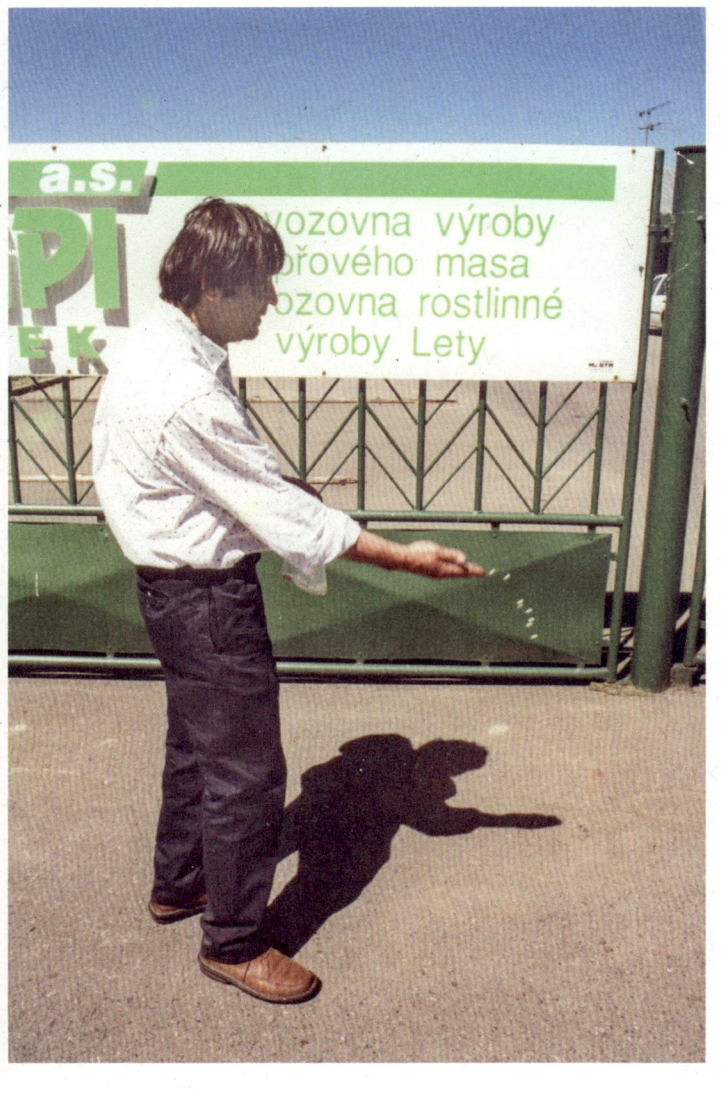

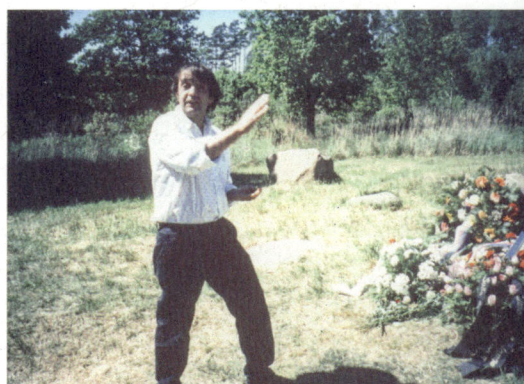

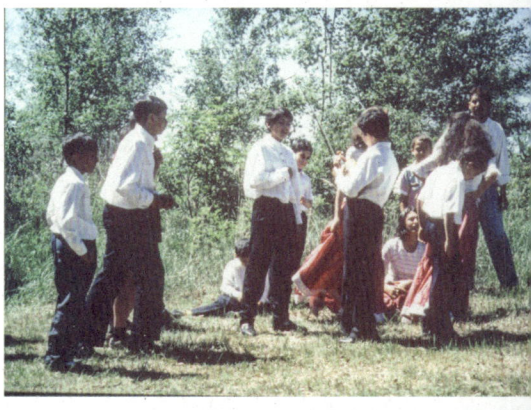

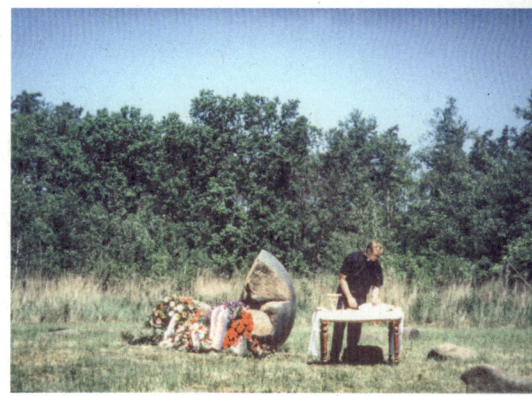

During this performance, Alfred Ullrich throws "pearls before swine" while other descendants of Roma and Sinti survivors commemorate their murdered ancestors by laying flowers on their "graves", dancing, embroidering and sewing.

Ullrich's performance art is political. In his first action, Ullrich stood in front of the entrance gate to the Lety concentration camp and let pearls fall to the ground from his open hand. This was a reference to the scandal that the former death camp, the site of the mass murder of Roma and Sinti, was being used as a pig farm. As a keen observer, Ullrich challenges outdated views and behaviours, and often finds discrimination against the different and unknown in language and images.

The concentration camp in Lety u Písku (Czech Republic) was built as a prison and labour camp in 1940 and was converted into a transit camp for Roma and Sinti from Bohemia in August 1942. According to the Czech government, around 1,392 men, women and children were imprisoned in the camp until its closure in August 1943. Of these prisoners, 326 were murdered. Survivors, however, report that there were a much higher number of prisoners and victims in the camp. Most of the prisoners were deported to Auschwitz in 1943. During the Second World War, almost all Czech Roma and Sinti were murdered, with only around one in ten surviving. The industrial pig farm on the site of the camp was built in the 1970s. It was only after decades of protests and resistance actions by Roma and Sinti activists, including Alfred Ullrich and this performance, that the Czech government finally bought the pig farm in 2017. At the end of July 2022, demolition began to make way for a memorial and museum.

RESIST! Just Ask #1:
Alfred Ulrich in conversation with Karima Renes, Live speaker in *RESIST!*

It's Yours!

Robert Gabris
Insectology in My Body

2020

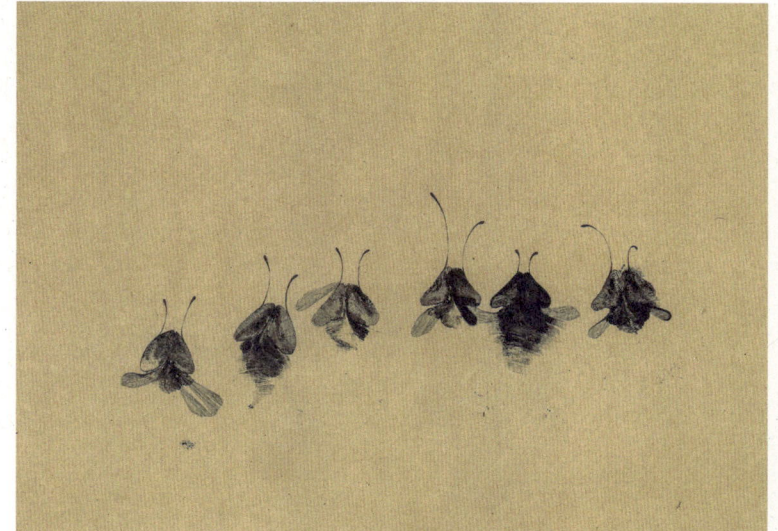

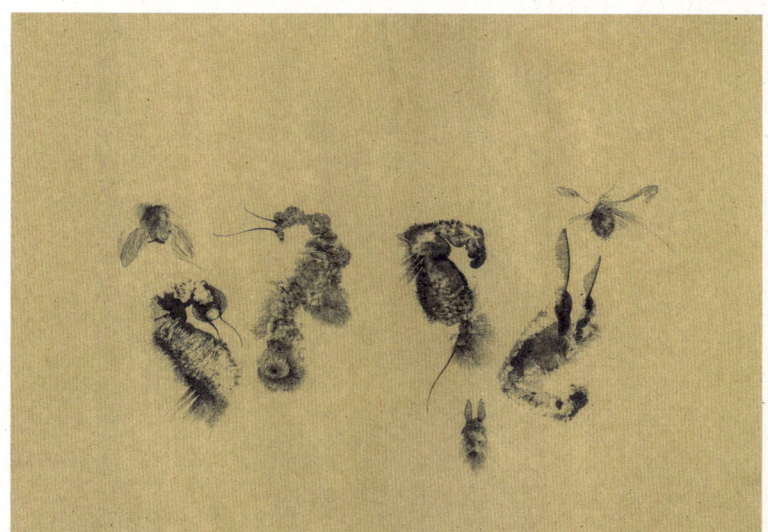

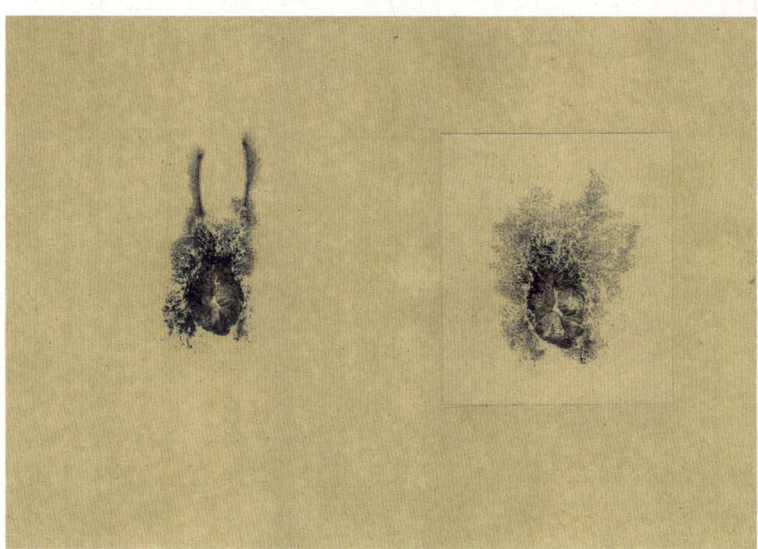

»The focus of my work centres around the bare human body, a tool that I reinterpret demonstratively. The constant change through drawing embodies my inner contemporaneity and queerness. The imagery created through this reflection demonstrates a subjective resistance to mainstream, normative thinking. In this series I used black ink to mirror print parts of my body, such as my hands, fingers, ears, and genitals. These drawings point to an entomological collection that examines the relationship between insects and humans. I meticulously dissect my body with a thin pen on paper, overdraw and redefine its shapes. I draw the state of being rejected as an object of disgust. On the other hand, there is also an element of glory in the fact that it is always associated with the fear of non-humanity.

My body and identity are in constant motion. This is the only thing I can find after years of searching for a reference to the topic of Roma resistance. My identity has no significant ethnological attributes and I distance myself from previous anthropological research. I don't emigrate, I don't assimilate, I don't integrate. If you want to identify my fingerprints, you have to go through my Insectopia.« *Robert Gabris*

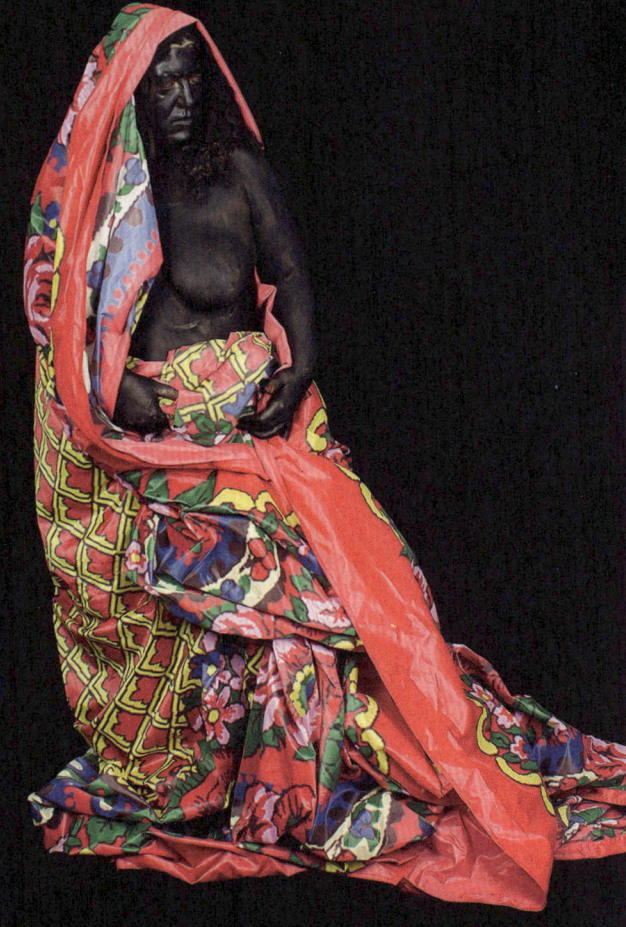

Emília Rigovà
Crossing B(l)ack
2017

The inspiration for this work is the author's light skin colour, which allows her to pass as non-Roma in society. The self-portrait is a declaratory act of making herself visible as a Roma woman while simultaneously styling herself as a Black Madonna – in other words, an iconic female figure with whom Roma identify.

RomaMoMa
Manifesto

ERIAC — European Roma Institute for Arts and Culture e.V.
Reinhardtstraße 41 - 43. Ground floor, street entrance, DE -10117 Berlin
eriac@eriac.org

RomaMoMA
A European Manifesto for Roma Cultural Inclusion

Where are the transnational spaces and institutional infrastructures for Roma cultural production? How will the Roma people and the Roma contributions become recognized in the (art-) history of Europe? Where are the institutions for whom diversity means true cultural inclusion of the largest minority in Europe?

The RomaMoMA Manifesto addresses the vicious circle that paralyzed Roma arts for over a millennium, prohibiting a truly diverse European cultural scene, and hindering the development of democratic societies.

Status quo

Roma are the largest and at the same time most vulnerable minority of Europe (10-12 million people). The social inclusion of Roma is impossible without cultural inclusion, yet the more than a millennium long cultural contribution of Roma to European societies, and national cultures is denied. Roma arts and culture have been misinterpreted and racialized as ethnic, naive and primitive. Roma cultural heritage is inaccessible and in -danger – stored in basements, archives and storages – without presentation and preservation strategies.

To this date, European majority institutions failed to include Roma arts and culture into their permanent programming. This cultural exclusion, and the missed opportunity of recognizing the vast contribution of Roma to European life and history has long lasting and devastating results: It relegates Roma people to the deprived – social, economic, political, and cultural periphery of Europe.

A change in cultural policy and practice is overdue. The transformation – as many times in history – must begin in the cultural field:

Alliance of Institutions for European Roma Cultural Inclusion

ERIAC is launching an Alliance of Institutions for European Roma Cultural Inclusion to conduct a policy change. We invite all public institutions in Europe working with arts and culture – museums, concert halls, academic institutions, cultural decision-makers, to reshape museum protocols and join the **Alliance of Institutions for European Roma Cultural Inclusion! Start the change within your own institution/ organization!** Join the alliance and commit to an institutional operation and programming that ensures the long-term cultural inclusion of Roma first into our culture and then into our societies. See the list of public institutions who ERIAC has already partnered with in the past for Roma cultural inclusion and contact ERIAC (eriac@eriac.org) with your institution`s Roma inclusion policy to receive the certification, the membership package and the expertise you need (if any). For more information visit www.eraic.org/romamoma.

Performing a Roma Modern and Contemporary Art Museum: RomaMoMA

RomaMoMA[1] is a transnational, collaborative and discursive art project of the European Roma Institute of Arts and Culture (ERIAC) and OFF-Biennale Budapest. It is a platform to envision and discuss the possible forms of a Roma museum of modern and contemporary art that will

---

[1] RomaMoma is not a new idea. We honour the many intellectuals and institutions since the beginning of Roma authorship - both Roma and non-Roma - who attempted to call for a similar initiative, before. The notion of the Roma Museum and its long, oppressed and invisible cultural history is the core and genealogy of this RomaMoma initiative.

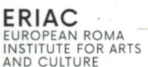

European Roma Institute for Arts and Culture e.V.
Reinhardtstraße 41 - 43. Ground floor, street entrance, DE -10117 Berlin
eriac@eriac.org

spread in time and space through a series of exhibitions, discussions, and art projects. It will invite Roma and non-Roma artists, cultural experts, scholars and civil society. RomaMoMA is to perform an institution which, hopefully one day, materializes into a cutting-edge agent of the contemporary arts and culture scene. RomaMoMA is guided and supported by the think-tank, which is assembled of experts of various fields of art and the humanities, in order to exchange ideas on the necessity and possible roles of a transnational museum of Roma contemporary art, and to come up with a collective proposal for the institution of such a museum.

Members of the RomaMoMA Think-tank

André Jenő Raatzsch (artist, Documentation and Cultural Centre for German Sinti and Roma, Heidelberg/RomArchive project), Jana Horváthová (Director, Museum of Romani Culture-Brno) Delaine Le Bas (artist), Ethel Brooks (Professor at Rutgers University, Department of Women and Gender Studies), Ian Hancock (Professor at the University of Texas at Austin, Department of Linguistics), Achille Mbembe (Professor at University of Wits Witwatersrand, Institute for Social and Economic Research), Maria Lind (curator, writer, art critic, co-curator of the 2019 Biennial in Timisoara), Tímea Junghaus (art historian, curator, executive director of ERIAC), Rashida Bumbray (curator, director of Culture and Art Program of the Open Society Foundations), Emilia Rigova (artist, head of Roma arts and culture Department at University of Matej Bel, Slovakia, Banská Bystrica), Angela Kocze (Director of Romani Studies Program, Central European University), Julia Ferloni (curator, MUCEM, Marseille), Kader Attia (artist and scholar), Vera Marusic (curator, Rautenstrauch-Joest-Museum in Köln) and Nanette Sneop (Director, Rautenstrauch-Joest-Museum in Köln), Denisa Tomkova (art historian, scholar, curator)

ERIAC has already partnered with the following institutions for Roma cultural inclusion

Maxim Gorki Theater, Berlin
Volksbühne, Berlin
Rautenstrauch-Joest-Museum, Köln
Villa Romana, Florence
Tensta Konsthall, Stockholm
MUCEM, Marseille

Supported by

ERIAC
OFF-Biennale
European Cultural Fund (ECF)

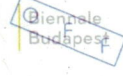

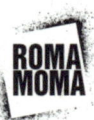

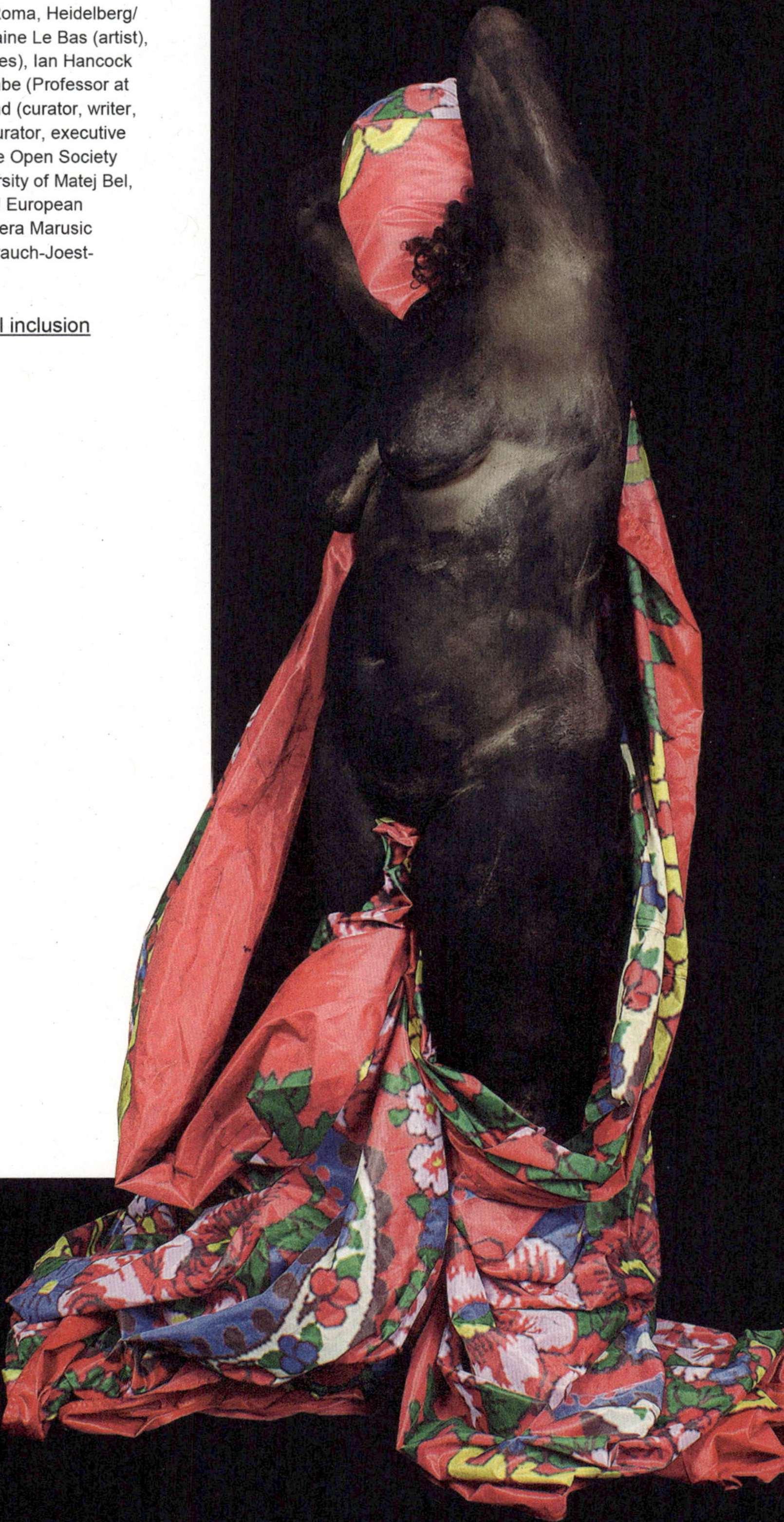

Conversation:
Roma Resist!

A conversation with **Tímea Junghaus**, director of the European Roma Institute for Arts and Culture (ERIAC) and curator of the *It's Yours!* space *Roma Resist!*

This conversation was part of the online programme *RESIST! DIGITAL*, which was launched due to Covid restrictions.

Nanette Snoep: There are 10 to 12 million Roma living in Europe. This is the largest minority on the European continent: a multinational, multilingual, and multireligious community that are dispersed, stateless, and subject to discrimination. Tímea Junghaus, you are the director of the European Roma Institute for Arts and Culture (ERIAC). We invited you to curate your own space with works by Roma artists as part of *RESIST!* What is your artistic approach – and how is it reflected in your contribution to the exhibition?

Tímea Junghaus: I am an art historian and curator; my task as ERIAC director is to seek acknowledgement for Roma art and culture in Europe. My activism and my involvement in contemporary art ultimately form part of my self-actualisation as a Roma woman: my practice is informed by my community's political stance against racism, sexism, and all forms of exploitation. Against this background, it was a very interesting, even radical experience to design the *It's Yours!* space. **The space was created with no reference to usual museum practice: there was no pre-set theme, no pre-set framework, no pre-set institutional curatorial agenda. Other museum spaces would do well to consider this approach. Breaking away from all these common practices is a radical act. For the Roma, this offer is an expression of respect and trust; the museum is thus acknowledging our self-determination. All this potential for self-definition, the freedom you gave us, was crucial – and brings with it a great responsibility.**

Snoep: Art historian, curator, activist: which of your roles is most important to you?

Junghaus: I don't see any divisions between these roles. Sometimes it's street activism in the different *mahalas*, as we call a neighbourhood or a settlement in the Romanes language. Sometimes it's a matter of access to water, sometimes it's a diplomatic meeting with representatives of the Council of Europe or a fascinating discussion within the community. But this is not specific to the Roma context; I know other curators who juggle similar roles.

Snoep: In interviews and articles, you repeatedly address the consequences of colonisation. From your perspective, what connects the history of anti-colonial resistance in the Global South with colonial continuities and the resistance of the Roma here in Europe?

Berlin & Cologne, Germany 22/01/2021

Junghaus: It is an important and highly political act to place the Roma at the heart of the post-colonial struggle in which they have participated since the 1960s. We are talking about a colony of 12 million people – a number that is constantly being challenged by academics and contemporary historiography. The history of the Roma people, like that of the Global South, is the history of an oppressed and hidden genealogy that goes back 600 years. During this time, the Roma have lived on the European continent and contributed to politics and culture – while also experiencing discrimination, expulsion, persecution, and genocide. This includes 500 years of Roma slavery in Romania as well as 500,000 Roma victims of the Holocaust. These victims were not acknowledged until 1982, and there has been no compensation to date. All this corresponds to colonialism as a strategy of the white majority to maintain asymmetrical power relations in economic, political, and cultural life. Consequently, knowledge about the Roma tends to be produced without any contribution from the Roma themselves; for example, the discipline called "Roma Studies" exists without any input from Roma academics. Or consider how the Roma are denied access to their cultural heritage, or the way Roma issues are discussed in the EU today: there is talk of "solving the G-word problem" or "the Roma issue"; in this discourse, devastating problems – housing, segregated education, health, work – are presented as inevitable by-products of an imagined Roma culture.

Snoep: Namibian politicians Esther Utjiua Muinjangue and Ida Hoffman, who designed an *It's Yours!* space for *RESIST!*, as you did, also say "Not about us without us!" But so-called ethnographic museums in the West are by definition institutions that are not based on self-representation. Did you have any reservations about participating in our exhibition on behalf of the Roma?

Junghaus: It is well known in the Roma community that the ethnographic museum is a *benga*, Romanes for »devil«. It is hell for Roma culture. We can go to an ethnographic museum in almost any European capital and see our ancestors there. But what we find next to photos are not their names; what we see next to installations of tents, caravans, and clothes are not the names of the campsites but those of the ethnographers or anthropologists. Roma authorship and history are thus vehemently denied, not to mention the problematic role of Nazi museum archives. This is precisely why I did not hesitate to accept the invitation: if there really is to be a decolonial practice, then it must take place in the ethnographic museum. The artists I invited, though, really did feel ambiguous about the project.

Snoep: You titled your *It's Yours!* space *Roma Resist!* What is the meaning of the title?

Junghaus: This title, complete with exclamation mark, is really important. As soon as enough critical Roma intellectuals started to break away from the historical image we had been taught, we realised: our history is not a story of victimhood, but one of survival, resilience, and true resistance. It is not widely known, but the only uprising during the Holocaust in Auschwitz was instigated, fuelled, and organised by the Roma: that is why we celebrate May 16 as Roma Resistance Day. Because many of our ancestors were undocumented, our history remained unwritten: the violence, the minor and major genocides. Our own historiography documents feats of heroism, uprisings, escapes, protests, interventions, and participation in the partisan movement. In positive terms: I think resistance is a well-established method of cultural survival – for example, when knowledge is passed on to younger generations without any infrastructure. We are a very resilient community. And a growing community in an ageing Europe.

Snoep: In most ethnographic collections, people from the communities where the collections come from, still remain unknown and anonymous. In this exhibition, we try to honour the names of those who have been fighting against colonialism for 500 years. What mattered most to you personally in the context of this exhibition?

Junghaus: A truthful encounter between Roma and non-Roma. The message is: healing can begin here. Here, in encounters like these. Both sides need it. After all, the colonial act and violence have caused damage not only to the victims but also to the oppressors.

Snoep: Healing also means reconciliation. Public conversations about decolonisation and the restitution of looted art mostly revolve around the Global South. What is the status quo with regard to Roma artefacts in museums?

Junghaus: The future of Roma culture depends on repatriation. But mentioning it is political suicide. You see, the Roma are a national minority – in almost every European country. As I said, 600 years of our culture and history in Europe are archived in national and ethnographic museums. We at the European Roma Institute for Art and Culture have therefore created a database. Since day one, we have been trying to collect artefacts. So far, we've been able to locate 33,000 objects in national collections across Europe. Some colleagues are extremely helpful, sharing their entire archives with us; others refuse to cooperate with an NGO. Most of the 33,000 works are in storage, with the Roma and the wider public denied any chance of access. Do not forget that we are talking about a huge number of objects here – produced by a minority that does not participate in cultural life, by artists who are considered by the majority as "self-taught", "naïve", "uneducated". Then there is this giant gap regarding ethnographic museums: they don't usually collect contemporary art as such, right? So, since the 1960s, they have focused on traditional art. We Roma consider these traditional trades – blacksmithing, goldsmithing, embroidery – as contemporary forms of artistic expression, but in ethnographic museums, they are catalogued under the names of the "collectors" and "ethnographers" rather than the artists. This is really outrageous. **The restitution process as we see it is irreversible. There is no museum space, no infrastructure in which we could house these artworks. But first, we must have restitution in our minds.**

Snoep: What does that mean?

Junghaus: According to manuscripts and written documents, Roma communities first appeared in Europe around the fifteenth century – but there are traces of Roma groups on the European continent dating from the twelfth and thirteenth centuries. They inspired Northern Renaissance artists to illustrate the multiculturalism of their era. The Roma were first depicted as a pagan minority, later as mercenaries. Nineteenth-century artists who couldn't travel to Africa, the Caribbean, or Tahiti would look for exoticism closer to home: the Roma. Here, they found "their" Blacks: the Roma thus became the counterpart of the so-called "primitives" in Africa and Asia. This becomes very clear in European modernism: there is Genella Lowell, for instance, the famous Roma model of the French sculptor Auguste Rodin. She is very well-known in the Roma community as a musician and muse. In the nineteenth century, Roma people served as models for the Austrian painter August von Pettenkofen; the flamenco dancers of Seville inspired Spanish painting. They all contributed to European art history. It is up to us professionals, art historians, writers, and theorists, to reveal this and thus promote decolonisation in our minds..

Snoep: The centre of your space is dedicated to a series of photographs taken by the German anthropologists and "racial scientists" Robert Ritter, Eva Justin, and Sophie Ehrhardt. These are very violent images. What was your motivation for displaying them – and what do they represent?

Junghaus: The horror of these images is precisely where I started. I just took another look at the captions and was struck again by the fact that the photos are not from the 1930s; they were taken in 1951. These anthropologists collected human body parts, hair, and casts of Roma victims to display in their *Wunderkammer*: to represent them as a "race". They continued to teach at German universities. Some of the casts are still in an archive at the Eberhard Karls University of Tübingen – with bits of hair and eyebrows stuck to them. I see it is a great achievement to have gained access to the archive cabinet. Three of these heads are now on display in the Roma Museum in Brno. The Sinti community is extremely traditional when it comes to objects belonging to the victims: out of respect for the deceased, they are not supposed to be exhibited. Documentation centres therefore illustrate the Holocaust against the Roma with photos of the original objects. But I personally think we should change that. I also believe that the traditional museological approach – from lending to access to cataloguing to presentation – is utterly outdated. We know that museums are in a crisis with regard to the role of minorities. I welcome this crisis; it is transformative. I hope minorities can support museums with their solutions. Institutions like ours can change the world by showing that material heritage is at risk. Today, it is invisible, hidden away in state collections. But we can participate in the process of re-appropriation, of renaming, and of celebrating the creators. In this way, we can help to decolonise institutions.

Snoep: Celebrating creators and revealing cultural heritage is precisely what your *It's Yours!* space does. What criteria did you use to select artists for *Roma Resist!*? What stories do their works tell?

Junghaus: When I first saw the intricate floor plan for *RESIST!*, I knew it was nothing like the traditional white cube museum setting. With this unusual space in mind, I sought out artists who could enter into dialogues with other minorities, other peripheries, other decolonial struggles. Take Emília Rigová, who is currently teaching at the Academy of Fine Arts in Banská Bystrica. Her work *Crossing B(l)ack* is a self-portrait in which she poses as Kali Madonna, an iconic figure in Roma mythology – the matriarch Kali Sara from whom we all descend. Rigová thus reflects on her light skin colour, visually revealing her Roma identity, while also exploring the stereotypical image of the Black Madonna or the "G-word Madonna".

Another work is Robert Gabris's *Insectology in My Body*: the photograph is a still from a performance staged as part of his scholarship at the Villa Romana in Florence. The performance involved him pressing various body parts onto paper and adding meditative, fluid lines, a typical stylistic device and form of expression in his work. The viewer can make out images of various body parts, of hands and fingers and ears and genitals. The patterns and sizes of the prints are reminiscent of an insect collection. Gabris has written a statement about this, in which he reflects on what it means to be invited by an ethnographic museum. He felt torn about the invitation. "The focus of this work is the bare human body," he writes. "It is my tool, that I reinterpret demonstratively. My work critically engages with identity issues by confronting different groups excluded from society. My work proceeds from new experimental forms of drawing as forms of resistance to exclusion and racism."

Another artwork in our space, Alfred Ullrich's 2000 performance called *Pearls Before Swine*, shows the artist casting pearls before a pig farm in Lety in the Czech Republic. It is located at the site of a camp where the Roma were gathered during the Holocaust before being loaded onto the trains that would take them to German camps. This performance was very important; it received a lot of media attention. Only two years ago, the Czech government finally announced that the pig farm would be closed and a memorial built. The construction process began last year.

The textile piece *Miri Daj* (My Mother) by Małgorzata Mirga-Tas is also part of *Roma Resist!* Like all her works, it depicts the traditional life of the community's members. She reproduces the entirety of the original scene, from the figures' clothing to their jewellery, using patches of fabric. Her artworks portray the Roma woman as the head of the household, the creator of these beautiful, shiny objects. This style of patchwork was historically used by the Roma to exchange information between different communities and camps.

Selma Selman's performance is entitled *You Have No Idea*. The artist returned to this piece in the context of the Black Lives Matter movement. Her statement forms an integral part of it. She writes: "This performance is very personal: it is my frustration brought to life. You have no idea. You have no idea about my life as a whole. You do not know who I am; nor do you know my joy or my sorrow. You don't know if there is pain in my life or not, or how I feel when performing this piece in front of a live audience. You have no idea. Although this piece relates to the specific circumstances of my life, I believe it has a universal message." Selman graduated from the University of the Arts in Bosnia, received a full scholarship from Syracuse University, NY, and was named best young Bosnian artist of 2014. During the pandemic, she returned to the city of her birth and founded a Roma museum next to her family home. Her performance art is celebrated all over Europe and in the USA.

Snoep: Do the artists you have chosen define themselves as "Roma artists"? And what does this label even mean?

Junghaus: I see "Roma art" as an institutional outcome of the Roma cultural movement. The label is a legitimate term: it acknowledges the movement. It suggests counterculture, authentic Roma voices. The artists don't have to agree with me on this. But they are part of the contemporary art crowd who openly acknowledge their Roma origin and treat it with respect. We are in a cultural war for the acknowledgement of Roma art. This term will continue to be used until we receive the equality and recognition we deserve. That's why we need to join forces with other peripheries and other minorities. In a world of Orbáns and Trumps and Le Pens, we need a global movement for effective counter-propaganda. We need to reach out to the youth on an emotional level. We need to unite all marginalised groups and allies of different minorities – in an intersectional way, including race and class, gender, and sexual orientation – in order to find an effective language against hate and for humanity. And I think "Roma art" is a useful term in this context.

Snoep: Cologne has a Roma and Sinti community of its own. What would you like to tell the Sinti and Roma who visit the exhibition?

Junghaus: I invite all Sinti and Roma to learn the names of our wonderful artists who are exhibited in this space and to pass them on as our history to the next generations. We are a community of 12 million people with 26 subgroups; I myself am a mixture of Sinti and Roma, my name is Sinti. I come from a family of Sinti circus artists and musicians. Of course, we also have a lot of history and cultural heritage that separate us. But only united can we grow. We must support each other and take care of each other – for example, by celebrating our culture and our artists. That is our responsibility. **Every single step we take together for an exhibition in the public space is another step towards a Roma museum.**

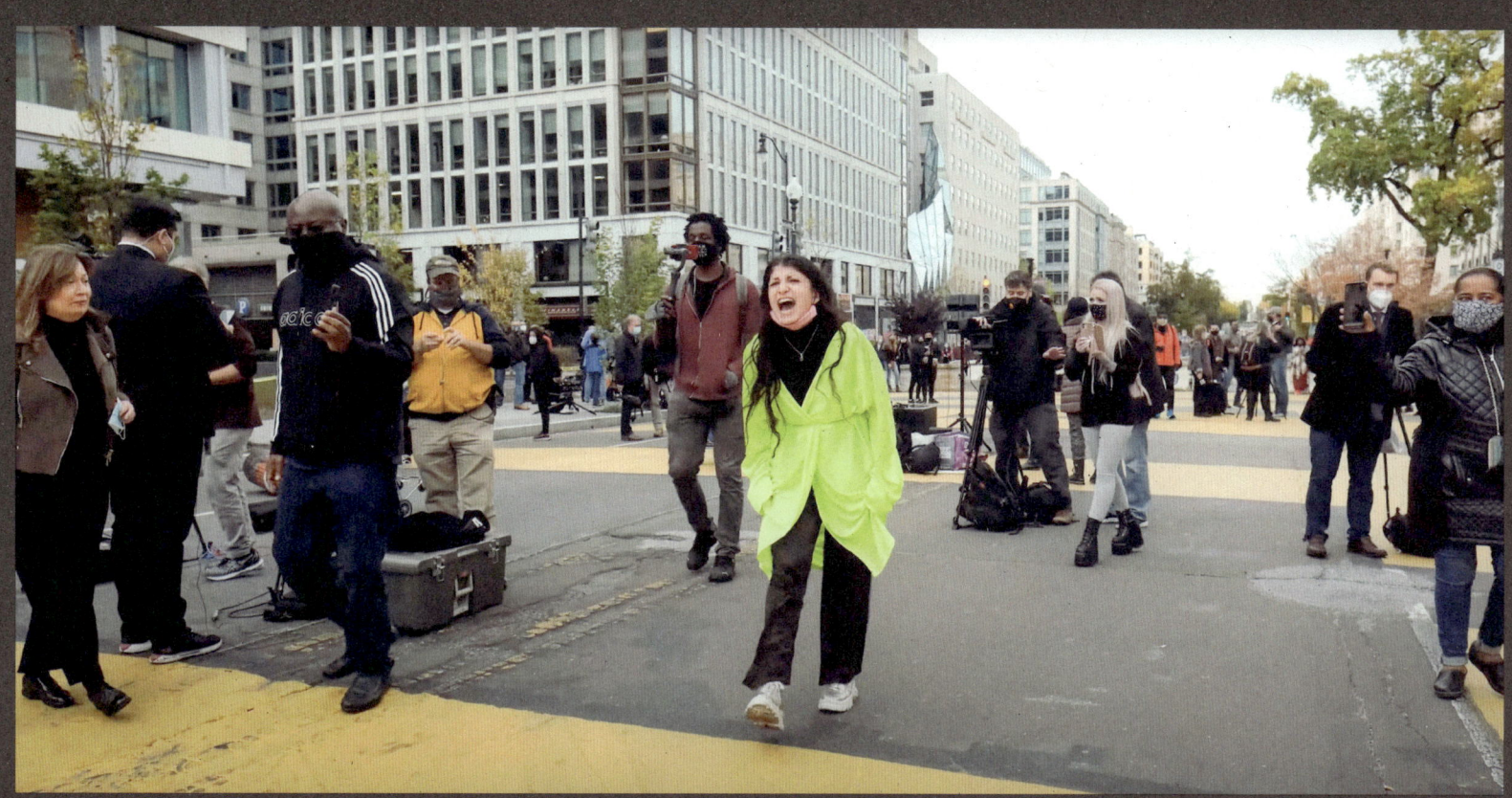

Selma Selman: *You Have No Idea*
3/11/2020, US Presidential Election Day, performance between BLM Plaza and the White House, Washington, DC, video, 5 min.

Washington, USA 03/11/2020

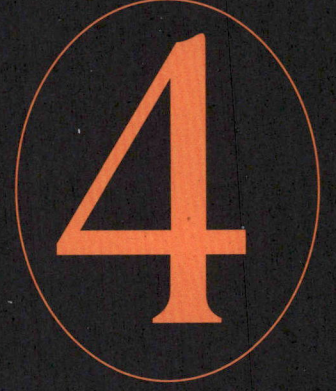

»and when we speak we are afraid
our words will not be heard
nor welcomed
but when we are silent
we are still afraid.

So it is better to speak.
remembering
we were never meant to survive.«

Audre Lorde A Litany of Survival, 1978

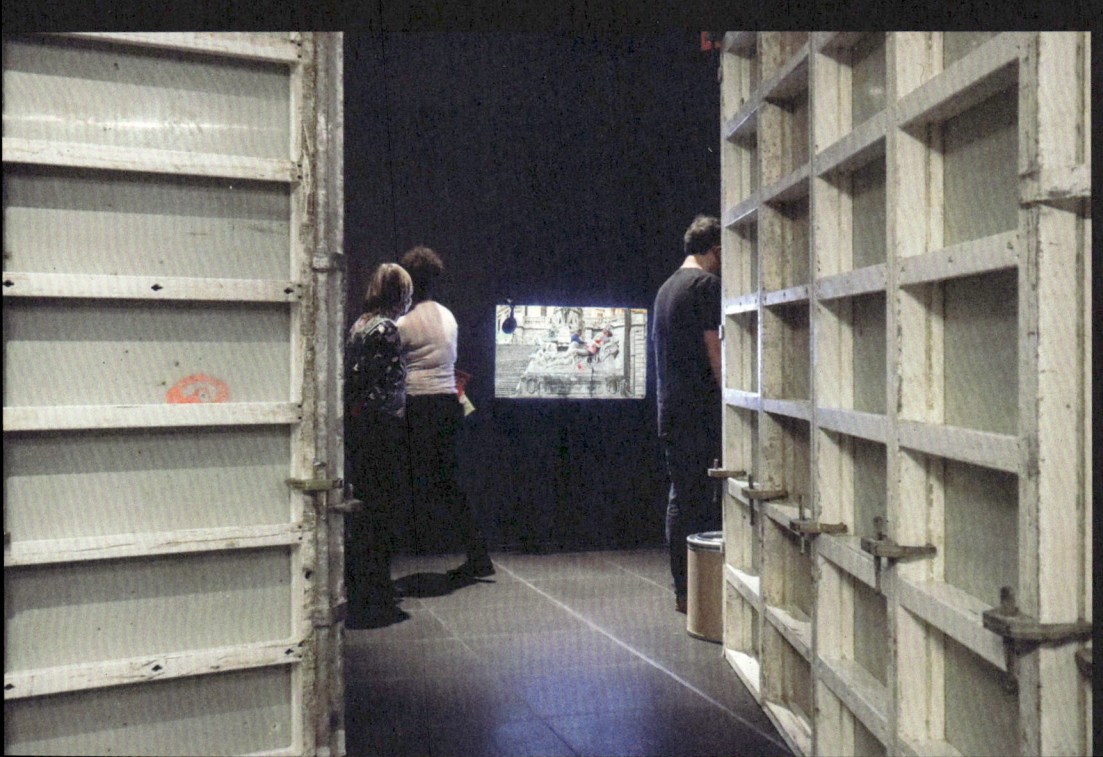

Trauma and Transformation

Psychologically, slavery and colonialism left deep traces and scars in the collective and individual memories of everyone they touched. For Grada Kilomba, an artist and theorist featured here, colonialism has never ended. *"It is like a ghost that keeps haunting our present and future, always interrupting because history has not been told 'right'."* Racism is intertwined with every structure in society, and its mechanisms can only be understood by learning about the past. The Caribbean-French psychiatrist Frantz Fanon, a writer and pioneer in decolonisation, describes his own experience of racism as an *"amputation, a cut or a haemorrhage"*. This wound is repeatedly reopened by the memory of colonial oppression, by crimes such as police violence against Black people and People of Colour, by the many monuments honouring colonial masters that still exist – and also by ethnological museums, which have come under increasing criticism in recent years as potentially hurtful to those affected. Everyday racism and the almost indescribable "micro-aggressions", traumatic for both adults and children, are often ignored or even actively denied by Whites.

In her video artworks, the Afro-American artist Kara Walker intimately examines the "unspeakable": the traumas of slavery. This is also evident in the important novel by Afro-American author Toni Morrison, Beloved, whose protagonists try to repress their traumatic memories of the past. They do not succeed. In an interview about her novel, Morrison said: *"I thought this has got to be the least read of all the books I'd written because it is about something that the characters don't want to remember, I don't want to remember, black people don't want to remember, white people don't want to remember. I mean, it's national amnesia."* Morrison emphasises the need to address traumatic history so as to create a new personal and collective self-image.

The works of the five artists in this section are very personal. They deal with traumatisation triggered by the collective (inherited) experience of colonial violence – be it the oppression of the First Nations in Canada, transatlantic slavery or the ongoing confrontation with stereotyping and racism. Only by reappraising and collective witnessing do we have a chance to understand what happened and to combat the despair of recurrent trauma.

»And no matter, for the sadness was at her center, the desolated center where the self that was no self made its home.«
Toni Morrison _{Beloved, 1987}

Tania Willard
The Protectors You Never Had, 2013

Canada 1813–1996
RESIDENTIAL SCHOOLS

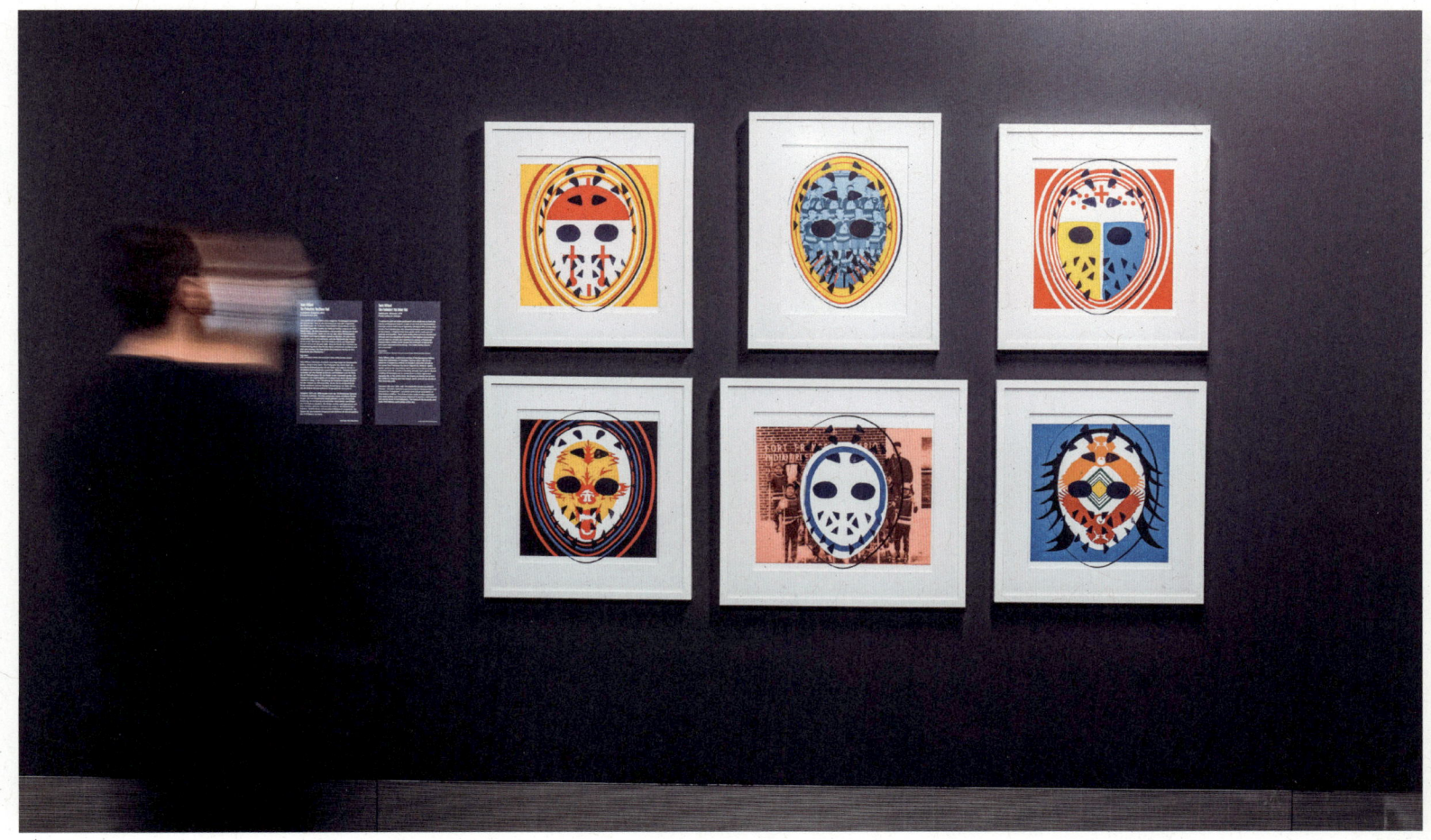

Between 1831 and 1996, over 140 residential schools operated in Canada – state-sponsored Christian institutions aimed at the "integration", conversion, and cultural assimilation of First Nations children. These children were usually forcibly separated from their families and frequently subjected to isolation, mistreatment, and sexual abuse in these institutions. First Nation communities still bear the scars of this traumatic past to this day. In May 2021, investigations of the soil behind the Kamloops Indian Residential School in Tania Willard's hometown revealed the remains of 215 children– former students who had been buried there while the school was still in operation. It is assumed that the children died of abuse, disease, and neglect. During the following months, the bodies of hundreds more children were found, buried on the grounds of residential schools all over the country. In June 2021, the Canadian government made September 30 the National Day for Truth and Reconciliation. The day honours the children who never returned home and survivors of residential schools, as well as their families and communities.

Tania Willard, artist, curator, and member of the Secwepemc Nation, combines Canadian hockey culture with the experiences of Indigenous children in Christian residential schools in her series *The Protectors You Never Had* (2013). Willard's "goalkeeper spirits" or "goalie spirits" allude to the way that hockey served as a substitute for parental protection and positive role models at residential schools. Team sports offered children a sense of belonging and an escape from their strictly regimented everyday life. In the artist's mind, the hockey masks are shields that protect the children's integrity and help them – now as adults – to ward off the ghosts of their traumatic pasts.

»I wanted to posit an Indian goalie spirit who would save us from the trauma of residential schools. In light of the Truth and Reconciliation hearings and the testimony of legendary Aboriginal NHL hockey players like Fred Saskamoose who discussed physical and sexual abuse at the schools, I imagined that these goalie spirits could ward off sadness and injustice. There were hockey teams at many residential schools and the popularity of hockey in First Nations communities and on reserves remains as a testament to spaces at residential schools where children could escape the onslaught of oppression and could celebrate and be strong. The Indian hockey story is one of survival.« *Tania Willard*

»Do you know what the difference is between a residential school and a public school? The answer: there are no cemeteries.«
Lawrence Paul Yuxweluptun

Courtesy of private collection, Cologne

Kara Walker
8 Possible Beginnings or:
The Creation of African-America, 2005

Video, 15:57 min.

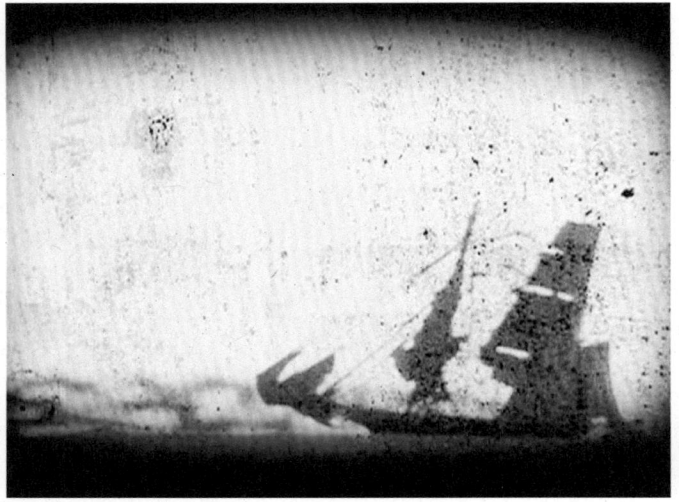
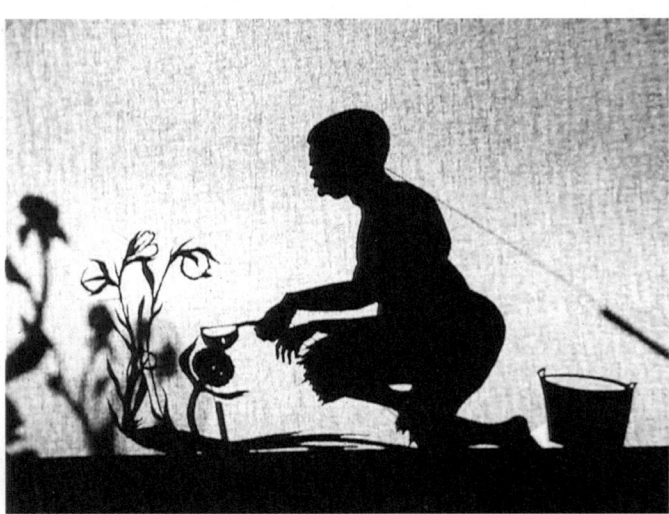
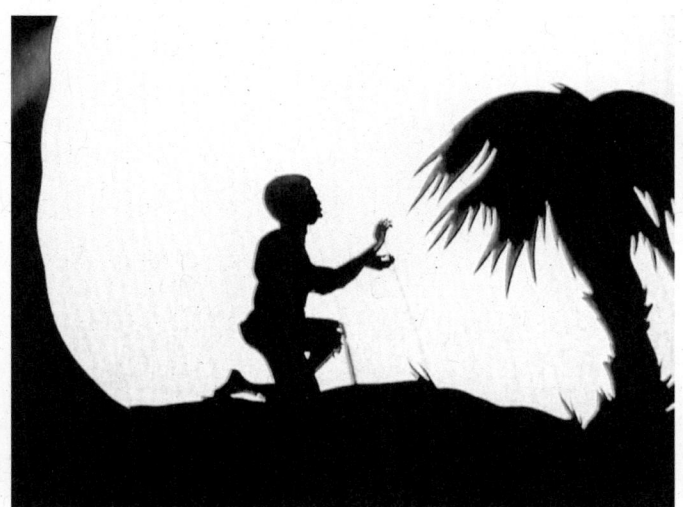
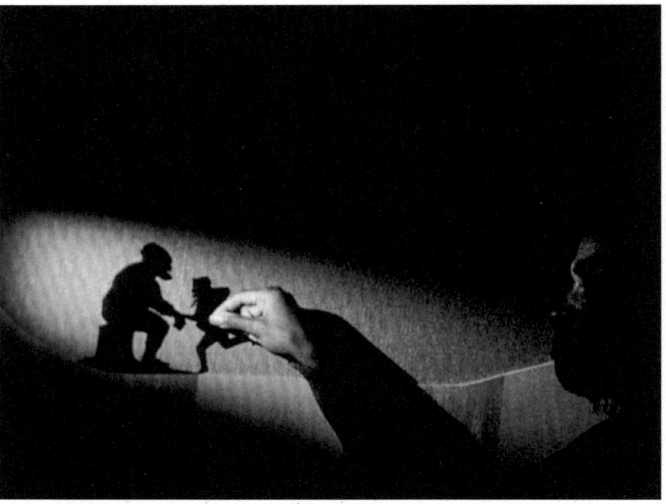
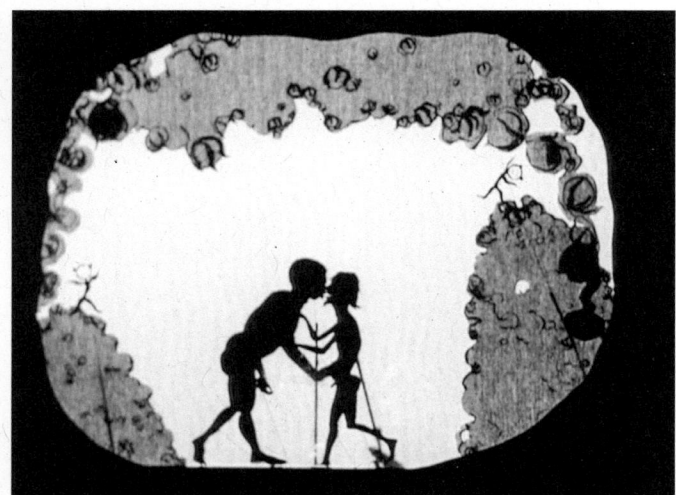

The African-American artist Kara Walker is particularly well known for her black cut-paper silhouettes. What initially seems like a nostalgic shadow play proves upon closer inspection to be an unsettling examination of slavery and racism in North America. These images unflinchingly confront repressed fears and the traumas of slavery.

The silhouettes of Black and white bodies that collide in Walker's work are characterised by exaggerated racialised and sexualised physical stereotypes. The nightmarish aesthetic and phantom nature of the video works *Testimony* and *8 Possible Beginnings* challenge the viewer to bear witness to the disturbing events deeply etched into the collective memory of the African-American population. By visually unleashing traumatic Black experiences, Walker presents a discourse of the unspeakable that references the horrific accounts of physical, psychological, and sexual abuse left unvoiced by formerly enslaved people.

By re-staging the violence of slavery as a shadow play, Walker creates a space to process historical traumas – without ever offering a solution.

Testimony: Narrative of a Negress Burdened by Good Intentions, 2004

Video, 08:49 min.

»If this is what is inside of me, then nobody is safe.«
Kara Walker

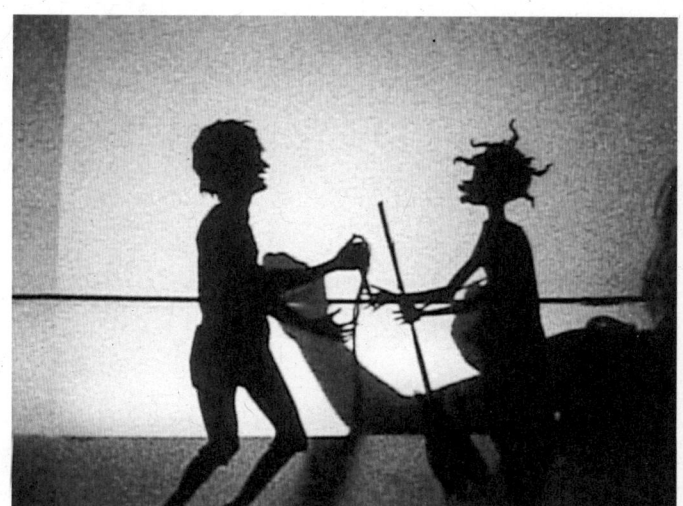

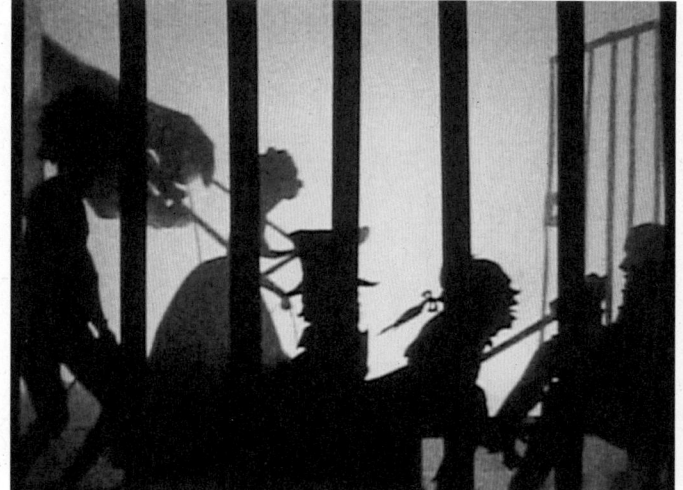

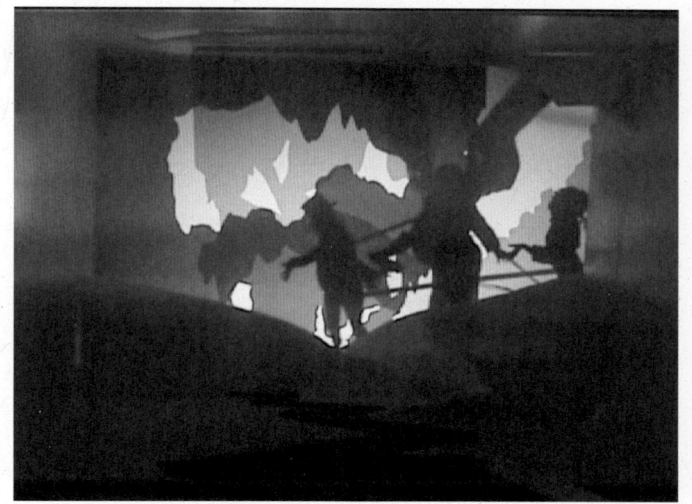

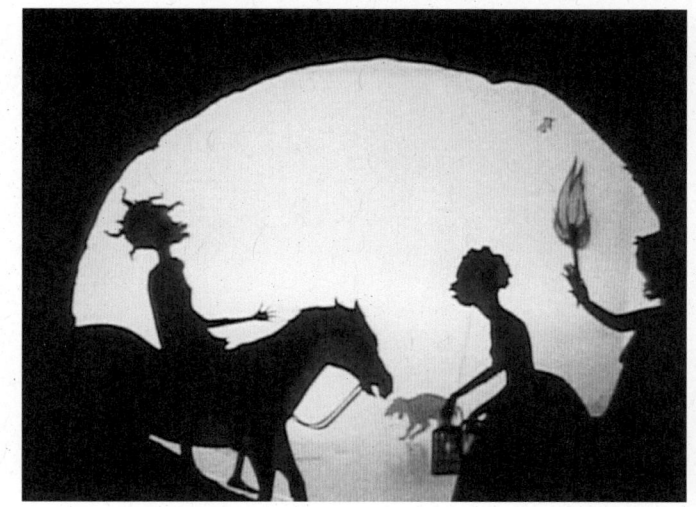

Courtesy of Sprüth Magers and Sikkema Jenkins & Co

SNARE FOR BIRDS
Kiri Dalena, Artist in Digital Residence

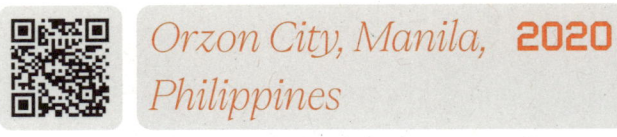

Orzon City, Manila, Philippines 2020

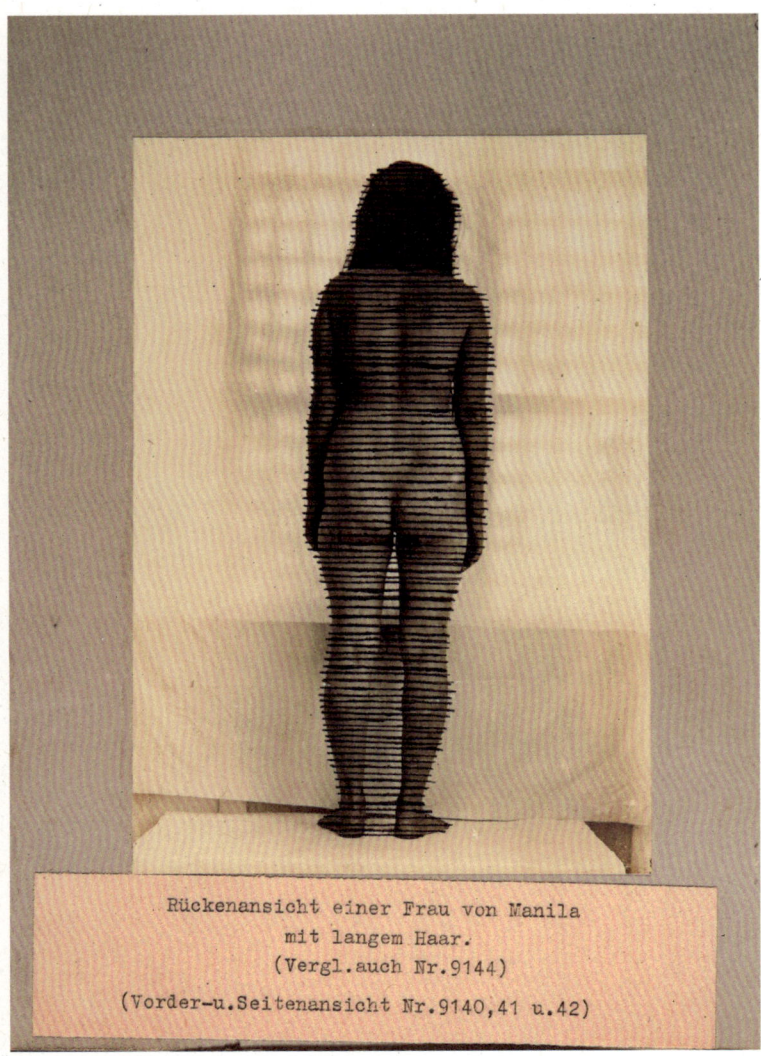

Kiri Dalena, *Women (Strike through)*, processed photography from the RJM collection, 2020

Kiri Dalena, *Mourning and Resistance (Blacking out)*, processed photography from the RJM collection, 2020

»To hide or to reveal, to awake or to let slumber, to intervene or not to intervene? What to make of these photographs and the thousands of questions that they carry? The choice should never be yours alone. It should have always been ours.« *Kiri Dalena*

"These are photos of us immobilised, trapped, imprisoned, threatened, violated, collected, enslaved, killed, and reordered," explained Kiri Dalena – a visual artist, film-maker, and human rights activist who lives and works in the Philippines – when we invited her to participate in a digital residency in winter 2020 which involved working with our collection of colonial photographs taken during the Philippine-American war (1899–1902). Kiri Dalena kept a kind of diary on her blog, *snareforbirds*, which could be accessed from within the *RESIST!* exhibition. The results of her research were presented in the exhibition *Counter Images* at the RJM, which opened in December 2021.

"My work began with two names that I couldn't pronounce properly, Dean Conant Worcester and Georg Küppers-Loosen, and an inventory of 3,781 photographs relating to the Philippines that were taken and collected by these men over a hundred years ago.

My exposure to images from the early years of the American conquest of the Philippines mainly involved photographs from the Philippine-American war (1899–1902). They were landscapes of trenches strewn with the bodies of Filipino revolutionaries. However, in this collection of historical photographs of the Philippines from the Rautenstrauch-Joest-Museum, taken between 1887 and 1907, there are few traces of the war. Instead, the collection is filled with carefully annotated pictures of living people, identified, filed, and organised according to location and ethnicity. On the one hand, I should have revelled at this encounter with images of our people from that period. Our flesh and manner of dress, our visible infections, wounds, and scars, all meticulously documented and framed. But on the other hand, these very same images were disturbing. I kept searching, seeking to understand and articulate what it was that troubled me about these pictures. A hundred years ago, our people were made to keep still while their photographs were taken. I hope that by returning to and rewriting these photographs, I can contribute to the articulation of a living resistance."
Kiri Dalena, Orzon City, Manila, 2020

On the series *Women (Strike Through):*
"One of the most widely condemned series in the archive is that of women made to undress for photographs. Research suggests that Dean Worcester may have wanted to distance himself from these photographs and so limited the circulation of these photos. […] Should we hide them from the public, but still be able to peek at them within our closed circles? I believe that this is what Worcester did. I wanted to do the opposite. What could we do with these photographs? Who would be exposed and diminished if these images surfaced?"
Kiri Dalena

On the series *Mourning and Resistance:*
"Blacking out selected figures or areas of the photographs with ink is not meant to erase but to blanket the figures underneath, to protect them. […] I painted over the Filipino women's light-coloured clothing with black ink. I did so to convey mourning – but wasn't black already a colour of resistance back then, too?" *Kiri Dalena*

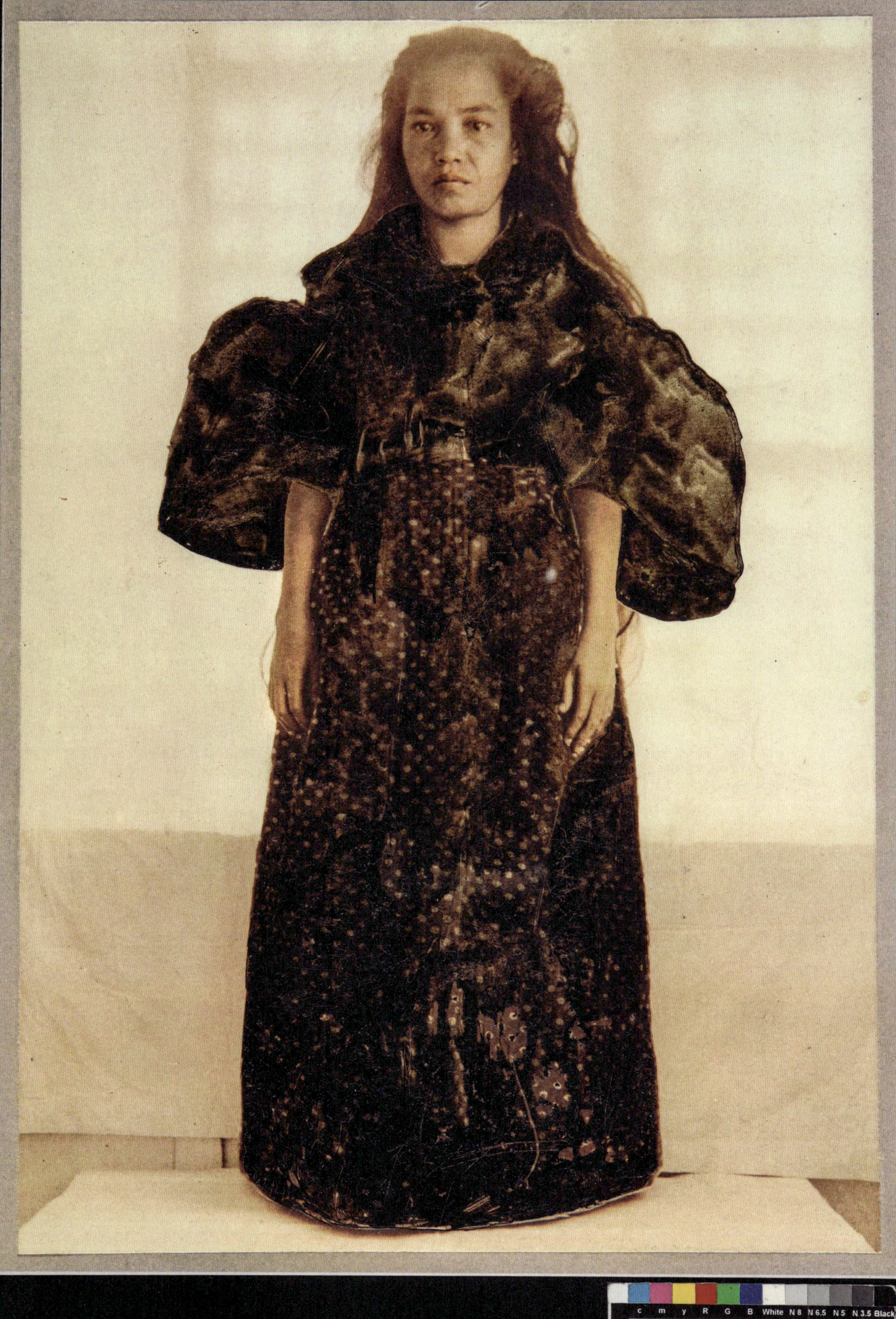

Mohammed Laouli
Les Sculptures n'étaient pas blanches, 2020

Performance, video, 15:54 min.

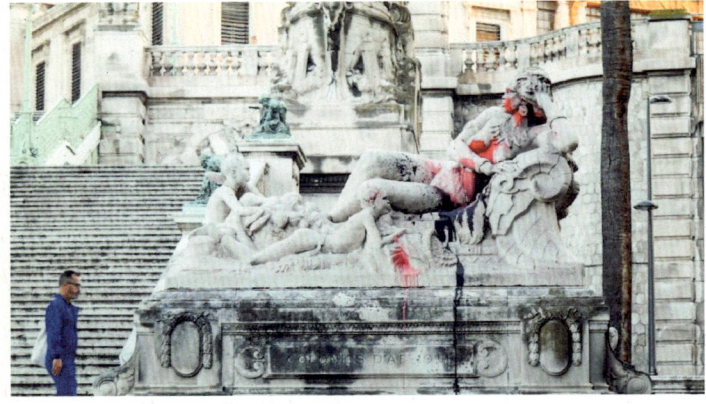
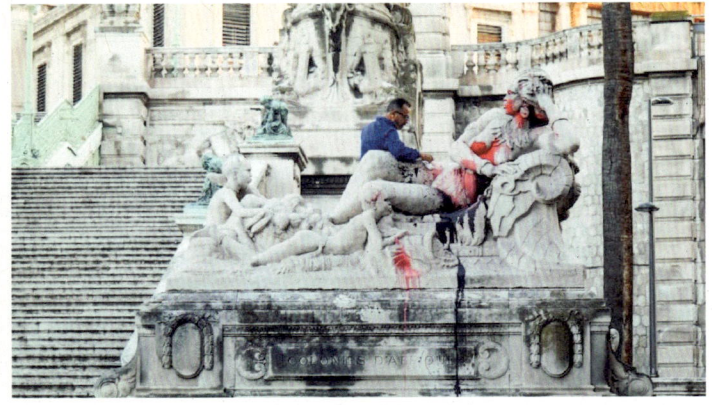
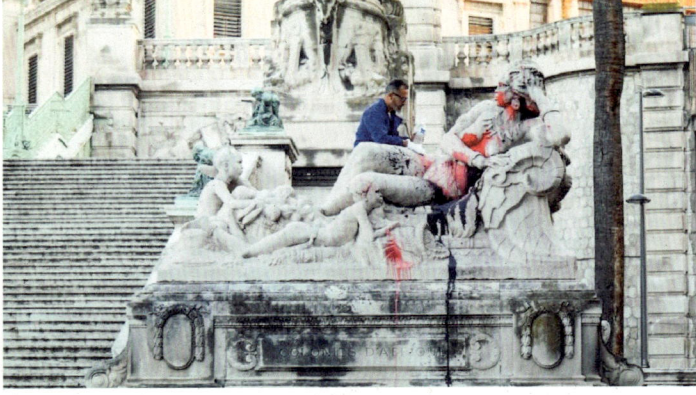

»One day I was walking past this sculpture in Marseille and saw that it was covered in red paint. I decided to take care of this sculpture, Colonies d'Afrique. I treated it with gentle, caring gestures to distance myself from the old power structures.« *Mohammed Laouli*

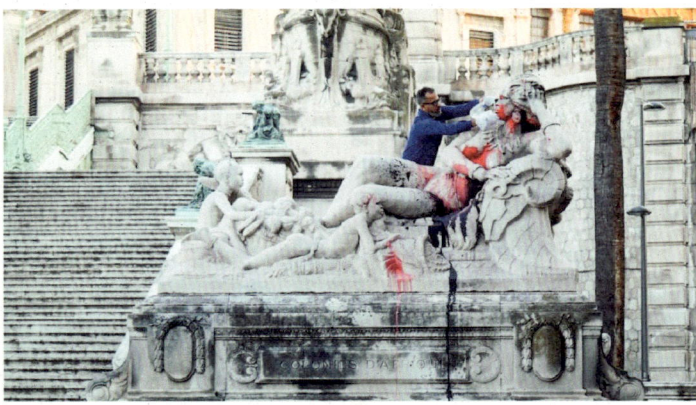
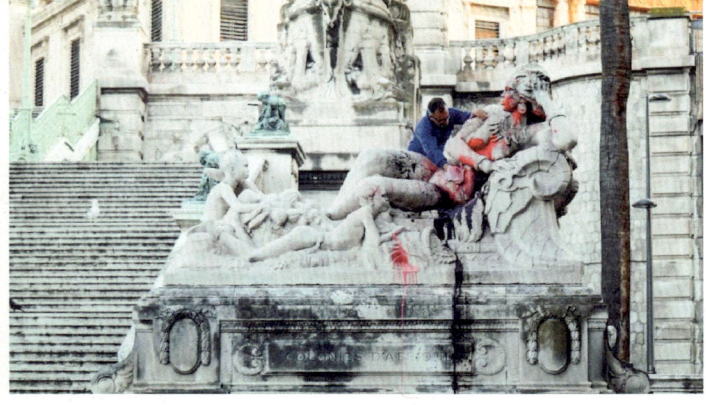

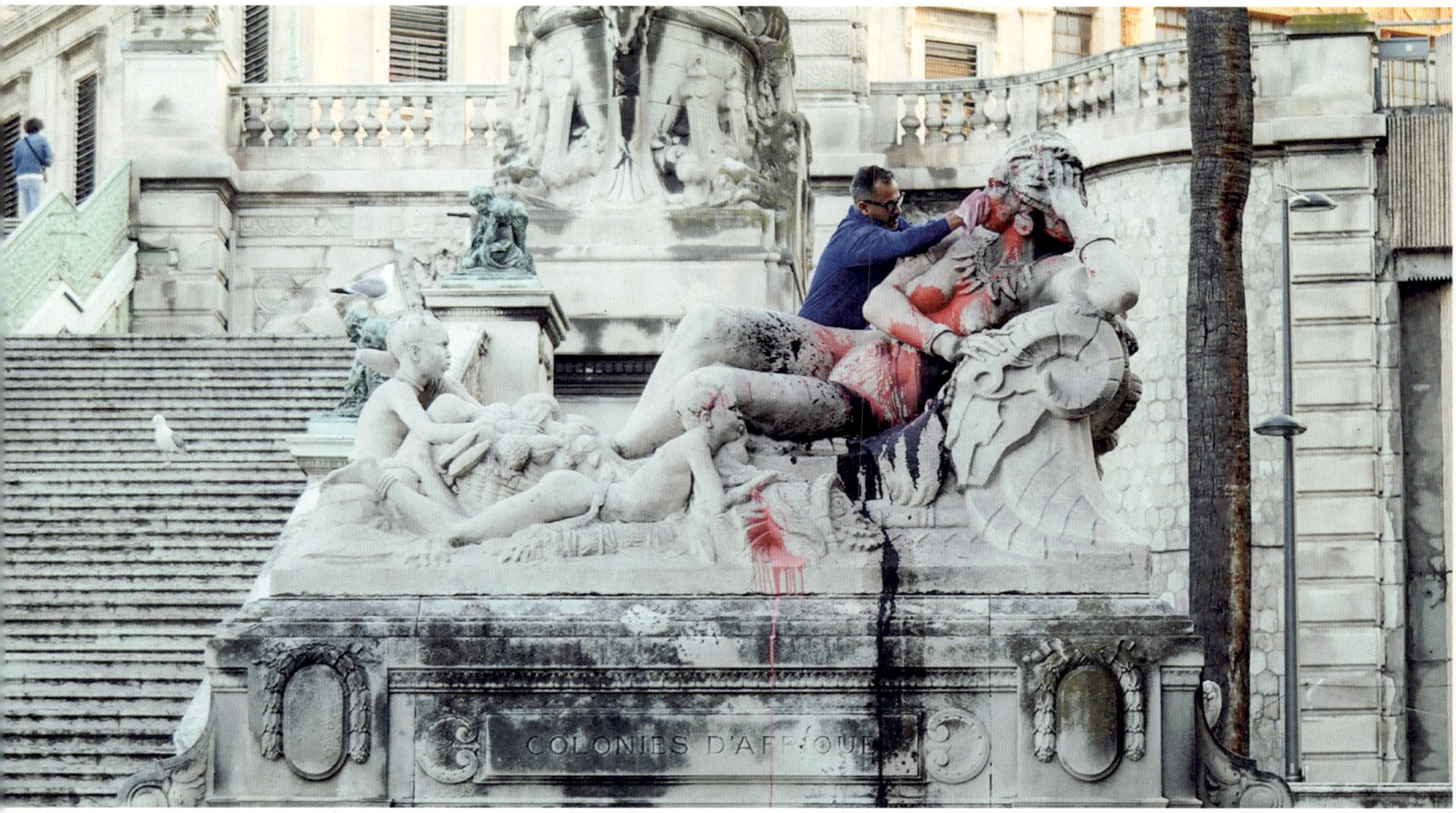

Marseille, France — 30/06/2020

The video *Les Sculptures n'étaient pas blanches* (The Sculptures Weren't White) examines the traces of colonialism in Marseille. It is summer 2020: on the steps of the Marseille-Saint-Charles railway station we see a man in blue overalls – Mohammed Laouli – cleaning a colonial monument. His clothing is reminiscent of the stereotype of Maghrebi migrants who came to clean and rebuild France during its thirty-year post-war boom. Titled *Colonies d'Afrique* (Colonies of Africa), the colonial monument that the artist is cleaning was inaugurated at the opening of the 1922 Colonial Exhibition in Marseille. It depicts a prostrate, nude woman, an allegory of the French colonies in Africa. Traces of red paint cover the sculpture, evidence of a demonstration by Black Lives Matter activists that took place on June 30, 2020. Is the artist trying to remove the traces of structural colonial violence and postcolonial rage in France in a kind of cleansing ritual?

Courtesy of the Artist

Grada Kilomba
Plantation Memories, 2018

Performance, 14:14 min., Music: Geisbaba; Cast: Martha Fessehatzion, Moses Leo, Michael Edode Ojake, Araba Walton, Sara-Hiruth Zewde

»I told her how it is being Black here and that it is not easy for me to always be the only Black person. She said: ›I don't think that you are Black, for me, you are not Black. [...]‹ When people like me say that I'm not Black. When they dislike me, they say that it's not because I'm Black. Either way, I am trapped in their racism.«

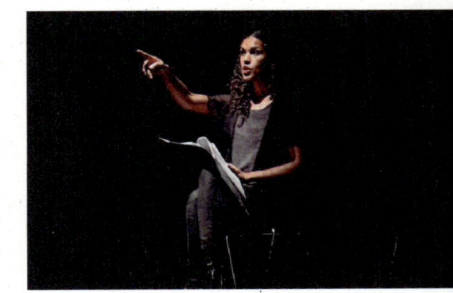

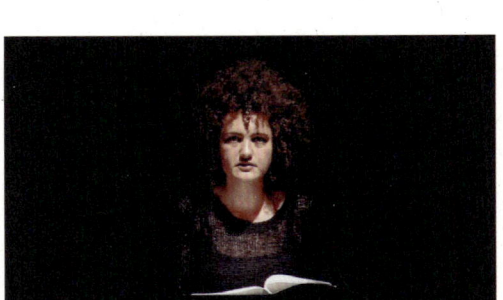

»They see you and the first thing that crosses their mind is to check 'Where is she from?' – without even knowing me. I am categorised as a race that doesn't belong here. [...] One is Black or German, not Black and German.«

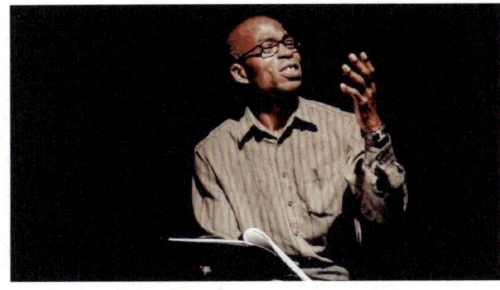

The room is dark. The only people visible are the five actors sitting side by side on stage, holding Grada Kilomba's book in their hands. Their reading of Plantation Memories: Episodes of Everyday Racism, which was published in 2008 and staged as performance for film in 2015, focuses entirely on the voices of the performers, the text, and the act of reading aloud. In it, the psychologist and artist Grada Kilomba psychoanalyses episodes of everyday racism, reflecting on the connections between colonialism and trauma as well as on the violent nature of racist thinking.

In her book Plantation Memories, Kilomba analyses the colonial logics of exoticisation, othering, and the racist bullying of Black people and people of colour. In doing so, she deconstructs the workings of white dominance by analysing the exclusion mechanisms of (academic) knowledge production – and thus revealing who is able to speak and write in the first place. At the same time, she explores processes of transformation and healing, focusing on subjectification through speaking, writing, and community care.

»There is a palpable fear that the colonialist will have to listen when the colonial subject speaks. This would mean an unpleasant confrontation with ›other‹ truths. Truths that were denied, repressed, and kept as secrets.«
Grada Kilomba

»Die schöne N.‹, she kept saying. An odd combination of words in which a positive word – beautiful – is followed by a very traumatic one. It is a game of sweet and bitter words that makes it hard to identify racism. [...] The first masquerades the second, the second, however, asserts my position as inferior in relation to whites. [...] When the N-word is spoken, one is not only referring to a colour, but to a chain of racist insults that become associated with the word itself. [...] The game of sweet and bitter words is a very part of racism itself..«

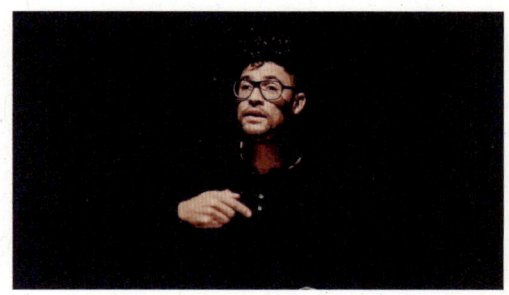

»It is not that we have not been speaking, but rather that our voices, through racism, have been systematically silenced. This impossibility illustrates how speaking and silencing emerge as an analogous project. The act of speaking is like a negotiation between those who speak and those who listen, that is, between the speaking subjects and their listeners. Listening is, in this sense, the act of authorisation towards the speaker. One can (only) speak when one's voice is being listened to. And those who are listened to are also those who belong, while those who are not listened to become those who ›do not belong.‹«
Grada Kilomba

Belkis Ayón
The Sleeping Woman, 1995

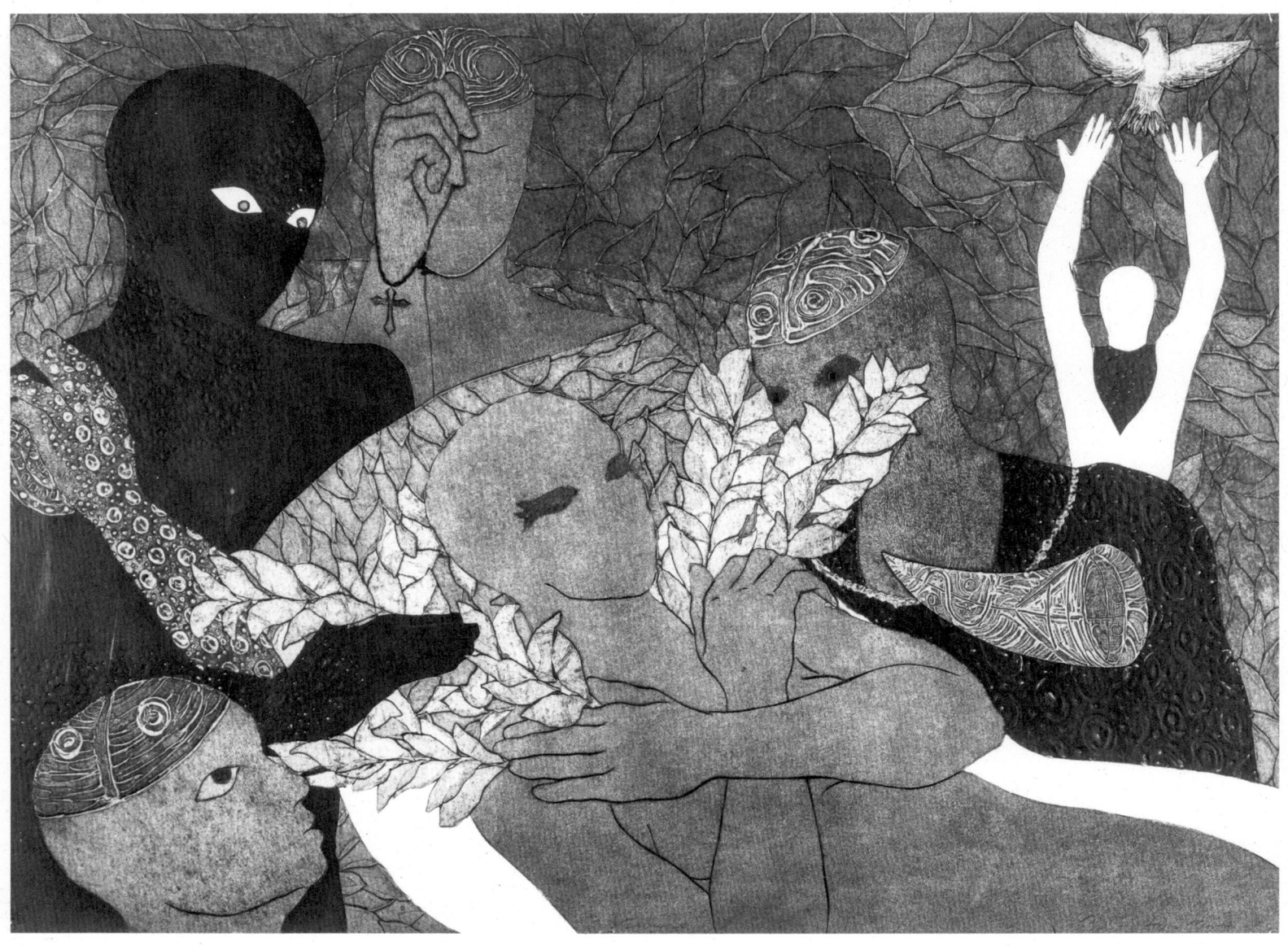

»The image of Sikán dominates in all my works because she, like me, lived and still lives in anguish, looking for a way out – through me« *Belkis Ayón*

The Abakuá is an Afro-Cuban all-male secret society that dates back to the nineteenth century. It is believed that this secret society was founded by enslaved men who had survived the brutality of the Middle Passage and enslavement. This society provided its members with mutual aid and protection from the cruel realities of slavery. They are not one of the syncretic mystical groups based on Catholicism that are so common in Cuba; rather, Abakuá harks back to the Ekpe or Ngbe religion, originating from the Cross River region in present-day Nigeria.

The Afro-Cuban artist Belkis Ayón began exploring Abakuá mythology in large-scale prints in the 1990s. The female figure of Sikán occupies a central position in her work: the princess – the only woman in Abakuá lore – was sentenced to death for revealing the religion's secrets to her partner, who came from another nation.

Ayón always depicts Sikán without a mouth and with a piercing gaze. This can be read as a metaphor for political censorship and the oppression of women in a culture dominated by patriarchy and machismo. Strikingly, Sikán bears the features of the artist herself, who took her own life at the age of 32. Ayón's symbolically charged work also reveals an intense engagement with Afro-Cuban traditions and history, which she cites in her mysterious images from a woman's perspective, empowering female figures in contradiction to the political norms and economic conditions of her time.

*Untitled
(Sikán with Goat)*, 1993

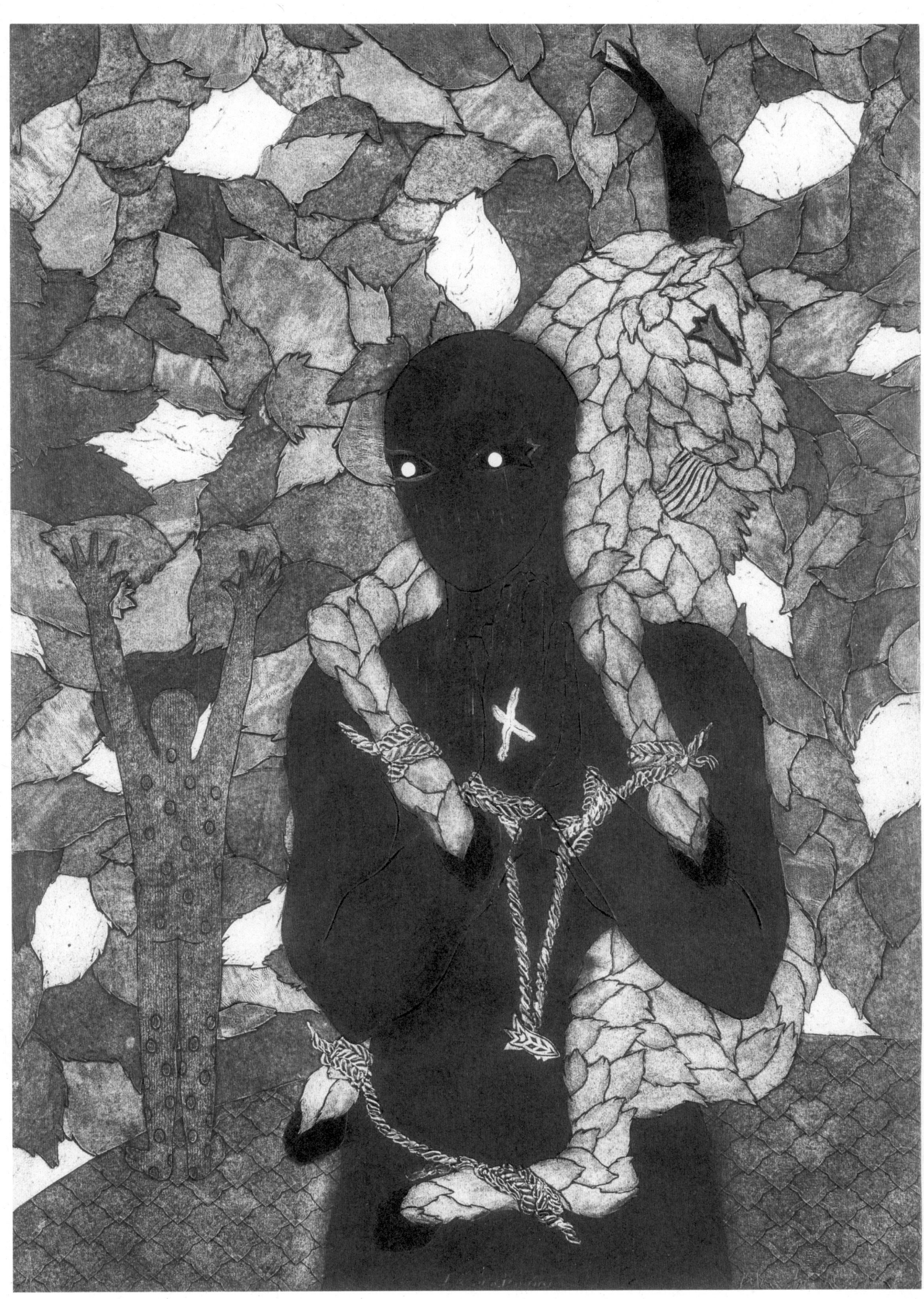

Luiza Prado de O. Martins
For Those Who Stand at Shorelines, 2019–2020

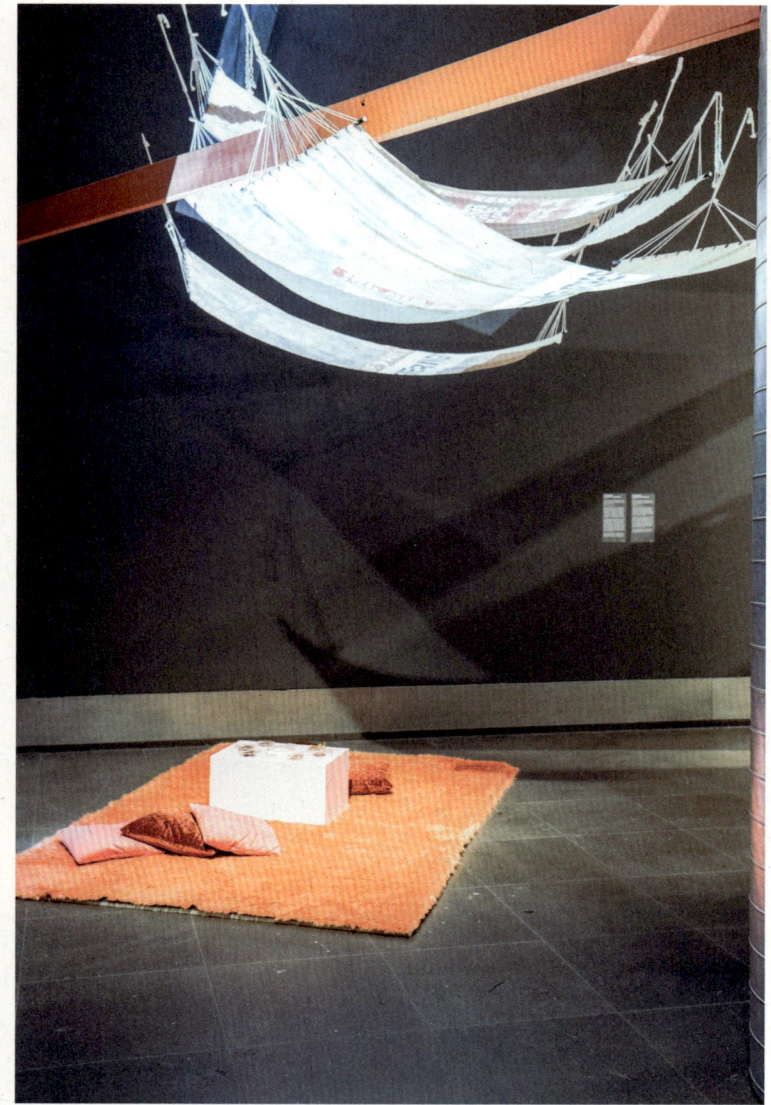

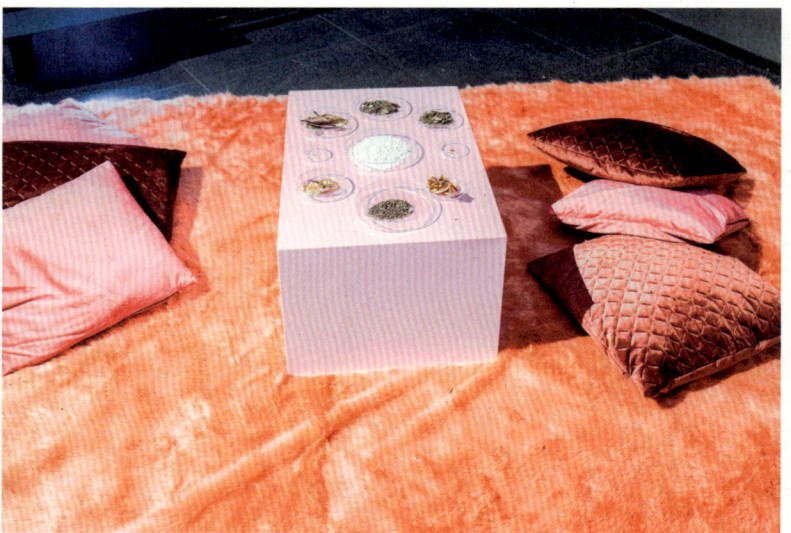

The title *For Those Who Stand at Shorelines* is inspired by Audre Lorde's poem "A Litany of Survival", in which the African-American poet puts into words the permanent struggle for survival of marginalised and vulnerable communities.

In response to centuries of colonial violence against Indigenous communities in the Amazon, Brazilian artist Luiza Prado de O. Martins creates a space to enable counter-practices of networking, community building, and solidarity as a means of overcoming trauma and building resilience. The artist invites visitors to enter this "girly" space and lie down on a cosy carpet covered with pink cushions or to sit at a small pink table with petri dishes containing seeds and plants. Projected onto a ceiling of hammocks – the Portuguese word for hammock is *rede*, which also means "mesh" or "network" – is a GIF essay exploring the link between plant-based birth control and anti-colonial protest: certain plants were used by Indigenous communities in the Amazon to prevent or abort pregnancies as a subversive form of resistance. At the same time, the artist's essay highlights the continuities of colonial violence by describing the neo-fascist policies of Brazilian President Jair Bolsonaro, which systematically attack marginalised groups and destroy their livelihoods.

»Decolonisation is not an individual choice; it demands collective, sustained, committed work. Let us feed these visions for a future of blue skies and open paths. Let us nourish each other with responsibility, care, affection, and patience.« *Luiza Prado de O. Martins*

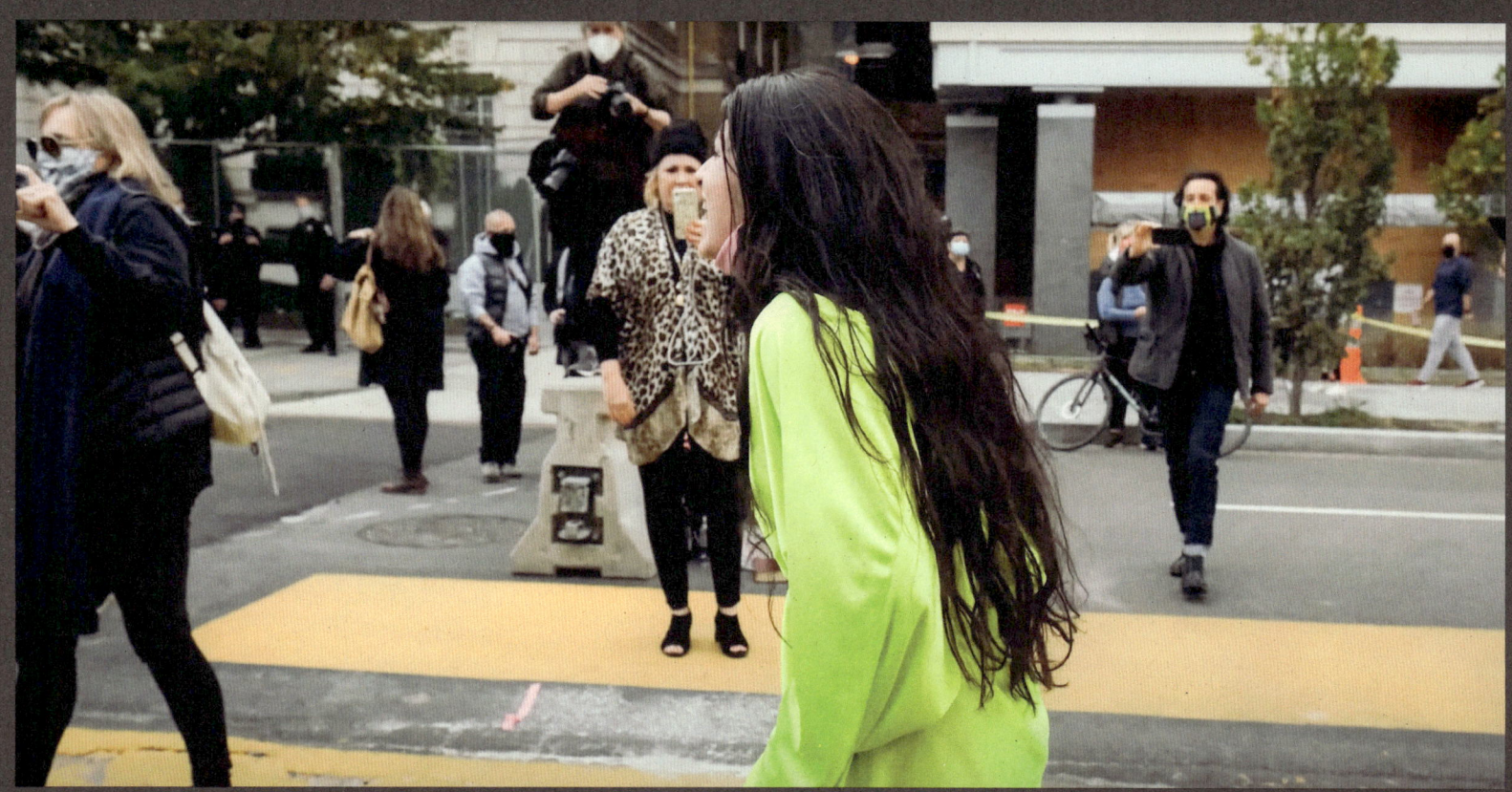

Selma Selman: *You Have No Idea*
3/11/2020, US Presidential Election Day, performance between BLM Plaza and the White House, Washington, DC, video, 5 min.

Washington, USA 03/11/2020

Our collaboration with In-Haus e.V., a grassroots organisation from the Kalk district of Cologne, shows how a cooperation can evolve over time if the partners are able to gradually build trust in each other. With its director Elizaveta Khan, the organisation and all its members have a prominent voice in Cologne, which we [the editors of this book] soon became aware of when we arrived in Cologne in 2019. We invited In-Haus e.V. to work with us as part of a participatory collaborative project: an open space called *Die Baustelle*, which launched in December 2019. Together with Cologne grassroots organisations, we wanted to think about how we could transform the RJM into a transcultural, multivocal, democratic space of exchange. Due to the Covid-19 pandemic, *Die Baustelle* had to close shortly after it opened. Despite this, we wanted to make sure that the large and now empty exhibition hall where *Die Baustelle* stood would still be put to good use. This led to In-Haus e.V. utilising this space at the RJM to host its language courses for refugees and immigrants, since Covid restrictions prevented the use of its own facilities. A genuine collaboration began from that moment in 2020, which also resulted in In-Haus e.V. curating this autonomous space for *RESIST!*

It's Yours! space: a space in a space

The exhibition *RESIST!* was an organic space of resonance and dissonance in a state of constant change. In the public, hegemonic space of the RJM, which, like other ethnological museums, is a place with highly asymmetrical power relations, *RESIST!* sought to make repressed and silenced stories and histories from the Global South as well as marginalised voices heard. With Esther Utjiua Muinjangue, Ida Hoffmann, Peju Layiwola, Tímea Junghaus, and In-Haus e.V with Elizaveta Khan, artists, curators, and activists who are directly affected by the topic of resistance were invited to create a non-hierarchical space in the museum to present conflicts, protests, and wounds, insofar as this is possible in a museum setting. Within the *RESIST!* exhibition space, they have taken the floor and curated their own autonomous *It's Yours!* spaces, places of agency and self-determination.

p. 064 Not about Us without Us
p. 094 Benin 1897
p. 138 Roma Resist!
p. 170 No Resistance Fits in a Box or a Museum

"It's Yours" Room

In-Haus e.V.
No Resistance Fits in a Box!

No resistance fits in a box, or in a museum. For us it is clear: no form of resistance fits into a museum and to depict any is not our goal. We do not present conclusive truths, messages, 'stories' or 'cultures'. We do not see our role as deciding where 'the audience' begins and 'the exhibition' ends. We engage in the process of addressing internal and external contradictions and oppositions, of pointing to perspectives and contexts, and of bringing different ways of hearing, seeing, feeling, and reading into and out of the museum. The installations as well as their realization are shaped by the interplay of the idea, the space and the interactions of people in and with the museum that take place.

Resistance must want to be seen. That is why part of our contribution is designed to work only when "the audience" becomes active and uses the codes. Resistance is multifaceted. Following the motto "The head is round so our thinking can change direction," our It's Yours! space is a physical and a metaphorical space that encourages engagement with the daily handling of inner and outer resistance. Resistance is everywhere in Cologne. We take up different formats, and build another installation in Cologne-Kalk.

In-Haus e.V., 2020

In-Haus e.V.

As a new German organization, we are committed to a post-migrant society in a democratic republic. Often we are not included in the domestic "we". But we stand against it: This is our country, too. This is not possible without resistance, this is not possible without opposition. Internal and external, own and foreign resistant perspectives, movements and actions are therefore always there. To perceive them, to pay attention to them, to take a stand, to show solidarity, to ask questions, to remain curious – panta rhei is the symbol for our actions.

Exhibition handout of the introductory text to the It's Yours! space
No Resistance Fits in a Box!

Cologne, Germany — November 2020

ART

We address inner and outer contradictions and resistance, highlight perspectives and contexts, and bring different ways of listening, seeing, and reading into and out of the museum.

IS

Refusing to confront the continuities of racism and colonialism leads to a failure to acknowledge the violent conditions that exist within the German culture of remembrance. Consequently, it is vital to understand postcolonial developments in order to recognise the influence of contemporary power relations and ways of thinking in German society.

ALWAYS

The general belief is that the colonial era ended with the independence of most colonised states. However, the fact that the conditions of domination and exploitation on which colonisation was based are still in effect today seems to have been forgotten. And the reality that our modern world and economic order is closely linked to the colonial era is all too rarely considered.

A STATEMENT.

The installations and their realisation are shaped by the interplay between the idea, the space, and the human interactions in and with the museum.

COLLECTING TOO.

No resistance fits in a box or in a museum. For us it is clear: no form of resistance fits in a museum and it is not our aim to merely display these forms. We want to stimulate new thought processes: our heads are round so that our thoughts can change direction.

WE ARE NOT THE CENTRE OF THE WORLD.

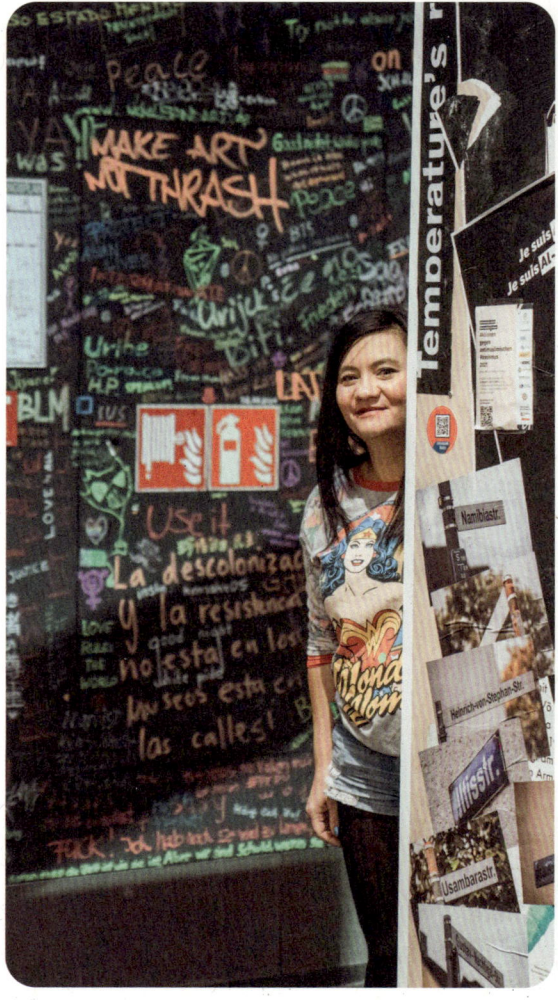

Elizaveta Khan
An activist, social worker, and social pedagogue, director of In-Haus e.V. in Cologne, lecturer in social work at various universities, speaker on the topics of postcolonialism, disintegration, empowerment, and intersectionality, member of the Integration Council of the City of Cologne, board member of the *KalkGestalten* community foundation. Khan describes herself as being "in a powerful professional situation as a foreigner on the Integration Council of the City of Cologne, with experience in resisting injustice and advocating for democracy and solidarity".

»Representative democracy needs representatives.«
Elizaveta Khan

A look back on In-Haus' participation in *RESIST!*

Elizaveta Khan

Cologne, Germany — September 2022

The grass roots organisation In-Haus e.V. about their *It's Yours!* space *No Resistance Fits in a Box or a Museum*

The Idea

"Whether I live or die is irrelevant. We must continue to work to make the world a better place for all people – each with his or her contribution and according to his or her possibilities." These sentences come from the Nigerian author, civil rights activist, television producer and environmentalist Ken Saro-Wiwa, who was executed before the eyes of the world in 1995.

While here we engage in various resistance activities without fear and protected, thousands of activists, journalists, political dissidents, environmental activists, people who stand up for others, are subject to repression. They live in exile, sit in prisons, they are tortured and threatened with death, they ignore if they will see their families and friends again, they do not know if and how they will live to see the next day. And yet they take up this fight for human rights, for equality and freedom. They remain resistant. And they always have.

So what could our contribution look like here? The sentence "Oh, we can't do anything on our own" is not true – because individuals as well as initiatives and organisations, up to the International Court of Human Rights, show that we can and must do something!

Resistance does not mean "against", resistance means "for". Resistance means standing up for democracy and for human rights. Our most important tool is solidarity, which activists must rely on. Let us not allow human rights violations before the eyes of the world to become more and more normal, an everyday practice. Let us also remain resistant and support each other in a worldwide network of commitment and solidarity. And let us stand up – for a democratisation of the Occident.

"We are all facing history," said Ken Saro-Wiwa in his closing remarks before he was sentenced to death.

The *It's Yours!* space
No Resistance Fits in a Box

We, Mona Leitmeier, Rita Bomkamp, Salman Abdo, Elizaveta Khan and Sae Yun Jung from In-Haus, accepted the RJM's invitation to curate one of the *It's Yours!* spaces. For us, resistance is loud, strong, and violent but also delicate, quiet, invisible, or often made visible, especially under aspects of power, in order to discredit them in turn. We approached the design of the *It's Yours!* space with these thoughts in mind.

The main room was arranged like a box with walls that were 11 m² tall. We painted, affixed, and labelled the walls with resistance slogans. We designed content for both the inside and the outside of the box. Inside the box, we depicted the inner or intimate side of resistance by formulating yes-no sentences that motivated the visitors to position themselves accordingly. The aim was to confront visitors with their own resistance, dilemmas, and contradictions. On the outer side was an installation by Sai Yun Jung that could be activated with the Artvive app, an augmented reality tool that linked the visitors to our space in Cologne-Kalk.

Via QR codes and headphones, visitors were able to listen to *RESIST!* statements from a wide variety of people, including other *It's Yours!* curators. We interviewed people involved in local initiatives such as "Keupstraße ist überall" and "Herkesin Meydanı - Platz Für Alle", who are fighting for the erection of a memorial in Cologne for the victims of the series of murders committed by the NSU, the "National Socialist Underground", a neo-Nazi terrorist organisation. Between 2000 and 2006, the NSU carried out two racially motivated bombing attacks in Cologne. The attacks killed 9 people, as well as a policewoman and injured 22 people, with some incurring serious injuries (2001 Probsteigasse, 2004 Keupstraße). The fight to have a memorial is a form of resistance for the activists. Their resistance is rooted in the fact that the majority of the German population and authorities had turned a blind eye to these racially motivated murders, saying things like "The migrants are killing each other" and "Germans have nothing to do with it". Despite the investigators admitting early on that the victims had names and looked like they did not have a German passport, they ruled out racist motives for the crimes, made no connection to the previous murders and assumed that the victims were drug dealers and that they were killed for that reason.

In addition to these testimonies, we also wanted to hear the perspective of those who have a resistance biography themselves. As language plays an important role in our German courses at In-Haus e.V. and language is also a form of resistance, it was important to us to let people tell their stories in their native language.

However, the crucial part of our space (see image p. 175) was formed by two walls that were both part of our *It's Yours!* space and part of the museum itself. These walls, which functioned like a chalkboard, were an invitation for visitors to write their points of view and criticism. In addition, we asked the other artists and activists involved in *RESIST!* for their statements of resistance, which we displayed on another wall of our space as well as on the exhibition floor.

We were also keen to bring the content of the exhibition into the public sphere (see pages 176–177). We, therefore, set up a "satellite" on Ottmar-Pohl-Platz in Cologne-Kalk, the headquarters of our association. It served as a vigil for all activists in Cologne and worldwide and was present for the duration of the exhibition.

Parallel to the exhibition, we created a website, resist.ihaus.org, on which we explored the following questions:

How can civil society get involved? How can political and artistic actions remain present in the public space when demonstrations, concerts, exhibitions, etc., are so restricted by state measures or when freedoms are curtailed to such an extent that such activities are hardly possible? How can debates be held when around 90% of the "majority" seem to hold one opinion? How can diversity become visible when homogeneity is enforced? The homepage takes up all these issues and records all the *RESIST!* statements that were made during the exhibition, but also beyond the duration of the exhibition. In addition, information on various resistance movements, initiatives and organisations is recorded and constantly expanded on this page.

Resistance is everywhere and at all times

We saw our contribution to the *RESIST!* exhibition as an invitation to reflect on thought processes in this space, to see things anew, to listen, to engage with different perspectives and thus to develop an understanding of the realities of life that are characterised by resistance and contradictions. Those who visited our space, therefore, had to reflect and make connections themselves.

It was clear to us that no form of resistance would fit into a museum, and we did not want to depict it here. We didn't want to present any conclusive truths, messages, "stories", or "cultures". Instead, we wanted to emphasise both the processual nature of our work and the dialogue with visitors and focus on internal and external contradictions and resistance. With our installations, we wanted to point to perspectives and contexts and bring different ways of hearing, seeing, feeling and reading into and out of the museum. The installation was the result of an interplay of ideas, space and people's interactions in and with the museum.

Resistance has to want to be seen. That is why part of our contribution was designed in such a way that it only works if "the audience" becomes active and uses the QR codes. Resistance is multi-layered. Following the motto "The head is round so that our thinking can change direction", our contribution to *It's Yours!* was a physical and metaphorical space that encouraged visitors to think about how to deal with inner and outer resistance.

More information at:
resist.ihaus.org

Conversation:
No Resistance Fits in a Box!

A conversation between Nanette Snoep, director of the RJM, and Elizaveta Khan, director of Cologne-based organisation In-Haus e.V., about bureaucratic hurdles to participation, colonial continuities, and her *It's Yours!* space. This conversation was part of the online programme *RESIST! DIGITAL*, which was launched due to Covid restrictions..

Cologne, Germany
25/01/2021

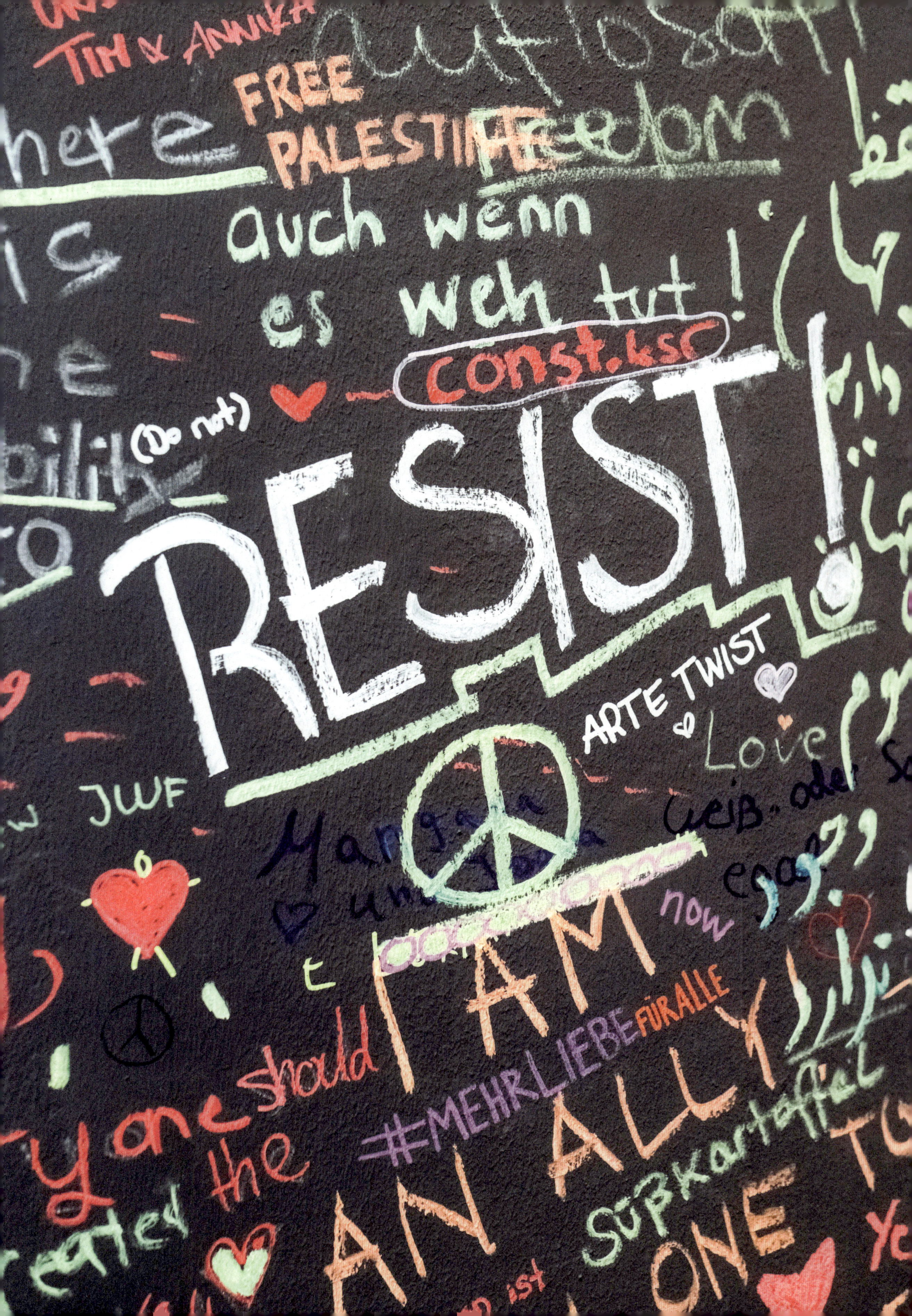

TIN & ANNIKA
FREE PALESTINE Freedom
here
auch wenn es weh tut!
const.ksc
(Do not)
RESIST!
ARTE TWIST
Love
JWF
weiß oder
now ega?
I AM
#MEHRLIEBEFÜRALLE
should
AN ALLY
y one
the
Süßkartoffel
ONE

RESIST!–Box

Some of In-Haus' activities also took place outside the museum: On Ottmar-Pohl-Platz in Kalk, an economically disadvantaged district in the east of Cologne, they set up a *RESIST!* box in which everyone was invited to leave their personal stories and thoughts on the subject of resistance throughout 2021. A selection of oral accounts recorded in the *RESIST!* box can be read on the following pages.

More information about the project and the audio statements at: resist.ihaus.org

Why do we need RESIST!?
Feodora

RESIST!, because unfortunately, most people survive by destroying others. But for what? Beneath the surface we are all raw and vulnerable. *RESIST!*, for a friendlier world! *RESIST!*, for a pluralistic society with shared values and a shared understanding of the law that applies to everyone. With this in mind: ›Time for outrage!‹, as Stéphane Hessel declared, because: ›To create is to resist. To resist is to create.‹«

Strong Women
Delshad

I found *RESIST!* in the history of the women of my country. This is a country where the response to the truth is the death penalty, where the death penalty is issued like a parking ticket. I'll name a few names:

Atena Daemi **calls for the abolition of the death penalty. Court verdict: seven years' imprisonment. In a letter from prison, she wrote: »My voice cannot be silenced by your cruel and unjust actions.«**

Narges Mohammadi, **human rights activist, has been sentenced to five years in prison twice. For what? »Assembling and carrying out crimes against national security.«**

White Wednesdays, **are a group of young women who come together to protest against the compulsory hijab and promote freedom of choice when it comes to clothing.**

Well, there are a lot of names, but these are a few, really just a few – a small proportion of the people who resist in their own way and whose names also represent civil courage. I would like to conclude by saying that the term »resist« in my country is a hard, arduous, and sometimes seemingly endless struggle. And I hope that one day it will come to an end.

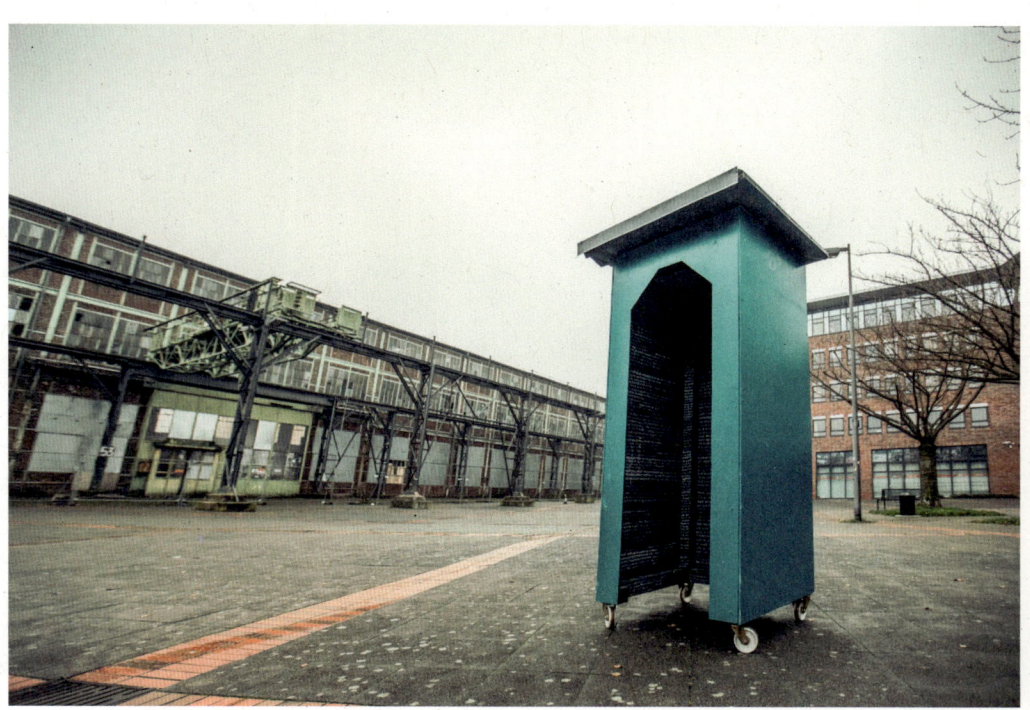

RESIST!-Box, Ottmar-Pohl-Platz, Cologne Kalk

Resilience
Yahya

I come from a place where resistance is seen as a crime that must be punished. During my life in Mauritania, my resilience has helped me to survive times when I felt weak. I was able to evade all attempts to silence me by force. My resilience enabled me to push through my emotional pain and to keep raising my voice instead of thinking about giving up. Through resistance, I have reached a point where I can say: I am here and I deserve to be proud of myself, my thoughts, and my decisions. In the course of my life, I have realised that through resistance I can break the silence. I have realised that keeping silent about violence is a greater crime than resisting. Through resilience, I was able to face my fears with courage. It was the candle that led me on the path to freedom. Resistance makes the impossible tangible. If I had to define my life in one word, it would be resistance.

Fear
Jarek

Fear that takes away space. Dehumanisation that serves to violate human dignity. Lack of respect for others is a simplistic form of communication. Look deep into a person's soul and just let them be.

Resistance
Maria

For me, this means that I am committed to ensuring that we can live in a society that does not tolerate discrimination and exploitation. A society in which I, like all people who want to live here, can live in dignity. And that currently means that we have to combat the gap between rich and poor, as well as violence against women and FLINTA (female, lesbian, intersex, trans and agender) people, racism, the climate catastrophe, global exploitation, and wars – by doing things such as stopping the production of weapons. For me, this means that we have to rethink the neoliberal economic model. If we do not take this path and do not use the pandemic to completely reconsider our approach, to say goodbye to permanent growth, we will either perish in floods, storms, and fires, or in sexualised and racialised violence in wars on the streets or at home.

The pandemic could be a wake-up call, **but only if we come face to face and truly see each other, care for each other and fight for a different model of society founded on feminist principles, if we stand up and do something about it. Resistance is important on both a small and a large scale** – to do everything we can to ensure that nothing remains as it is.

The future is feminist. **Let's abandon patriarchal values such as higher, better, more digitalised, faster, more brutal, more domineering – and instead become more mindful, more social, more diverse, more intersectional, and more human.**

This way of thinking and collective experience is the basis for any kind of resistance for me. **Feminism is a huge movement worldwide. It's the struggle against domination and violence and death for freedom and solidarity. Resistance is daring to have a nuanced opinion – and standing up for it.**

White Cars
Zehava

The white lane is closed,
An allegory on the way home
Mama closed her heart
And said: You,
Look at you, it's like you're dead.
The white lane, the way back.
Mama said: It's over (until you get married,
you have nothing to come back for,
And if Papa was still alive)
We'd sit *Zehava* for you.
I came,
with two suitcases, two children
And I went.
Over the Yabok Pass,
Between the chunks of white cars,
With a collection of leftover memories,
into another life,
I bought,
I collected.

Dilemma
Şaristan

The situation looks gloomy, and it appears that there is nothing you or I can do. This is a dilemma that is not unique to our time. History can show us the way to those who have felt exactly the same. Everyday people who felt forced by injustice to act and challenge those who had the power. It is our right and our moral obligation to protest against unjust political, economic, or social conditions. Many of the rights that we take for granted are the result of human rights protests – women's rights, workers' rights. It has always been a struggle to bring about change, but it is achievable.

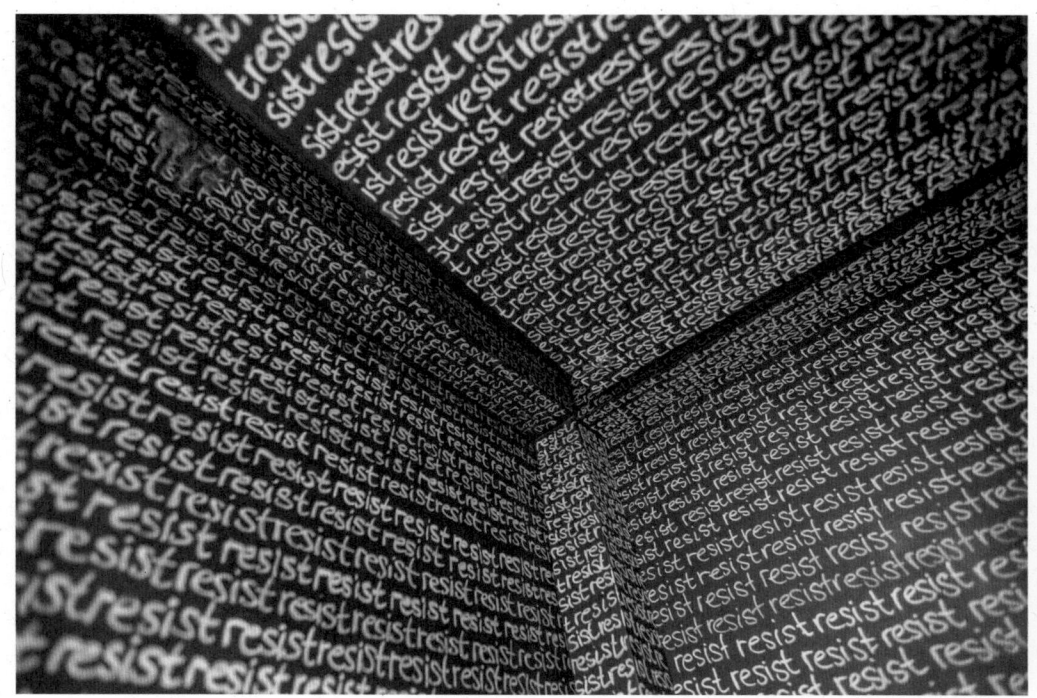

RESIST!-Box, Ottmar-Pohl-Platz, Cologne Kalk

Language
Alexandra

I remember a story when I had been in Germany for just under two months and had already started at the Russian theatre. We were rehearsing Anne Frank and I went down to the train station in Cologne at 10 o'clock in the evening and waited for my train.

There were two girls sitting on the back of a bench with bomber jackets and Buffalo shoes. And at some point, I realised that these girls were getting closer and closer. Coming up behind me. I didn't think much of it and kept walking a little further. And then, at some point, I realised they were pushing me towards the track. I turned around, and one of the girls said something in German. And because at that time the only German I knew was »Hitler kaputt« and »Hände hoch!« [»Hands up!«], I said: »I don't understand German. I don't understand German.« Very original. And she was so perplexed. She looked at me, lunged towards me, and slapped me in the face. And I was ... I don't know, I was only 15 years old – something came from my gut. I don't even swear at all. But some crude swear words »[***suka bljad]« came out of me. I said them to her face, then a second girl came and gave me another slap.

And then we started to wrestle. Really! At some point, the train came and they ran off. They had two big dogs with them, and I stood there like a drowned rat and started to cry. Not because I was hurt, but simply because I was so angry. I thought to myself, this can't be happening. I've come to this country, I didn't even want to come here, and now I'm getting slapped in the face, just because I don't speak your language. Then I sat on the train and people gave me tissues, and I was just so angry inside and I swore to myself: I will learn this language and I will fight back. Not with my hands, but with my words, if I need to.

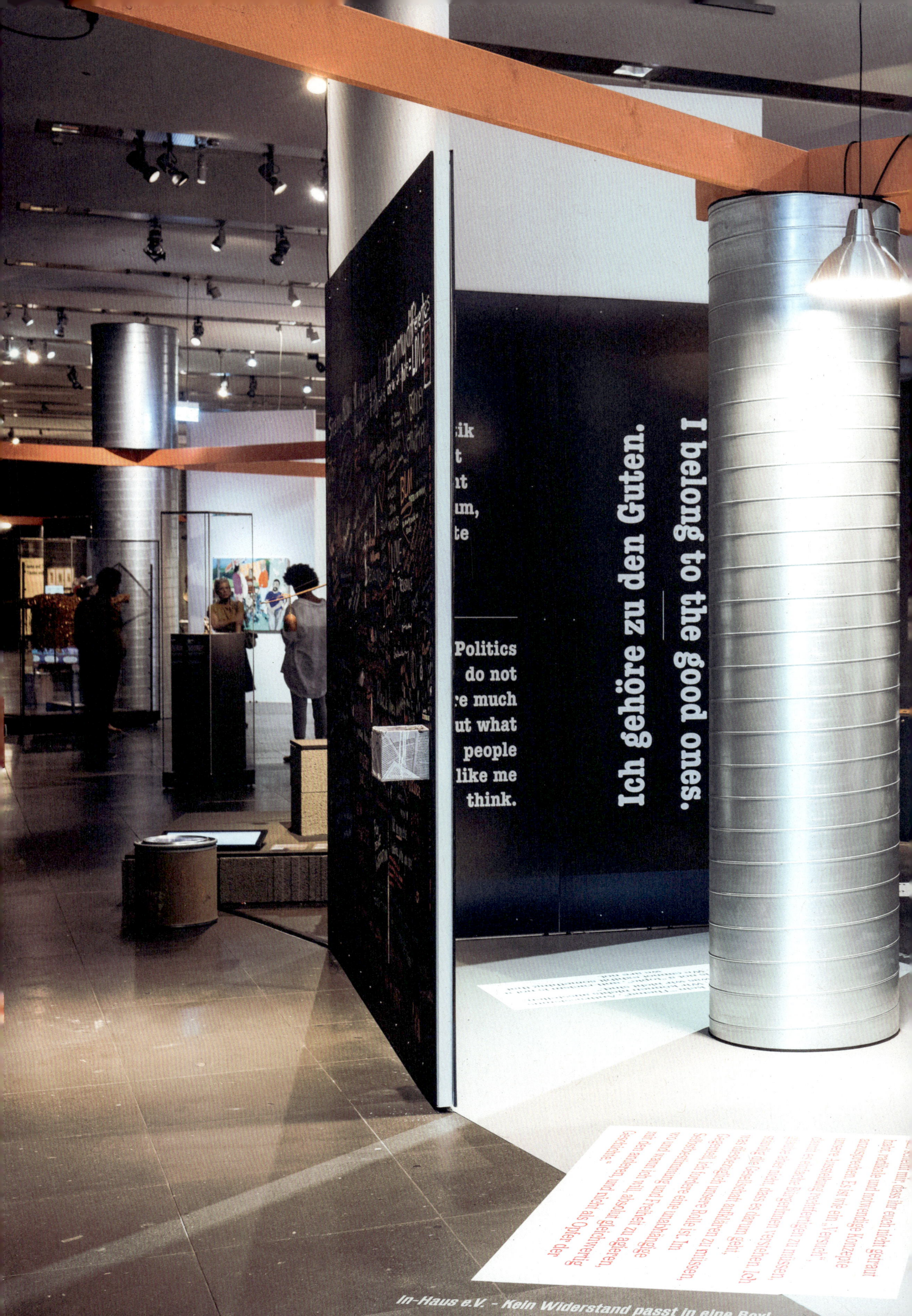

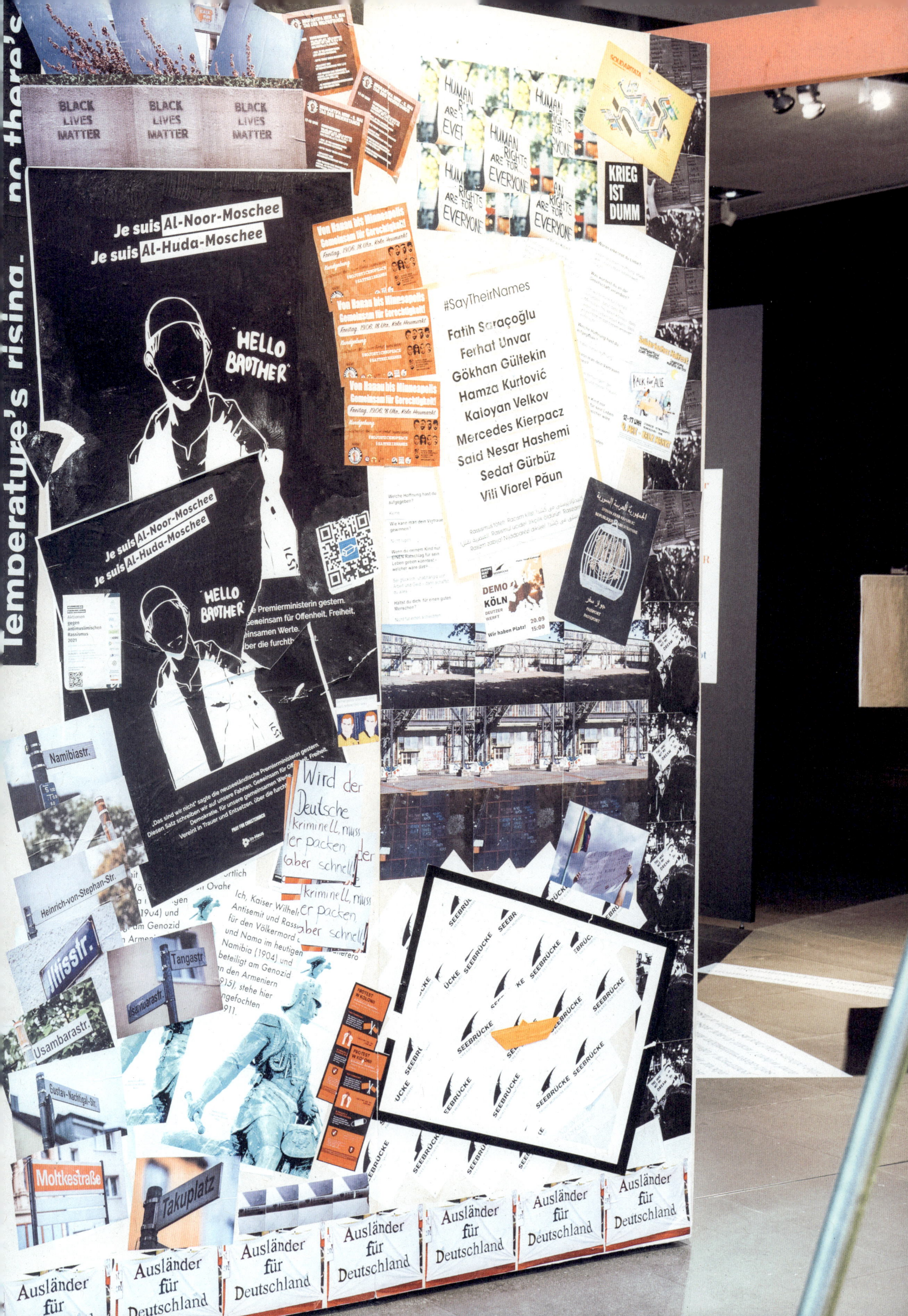

BLACK LIVES MATTER
Artist in Residence: Francis Oghuma

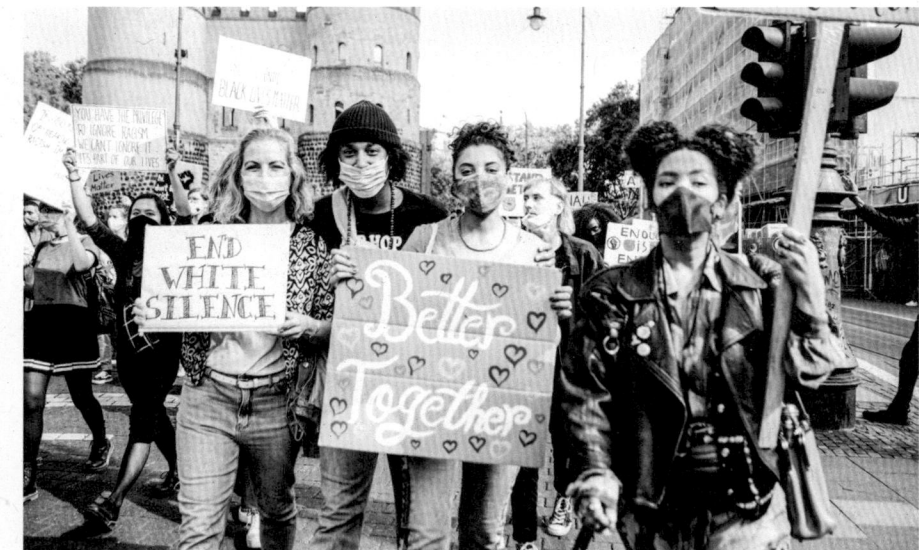

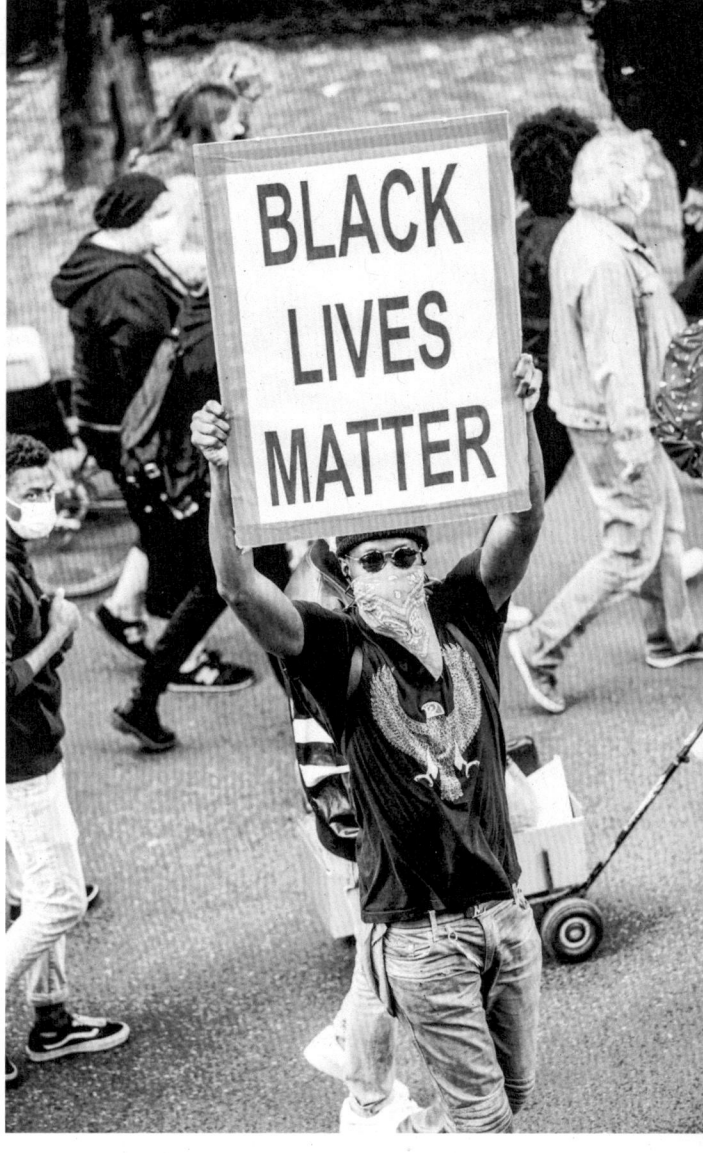

»The fact that we have to remind our fellow citizens that Black Lives Matter shows how big the problem is and how deeply racism is embedded in the fabric of our society.«

A protestor in the Cologne BLM demonstration on 6 June 2020

The Black Lives Matter demonstration in Cologne on June 20, 2020 took place in the wake of the murder of the Black American George Floyd, who was killed by a police officer in Minneapolis on May 25, 2020. More than 10,000 people from Cologne demonstrated the day after Juneteenth, the day commemorating the liberation of enslaved people in the USA – which in 2020 was marked by worldwide Black Lives Matter protests against racism and police violence. The Nigerian photographer Francis Oghuma, who is based in Cologne and was an artist-in-residence for *RESIST!*, documented the Black Lives Matter movement in Cologne and North Rhine-Westphalia: his photographs and interviews were shown in the exhibition.

Cologne, Germany 06/06/2020

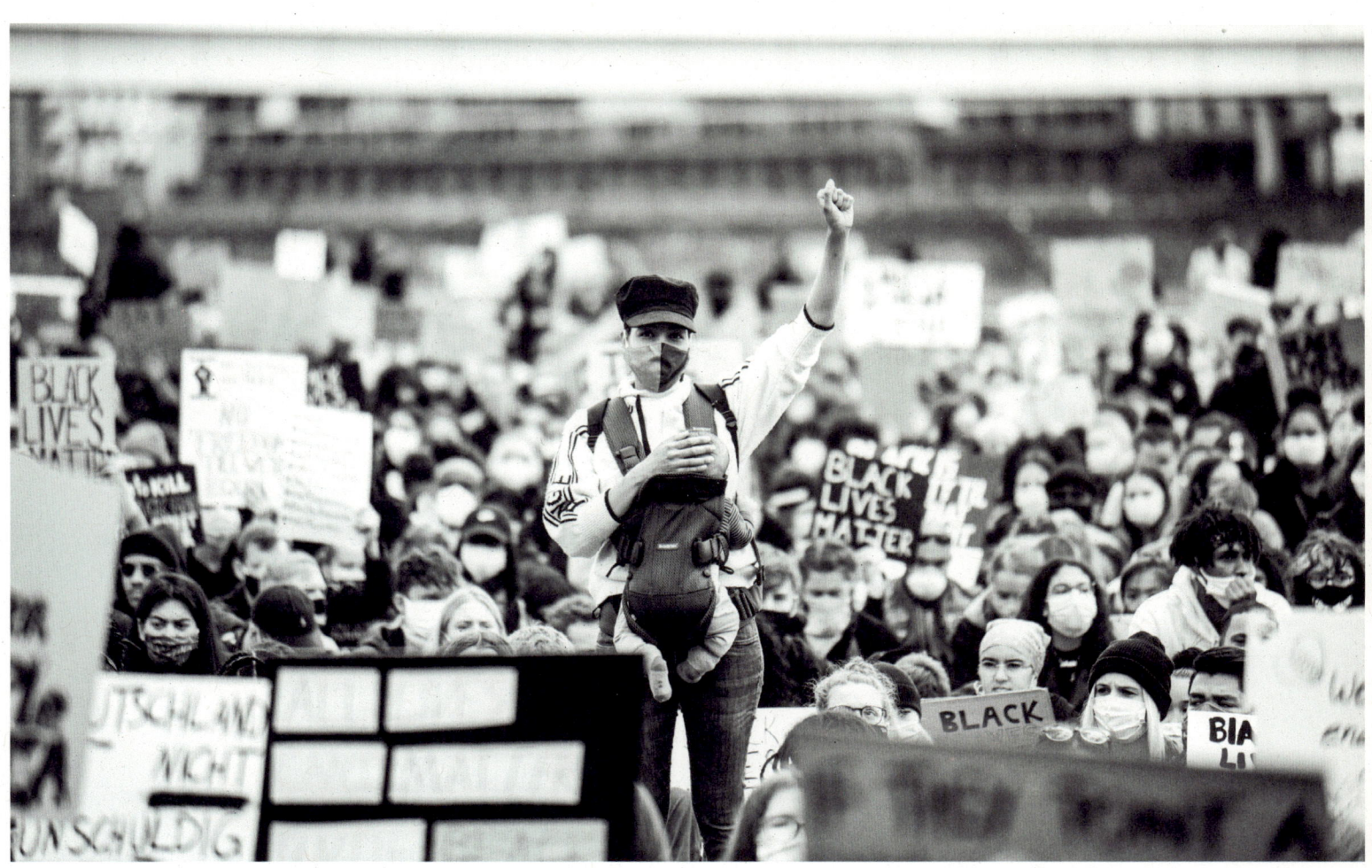

»I've realised that racism denies us countless opportunities. Even if we give 300 per cent, that sometimes isn't enough. Whether consciously or unconsciously, we are robbed of our time and quality of life. It's unfair, exhausting, and makes me furious. If there was no more racism, we would finally have time to deal with the normal everyday issues in life..«

A protestor in the Cologne BLM demonstration on 6 June 2020

[RESI)STANCE | ONE SHOT

Artists in Residence: Bahar Gökten and Daniela Rodriguez Romero Dance Performance

Video, 34:07 min., Direction, Camera and Postproduction: Young-Jean Maeng

 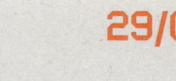

Cologne, Germany 29/01/2021

For the launch of the digital programme *RESIST!* on 29.01.2021, dancers from Bahar Gökten and Daniela Rodriguez Romero's group were invited to performatively open the exhibition. The dancers, who also took part in the interdisciplinary research workshop in August 2020, developed their own choreography for each chapter.

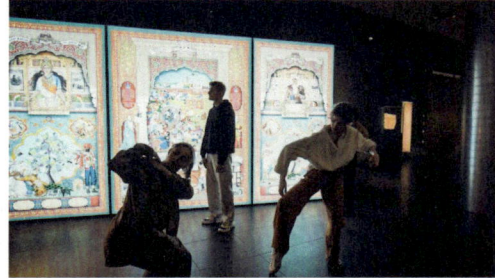

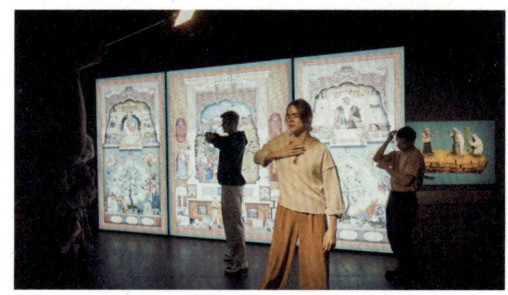

In preparation for the exhibition *RESIST! The Art of Resistance*, the dancers and choreographers Bahar Gökten and Daniela Rodriguez Romero conceived and directed a first informal-formal interface format: an interdisciplinary research on the traces of anti-colonial and post-colonial resistance, which traces the synergy of urban dance art and cultural anthropology. From 03–09/08/2020, 27 young dancers from the local dance scene took on the role of movement researchers to spend a week at the museum with staff members and invited guest speakers. In so-called movement laboratories, the urban dancers investigated the artefacts in the museum's collection that were to be featured in the *RESIST!* exhibition. The process was recorded in the form of a documentary film and shown in the exhibition.

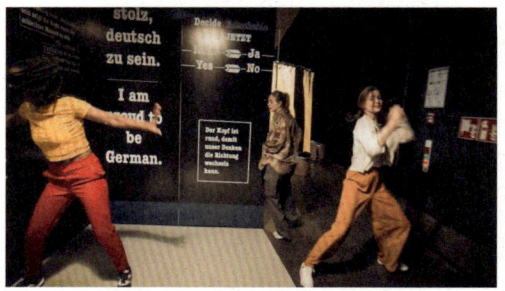

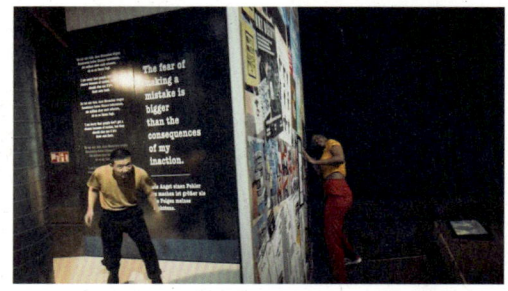

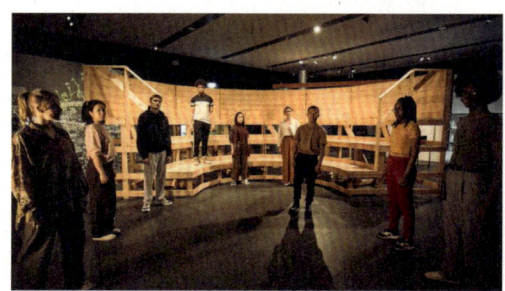

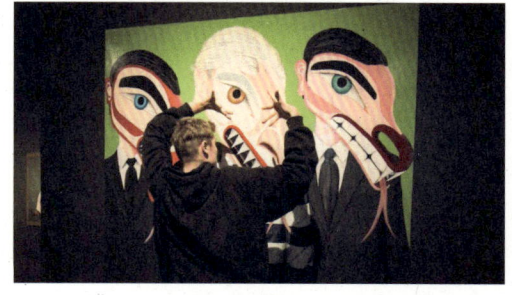

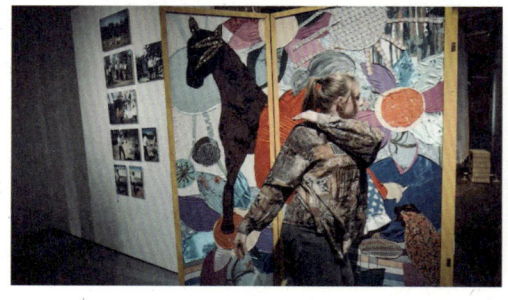

[RESI)STANCE | RESEARCH:

In preparation for the exhibition *RESIST!* August 2020; Artists in Residence: Bahar Gökten and Daniela Rodriguez Romero; video, 09:02 min, Director, cinematography and post-production: Young-Jean Maeng

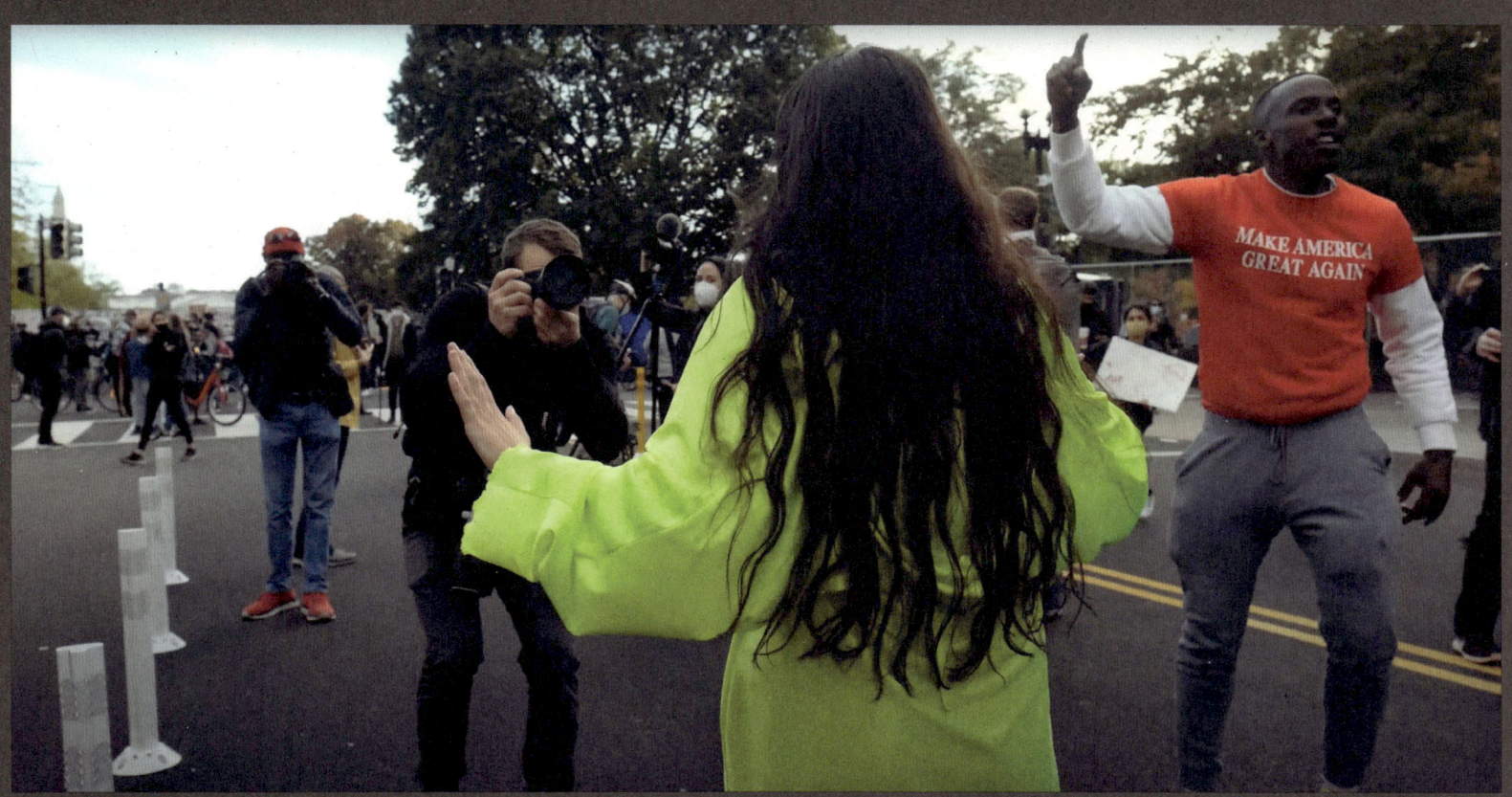

Selma Selman: *You Have No Idea*
3/11/2020, US Presidential Election Day, performance between BLM Plaza and the White House, Washington, DC, video, 5 min.

Washington, USA 03/11/2020

DANCE RESIST!

A Choreographic Interpretation of the Five Chapters of the Exhibition

Video, 8:40 Min., Direction, Camera and Postproduction: Young-Jean Maeng; Dance/Choreography: Emilie Pesch, Enting Zhang, Johann Bae, Kevin Claudio Ponge Kassoma; Filmcrew: Tim Junge, Simon Federlein, Cathalina Roldan

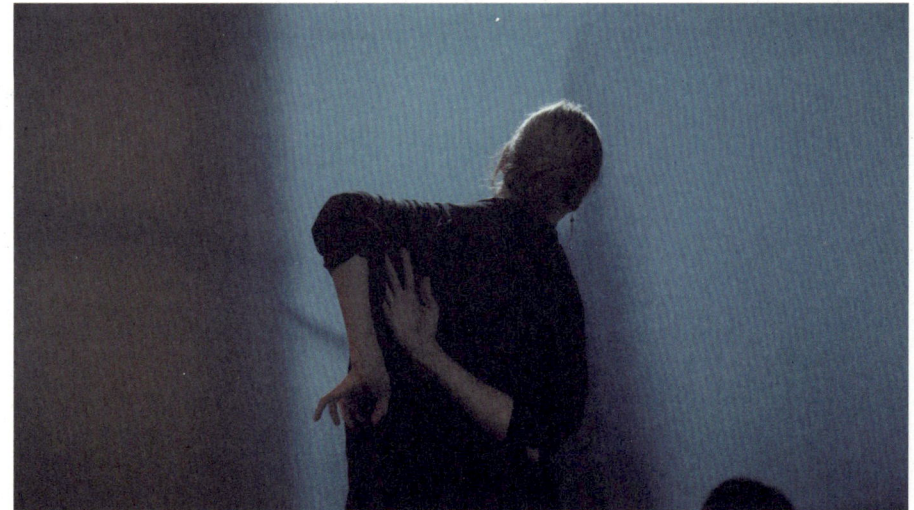
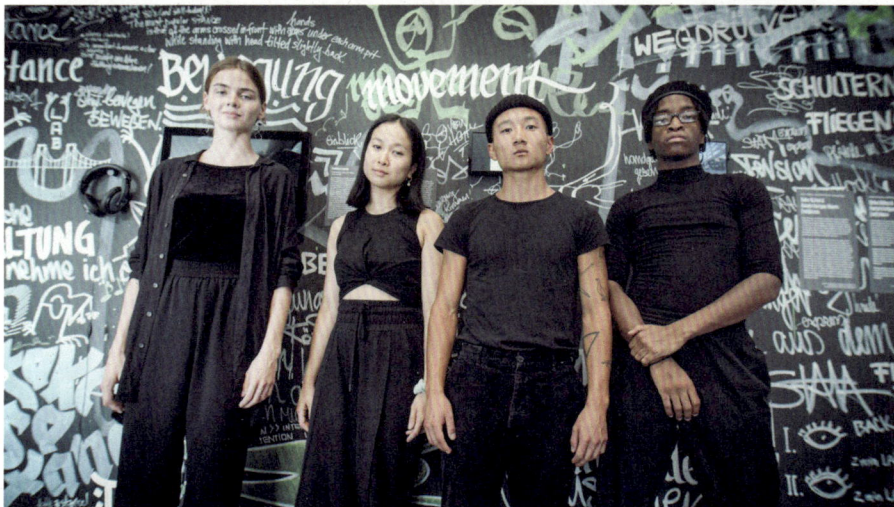
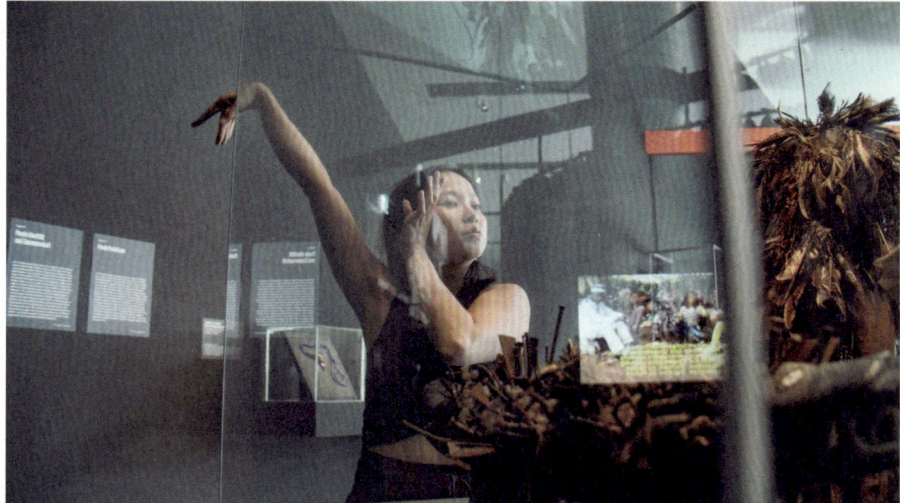
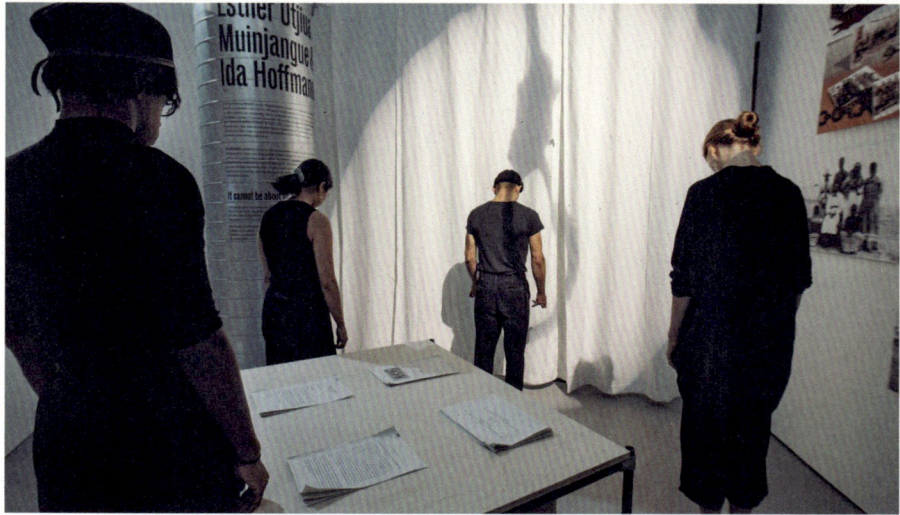

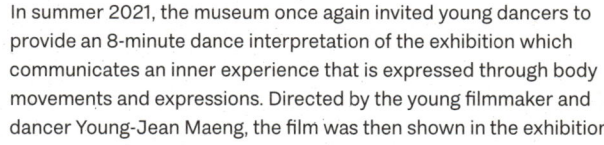

Cologne, Germany — **July 2021**

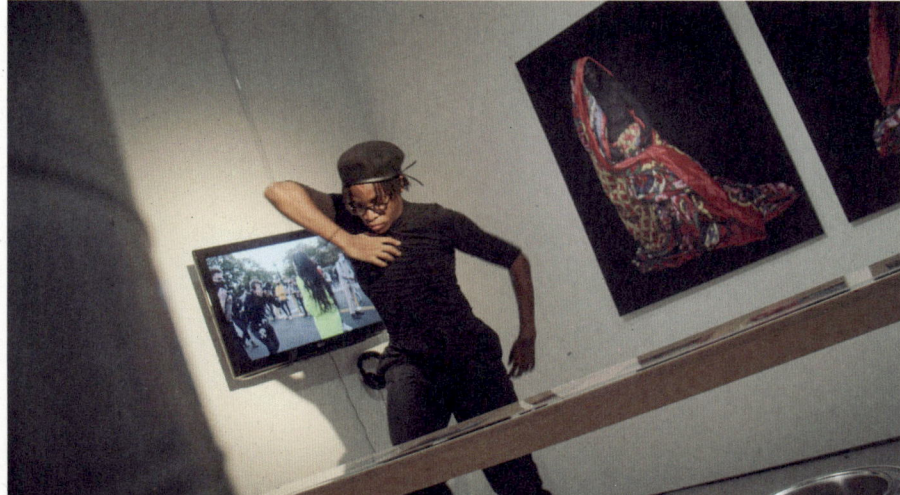

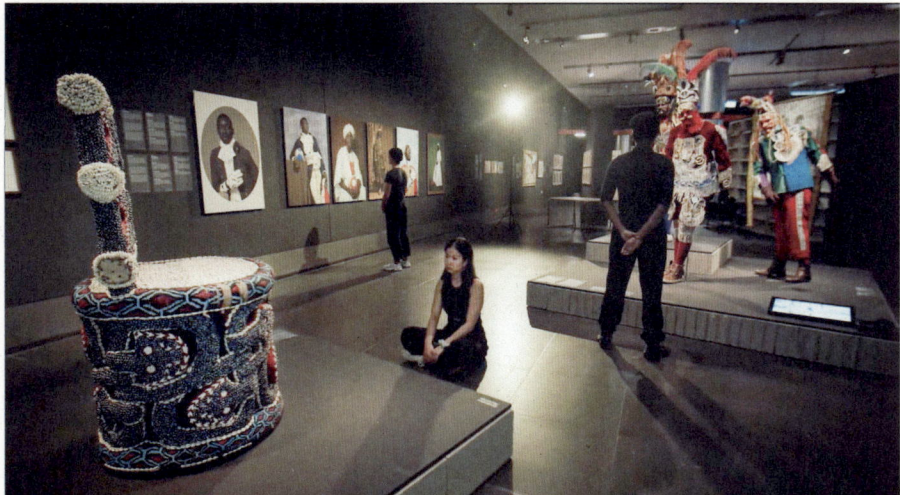

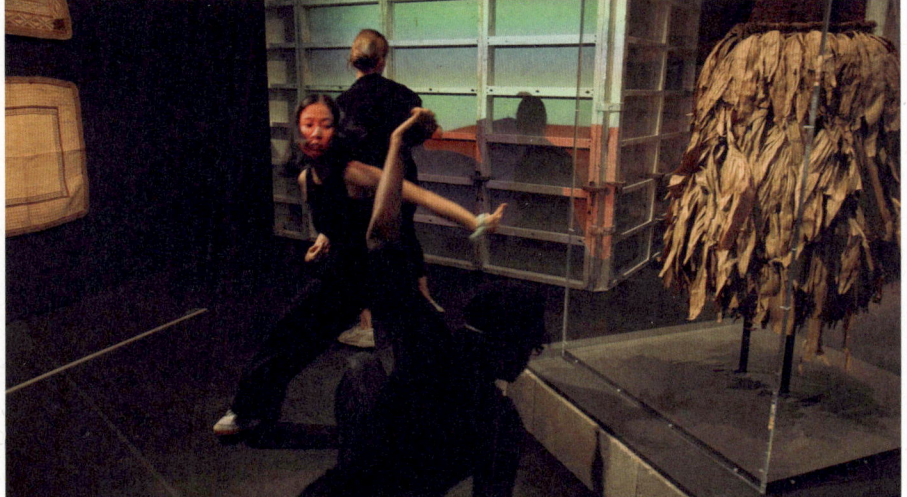

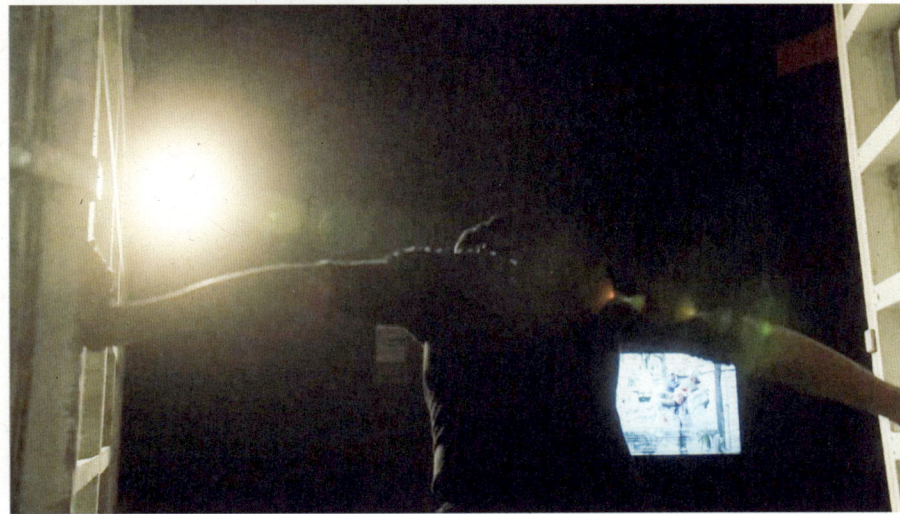

In summer 2021, the museum once again invited young dancers to provide an 8-minute dance interpretation of the exhibition which communicates an inner experience that is expressed through body movements and expressions. Directed by the young filmmaker and dancer Young-Jean Maeng, the film was then shown in the exhibition.

»Caring for myself is not self-indulgence, it is self-preservation, and that is an act of political warfare.« *Audre Lorde* *A Burst of Light, 1988*

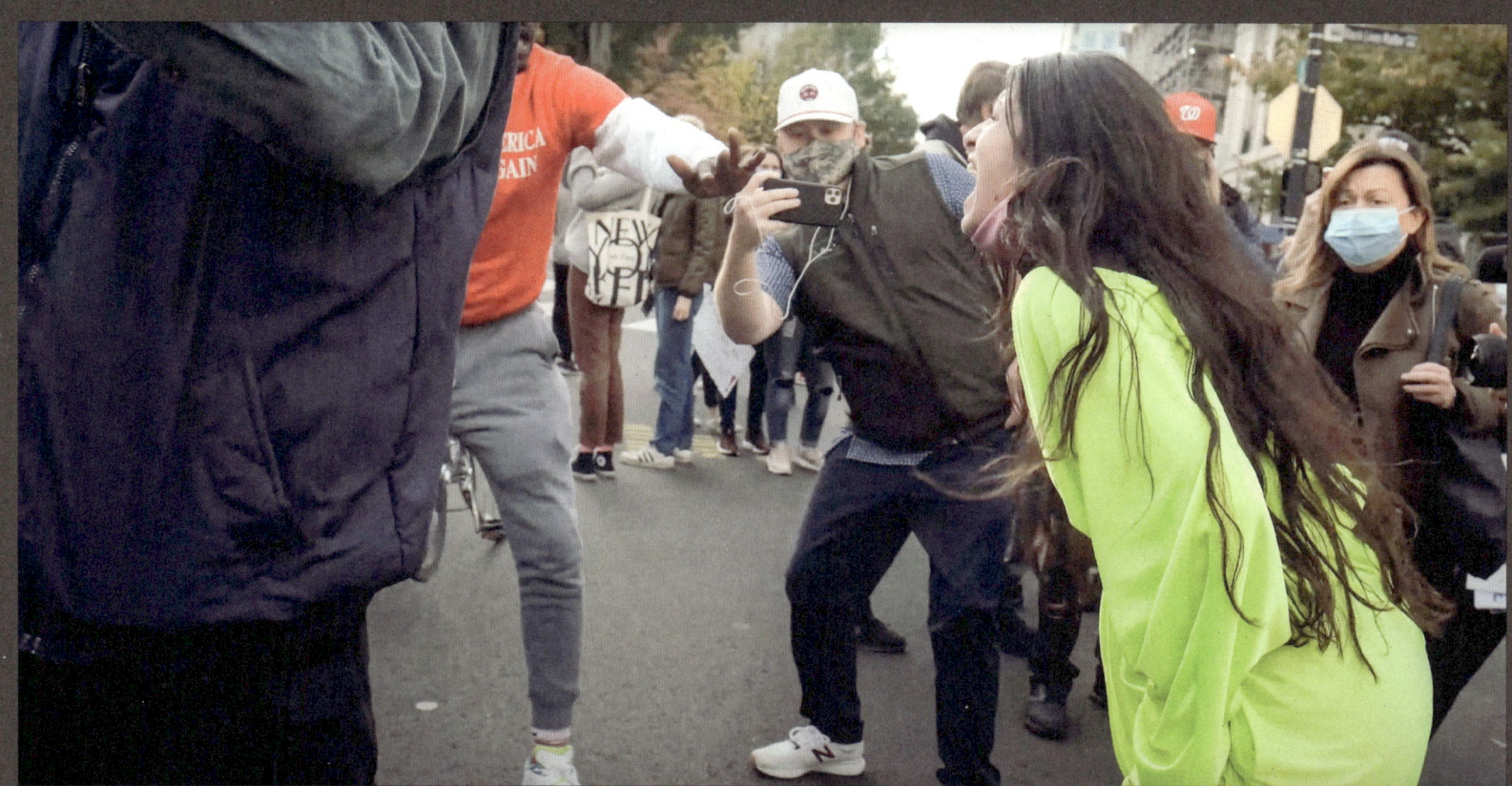

Selma Selman: *You Have No Idea*
3/11/2020, US Presidential Election Day, performance between BLM Plaza and the White House, Washington, DC, video, 5 min.

»This performance is very personal: It is my frustration brought to life. You have no idea. You have no idea about my life as a whole. You do not know who I am; nor do you know my joy or my sorrow. You do not know whether there is pain in my life or not, or how I feel at that moment. You have no idea, no idea ...« *Selma Selman*

Washington, USA 03/11/2020

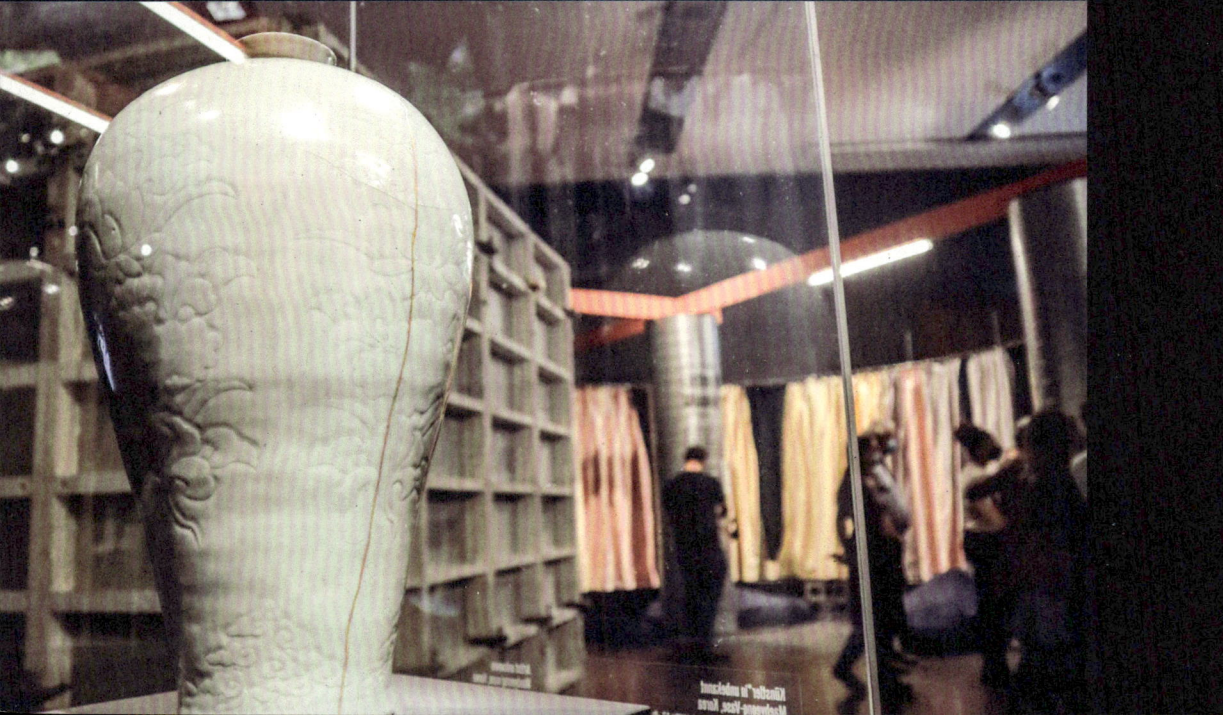

Cultural Resilience or the Art of Survival?

"The number of people who are busy repairing something is absolutely astonishing. It is a massive fact of everyday life. And for sure something must be going on in these constant permanent actions of repair or if you want reparation. Some forms of knowledge must be invented in the process through which people are constantly trying to put back together that which has been broken, whether intentionally or not. And it strikes me to which extend the earth is in need of repair, of care and of maintenance." The School of Resistance, Achille Mbembe in conversation with Milo Rau, 2020.

Colonialism has left deep traces in collective and individual memory. According to the French-Algerian artist Kader Attia, covering up and concealing these wounds does not help to heal them – especially as they are repeatedly torn open by the continuity of violence. Rather, the way to healing lies in showing the wounds. Harsh and inhumane measures were taken to spread European languages and Christian religion and culture. The enforcement of cultural dominance interrupted and eradicated whole fields of knowledge and practices; some survived in hiding. How to deal with this legacy today? The art of resistance reveals the incredible capacity of humanity to fight for its freedom and to overcome catastrophic oppression and trauma. This is shown by the Brazilian artist Ayrson Heráclito, who tries to transform the traumatic memory of slavery with a Candomblé ritual. Resistant counterculture finds expression in the art of the everyday, the hidden, the quiet, but also in the art of inexhaustible protest and solidarity – as shown, for example, in the history of the anti-apartheid protests. It is a resistance that appears in the most diverse cultural forms: in dance, songs and music, pop culture, writing, storytelling, poetry and painting.

But the art of resistance also lies in reviving suppressed and forbidden languages, techniques and art forms, such as the examples shown from the Pacific: here, despite German, Japanese, British and Australian colonial rule, traditional types of music, monetary systems, and crafts are presently resurging and community museums and numerous other initiatives are called into life.

This recourse to collectively shared narratives and practices is a crucial resource for strengthening the social fabric and psychological resilience of the community. It attempts to operate outside colonial dynamics and power structures. Especially the younger generation and many minorities transform forms and practices from the past, reinventing them in music, fashion, language and dance. YouTube, Instagram and TikTok are often used to spread these ideas and create communities. Afrofuturism, as Black empowerment in film, literature, art and music, also creates spaces in which racism and discrimination are overcome and Black people can empower themselves by inventing entirely new science fiction worlds. The aim is to build and own new narratives, freeing oneself from mainstream and white narratives and envisioning self-determined futures.

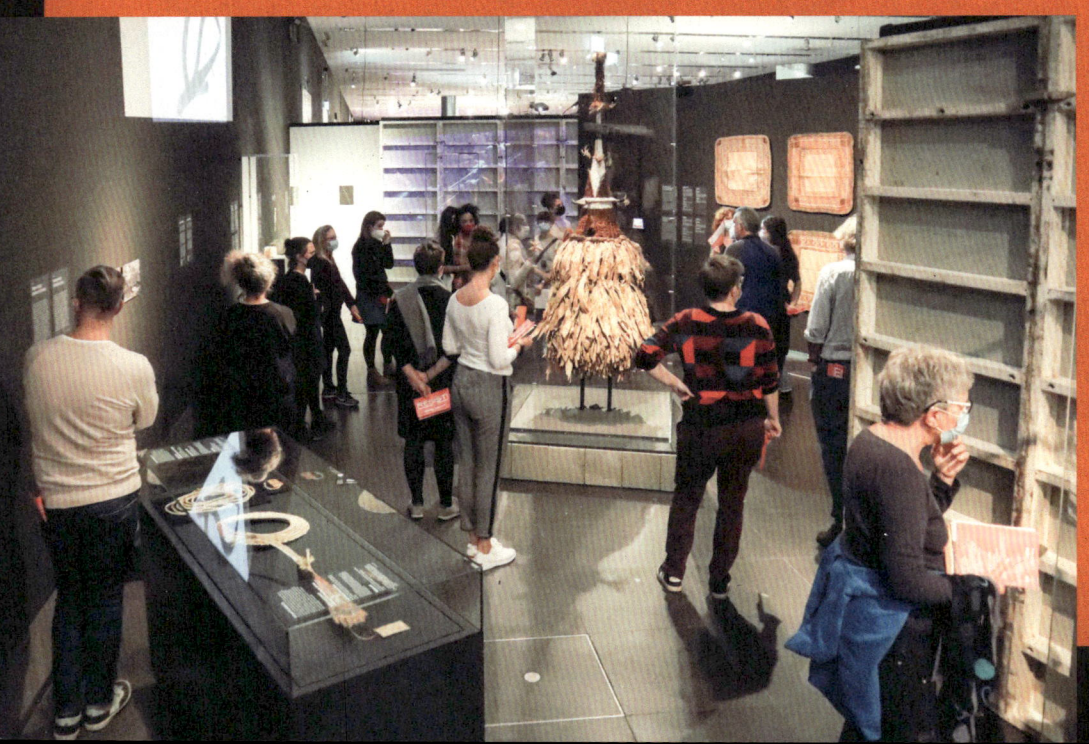

Mirror of Colonial Horror

Kareau or "scare-devil" depicting a European soldier, Nicobar Islands, Bay of Bengal, India, ca. 1900, maker and owner not recorded

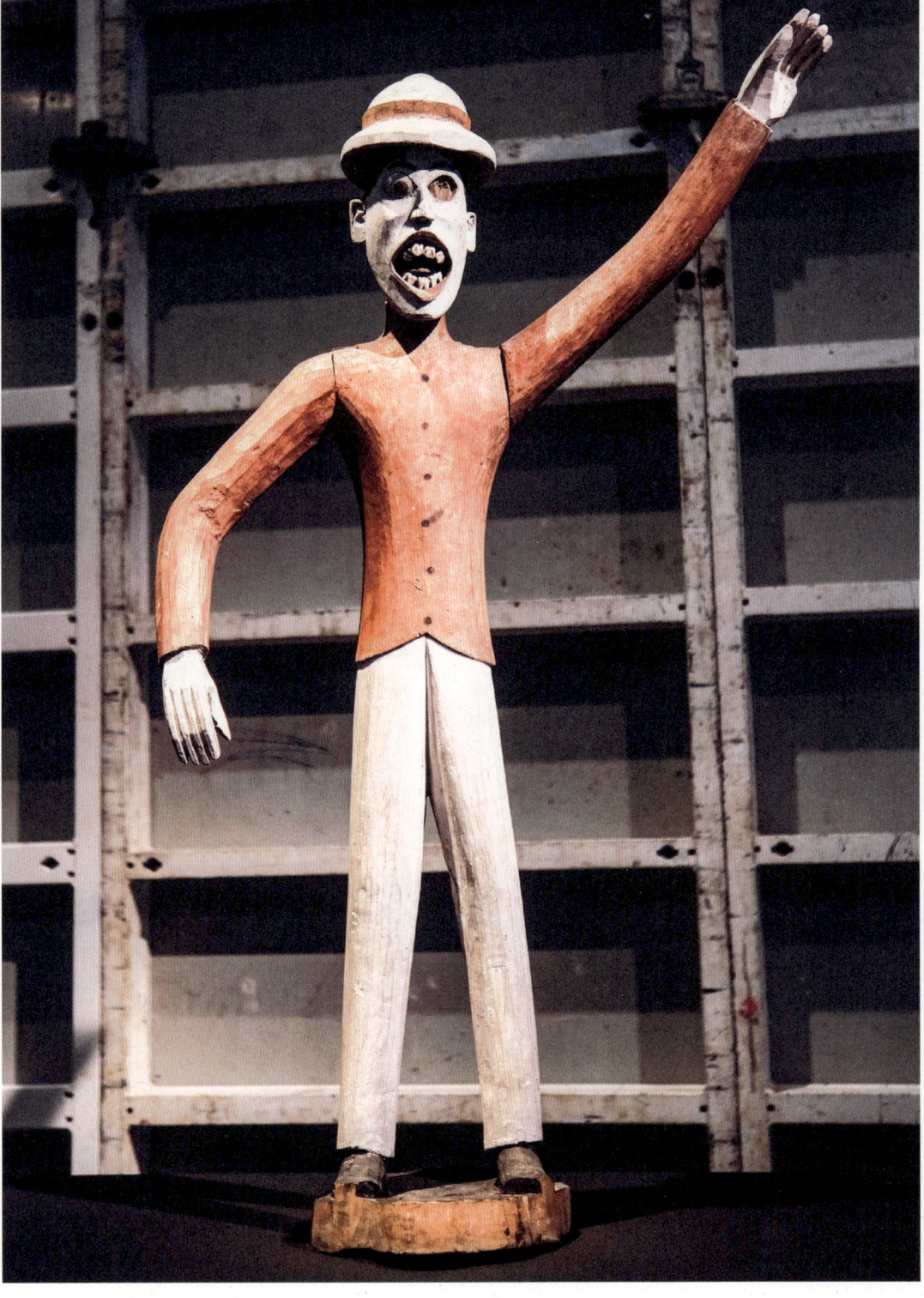

Collection RJM No. 23331; The exact provenance of this figure is unknown, the museum acquired it in 1909 from the Hamburg trading house Umlauff

For the people of the Nicobar Islands, the Europeans who began travelling to this transport hub in the Indian Ocean in the seventeenth century were initially just a new set of trading partners. Missionaries sent to convert the islands into colonial outposts failed due to resistance from the islanders. In the nineteenth century, the Danes, Austrians, and Prussians all tried unsuccessfully to occupy the islands before they were incorporated into British India in 1869. While this *kareau* figure reflects the horror and terror spread by British soldiers, it also subverts the power of the foreign soldier it represents. This imposing character turns the colonial gaze back on itself, for the "savage" depicted here is a European soldier. Displayed at the entrance to a home, the figure was believed to ward off the calamities and diseases brought to the islands by the colonial occupiers. *Kareau* are often frightening in appearance, taking the form of mythological creatures wearing European elements such as top hats, turbans, rifles, or uniforms. This appropriation of foreign attributes reflects a form of ritual resistance against the superiority of the colonisers. *Kareau* were not for sale, as they were closely linked to their owner's well-being. The sculptures could protect the house as a kind of extension of their owner and served as a memorial after their death.

Ayrson Heráclito
O Sacudimento da Maison des Esclaves em Gorée
O Sacudimento da Casa da Torre, 2015

Performance, two-channel video installation, 08:32 min.

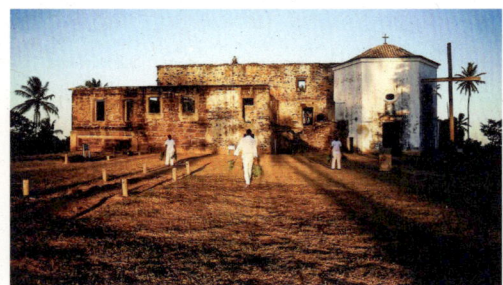
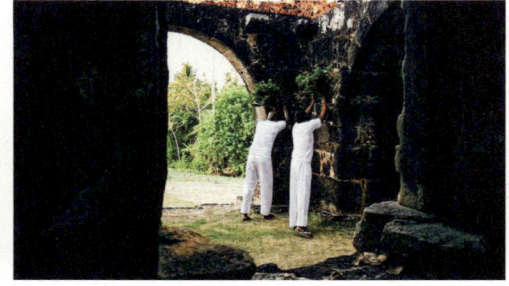
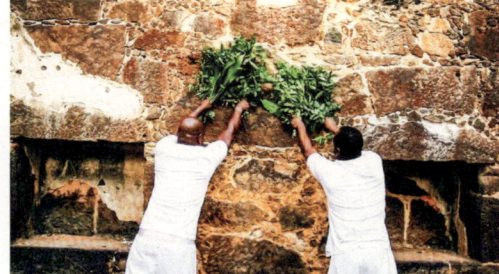
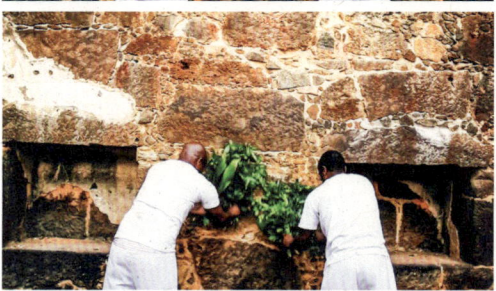
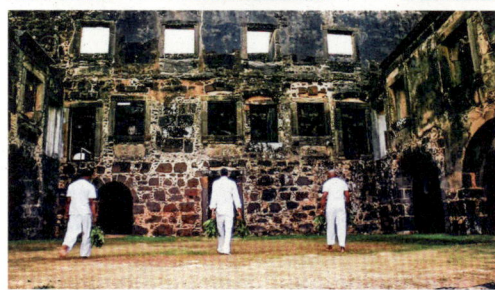
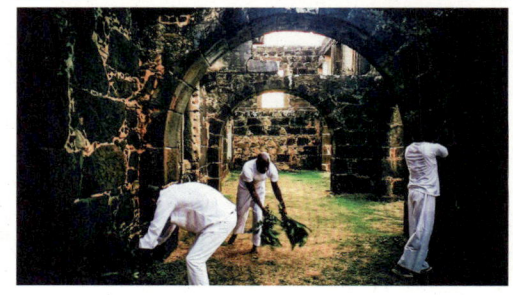

»When I ›shook‹ the Casa da Torre, I wanted to purge our historical past; I wanted to ›shake up‹ history, to make the past present through the act of shaking. [...] I evoke history, spell it out, in order to then intervene in it as an artist and as a man, to suppress it, not from memory – for us, remembering the past is essential in order to act on it and make sure that it does not repeat itself – but from everyday practices by overcoming it.« *Ayrson Heráclito*

Gorée, Senegal &
Salvador de Bahia, Brazil

2015

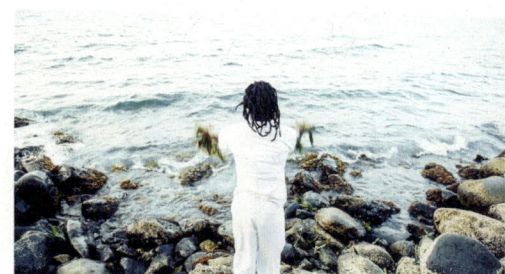
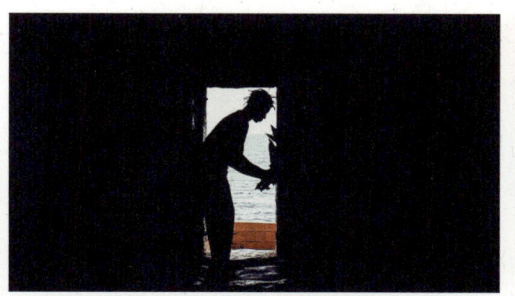
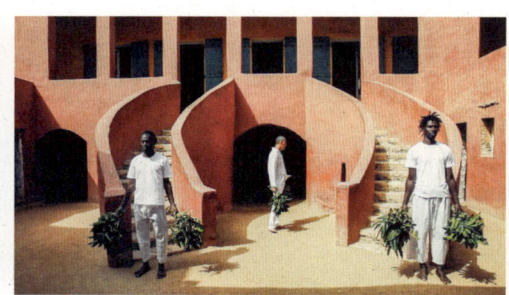
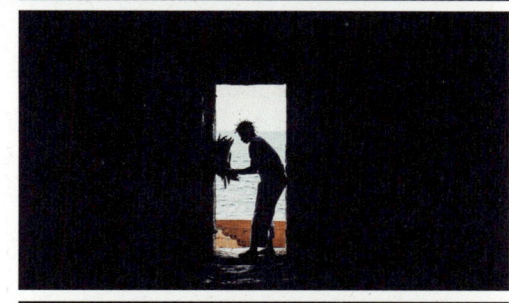
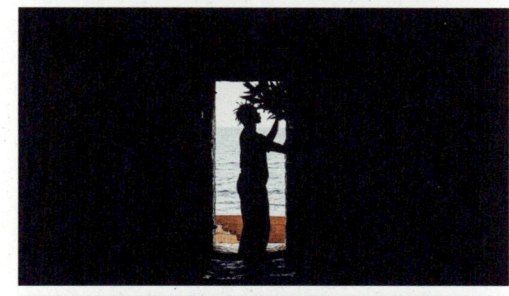
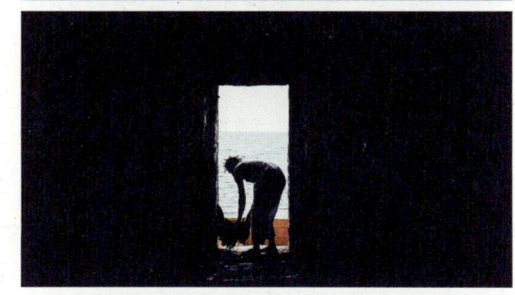
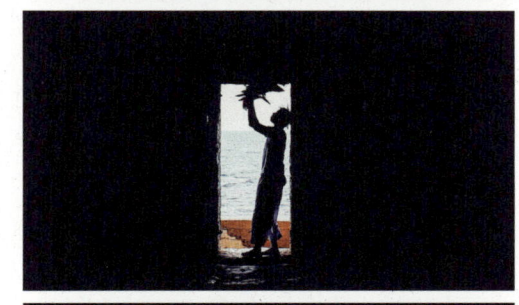
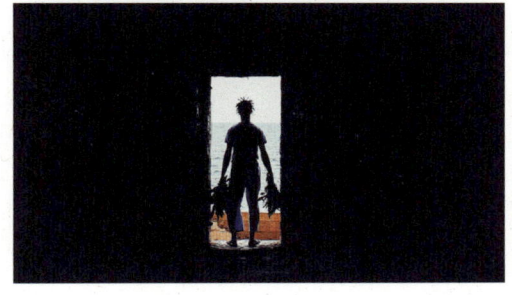

The shaking of the Casa da Torre (left) and the Maison des Esclaves (right) forms a diptych whose central theme is the ritual cleansing of two significant places that symbolise the tragedy of the transatlantic slave trade and colonisation. One site is on the island of Gorée, a few kilometres off the coast of Dakar, Senegal, where enslaved Africans were imprisoned before being deported to the Americas. The other site is located on the north coast of the Brazilian city of Salvador de Bahia, one of the largest administrative centres of the Portuguese colonial system. The Maison des Esclaves (the island of Gorée) represents the violence of separation and non-return, while the Casa da Torre (Salvador de Bahia) signifies the violence and trauma of arriving in the "New World". In the Afro-Brazilian tradition of Candomblé, which has its roots in the Vodou religion from West Africa, the "shaking" or "brushing" of sacred leaves all over the building serves to drive away the spirits of the deceased so that they cannot harm people. This is a form of a spiritual cleansing. "When I "shook" the Tower House, says Ayrson Heráclito, the only *Egun* [spirit of a deceased] that was there, that those walls were pregnant of even after so many years, was the slave master; moreover, the only *Egun* there, who haunted me, remaining among us, migrated from the Casa da Torre, his castle or fortress, migrated and seeped into the whole social fabric of Bahia; but not only that: it was the coming violence of slavery and the old colonial system, which bequeathed to us an extreme inequality and also as its fruit, poverty." In an attempt to free himself from the ghosts and phantom pains of colonialism and to heal the colonial wounds of the present, Heráclito returns to historical sites of colonial suffering.

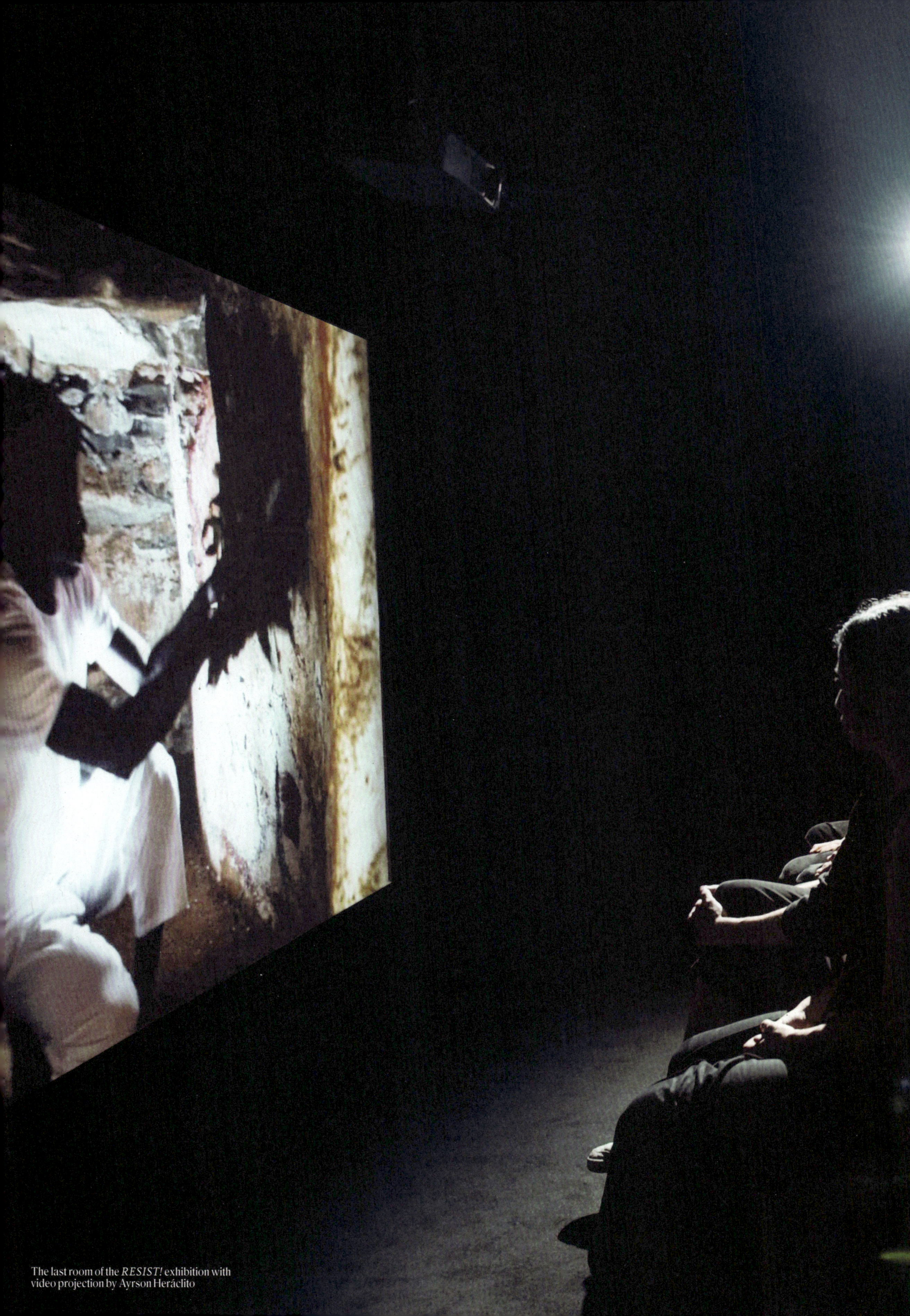

The last room of the *RESIST!* exhibition with video projection by Ayrson Heráclito

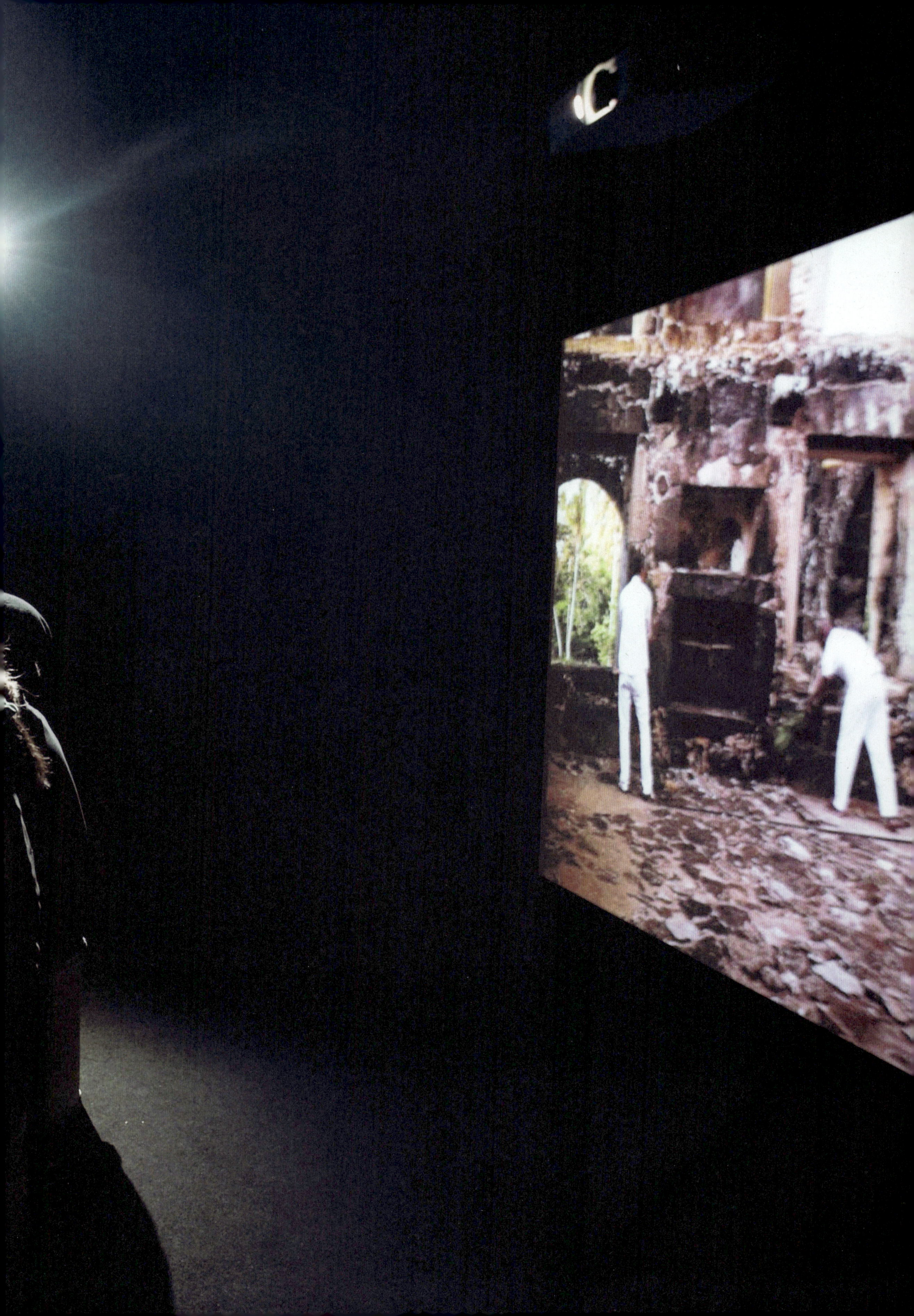

Kader Attia
Repaired Broken Mirror, 2017

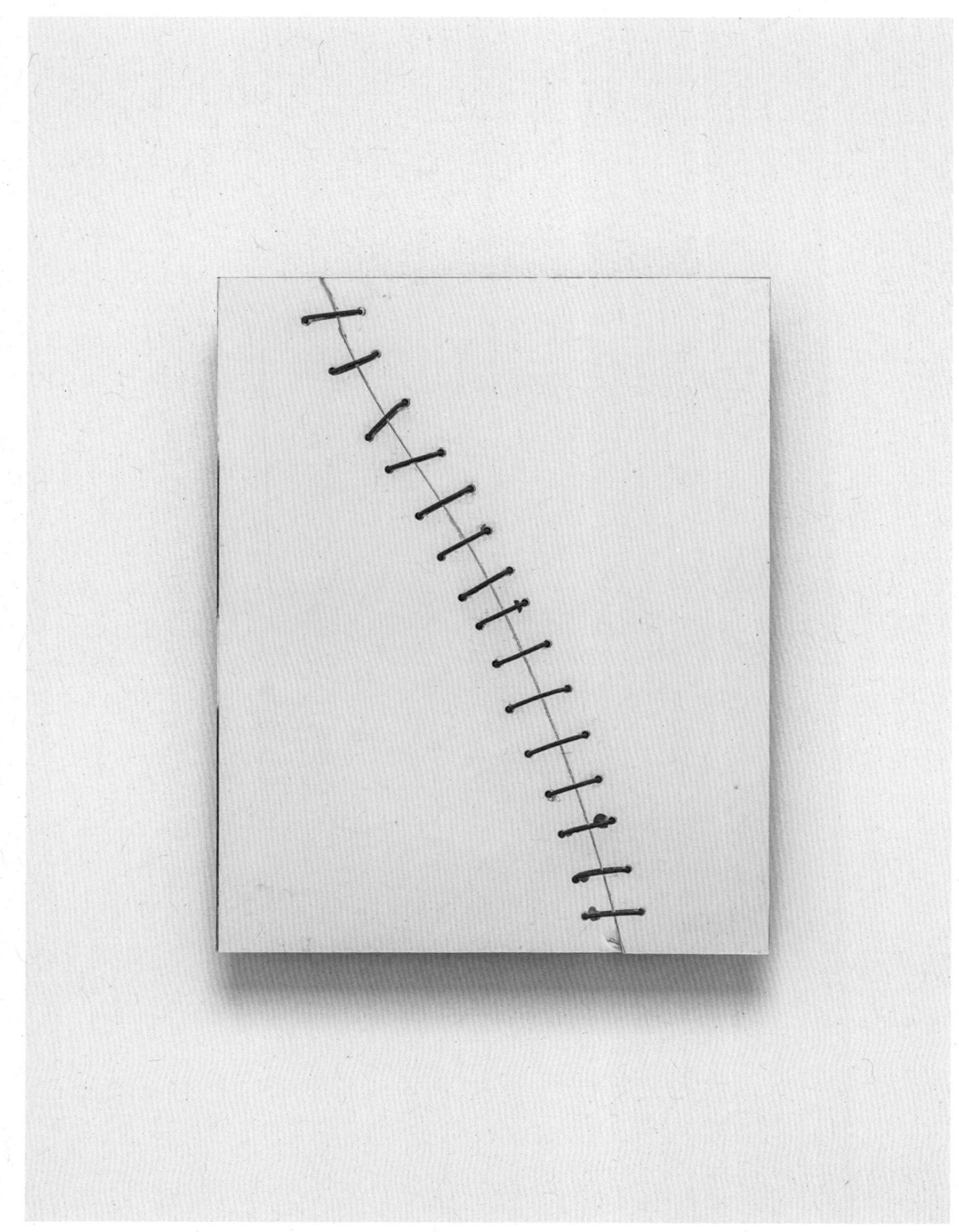

»You're not only looking at a repair but an injury. The word ›repair‹ is an oxymoron. Every repair is entangled with the injury – you cannot separate the two.«
Kader Attia

Western concepts of repair often aim to erase all signs of damage, to make the restored object seem as intact as it had been before it fell apart, before its demolition or destruction. In contrast, another form of repair – as exemplified by the Japanese *kintsugi* technique (roughly translated as "joining with gold") – aims to deliberately highlight cracks instead of covering them. The method involves repairing and reassembling damaged objects, but without trying to restore them to their prior wholeness. *Kintsugi* thus enhances the individuality and special character of the repaired object. The visible injury becomes part of the object, like in Kader Attia's repaired mirror, which reflected visitors' faces as they passed in front of it and entered the final room of the exhibition *RESIST!*

Thus, rather than hiding colonial trauma and regarding the legacy of colonialism as an obstacle, the museum – and in this context the exhibition *RESIST!* – seeks to find new ways of dealing with the "problem" of colonialism and coloniality instead of perpetuating the museum's "aphasic" relationship with its colonial past.

RESIST! aims to facilitate a conversation and to create a museological space of negotiation. But can colonial wounds be healed? Can these traumatic ruptures and cracks be repaired in an ethnological museum? Rather than healing colonial wounds, which is probably an impossible task, *RESIST!*'s museological practice of repair is to expose these wounds and to call for their recognition.

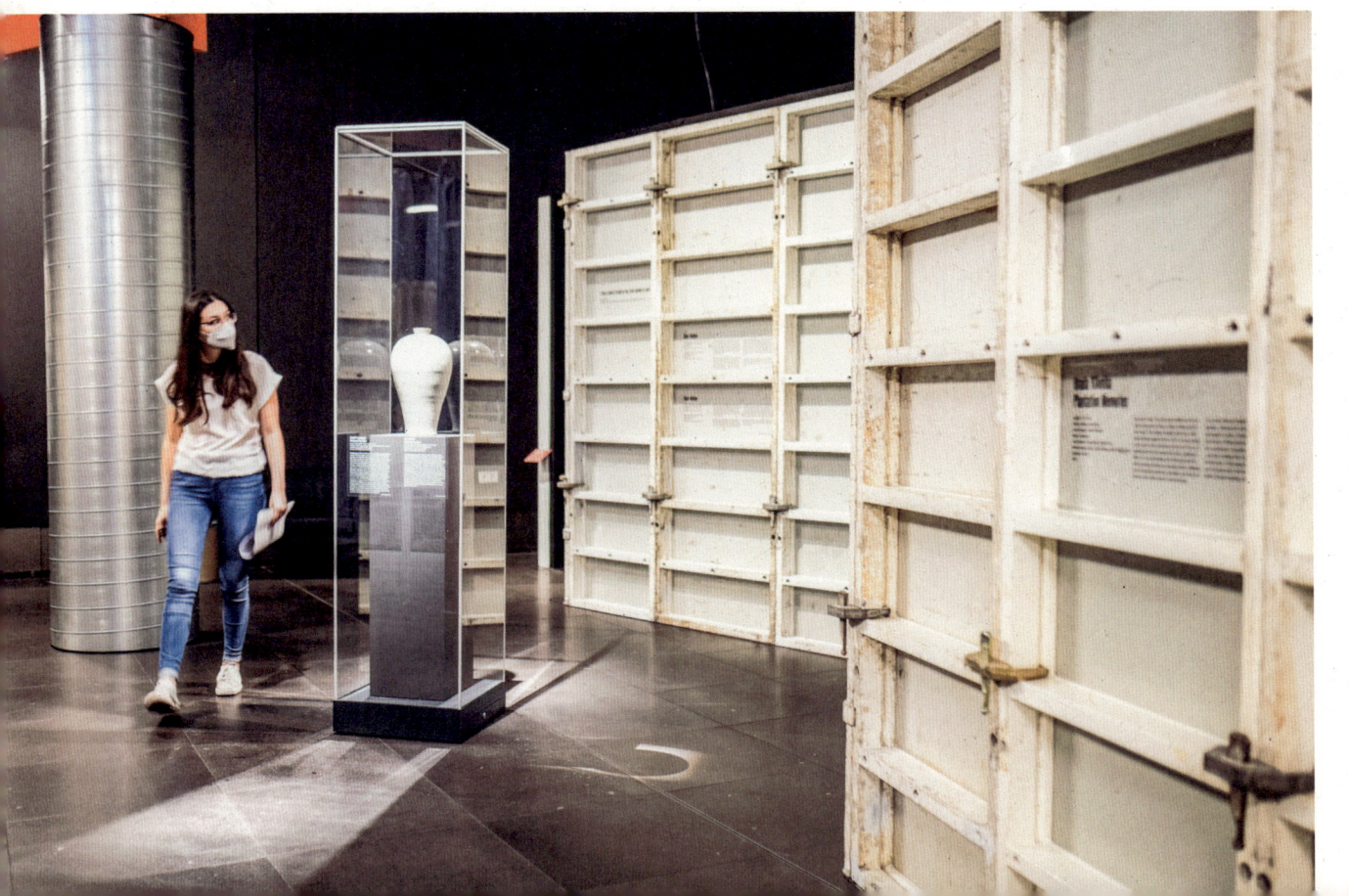

»The choice to work against the grain, to challenge the status quo often has negative consequences. And that is part of what makes that choice one that is not politically neutral.«
bell hooks *Teaching to transgress: Education as the practice of freedom, 1994*

It's Yours! curators

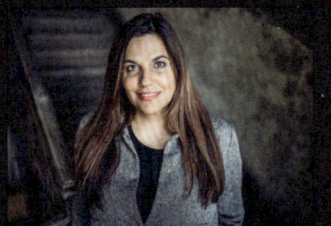
Tímea Junghaus
*1975, Budapest, Hungary

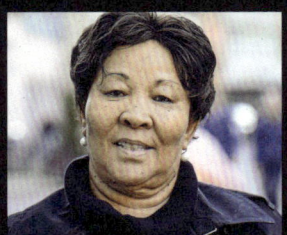
Ida Maria Magdalena Hoffmann
*1947, Karasburg, today Namibia

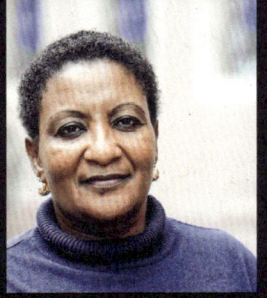
Esther Utjiua Muinjangue
*1962, Windhoek, today Namibia

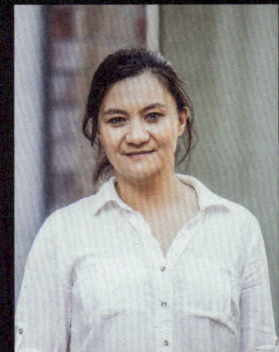
Elizaveta Kahn
*1982, Moscow, former Sowiet Union

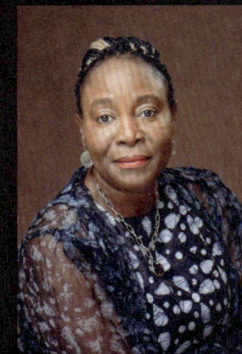
Peju Layiwola
*1967, Benin City, Nigeria

Artists

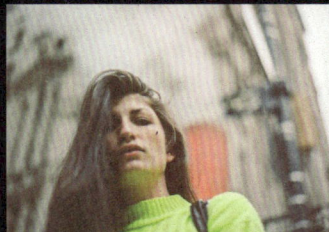
Selma Selman
*1991, Bihac, Bosnia and Herzegowina

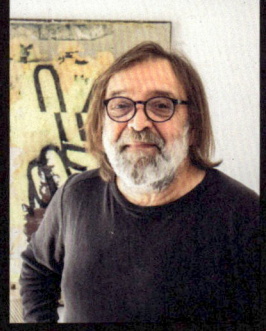
Alfred Ullrich
*1948, Schwabmünchen, Germany

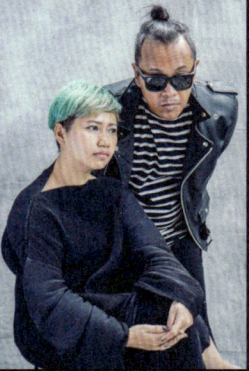
indieguerillas
Miko Bawono
*1975, Kudus, Indonesia
Santi Ariestyowanti
*1977, Semarang, Indonesia

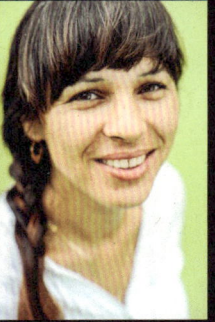
Małgorzata Mirga-Tas
*1978, Zakopane, Poland

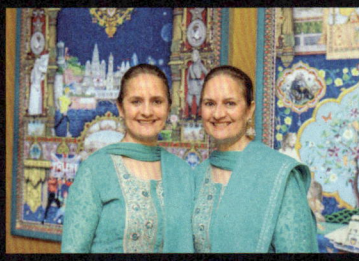
Amrit und Rabindra Kaur Singh
*1966, London, UK

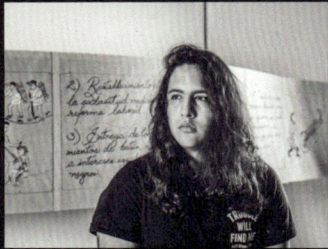
Diego Sandoval Ávila
*1993, Mexico City, Mexico

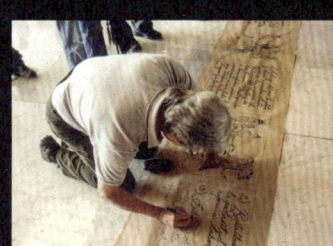
Juan Manuel Sandoval Palacios
*1948, Mexico City, Mexico

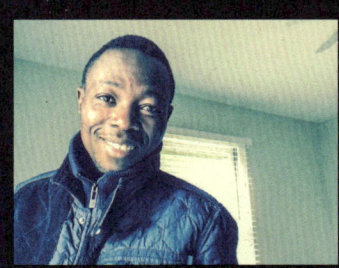
Jimoh Ganiyu
*1978, Ibadan, Nigeria

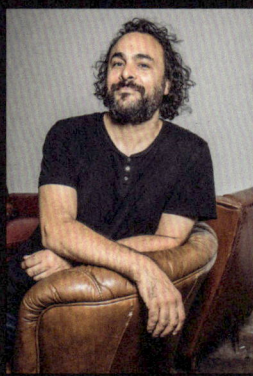
Kader Attia
*1970, Dugny, France

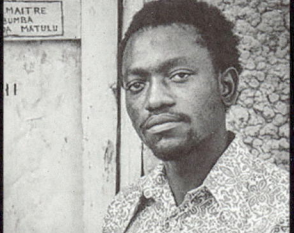
Tshibumba Kanda Matulu
*1947, Lubumbashi, Democratic Republic of the Congo

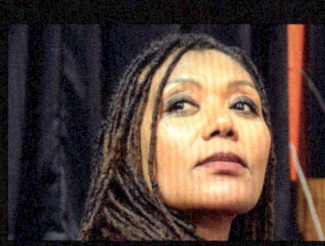
Patricia Kaersenhout
*1966, Den Helder, Netherlands

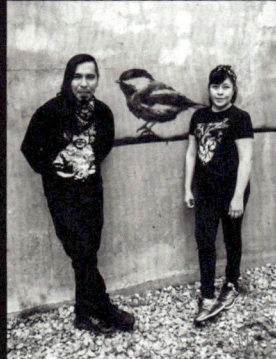
Lapiztola
2006, Oaxaca, Mexico

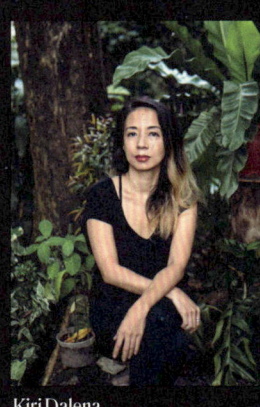
Kiri Dalena
*1975, Manila, Philippines

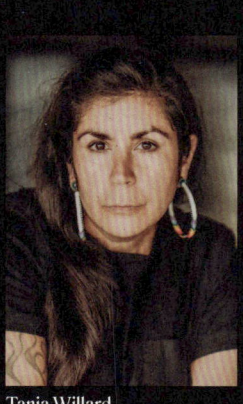
Tania Willard
*1977, Kamloops, Canada

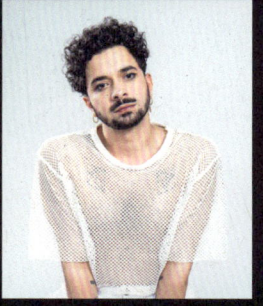
Robert Gabris
*1986, Hnúšta, Slowakia

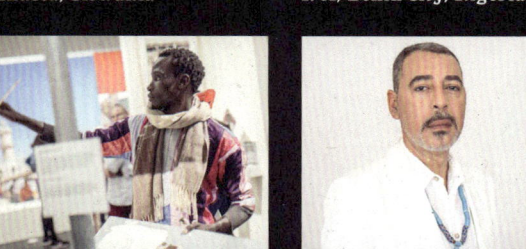
Monday Midnite
*1961, Benin City, Nigeria

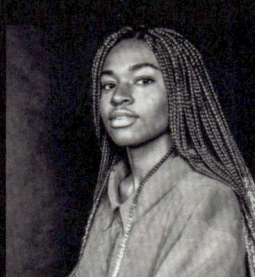
Nwakuso Edozien
*1996, Lagos, Nigeria

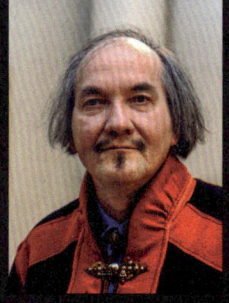
Keviselie/
Hans Ragnar Mathisen
*1945, Áhkkánjárga/Narvik, Norwegia

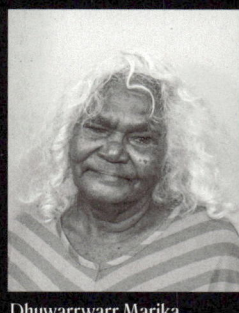
Dhuwarrwarr Marika
ca. 1945, Region Miwatj, Australia

Mamadou Sall
*1980, Rufisque, Senegal

Ayrson Heráclito
*1968, Macaúbas, Brazil

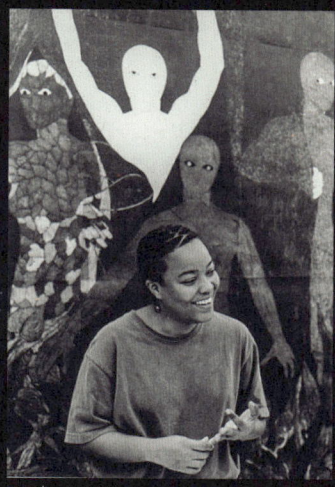
Belkis Ayón Manso
*1967; †1999, Havanna, Cuba

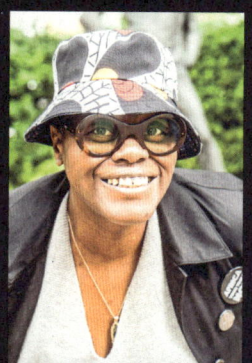
Rokia Bamba
*1976, Brussels, Belgium

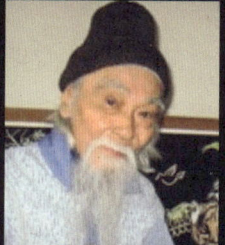
Huỳnh Văn Thuận
*1921, Saigon, Vietnam;
† 2017, Ho Chi Minh City, Vietnam

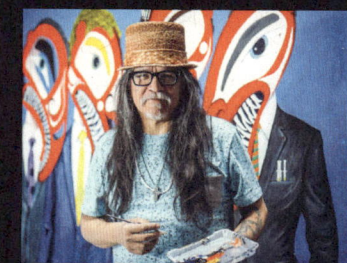
Lawrence Paul Yuxweluptun
*1957, Kamloops, Canada

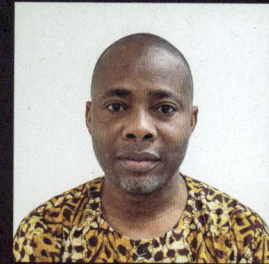
Alao Lukman
*1981, Jos, Nigeria

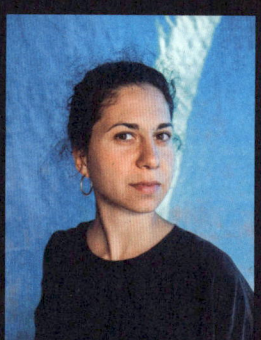
Bahar Gökten
*1986, Esslingen a. Neckar, Germany

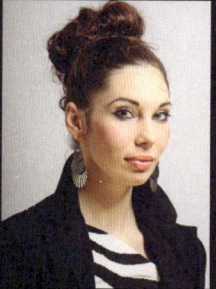
Daniela Rodríguez Romero
*1983, Biberach a.d. Riss, Germany

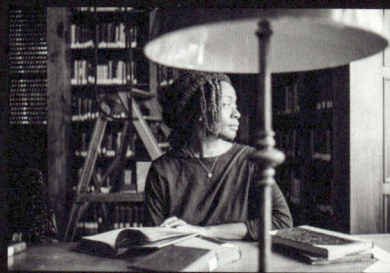
Kara Walker
*1969, Stockton, USA

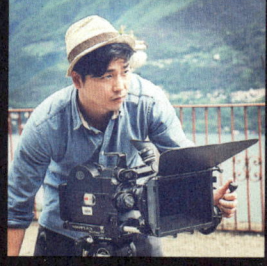
Young-Jean Maeng
*1987, Cologne, Germany

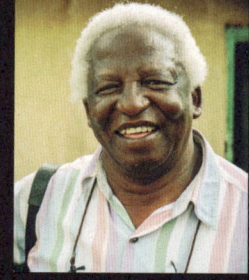
Peter Magubane
*1932, Johannesburg, South Africa

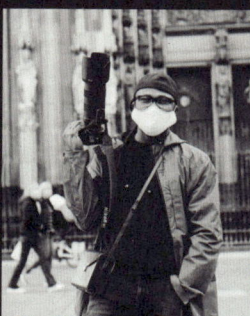
Francis Oghuma
*1985, Lagos, Nigeria

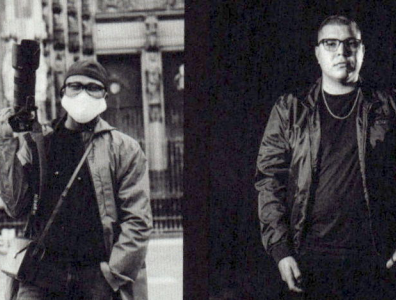
Ernesto Yerena Montejano
*1987, El Centro, CA, USA

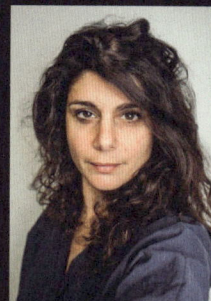
Nura Qureshi
*1977, Bremen, Germany

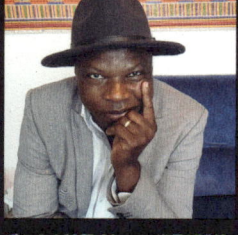
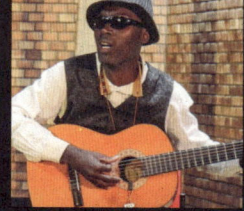
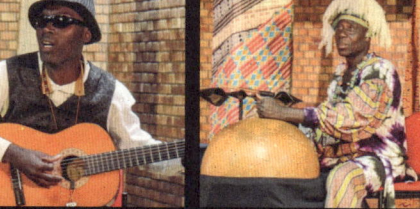
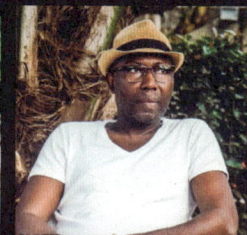

Compagnie GAKOEKOE
Gaëtan Noussouglo (*1966), Eustache Bowokabati Kamouna (*1970), Anani Gbeteglo (*1957), Roger Atikpo (*1972), Marcel Kodjovi Djondo (*1967), Florisse Adjanohoun (*1971). Togo, France, Belgium.

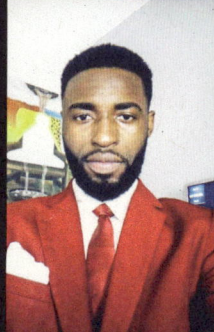
Franky Mindja
*1994, Yaoundé, Cameroon

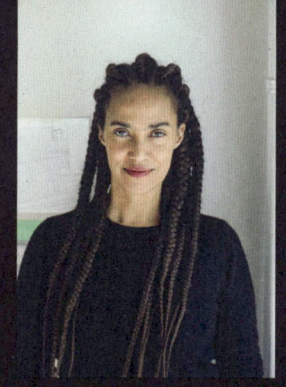
Grada Kilomba
*1968, Lisbon, Portugal

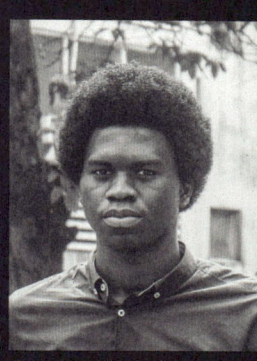
Osaze Amadasun
*1994, Abia State, Nigeria

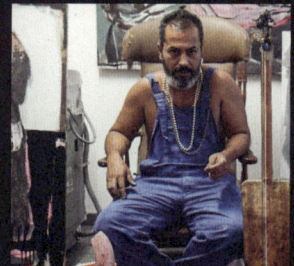
Mohammed Laouli
*1972, Salé, Morocco

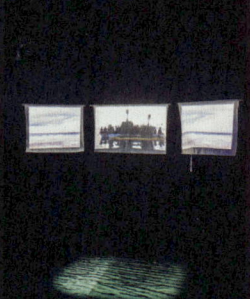
Wantok Music Foundation

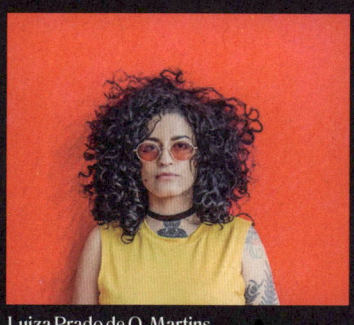
Luiza Prado de O. Martins
*1985, Rio de Janeiro, Brazil

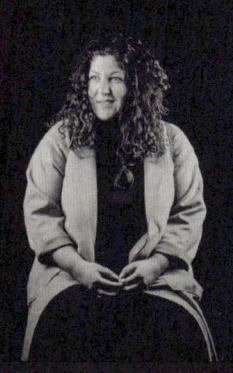
Emília Rigová
*1980, Trnava, Slovakia

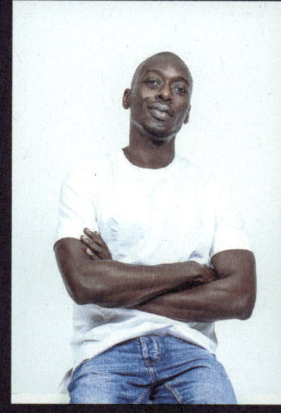
Omar Victor Diop
*1980, Dakar, Senegal

Editors

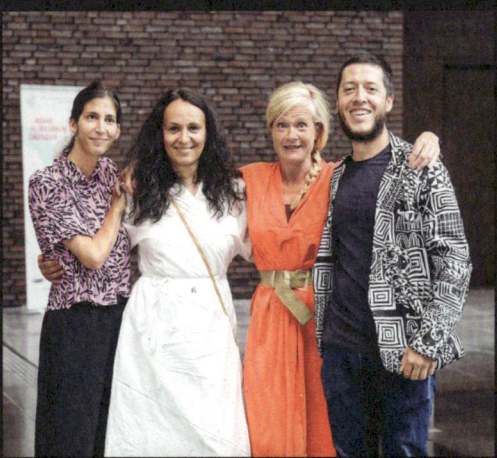

left to right: Hauth, Marušić, Snoep, Márquez García

Nanette Snoep has been director of the RJM since 2019 and is the initiator of the exhibition *RESIST! The Art of Resistance*. Under her direction, the RJM restituted 92 artworks from the Benin Kingdom to Nigeria in 2022. From 2015 to 2019, she was director of three ethnological museums in Leipzig, Dresden and Herrnhut. Under her leadership, in 2017 the first return of ancestral remains to Hawaii from the State of Saxony took place, actions that led to other ancestral remains being returned from these museums. In 2018, she initiated the exhibition *Megalopolis: Voices from Kinshasa* which gave carte blanche to a collective of artists, filmmakers and writers from Kinshasa. From 1997 to 2015, she was chief curator of the collection for Global History of the Quai Branly Museum in Paris, where she curated amongst others an exhibition about the history of racism, *Human Zoos. The Invention of the Savage*, for which she received in 2012 the award *Globes de Cristal – Art et Culture* for the best exhibition of the year in France. In 2022, she was honoured with the *Kenneth Hudson Award for Institutional Courage and Professional Integrity* as part of the *European Museum of the Year Prize*.

Vera Marušić joined the RJM in November 2019 as consultant to the director and in charge for program and strategic planning. Previously, she worked as a project coordinator and curator in international and interdisciplinary projects in the cultural/art fields and in higher education. In 2015, she curated *RomAmoR, a Tribute to Roma and Sinti Cultures* for the European Center for the Arts Hellerau in Dresden. From 2015–2019, she worked on the repositioning of the three ethnological museums in Saxony, which included in particular the ethical and legal discussion of restitution requests in the context of human remains and cultural objects from contexts of colonial injustice. In Cologne, she is continuing her work on the implementation of diversity-sensitive and power-critical decolonization processes.

Lydia Hauth is an ethnologist and cultural manager and has been working at the RJM since 2019. There she was responsible for the realisation of the exhibition *RESIST! The Art of Resistance*. From 2014–2018 she worked at the Grassi Museum of Ethnology in Leipzig where she coordinated and curated several participatory and international exhibition projects as part of the *Grassi invites* series and was responsible for the coordination of the international project *Megalopolis: Voices from Kinshasa* with 28 artists from Kinshasa.

Ricardo Márquez García is a Colombian cultural mediator and researcher and currently lives in Cologne. For four years (2014–2018) he lived, researched and taught in Cameroon, first in the capital Yaoundé and then in the west of the country in Dschang. From 2020 to 2022 he worked as a junior curator at the RJM and has been a doctoral student in the Cluster of Excellence at the University of Bonn Center for Dependency and Slavery Studies. In his work as a junior curator, he coordinated the special exhibition *RESIST! The Art of Resistance*.

»*RESIST!* is not a special exhibition!«
Comment left by a visitor to the exhibition, October 2021

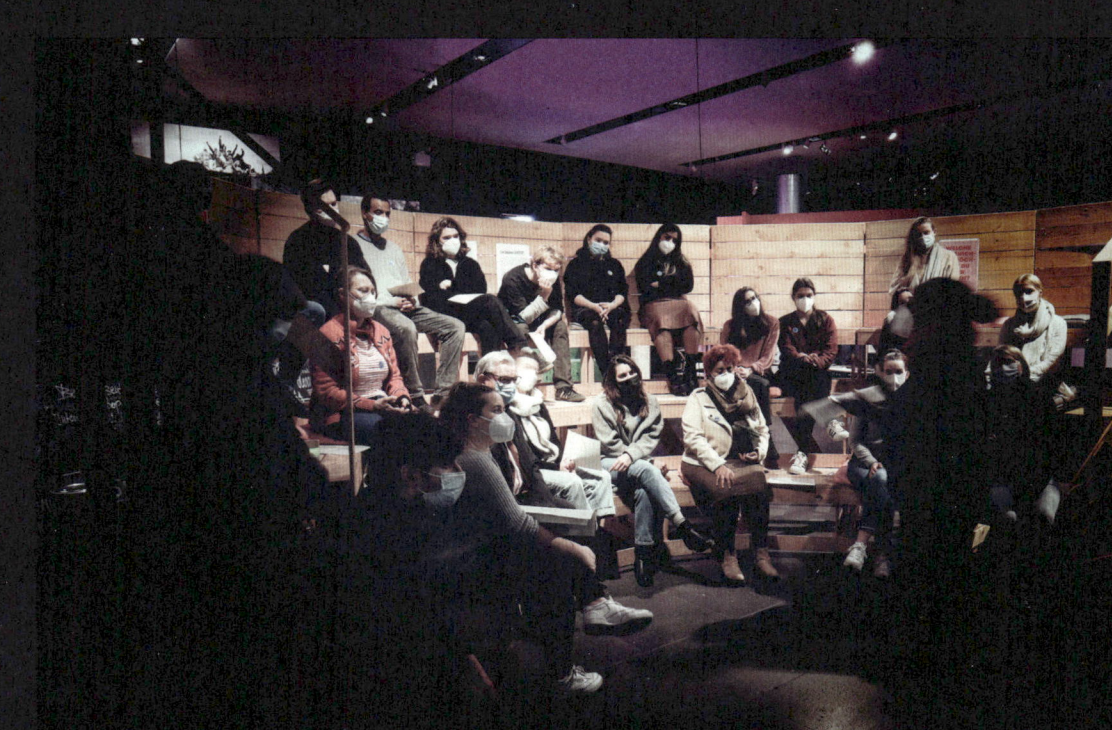

Credits

pp. 024, 028, 030, 037, 040, 093, 104–105, 126, 128, 135, 140, 142–143, 180–181, 190, 199: Exhibition views from ©RJM, Photos: Silviu Guiman; pp. 062, 076, 086, 108–109, 132, 154, 192, 205: Exhibition views from ©RJM, Photos: Tijmen Snoep; pp. 025, 085, 125, 137, 153, 169, 185, 189: All video stills from You Have No Idea, ©Selma Selman; pp. 018–021: Reflection raumlabor, ©raumlaborberlin; pp. 026–027: Video stills from the film Mozambique ©RTP Arquivos; p. 031: The Beheading of Atahualpa in Cajamarca ©SLUB Dresden/Deutsche Photothek/Regine Richter; p. 032: Video stills from film on the 239th Anniversary of the Revolution of Túpac Amaru, ©Coraje Inka TV; pp. 033–035: Amistad Portraits, William H. Townsend, ©Beinecke Rare Book and Manuscript Library, Yale University; pp. 036–037: Portrait of Chief Charles Taku in front of the sculpture, ©RJM, Photo: Francis Oghuma; p. 038: Visit of the Bangwa delegation, ©RJM, Francis Oghuma, Vera Marušić; pp. 040–041: Jallianwala: Repression and Retribution, ©Singh Twins; pp. 042–043: Are you Calling me a Dog?, ©Nura Qureshi; pp. 045–049: Photos Peter Magubane, ©Peter Magubane; p. 046: Videostills from [Resi]stance One Shot, ©Young-Jean Maeng; pp. 050–053: Posters Medu Art Ensemble, ©The Art Institute of Chicago; p. 054: Why Should an Indian Woman have to Bleach her Hair to be Accepted?, ©Collection Christian Feest; p. 054: Protect Sacred Water, ©Ernesto Yerena; p. 054: We the resilient, ©Ernesto Yerena, Photo of Ayşe Gürsöz; p. 055: Wounded Knee Run, Pine Ridge Indian Reservation, SD, USA, ©Collection Christian Feest; p. 055: One with the Earth, Anthony Gauthier, Institute for American Indian Art, Santa Fe, NM, USA, ©Collection Christian Feest; p. 056: Photo ghost dance garment, edited, ©RJM; p. 057: The Intellect, Lawrence Paul Yuxweluptun, ©Private Collection Cologne, ©RJM, Photo: Silviu Guiman; p. 058: Patrice Lumumba during the ceremony to celebrate the independence of the Congo on 30/06/1960; p. 060: Painting of Patrice Lumumba, Tshibumba Kanda Matulu, ©Nationaal Museum van Wereldculturen, NL; p. 061: The Defence of The Maize, Lapiztola, ©RJM, Photo: Francis Oghuma; p. 062–063: Códice de Ayotzinapa, Diego Sandoval Ávila, Juan Manuel Sandoval, ©RJM, Photo: Francis Oghuma; p. 066: Portrait Esther Utjiua Muinjangue, ©Ingo Schneider; p. 066: Portrait Ida Hoffmann, ©Ingo Schneider; pp. 077–082: All posters on the genocide, ©Esther Utjiua Muinjangue, Ida Hoffmann, Asser Karita; pp. 083–084: Video stills from documentary with Esther Utjiua Muinjangue and Ida Hoffmann, ©Esther Utjiua Muinjangue, Ida Hoffmann; p. 083: group Photo, ©Esther Utjiua Muinjangue, Ida Hoffmann; p. 088: Video stills from Les Racontottes, ©Compagnie GAKOEKOE; p. 091: Video stills from Body Games, Capoeira and Ancestry, ©Richard Pakleppa, Matthías Röhrig Assunção, Christine Dettmann; pp. 096–103: Video stills from Untangle the Threads, ©Salman Alkhir Abdo, Fadi Elias; p. 097: Portrait Peju Layiwola, ©Kunle Ogunfuyi; p. 106: The Close Relationship between Past and Present, ©Nwakuso Edozien; p. 106: Double Standard, ©Jimoh Ganiyu; p. 107: Bini Playing Cards, ©Osaze Amadasun; p. 107: Video still from 1897, ©Monday Midnite; p. 113: Peju Layiwola with memorial head, ©RJM, Photo: Tijmen Snoep; p. 116: Opening I MISS YOU, ©RJM, Photo: Francis Oghuma; p. 117: Hand Peju Layiwola, ©Vera Marušić; p. 119: Video stills from Restitution of the Benin court artworks, ©Young-Jean Maeng; p. 121: Video still from Untangle the Threads, ©Salman Alkhir Abdo, Fadi Elias; pp. 123–124: RESIST! All in one, ©RJM, Photo: Francis Oghuma; pp. 129–131: Project Diaspora, ©Omar Victor Diop, Galerie MAGNIN-A; pp. 132–133: Objects of Love and Desire, ©Patricia Kaersenhout, private collections Cologne and Rotterdam; p. 134: Comic Manga Bell and his Anti-Colonial Petition, ©Franky Mindja, Initiative Perspektivwechsel e.V.; p. 135: Photos Njoya, ©Photographic Collection RJM; p. 136: This Hegemony Life ©indieguerrillas, Mizuma Gallery; p. 141: Portrait Tímea Junghaus, ©Nihad Nino Pušija; p. 144: Pearls before Swine ©Alfred Ullrich; p. 145: Insectology in my Body, ©Robert Gabris; pp. 146–147: Crossing B(l)ack ©Emília Rigovà; p. 157: The Protectors you Never Had, Tania Willard, Private Collection Cologne, ©RJM, Photo: Silviu Guiman; pp. 158–159: Video stills from Kara Walker, ©Kara Walker, Courtesy Sprüth Magers and Sikkema Jenkins & Co; pp. 160–161: Photographies Kiri Dalena, ©Kiri Dalena; pp. 162–163: Video stills from Les Sculptures n'étaient pas blanches, ©Mohammed Laouli; pp. 164–165: Video stills from Plantation Memories, ©Grada Kilomba, Goodman Gallery; pp. 166–167: Collagraphs Belkis Ayón Manso, Belkis Ayón Estate, Havana, Cuba and Ludwig Forum Aachen, loan from the Peter and Irene Ludwig Foundation, Photo: ©Carl Brunn; p. 168: For Those who Stand at Shorelines, Luiza Prado de O. Martins, ©RJM, Photo: Silviu Guiman; p. 172: Portrait Elizaveta Khan, ©Salman Alkhir Abdo; pp. 177–179: Kalk Box In-Haus e.V., ©Salman Alkhir Abdo; pp. 182–183: Demo Black Lives Matter, ©Francis Oghuma; p. 184: Videostills from [Resi]stance, ©Young-Jean Maeng; pp. 186–187: Video stills from dance video, ©Young-Jean Maeng; p. 195: Photo kareau, ©RJM, Photo: Francis Oghuma; p. 198: Repaired Broken Mirror, Kader Attia and Gallery Nagel Draxler Berlin/Köln/München; pp. 194–195: Video stills from O Sacudimento da Maison des Esclaves em Gorée/O Sacudimento da Casa da Torre, ©Ayrson Heráclito; p. 202: Portrait Selma Selman, ©Irfan Brkovic; Portrait Emília Rigovà, ©Emília Rigovà; Portrait Tania Willard, ©Kyla Bailey; Portrait Kara Walker, ©Ari Marcopoulos; Portrait Dhuwarrwarr Marika, ©Buku-Larrŋgay Mulka; Portrait Małgorzata Mirga-Tas, ©Małgorzata Mirga-Tas; Portrait Alfred Ullrich, ©Anna Dietze; Portrait indieguerrillas, ©indieguerrillas, Mizuma Gallery; Portrait Franky Mindja, ©Franky Mindja; Portrait Singh Twins, ©Singh Twins; Portrait Juan Manuel Sandoval Palacios, ©Juan Manuel Sandoval Palacios; Portrait Diego Sandoval Ávila, ©Juan Manuel Sandoval Palacios; Portrait Jimoh Ganiyu, ©Jimoh Ganiyu; Portrait Kader Attia, ©Camille Millerand; Portrait Tshibumba Kanda Matulu, ©Tshibumba Kanda Matulu; Portrait Patricia Kaersenhout, ©Patricia Kaersenhout; Portrait Lapiztola, ©Lapiztola; Portrait Kiri Dalena, ©Kimberly de la Cruz; Portrait Nwakuso Edozien, ©Nwakuso Edozien; Portrait Robert Gabris, ©Robert Gabris; Portrait Monday Midnite, ©Monday Midnite; Portrait Mamadou Sall, ©Mamadou Sall; Portrait Ayrson Heráclito, ©Tiago Sant'Ana; Portrait Omar Victor Diop, ©Fondation Louis Vuitton; Portrait Grada Kilomba, ©Filipe Avila ; Portrait Osaze Amadasun, ©Osaze Amadasun; p. 203: Portrait Belkis Ayón Manso, ©Werner Gadliger; Portrait Rokia Bamba, ©Rokia Bamba; Portrait Tímea Junghaus, ©Nihad Nino Pušija; Portrait Lawrence Paul Yuxweluptun, ©Amanda Siebert; Portrait Alao Lukman, ©Alao Lukman; Portrait Young-Jean Maeng, ©Young-Jean Maeng; Portrait Peter Magubane, ©David Meyer-Gollan; Portrait Bahar Gökten, ©Aras Gökten; Portrait Daniela Rodríguez Romero, ©Daniela Rodríguez Romero ; Portraits In-Haus e.V., ©Salman Alkhir Abdo; Portraits Company GAKOEKOE, ©Compagnie GAKOEKOE; Portrait Francis Oghuma, ©Francis Oghuma; Portrait Ernesto Yerena, ©Ernesto Yerena; Portrait Nura Qureshi, ©Nura Qureshi; Portrait Esther Utjiua Muinjangue, ©Ingo Schneider; Portrait Ida Hoffmann, ©Ingo Schneider; Portrait Huỳnh Văn Thuận, ©Huỳnh Văn Thuận; Portrait Peju Layiwola, ©Kunle Ogunfuyi; Portrait Keviselie/Hans Ragnar Mathisen, ©Keviselie/Hans Ragnar Mathisen; Portrait Luiza Prado de O. Martins, ©Luiza Prado de O. Martins; Portrait Mohammed Laouli, ©Faycal Ben; p. 204: Group photo, ©Francis Oghuma

Imprint

Publication

This book was published on the occasion of the exhibition RESIST! The Art of Resistance at the Rautenstrauch-Joest-Museum, Cologne / Germany 01/04/2021–09/01/2022.

©Rautenstrauch-Joest-Museum and Verlag der Buchhandlung Walther and Franz König, Köln

Editors: Nanette Snoep, Vera Marušić, Lydia Hauth, Ricardo Márquez García

Concept and Text Editing: Nanette Snoep, Vera Marušić, Lydia Hauth, Ricardo Márquez García

Image Editing: Ricardo Márquez García, Nanette Snoep, Vera Marušić, Lydia Hauth

Authors: Nanette Snoep, Vera Marušić, Lydia Hauth, Ricardo Márquez García, Esther Utjiua Muinjangue; Ida Hoffmann, Peju Layiwola; In-Haus e.V., Tímea Junghaus,

Translations: Alexandra Berlina, Laura Brandt, Paul Harris, Franceline Richert, Good and Cheap Translators

Proofreading: Good and Cheap Translators

Design: Marius Förster (operative.space)

Typefaces: Bely by Roxane Gataud (Typetogether); DuBois by Tré Seals (Vocal Type); Eiko by Caio Kondo (Pangram Pangram); Passenger Sans by Diana Ovezea, Samo Aćko (Indian Type Foundry); Quilombos by Émilie Aurat; Romana by Gustav F. Schroeder, Theophile Beaudoire

Cover: The Young Lions by Peter Magubane, 1976

Print: oeding print GmbH

Published by Buchhandlung Walther and Franz König, Ehrenstr. 4, 50672 Cologne

Bibliographic information published by the Deutsche Nationalbibliothek: The Deutsche Nationalbibliothek lists this publication in the Deutsche Nationalbibliografie; detailed bibliographic data are available in the Internet at https://dnb.dnb.de.

Printed in Germany

Distribution:
Germany, Austria, Switzerland
Buchhandlung Walther König
Ehrenstr. 4, D-50672 Köln
Fon +49(0) 221 20 59 6 53
verlag@buchhandlung-walther-koenig.de

Unites States and Canada
D.A.P./Distributed Art Publishers, Inc.
75 Broad Street, Suite 630
USA-New York, NY 10004
Fon +1(0) 212 627 1999
orders@dapinc.com

Outside the United States and Canada, Germany, Austria and Switzerland by
Thames & Hudson Ltd., London
www.thamesandhudson.com

ISBN 978-3-7533-0271-3

Exhibition

Curators *It's Yours!* Spaces: Esther Utjiua Muinjangue & Ida Hoffmann, Peju Layiwola, Tímea Junghaus, Integrationshaus (In-Haus e.V.) Cologne Kalk with Elizaveta Khan, Mona Leitmeier, Sae Yun Jung, Salman Abdo, Rita Bomkamp

Artists in Residence: Rokia Bamba (Music), Bahar Gökten und Daniela Rodriguez Romero (Urban Dance), Kiri Dalena (Colonial Photography), Francis Oghuma (Real Time Documentary)

Participating Artists: Christie Akumabor, Osaze Amadasun, Kader Attia, Belkis Ayón, Omar Victor Diop, Nwakuso Edozien, Robert Gabris, Company GAKOEKOE (Florisse Adjanohoun, Roger Atikpo, Marcel Djondo, Anani Gbeteglo, Eustache Kamouna, Gaëtan Noussouglo), Jimoh Ganiyu, Ayrson Heráclito, indieguerillas, Patricia Kaersenhout, Grada Kilomba, Mohammed Laouli, Alao Lukman, Peter Magubane, Dhuwarrwarr Marika, Tshibumba Kanda Matulu, Medu Art Ensemble, Luiza Prado de O. Martins, Małgorzata Mirga-Tas, Keviselie/ Hans Ragnar Mathisen, Monday Midnite, Franky Mindja, Lapiztola, Nura Qureshi, Emília Rigová, Mamadou Sall, Juan Manuel Sandoval, Diego Sandoval Ávila, Selma Selman, The Singh Twins, Alfred Ullrich, Huỳnh Văn Thuận, Kara Walker, Wantok Musik Foundation, Tania Willard, Lawrence Paul Yuxweluptun, Ernesto Yerena

Idea & Curator at large: Nanette Snoep, Director Rautenstrauch-Joest Museum, Cologne

Project Management: Lydia Hauth

Project Coordination: Ricardo Márquez García, Paloma Nana

Scientific Assistant: Nada Schroer

Exhibition Production: Agustina Andreoletti

Research & Editing: Caroline Bräuer, Anna Brus, Carl Deußen, Lucia Halder, Lydia Hauth, Clara Himmelheber, Yagmur Karakis, Oliver Lueb, Paloma Nana, Ricardo Márquez García, Vera Marušić, Sonja Mohr, Anne Slenczka, Nada Schroer, Nanette Snoep, Annabelle Springer, Stefanie Teufel

Public Programme: Agustina Andreoletti, Iris Kaebelmann, Lydia Hauth, Carla de Andrade Hurst, Ricardo Márquez García, Vera Marušić, Paloma Nana, Aurora Rodonò, Team of *RESIST!* Live Speakers

Concept & Coordination – Live Speaker & Awareness Programme: Carla de Andrade Hurst, Paloma Nana, Aurora Rodonò

Expert-Team Awareness & Mediation: Helene Batemona-Abeke, Daniel Brunsch, Esther Poppe

Team of Live Speakers: Aminata Estelle Diouf, Benjamin Chardey, Fatima Remli, Fatou Cissé Kane, Halima Kamara, Hanna Held, Jabbar Abdullah, Karima Renes, Keea Kauhanen, Lukas Herrmann, Marlène Tencha, Niki Vetter, Olga Drachuk-Meyer, Quyên Vo, Sarah Fatima Schütz, Sepiedeh Fazlali, Sophia Jia-Xin Liu, Tatjana Schnellinger

Library of Resistance: Aurora Rodonò, with team of Live Speakers

Process Rooms Young Rebels & Repair Atelier: In Cooperation with Coach e.V. and Jugendfreizeitwerk Köln e.V. Chorweiler

Production Assistants *It's Yours!* Spaces: Vanja Smiljanić, Camilo Sandoval

Exhibition Design: raumlaborberlin with Florian Stirnemann, Benjamin Foerster-Baldenius, Louise Nguyen, Sarah Bovelett & Thomas Quack

Graphic Design Exhibition: Thomas Quack

Exhibiton Construction: Tobias Eusterholz, Jan Schlake, werkstatt.global with Kai Heusmann, Milan Knell, Fabian Preuschoff, Götz Schneider

Conservation and Object Mounting: Birgit Depenbrock, Petra Czerwinske, Kristina Hopp, Stephanie Lüerßen, Christof Nakat

Collection Management: Christian Andert

Media Technology: Süleyman Atalayin, Agustina Andreoletti assisted by Dawid Liftinger

Lighting: Martin Leetz

Museum Archive: Susanne Kube, Annette Motz

Communication: Judith Glaser, Lydia Hauth, Vera Marušić

Communication Design: Elsa Westreicher

Translations Exhibition Texts: Alexandra Berlina, Laura Brandt, Paul Harris

Proofreading Exhibition Texts: David Frohnapfel

Interns & Supporters: Bianca Casini Monteiro, Floraine Bouyssi, Stephanie Zeiler, Marie Katharina Baur, Jana Schmitz, Lia Helguero Kandt, Lino Krukenberg, Tabita Ntanguen, Layla Pankratz, Paul Schmidl, Sarah Schütz, Judith Zweck, Heribert Bache, Tijmen Snoep, Romy Berthold, Paula Ulbrich, Julia Hahn-Klose

The project is funded by

German Federal Cultural Foundation, Peter and Irene Ludwig Foundation, F. Victor Rolff Foundation, Federal Agency for Civic Education, Museum Association RJM e.V., Program 360° Fund for Cultures of the New urban society program of the German Federal Cultural Foundation.

Deutschlandfunk was the media partner of the exhibition.

Particular thanks go to our partners and sponsors:

Funded by the German Federal Cultural Foundation

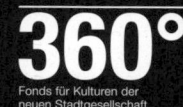

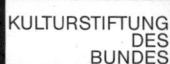

Peter und Irene Ludwig Stiftung

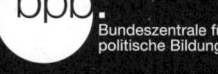

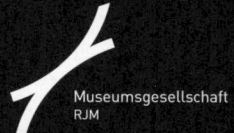

Media Partner:

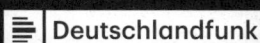

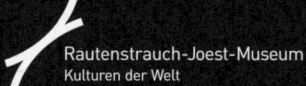
Rautenstrauch-Joest-Museum
Kulturen der Welt

Ein Museum der

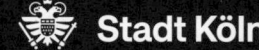
Stadt Köln

»Any decision that affects our heritage, our lives, must include us. We don't want to be merely spoken to; we want to be part of a dialogue. We want to tell our stories.«
Peju Layiwola It's Yours! curator RESIST!, January 2021

»›We are the voices of the people who died in 1904.‹ We are speaking on behalf of the skulls that are in Germany. And that is why we are saying: ›Not about Us without Us.‹«
Esther Utjiua Muinjangue It's Yours! curator RESIST!, January 2021

»In any case, we are all people from Cologne: [...] We position ourselves as new Germans and also want the recognition that goes with it. [...] Of course, that also means access to resources and, of course, political participation.«
Elizaveta Khan It's Yours! curator RESIST!, January 2021

»Our history is not a story of victimhood, but one of survival, resilience, and true resistance.«
Tímea Junghaus It's Yours! curator RESIST!, January 2021